The Making of the Modern World

VOLUME ONE

THE MAKING
OF THE
MODERN WORLD

General Editor
DOUGLAS JOHNSON
Professor of French History
University College London

VOLUME ONE

EUROPE DISCOVERS
THE WORLD

LONDON ★ ERNEST BENN LIMITED
NEW YORK ★ BARNES & NOBLE INC

First published 1971 by Ernest Benn Limited
Bouverie House, Fleet Street, London, EC4
& Barnes & Noble, Inc.
105 Fifth Avenue, New York, N.Y. 10003

Distributed in Canada by
The General Publishing Company Limited, Toronto

Book designed by Kenneth Day

Maps drawn by E. A. Chambers

Printed in Great Britain

ISBN 0-510-27350-5
ISBN 0-389-04128-9 (USA)

Contents

Maps

Introduction DOUGLAS JOHNSON

THE EVIDENCE about the past that is available to historians is always
growing and changing. But it is not this only that changes history;
what is perhaps more important is that historians are continually
changing the questions that they ask about the past. Things that
appear obvious and certain at one moment, lose these qualities;
assumptions change, perspectives alter, values extend. And there are
few areas of history where these changes have taken place so strikingly
as in the study of Europe's relations with the world that surrounds
the European continent. From thinking in terms of all history being
European history, or, more precisely, western European history,
there has developed a sense of complexity. We realize that it is
difficult to define Europe, whether geographically, politically, or
culturally. Periods which have been described as periods of European
unity, such as that of Hellenistic civilization or the Roman Empire,
are now seen as periods in Mediterranean, Asian, and African history.
Centuries of medieval European civilization are now seen to involve
considerable diversity, where different political and cultural units
such as the ideal of universal Christendom, the uncertain progression
of national monarchies, the various feudal principalities and city-
states, created a series of tensions rather than any simple consolidated
whole. This diversity is all the more apparent when one considers
Scandinavia, Lithuania, Hungary, and Poland, which received the
influence of Christianity and Roman law, as well as the Orthodox
principalities of Russia.

But if it has become more difficult to understand the full complexity
of the developments on the European continent, it has become easier
to recognize the richness of the world as a whole. The concept of
Europe as the chief centre of the world is one that must be scru-
tinized. Historians are beginning to understand the often-quoted
remark of Paul Valéry that Europe is only a western appendix to Asia.

This volume does not set out to provide a history of world
civilizations. Believing that the moment when Columbus, Vasco da

Gama, Magellan, and others made their voyages and discoveries is still a moment of great significance in world history, it examines some of the civilizations as they existed about that time. A second volume will consider the period of colonialism, when European States and techniques dominated many lands. A third volume will examine the end of this period and the developments associated with what has, perhaps loosely, been styled 'the end of Europe'.

1   The earth according to Ptolemy, from a reprint of his *Geographia* published at Ulm in 1482

The Discoveries ROBERT KNECHT

The State of Geographical Knowledge

EUROPEAN GEOGRAPHICAL KNOWLEDGE at the beginning of the fifteenth century was a mixture of theory, fable, and practical experience. Most of the theory went back to antiquity, particularly to Aristotle and Ptolemy. Aristotle supported the theory of the sphericity of the earth, which had already been evolved in the fifth century B.C., by demonstrating that only a sphere could throw a curved shadow on the moon in an eclipse. He believed, however, that there was only one continent balanced by an equal weight of ocean and that the distance across the sea from Spain to India (which Alexander the Great had reached) was not great. Claudius Ptolemaeus, who lived at Alexandria in the second century A.D., was a compiler of information rather than an original thinker. He became famous on account of his *Astronomy* or *Almagest* which elaborated upon the Aristotelian concept of the universe and of his *Geography* which comprised a gazetteer of place-names and the first known atlas. Though Ptolemy took enormous pains to determine the latitude and longitude of all known localities he was often wildly inaccurate about places outside the Mediterranean area. He underestimated the circumference of the earth and the length of an equatorial degree while exaggerating the east–west breadth of Asia. His world map showed how far geographical knowledge had advanced since Aristotle's day by depicting the three continents of Europe, Africa, and Asia. But Ptolemy showed the Indian Ocean as a landlocked sea and failed to give any guidance on the extent of the Atlantic.

During the early Middle Ages geographical theory became subordinated to Christian theology. This resulted in the flat earth theory advocated by the monk Cosmas and the *mappa-mundi* with Jerusalem as the centre of creation and the four Rivers of Paradise flowing from the Garden of Eden. Fortunately, ancient learning was kept alive by Muslim scholars like al-Idrisi, a gifted Moor from Ceuta who lived at the court of Roger II of Sicily in the twelfth century and produced

9

an exhaustive *Geography*. Curiously enough Ptolemy's *Geography*, which was known to the Arabs, was not discovered by Christian Europe till the fifteenth century, but his *Astronomy* was used from the twelfth century onwards and served to discredit the flat earth theory. The original contribution of the medieval schoolman to geographical knowledge was slight, but Roger Bacon's *Opus Majus* (1264) and Cardinal Pierre d'Ailly's *Imago Mundi* (*c* 1410) were important and influential works, the latter being Columbus' favourite bedside book. A most significant event in the development of medieval European geographical knowledge was the translation of Ptolemy's *Geography* into Latin in 1406. But if it was received with the greatest respect, it was not accepted uncritically by everyone. Pope Pius II, for example, repudiated the notion of a landlocked Indian Ocean in his *Historia Rerum Ubique Gestarum*.

Geographical knowledge at the beginning of the fifteenth century also rested upon a large body of myth. This should not be overlooked for it was widely accepted and helped to determine the programme of discovery. Much of this mythology went back to classical times; it originated in the works of Ctesias, in Pliny's *Natural History*, or in Solinus' even more mendacious *Polyhistor*. Other myths were of Christian or Muslim origin, but whatever their provenance they were nearly all about Asia. A most popular work of the fourteenth century, *The Travels of Sir John Mandeville*, peopled India with dog-headed men who snarled and barked, men who shaded themselves by lying on their backs and holding up a single huge foot, headless men with eyes in their stomachs, and other equally weird creatures. St Thomas the Apostle was supposed to have founded a large and prosperous Christian community in south-east India. Undoubtedly the most famous of all geographical legends was that of Prester John, a long-lived Christian monarch who ruled over an enormous kingdom of incredible opulence. Originally he was located in Asia, but about 1340 he was transferred to Ethiopia where the Portuguese looked for him more than a century later. Yet another legend which influenced African exploration was that of the River of Gold which was probably based on vague information about the Niger or Senegal carried across the Sahara by Arab caravans. The well-known story of Atlantis, originally told by Plato, was revived in the early Middle Ages as that of St Brandon who discovered enchanted isles off the west coast of

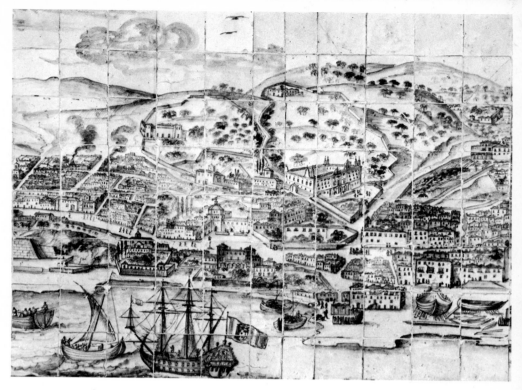

2   Lisbon in the sixteenth century

Ireland. St Brandon's island was one of several imaginary Atlantic islands shown on early maps. Others included Antillia or the Isle of the Seven Cities, said to have been discovered by refugees from the Moorish conquest of Spain in the eighth century, and the isle of Brazil which was not removed from Admiralty charts till 1873.

Finally, geographical knowledge at the end of the Middle Ages was based on a fair amount of first-hand experience. Medieval Europe was far from static. Although its roads were appalling and river transport was slow and expensive, thousands of people – merchants, artisans, students, clergy, pilgrims – were for ever on the move. Europe was also encircled by thriving sea routes. Some Europeans even ventured beyond the limits of their own continent. In the tenth century the Norsemen colonized Greenland and in the eleventh they accidentally reached an unidentified part of the New England coast (Vinland), but their achievement left only vague traces in Scandinavian epic poetry and had no influence on the discoveries. Far more important from our point of view were the journeys of European merchants and ecclesiastics to the Far East which began in the thirteenth century, after the Tatars had asserted their authority over the Mongols of central Asia and conquered China, establishing a tolerant and orderly régime. In 1245 John of Plano Carpini, a Franciscan friar, was sent by the Pope to the Mongol ruler at Karakorum in Outer Mongolia, and in 1253 William of Rubruck carried out a similar mission. About 1256 two Venetian merchants, Niccolo and Maffeo Polo, travelled to the court of Kubilai Khan at Peking where they remained for fourteen years. They then returned to Venice only to set off again, this time with Niccolo's son, Marco. By joining the khan's diplomatic service,

3   Henry the Navigator (to the right of St Vincent), a detail from the St Vincent panels, a Portuguese masterpiece of the fifteenth century depicting veneration of St Vincent by a group of Churchmen, soldiers, and burghers

Marco was able to travel widely in his dominions. In 1292 the Polos came home by way of the Malay peninsula, Sumatra, and India. During the next century more Europeans went to the Far East but only the names of the ecclesiastics are known. The fact that many merchants were amongst them is attested by a Florentine guide-book to the route from the Levant to Peking. It describes the stages of the journey, the means of transport, and the most suitable goods for the Chinese market. This state of affairs continued until the middle of the fourteenth century when the Ottoman Turks drove a wedge into Asia Minor severing the overland route to the East. But the memory of the medieval journeys lived on in works like Marco Polo's *Travels* or Odoric of Pordenone's more fanciful *Descriptio Orientalium Partium*.

The Reasons for Exploration

In the late nineteenth century it was fashionable to interpret the Age of Discovery as an aspect of the Italian Renaissance. The great French historian Michelet defined the Renaissance as 'the discovery of the world and of man', while Burckhardt in his classic work, *The Civilization of the Renaissance in Italy*, claimed that geographical curiosity was a feature of the Italian genius. But, as we have seen, the European urge to travel and interest in the rest of the world existed long before the Renaissance. The fact that most medieval travellers to the Far East and many of the great explorers of the Age of Discovery were Italians was due to their commercial preponderance in the Mediterranean which brought them into direct contact with the Muslim world and its neighbours. What was new in the fifteenth century was that countries which had so far played a relatively insignificant part in exploration began to send expeditions into uncharted seas. As a result, new lands were discovered, old superstitions shattered, and hitherto respectable theories disproved. Within a century and a half Europe found more or less the whole world as we know it today and established her ascendancy over many parts of it. If the Renaissance was not responsible, how are we to explain this belated and rapid expansion of Europe?

One thing is certain: the movement of expansion was not the result of population pressure. Although the population of Europe did begin to rise after the Black Death in the fourteenth century, its rate of increase was continually checked by epidemics, and did not reach a significant level before the eighteenth century. The number of Europeans who settled overseas during the expansion was very small. The total number of able-bodied Portuguese in the whole of the Portuguese Empire during the sixteenth century has been estimated at a mere 10,000. Although discovery was often the prelude to colonization, the early explorers were not interested in settlement; they always set off with the firm intention of coming home.

The Age of Expansion has been described as the sequel to the Age of the Crusades. There is some truth in this. Earlier efforts to defeat the Infidel in the Holy Land had failed and the Christian Powers planned to outflank him. By forming an alliance with Prester John they hoped to strike at 'the soft underbelly' of the Muslim world. The crusading spirit was nowhere more alive than in the Iberian peninsula where the *Reconquista* was still in progress, and no one was more imbued with it than Prince Henry of Portugal, known as 'the Navigator', who sponsored some of the earliest voyages of exploration. A contemporary chronicler tells us that the prince wished to investigate the extent of Moorish power, to convert pagans to Christianity, and to seek an alliance with any Christian rulers who might be found in Africa. But Henry also had another motive: he wanted to find the countries whence came the gold which reached Morocco across the Sahara 'in order to trade with them and so maintain the gentlemen of his household'.

The motives of the early explorers were mixed. When Vasco da Gama reached Calicut in 1498 he declared that he had come in search of 'Christians and spices'. In 1511 Albuquerque reminded his officers as they were about to attack Malacca of 'the great service we shall perform to our Lord in casting the Moors out of the country and quenching the fire of the sect of Mahomet . . . and the service we shall render to the king Don Manoel in taking this city because it is the source of all the spiceries and drugs.' Bernal Diaz went to the Indies 'to serve God and his Majesty, to give light to those who were in darkness and to grow rich as all men desire to do'. We have no reason to doubt the sincerity of these statements. Religion was important to the discoverers, but the objectives which they consistently pursued and the routes which they followed suggest that acquisitiveness was more often than not their primary motive. First and foremost they wanted gold, which was becoming increasingly scarce in Europe in the fifteenth century as governments tried to hoard as much of it as they could. There was also a growing demand for silver which the increased production of the German mines could not wholly satisfy. Furthermore, the Portuguese and the Spaniards wanted a direct share in the profitable trade in Eastern luxury goods.

Among the goods which reached Europe from the Far East during the Middle Ages spices were particularly important. They included not only condiments for preserving and seasoning food but also drugs, dyes, perfumes, and cosmetics. By the fifteenth century the bulk of this Eastern trade reached Europe by sea. The goods were carried by Arab merchants from places like Malacca in the Malay peninsula or Calicut on the Malabar coast of India across the Indian Ocean to ports along the Persian Gulf or the Red Sea, whence they were taken by boat or overland to markets in Egypt or the Levant. Here they were bought by Venetian merchants, who carried them the rest of the way to Europe. Thus, the Eastern trade route was not controlled from one end to the other by a single commercial interest; the goods were bought and sold several times over, each time becoming more expensive. Moreover, the various governments

4   Portuguese carracks of the sixteenth century, from a
painting by Cornelis Anthoniszoon

straddling the route imposed heavy tolls and duties so that the ultimate cost of the goods was far in excess of the price charged by the producers. Europe's only hope of obtaining Eastern goods more cheaply lay in circumventing the middlemen.

The timing of the Age of Discovery depended not only on motivation but on the achievement of a certain technological expertise. In addition to reasons for wanting to go overseas, Europeans needed suitable ships and navigational aids. The ships used by the early explorers were ordinary merchantmen, of which two main types existed in fifteenth-century Europe: the 'long ship', or galley equipped with oars and sails, and the 'round ship', including the carrack and the caravel, which depended on sail alone. Though fast and manœuvrable the galley was not suitable to distant exploration for it could not stand up to heavy weather and required a large crew which restricted the amount of space available for supplies and artillery. Despite these disadvantages the Mediterranean countries clung to it till the seventeenth century, which helps to explain their failure to take part in the discoveries. The round ship, which the Atlantic Powers preferred in the fifteenth century, was stronger, more capacious, and cheaper to run. Its combination of square and lateen rigs and its stern rudder made it reasonably manœuvrable. Furthermore, it could be equipped with powerful guns, a factor of enormous importance in the establishment of European ascendancy overseas. Amongst the various kinds of round ship that existed the early explorers tended to favour the caravel, a small coastal trader of about 60 to 80 tons. They had to use small ships for economic and practical reasons. The profits of exploration were too unpredictable to warrant large investments. Speed was essential if their supplies were to hold out, and they needed ships of shallow draught to explore coastal waters.

By the middle of the fifteenth century a number of navigational aids existed to help the explorer. The basic instrument was, of course, the magnetic compass which consisted of a piece of magnetized wire on a cardboard disc marked with a wind rose pivoting on a pin. The lead was used to take soundings and samples of the sea-bottom. Information provided by these instruments was recorded in pilotage books called 'rutters'. The marine or portolan chart provided an accurate picture of known coastlines. When a ship went out of sight

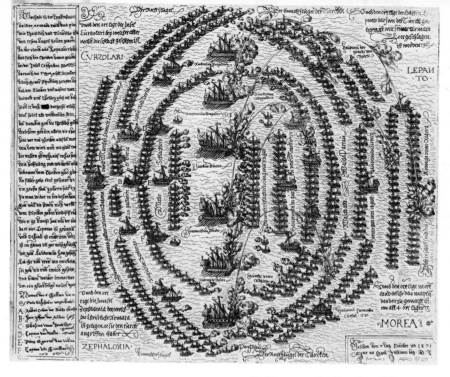

5 Galleys at the Battle of Lepanto

of land her master could ascertain her position by keeping a dead-reckoning. On a direct passage with a following wind this was a relatively easy matter dependent essentially on an estimate of the ship's speed. At first this was done simply by watching a piece of wood or other object float by; the log-line did not come into use before the sixteenth century. On an indirect passage a traverse-board was necessary to determine a ship's position. This was a wooden compass rose with eight peg-holes along each bearing. At the end of each half-hour of the watch a peg was placed in the hole corresponding to the ship's course and the results were noted down at the end of the watch. Accuracy depended, of course, on the correct use of the half-hour sand-glass by which time was kept. As long as European navigators worked mainly in coastal waters they had little need to observe latitudes, but once they ranged across the oceans they could not avoid doing so. Among the heavenly bodies which they could use in northern latitudes to fix their position, the

6 By the fifteenth century a number of navigational aids existed to help the explorer, among them the astrolabe, used to determine latitude

Pole Star was the most convenient; further south they had to use the sun. The astrolabe was used to find latitude in the fifteenth century, later the cross-staff was preferred. Among tables of the sun's declination which were available (but not often used by mariners) those of Abraham Zacuto were especially important. The first known navigation manual was the anonymous Portuguese *Regimento do estrolabio y do quadrante* of which the earliest surviving edition appeared in Lisbon in 1509. The problem of determining longitude was not satisfactorily solved till the eighteenth century. Even so, the Renaissance navigator could keep track of his position reasonably well.

Portuguese Exploration and Expansion

In the days of Henry the Navigator the trade in spices and other Eastern commodities seemed far beyond the reach of the Portuguese; it was bottled up in the Mediterranean and jealously guarded by the Venetians. Portugal was too weak to attempt any breach of their monopoly, so she looked for wealth in Africa. The programme of exploration sponsored by Henry the Navigator early in the fifteenth century was cautious. His captains did not leap into the unknown. They groped their way along the West African coast, carefully naming each cape, beach, and river as they went along. In 1434 Gil Eannes rounded Cape Bojador, and in 1442 Nuno Tristão sighted Cape Blanco. Two years later he discovered the mouth of the Senegal, while Dinis Dias reached Cape Verde. At first the Portuguese had to be satisfied with fish, sealskins, and seal oil, but as they moved beyond the Mauretanian coast they discovered more profitable forms of trade, notably ivory, gold-dust, pepper, and slaves. When Prince Henry died in 1460 the impetus behind the explorations flagged. The Portuguese had reached a difficult stretch of coast and viewed with apprehension the gradual disappearance of the Pole Star which they used to plot their course. Yet the reconnaissance of the African coast was not given up. In 1469 a private individual, Fernão Gomes, signed an agreement with the king of Portugal in which he undertook to explore 100 leagues of African coast annually for five years. His captains reached the Gold Coast in 1471 and within the next four years they got as far as the kingdom of Benin, which yielded numerous slaves and pepper of a high quality. The trade which they established with the Guinea coast proved so profitable that Spanish privateers tried to encroach upon it, but in 1479 the Portuguese were able to safeguard their interests in the Treaty of Alcaçovas.

So far Portuguese ambitions had not ranged beyond Africa, but in the 1470s they began to look further afield. The eastward shift of the West African coast south of Cape Verde seemed to augur well. Perhaps they had reached the southern extremity of Africa and were heading straight for the Indian Ocean? The discovery of the southerly trend of the coast beyond Malimba disillusioned them on this score, but they did not abandon hope of eventually rounding Africa. In the 1480s there was a great revival of enthusiasm in Portugal for discovery and overseas trade. King John II laid down savage penalties for foreign interlopers in the Guinea trade and tried to prevent information about the new discoveries from leaking out. At the same time a fort was built at São Jorge de Mina which effectively protected the Portuguese trade in gold, slaves, and pepper for a century and a

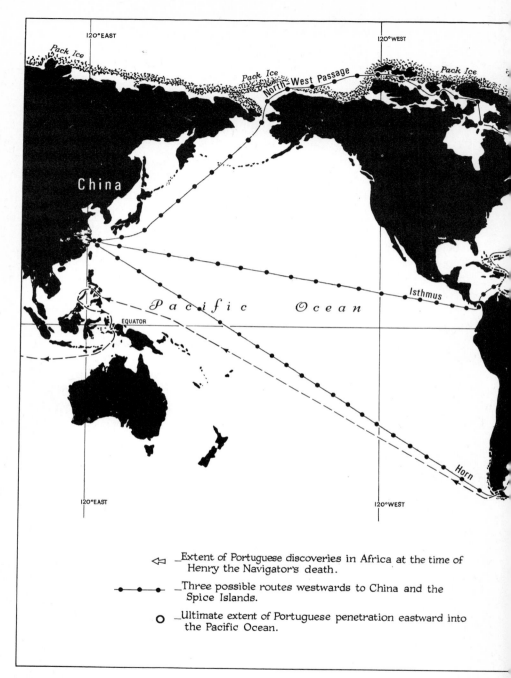

MAP 1   World map of the Discoveries   20

•••••••••••• —Bartolomeo Dias	◄—◄—◄ —Magellan
◄—◄—◄— —Christopher Columbus	┼—┼—┼— —Frobisher
------------ —Vasco da Gama	
+·+·+·+·+·+·+ —Amerigo Vespucci	

half. But John was not interested only in the Guinea trade; as a scholar he knew that there was a growing body of opinion favourable to a circumnavigation of Africa. Certain classical authorities like Strabo and Solinus did not agree with Ptolemy's view of the Indian Ocean and an increasing number of maps, including the famous world map of the Venetian monk, Fra Mauro (1459), showed Africa as circumnavigable.

To investigate the possibility of an extension of Portuguese maritime enterprise to the Far East, John II sent out a series of expeditions at his own expense and under capable navigators. Among the equipment which they carried were stone columns, called *padrões*, for erection at prominent points in newly discovered lands. Within four years Diogo Cão had explored another 1,450 miles of African coast, setting up his first *padrão* near the mouth of the Congo river and his last on Cape Cross, 22° south of the equator. In 1487 Bartholomeu Dias was ordered to go beyond this point. As he proceeded south he was forced into the Atlantic by bad weather until about latitude 40°S when he picked up the prevailing westerly wind and ran east, doubling the Cape without seeing it. After coasting along as far as the Great Fish river he was persuaded by his crew to turn back. Only then did he sight the Cape. He called it with good reason the Cape of Storms, but John II, realizing that Ptolemy had been proved wrong, renamed it the Cape of Good Hope. Meanwhile, the king had taken steps to find out about the countries which his sea captains hoped to reach. During the 1480s he sent out a number of agents to the Middle East to collect information about India and, if possible, to establish contact with Prester John. The most successful of these was Pero da Covilhan, who left Lisbon in the same year as Dias sailed for the Cape. Disguised as an Arab merchant, he travelled to Aden whence he reached Calicut by sea. After carrying out a tour of inspection of the ports of the Malabar coast, he went on to the great entrepôt of Ormuz in the Persian Gulf, thence to Sofala in south-east Africa, where he learnt that Africa could be circumnavigated. In 1490 he returned to Cairo and sent a full report to John II before going on to Mecca disguised as a pilgrim. Eventually he reached Abyssinia where he spent the rest of his life in the service of the emperor.

Ten years elapsed between the discovery of the Cape of Good

7   The Jeronimo Monastery built at the mouth of the
Tagus by Don Manoel in thanksgiving for the discovery of
the sea route to India. Vasco da Gama is buried here

Hope and the departure of Vasco da Gama. This delay may have been
caused by political troubles in Portugal or by the need to collect
information about the Atlantic wind system. Da Gama's expedition
was certainly prepared with care. He was given new maps, reports,
astronomical instruments, and declination tables for using the sun
instead of the Pole Star. Dias supervised the design of two of his four
ships, contributed some of his own men to their crews, and accompanied the expedition on the first lap of its journey down the African
coast. Considering that da Gama was a soldier, not a professional
seaman, his navigation proved remarkably accurate and must have
been based on reliable information. Instead of following the African
coast in the teeth of the south-easterly trades, as Dias had done, he
swung out into the Atlantic beyond Cape Verde and caught the
prevailing north-westerly to the Cape, a course which was to be
followed by generations of sailing-ships. After spending a record
ninety-six days at sea his fleet anchored 130 miles north of the Cape.
Da Gama rounded it with about as much difficulty as Dias, though in
slightly better weather. Beyond the Great Fish river he hugged the
coast of Natal and eventually reached Moçambique.

Da Gama's arrival at Moçambique opened a new phase in Portu-

8 Vasco da Gama (1460–1524)

guese enterprise. Whereas hitherto the explorers had been obliged to advance into the unknown without charts or the aid of native pilots, they now found themselves in a well-developed trading area presenting no serious navigational obstacles or superstitious fears. The difficulties that faced them were of a different sort: they had to wrest a share of the Eastern trade which the Arabs regarded as their own preserve. Da Gama was not the first European to attempt this. As Covilhan had discovered, some Italian, French, and Dutch merchants were already making use of the Arab ships which plied between Egypt and the west coast of India. They were too few, however, and their efforts were not sufficiently co-ordinated to give the Arab merchants much cause for anxiety. But da Gama's expedition was another matter; it represented the first organized attempt by a European government to break their commercial monopoly. The Portuguese knew what to expect: his ships carried twenty guns between them and his men were armed. An unfriendly reception awaited them almost everywhere in south-east Africa and at Mombasa they had to shoot their way out of the harbour. On the other hand, at Malindi, da Gama managed to secure the services of Ahmed ibn Majid, the best Asian navigator of his day. As a result he crossed the Indian Ocean safely, arriving at Calicut in May 1498.

24

Because of the discovery of the Cape route to the East the interest of the Portuguese in Africa declined. They continued to trade with Guinea, and established settlements along the west and east coasts, notably in Angola and Moçambique, but they did not penetrate far inland. An exception was Antonio Fernandes who, in 1514, travelled inland from Sofala in search of the Monomotapa and the legendary wealth of his kingdom. Trading factories dealing in ivory were later set up on the Zambezi and it was from one of these that Gaspar Bocarro travelled to Kilwa in 1616, discovering Lake Nyasa on the way. The only part of the African interior with which the Portuguese established fairly close relations was Ethiopia. An armed expedition was sent to help its ruler in 1541, and sixteen years later the Jesuits established a mission there which lasted till almost the end of the century.

The reception which awaited da Gama at Calicut was distinctly cool, for the goods which he had brought with him were of no interest to the Indians and the Arab traders put pressure on the local ruler, the Samuri, to deny him trading facilities. Yet by sheer persistence he managed to collect a cargo of spices valuable enough to justify his enterprise. His return voyage across the Indian Ocean was bedevilled by storms, headwinds, and sickness, but conditions improved after he had rounded the Cape. By the time he reached Lisbon, in September 1499, he had spent 300 days at sea and lost half his company. Yet the Portuguese Government did not feel that his efforts had been wasted. Within six months an expedition of thirteen sail and 1,500 men set off under Pero Alvares Cabral with the object of establishing a trading base at Calicut. The Samuri, however, refused to co-operate and after a violent dispute Cabral sailed down the Malabar coast to Cochin where he obtained permission to set up a factory. Though he lost all but five of his ships, he too had reason to feel pleased with himself for he took home a precious cargo of assorted spices and medicinal drugs. In 1502 da Gama led another expedition to India in the course of which he bombarded Calicut and defeated an Arab fleet.

Exploration was now giving way to market imperialism. The Portuguese were neither rich nor numerous enough to compete with the Arabs by purely commercial means; all they could do was to destroy their trade by force. So they decided to set up a permanent fleet in the Indian Ocean and a network of commercial and naval bases. The Arabs, seeing that their monopoly was threatened, dispatched a large fleet to annihilate the interlopers, but it was defeated off Diu in 1509 and subsequent Arab attacks also failed. The Portuguese were thus able to carry out their plan for an armed take-over of the spice trade. Under the able direction of Afonso d'Albuquerque they established bases at Socotra and Hormuz, thereby gaining control of the western extremities of the Arab trade. In 1510 they seized the island of Goa and in the next year Malacca, whence they were able to control traffic across the Bay of Bengal. The absence of timber supplies on the Red Sea and the Persian Gulf has been blamed for the failure of the Arabs to protect their interests, but the real cause of their failure lay rather in their outmoded techniques of naval warfare. Whereas the Portuguese used sailing-ships equipped with powerful guns, the Arabs continued to rely mainly on galleys, and clung to the old method of ramming and boarding.

The secret of European ascendancy in Asia was superiority of fire power. Artillery was known in Asia long before the coming of the Portuguese, but in the fifteenth century European technology

9   Vasco da Gama meets the Samuri of Calicut in 1498

advanced rapidly so that the armament of the Portuguese ships took the Asians completely by surprise. The *Rajavali* describes the arrival of the Portuguese in Ceylon as follows:

> and now it came to pass that a ship from Portugal arrived at Colombo, and information was brought to the King that there were in the harbour a race of very white and beautiful people who wear boots and hats of iron and never stop in any place. They eat a sort of white stone and drink blood. And if they get a fish they give two or three *ridé* in gold for it, and besides, they have guns with a noise like thunder and a ball from one of them, after traversing a league, will break a castle of marble.[1]

The gunned ship developed by the Atlantic Powers of Europe was of crucial significance, for nothing could resist it east of the Cape. 'At the rumour of our coming', wrote Albuquerque to the king of Portugal in 1513, 'the [native] ships all vanished and even the birds ceased to skim over the water'. Within fifteen years of their arrival in the Indian Ocean the Portuguese destroyed the naval power of the Arabs and their king could justifiably claim the title of 'Lord of the Conquest, Navigation, and Commerce of Ethiopia, Arabia, Persia, and India'. But it must be stressed that the superiority of the Europeans was confined to the sea. On land, as Albuquerque well understood, they were highly vulnerable, for they had not yet developed an effective field-artillery capable of compensating for their numerical weakness. How could they hope to subdue a monarch like Krishna Raya who went to war in 1520 with 703,000 infantry, 32,600 cavalry, and 551 elephants? So the Portuguese carefully refrained from attempting to dominate any part of the Indian mainland.

The commercial activities of the Portuguese lie outside the scope of this chapter. We are concerned with discovery not with trade, but in the period of European expansion the two activities were so closely related as to be virtually indistinguishable. The Portuguese were only interested in discovery as a means to wealth. Where there was no profit to be made they did not trouble to go. The maps they wanted were maps of the spice routes, not of the Indian mainland which they could not hope to conquer. Exploration of areas without promise of gain was left to private individuals motivated by religious zeal or mere curiosity. Two such individuals were the Jesuits Benedict Goes, who travelled from India to China by way of Afghanis-

[1] C. M. Cipolla, *Guns and Sails in the Early Phase of European Expansion, 1400–1700*, p. 107.

27

tan in 1602, and Antonio de Andrade, who crossed the Himalayas into Tibet in 1624. But in general the Portuguese soon came to regard India as merely a convenient stage on the way to places of greater profit further east, for Malacca stood on the western edge of another important trading area controlled by the Chinese and the Japanese.

The Portuguese were particularly keen to get to the Moluccas or Spice islands, but locating them was not a simple task. Late medieval European maps of this part of the world were worse than useless. On the basis of information handed down from antiquity or derived from Marco Polo's *Travels*, they either fused the Malay peninsula and the East Indies into one huge peninsula or put in a purely imaginary archipelago. Fortunately for the Portuguese a Javanese map of Indonesia fell into their hands in 1510. Three years later they reached the Moluccas and made an agreement with the sultan of Ternate, the main clove-producing island. In 1517 a Portuguese fleet reached Canton in China and celebrated the occasion by firing its cannon. This only terrified the Chinese and confirmed the dreadful stories they had heard about the 'barbarians with the big nose'. Even so, they allowed the Portuguese to settle at Macao in 1556. The Portuguese also reached Japan, but finding its produce relatively disappointing they did not trouble to explore the country further, being content with an annual voyage from Nagasaki.

The Atlantic and Columbus

European expansion in the fifteenth century was not limited to one direction, nor was it the preserve of a single nation. The Portuguese discovery of the Cape route to India and the Far East coincided with exploration of the Atlantic in which Castile played a prominent role. Here again there was continuity with the early Middle Ages when expeditions had ranged far into the Ocean Sea. Iceland was reached from Ireland in the eighth century and colonized from Norway in the ninth, while Greenland was settled from Iceland in the tenth. Archaeology has revealed that the Greenland settlement still existed in the late fifteenth century and continued to be in contact with Europe. During the eleventh century ships from Greenland reached Labrador and followed the North American coast as far as New England. Groups of islands further south in the Atlantic – the Madeiras,

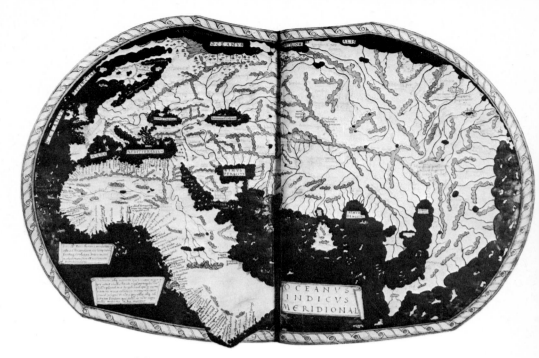

10 Map printed by Henricus Martellus, *c.* 1489, showing the world as Columbus probably conceived it before he sailed, with Asia according to Ptolemy and Marco Polo, Africa as revealed by Dias, and no New World

the Azores, and the Canaries – were known to Europeans in the fourteenth century and systematically settled by them in the fifteenth. Yet, in spite of their experience of Atlantic navigation, Europeans underestimated the ocean's size and did not suspect the existence of the American continent. Ptolemy had given the circumference of the world as only 18,000 geographical miles, while he had exaggerated the east–west breadth of Asia, errors which Marco Polo and Pierre d'Ailly had repeated in their works. No map, with the exception of the Vinland map (*c* 1440) whose authenticity remains questionable, gave even a rough idea of the real extent of the Atlantic.

As knowledge about the Atlantic increased during the fifteenth century a number of people began to toy with the idea of reaching Cathay by crossing the ocean westward. Since no one suspected the existence of an intervening continent, the main problem appeared to be the distance separating Asia from Europe. Paolo Toscanelli, the

29

Florentine mathematician and cosmographer, estimated this at a mere 5,000 miles, while Christopher Columbus reduced the figure to 3,500 miles! The problem of distance also seemed less forbidding as Atlantic islands capable of serving as stages *en route* were discovered and occupied. Yet Columbus did not gain support easily for his 'enterprise of the Indies'. Although he had had some experience of navigation (he had been to Guinea, Madeira, and possibly Iceland), his obscure Genoese origins and the high price that he placed on his services were not encouraging to possible patrons. After a delay of five years, however, Queen Isabella of Castile agreed to help him. He was authorized to discover and gain 'certain islands and mainland in the Ocean Sea', but the fact that he was only given three small ships, no letters of credence, no gifts suitable for a prince, and few arms suggests that he was not expected to find more than islands. Yet he was promised the office of Admiral, Viceroy, and Governor of his discoveries, a hereditary title of nobility, and a tenth of the profits that might accrue from them.

Columbus's small fleet, consisting of the *Niña* (60 tons), the *Pinta* (60 tons), and the *Santa Maria* (120 tons), left Palos on 3 August 1492. After a stop in the Canaries to repair the *Pinta*'s rudder, it resumed its journey on 6 September. The weather was fair and the wind favourable so that Columbus was able to proceed swiftly along the twenty-eighth parallel which he believed would

11   Christopher Columbus. A portrait attributed to Ridolfo Ghirlandaio

30

lead him to Cipango (Japan). Weed and flocks of birds soon indicated the proximity of land and on 12 October the expedition sighted Watling Island on the edge of the Bahamas group. Columbus was sure that Asia lay close at hand, but instead of continuing westward, he veered south and began threading his way through the islands. He received encouragement from the natives who told him of a rich and beautiful land to the south, which turned out to be Cuba. Columbus at first identified it with Cipango, but as its coastline seemed endless he concluded that it was Cathay and dispatched an embassy to the Great Khan. The discovery of Haiti in the weeks that followed did not upset him as islands were only to be expected off the coast of Cathay. The small pieces of gold which he got from the natives also served to convince him that he was within the Great Khan's commercial empire. So far everything had gone quite well, but when the *Santa Maria* was wrecked on a coastal reef, Columbus had to change his plans. He erected the fort of Navidad near Cape Haitien and left part of the *Santa Maria*'s crew to man it. Then, on 4 January, he set off in the *Niña* for home. At first the weather was good and he was able to make daily runs surpassing even those of his outward journey, but in February he ran into a terrible gale and had to take shelter in the Azores. An even worse storm almost engulfed him off the coast of Portugal. On 4 March, however, he arrived at Lisbon and in the next month appeared before Ferdinand and Isabella at Bárcelona, accompanied by a group of strangely attired natives unlike any previously known to Europeans, a living proof that he had achieved his purpose.

The king of Portugal treated Columbus's claims sceptically, yet he was anxious about Spanish activities in the Atlantic. To forestall any objections on his part, Ferdinand and Isabella applied to the Pope for confirmation of their ownership of Columbus's discoveries. Alexander VI, who was appropriately a Spaniard, was only too pleased to oblige as he needed their support in Italy. In the famous bull *Inter Caetera* he conferred on Spain

> all the islands and mainlands, found or to be found, discovered or to be discovered, westward or southward, by drawing and establishing a line running from the Arctic to the Antarctic Pole one hundred leagues west and south from any of the islands that are commonly called the Azores and Cape Verde.[2]

[2] J. R. Hale, *Renaissance Exploration*, p. 65.

Subsequently the Pope extended his grant to

> all islands and mainlands whatever, found or to be found . . . in sailing
> or travelling towards west and south, whether they be in regions
> occidental or meridional and oriental and of India.[3]

This so alarmed the king of Portugal that he opened direct negotiations with the Spanish monarchs, who agreed in the Treaty of Tordesillas to shift the line of demarcation 270 leagues further west. As they believed that Columbus had reached Asia, they could not see any disadvantage to themselves in the adjustment. But the king of Portugal knew better: the treaty gave him not only the only genuine route to the Far East but also most of the south Atlantic, including Brazil which was shortly to be discovered by Cabral on his way to India.

Columbus, meanwhile, had returned to the West Indies at the head of a much more ambitious expedition comprising seventeen ships and 1,200 men. Its purpose was obviously to establish a settlement for the volunteers who accompanied him, including artisans, soldiers, farmers, and priests, carrying tools, seeds, and animals. After a prosperous passage, the fleet made landfall at Dominica and followed the curve of the Lesser Antilles as far as the north coast of Hispaniola. Finding that the Navidad settlement had been wiped out, Columbus founded a new colony on another site, but it was soon bedevilled by wars with the natives and internal quarrels. Lacking the qualities necessary to a colonial administrator, Columbus failed to impose discipline on his followers, who could only think of gold and slaves. Before he returned to Spain in 1496 he explored the south coast of Cuba and discovered Jamaica, 'the fairest island that eyes have beheld', but he did not try to go further west. Perhaps he was not really keen to make contact with the court of the Great Khan. Convinced as he still was that he had reached Cathay, he may have preferred to look for riches where the natives were tame and competition absent rather than to venture further afield where he might encounter powerful rivals.

While Columbus was looking for Cathay in the Caribbean, another attempt was made to find it further north. In 1496 John Cabot, a naturalized Venetian of Genoese origin, obtained a patent from Henry VII of England to sail to all parts of 'the eastern, western and northern sea' with a view to discovering

---

[3] J. H. Parry, *The Age of Reconnaissance*, pp. 151–2.

whatsoever islands, countries, regions or provinces of heathens and infidels in whatsoever part of the world placed, which before this time were unknown to all Christians.[4]

Since 1480 at least, Bristol merchants had organized expeditions to explore the North Atlantic and they had probably discovered New-foundland. Cabot presumably came to England because he had heard of their activities and felt doubtful about Columbus's claim to have reached the 'land of the Great Khan'. In May 1497 he sailed on the small bark, *Matthew*, and stayed away for three months. Where he went is not known for certain; one theory is that he landed on or near the coast of Maine and coasted as far east as Cape Race or Cape Breton. Be this as it may, he returned convinced that he had reached Asia and prepared another expedition to follow its coast to Cipango where 'all the spices of the world have their origin as well as the jewels'. Unfortunately, even less is known about Cabot's 1498 voyage than about his first, for he was never seen again. Contem-

[4] J. A. Williamson, *The Cabot Voyages and Bristol Discovery under Henry VII*, p. 204.

12   Columbus takes possession of Hispaniola. This etching combines two incidents: *left*, Columbus lands at Guanahani, dedicating the island to Our Lord (San Salvador); *right*, he meets the people of Hispaniola

porary maps, notably La Cosa's, suggest that he sailed far enough south to arouse the apprehensions of the Spaniards. But at least one of Cabot's five ships must have come back, for Englishmen no longer believed that they had found Asia after 1498; instead they referred to the 'New Land' or 'the New Found Land'.

In the spring of 1498 Columbus set off on his third voyage, this time with only six ships. His instructions were presumably that he should go to Hispaniola with supplies for the colonists. On reaching the Canaries, however, he divided his fleet: while three ships were sent to Hispaniola, he took the rest as far south as the Cape Verde islands and only then turned west. Columbus did this for two reasons: he had been advised that 'the majority of precious things come from a very hot region' and wanted to verify a rumour that a large land mass lay somewhere in the Western Ocean on the equatorial latitude. At the end of July he sighted the peaks of Trinidad, then the low-lying coast of Venezuela. At first he thought this was just another island, but the great volume of fresh water flowing from the Orinoco delta soon convinced him that he had found a large and hitherto unknown continent. His medievalism, however, got the better of his judgement for he declared that the river flowed from the Earthly Paradise. In the course of his journeys across the Atlantic he had noticed that his ships had climbed smoothly towards the sky west of the Azores and that the temperature had risen as they had drawn nearer to the sun. On the basis of this weird observation he concluded that the earth was pear-shaped, not spherical, and that the Earthly Paradise lay at the top of a stalk-like projection which rose towards Heaven at the equator. Yet Columbus did not try to reach this Paradise; instead he proceeded to Hispaniola where he found half the colonists in open revolt. In 1499 he was superseded and sent back to Spain in irons.

Although Columbus failed as a colonial administrator, he had not completely forfeited the confidence of the Spanish government, and in 1502 he was allowed to lead another voyage of discovery. His outward journey was the best he ever made: he took only twenty-one days to reach Martinique from the Canaries. After riding out a storm off Santo Domingo he made for Honduras, where he saw a large canoe carrying goods of a more sophisticated kind than he had so far seen in the Caribbean. But he did not follow up this first contact with the Mayan civilization of Yucatan, preferring to look instead

13 Map of Brazil, with natives, plants, animals, and birds

for a strait that would lead him to India. He followed the coasts of Nicaragua and Costa Rica and in January 1503 founded a settlement at Belem at the entrance to the modern Panama Canal. The hostility of the natives, however, obliged him to return to Hispaniola, but his four ships were not equal to the journey. Two had to be abandoned on the coast of Central America, while the other two only just managed to reach Jamaica without falling apart. While Columbus was marooned here, he informed the Spanish monarchs that he had been within ten days' march of the Ganges and within reach of mountains of gold. He was rescued a year later and returned to Spain, but he was broken in body and spirit and died in May 1506, probably still convinced that the lands that he had discovered were part of Asia.

Exploration after Columbus

Columbus was not alone in exploring the coast of South America. In 1499 Vincente Yañez Pinzon discovered a great river which may have been the Amazon, but was probably the Orinoco, while Alonso de Ojeda explored the coast of Venezuela. In 1500, as we have seen, Cabral made the first certainly recorded landing in Brazil on his way to India. Then there was Amerigo Vespucci, a Florentine geographer and amateur navigator, who claimed to have made four voyages to the New World. The most important of these took place in 1501 when he explored the whole length of the Brazilian coast south of 5°S. It was mainly this voyage which caused the German geographer and humanist, Martin Waldseemüller, to consider Vespucci the true discoverer of the American continent and to name it after him. Vespucci was not, however, an explorer of the same calibre as Columbus; he was a good publicist and interpreter of discoveries. He showed beyond a shadow of a doubt that America stood as a barrier between Europe and Asia. But how wide was the barrier? This question was answered in 1513 when Vasco Nuñez de Balboa, following up an Indian report, crossed the Isthmus of Darien and saw the Pacific. Clad in armour, and with drawn sword, he waded into the water and standing breast-deep raised the banner of Castile.

Now that the west coast of America had been discovered it became necessary to find a way by which Atlantic shipping might reach the Pacific. The honour of finding such a route fell to Ferdinand Magellan, a Portuguese sailor of fortune, who had taken part in the

14 Magellan on his ship discovers the strait which bears his name in October 1520

siege of Malacca and had probably visited the Moluccas. In 1518 he persuaded the Emperor Charles V to authorize an expedition to the East Indies from the west. Magellan believed that a western passage might be found by following up Vespucci's third voyage to the southern extremity of South America, and the Spanish government was interested in his plan because it hoped that the Moluccas lay within the Spanish hemisphere as defined by the Treaty of Tordesillas. The meridian of 46°W which had been chosen as the dividing-line between the Portuguese and Spanish zones of overseas enterprise applied not only to the Western Hemisphere; it went right round the world, but no one knew exactly where the Moluccas were situated in relation to it, as longitude was not easily computed before the invention of the chronometer in the eighteenth century.

Magellan's fleet of five ships and 280 men left Spain in September 1519. Two months later they reached the coast of South America and followed it down as far as San Julian in Patagonia where they stopped for the winter. Here Magellan had to suppress a mutiny, and soon afterwards one of his ships was wrecked and another deserted. Nevertheless, he reached the strait that bears his name in October 1520 and negotiated its 320 treacherous miles in thirty-eight days. Then, on 28 November, he entered the broad waters of the Pacific, solving the riddle of westward passage. He now steered north along the coast of Chile until he caught a favourable wind, then struck out in a latitude well to the north of the Spice islands. As each day passed without land being sighted Magellan's men were reduced to eating rats and gnawing leather. Eventually they reached Guam in the Ladrones, where they did not find much refreshment. In April they reached Cebu in the Philippines, but Magellan allowed himself to be caught up in a local war and was killed with forty of his men. Fortunately he had accomplished his purpose; he had reached the Far East by a westward voyage and had succeeded where Columbus had failed. Sebastian del Cano took over command of the expedition. With only two ships left he sailed south to Borneo, and eventually reached Tidore in the Moluccas where the sultan welcomed him and allowed him to take on a cargo of cloves. The two ships then parted company: the *Trinidad* set out to cross the Pacific to Panama but was captured by the Portuguese; del Cano's own ship, the *Victoria*, returned to Spain via the Indian Ocean and Cape of Good Hope.

37

She arrived on 8 September 1522, almost three years after her departure, with a crew of only fifteen men. Thus ended the first circumnavigation of the world.

Magellan's voyage demonstrated the enormous difficulties attendant upon a westward voyage to the Spice islands. Its length was bad enough, but there were also the trade winds which blew unceasingly from the east between the Tropics so that it was much easier to sail from America to Asia than in the reverse direction. The Spaniards did not learn this lesson immediately: a second expedition to the Moluccas in 1525 ended disastrously and another from Mexico in 1527 fared no better. Saavedra, who led this last voyage, died as he tried vainly to beat his way back to Mexico against the trade winds and his crew surrendered to the Portuguese. In the light of these failures, Charles V, who needed money badly for his war with France, sold his claim to the Moluccas to Portugal for 350,000 ducats. This had the effect of reducing Spanish activity in the Pacific without stopping it altogether. In 1565 Lopez de Legaspi planted the first Spanish colony in the east at Cebu in the Philippines, and in the same year Andres de Urdaneta proved that an eastward journey across the Pacific was possible by pursuing a wide northern arc reaching as far as the forty-second parallel.

Magellan's discovery of a westward passage to the Far East did not rule out the possibility that another might exist in the Northern Hemisphere. The search for a north-west passage was started by John Cabot's son, Sebastian, in 1509. He reached latitude 67°N and may have penetrated Hudson's Bay, but ice and a mutinous crew obliged him to turn back. Another expedition, this time on behalf of King Francis I of France, was undertaken in 1523 by Giovanni da Verazzano. He wrote,

> My intention in this navigation was to reach Cathay and the extreme east of Asia, not expecting to find such an obstacle of new land as I found; and if for some reason I expected to find it, I thought it not to be without some strait to penetrate the Eastern Ocean. And this has been the opinion of all the ancients, believing certainly our Western Ocean to be one with the Eastern Ocean of India without interposition of land.[5]

Verazzano was an able surveyor. His account is the most accurate of all the early coastal voyages, but he made one serious mistake

[5] J. R. Hale, *op. cit.*, p. 71.

15   Sebastian Cabot, by S. Rawle

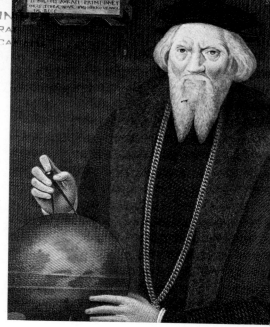

in the course of his reconnaissance of the North American coast from
Florida to Cape Breton. After missing the entrance to Chesapeake
Bay, he saw its broad waters beyond eastern Maryland and concluded
that it must be the Pacific – hence the feature called the 'sea of
Verazzano' which subsequently found its way into maps, causing
much speculation. In 1534 Jacques Cartier led an expedition to
Canada – probably with a view to finding a passage to the Pacific.
Though he soon discovered that the St Lawrence was a river, not a
strait, he was encouraged to persist in his efforts by stories that
reached him of three native kingdoms in the vicinity. He returned to
the same area in 1535 and again in 1541, when he and Roberval
planted the first French colony in Canada.

European expansion was essentially confined to the oceans and
coasts. The Portuguese, as we have seen, did not try to penetrate
Asia or Africa to any significant extent. They knew that their superiority lay in the gunned ship and that on land they were vulnerable.
They could not hope to conquer territory in Asia which was densely
populated and well defended by large armies. In Africa the geophysical conditions were an insurmountable barrier to white penetration. But in America conditions were different: the country was

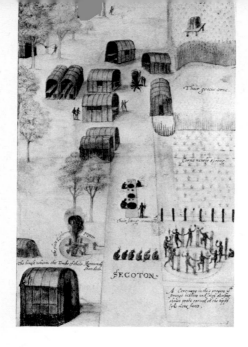

thinly populated, the natives were technologically backward, and the geophysical conditions were generally tolerable. Furthermore, the natives' power of resistance was undermined by their susceptibility to European infectious diseases, and some who were exploited by ruthless minorities like the Aztecs of Mexico were ready to welcome strangers as liberators. This exceptional combination of factors enabled Europeans to penetrate America in a way that would not have been possible elsewhere. The Spanish *conquistadores* who overran Central and South America were not explorers. They were for the most part unprincipled adventurers on the lookout for gold and slaves, but their activities cannot be overlooked in the present context as they contributed enormously to the process of discovery.

The settlement of Central America began in 1509 when the Spanish government issued two licences, one to Diego de Nicuesa for the settlement of Veragua, and the other to Alonso de Ojeda for that of what is now the north coast of Colombia. The two expeditions numbered over 1,000 men, but most of them succumbed to famine, sickness, and poisoned arrows. Reinforcements were sent from Hispaniola under a royal official, de Enciso, but the leadership was soon taken over by Balboa. Besides leading the expedition to the

Pacific coast, he founded a colony at Darien and subdued the Indians by a combination of force and diplomacy. In 1519, however, he was beheaded on a treason charge by order of the first royal governor of Darien, Pedro Arias de Avila, better known as Pedrarias. Though a ruthless and cruel tyrant, Pedrarias served the cause of discovery by carrying out a comprehensive reconnaissance of Nicaragua. Meanwhile, Diego Velazquez, the able and energetic governor of Cuba, sent a number of small expeditions to the north coast of Yucatan and the Gulf of Mexico. They came back with reports of a great empire, whose ruler Montezuma lived in a great city in a mountain lake. This, of course, was the rich and powerful Aztec state which dominated Mexico from sea to sea.

The conquest of Mexico began on Good Friday 1519 when Hernán Cortés and his force of 600 volunteers landed on the coast. To demonstrate his independence of the governor of Cuba, Cortés ordered his ships to be destroyed and founded the 'municipality' of Vera Cruz from which he obtained a new commission. He then led his band of adventurers from the tropical coastland to the high valley of Mexico. After defeating the Tlaxcalans, he made an alliance with them and advanced on Tenochtitlan (Mexico City). Unfortunately, we cannot linger over the colourful details of the Mexican conquest – the capture and death of Montezuma, the confiscation of his treasure, the terrible *Noche Triste*. Suffice it to say that it was rapid and complete. Much of the country was inevitably discovered during the conquest; even Popocatapetl, its highest peak, was climbed by an intrepid mountaineer. With Mexico at his feet, Cortés continued the search for a strait across Central America or for harbours suitable for Pacific exploration. Pedro de Alvarado led an expedition to Guatemala, while Cristobal de Olid was sent to Honduras. In 1533 a fleet sent out by Cortés discovered Lower California.

Meanwhile, rumours had reached the Spaniards in Darien of another native empire situated far to the south and high up in the Andes. This was the Peruvian Empire of the Incas. Its conquest was organized by a syndicate of three Spaniards who had settled in Darien: two soldiers of fortune, Francisco Pizarro and Diego Almagro, and a priest, Fernando de Luque, who provided most of the capital. After spending four years exploring the Pacific coast of South America as far south as Tumbes, Pizarro returned to Spain where he was given a favourable hearing by the Emperor Charles V and a capitulation appointing him governor of Peru for life. Then, after recruiting volunteers in his native Estramadura, he went back to Panama.

Pizarro had only 180 men and twenty-seven horses when he set off to conquer Peru in 1530, but he had the advantage that a war of succession had recently broken out among the Incas. In the autumn of 1532 he led a surprise attack on Cajamarca, capturing the usurper Atahualpa and killing most of his retinue. Finding themselves without their ruler the Incas ceased to resist, and in 1533 Pizarro was able to capture Cuzco, their traditional capital, and its treasure. Serious disputes soon arose among the conquerors, culminating in civil war and Pizarro's murder in 1541, yet exploration from Peru continued during these years. Expeditions were made eastward across the Andes and into the upper basin of the Amazon in search of a land reputed to overflow with spices. In 1539 Belalcazar travelled overland from Peru to the Caribbean by way of Colombia and the Magdalena River. Other journeys were made south of Peru in a vain search for another golden empire. Almagro set off in 1535 on a gruelling two-year march into Chile which ended in bitter disappointment. This did not deter Pedro de Valdivia from leading another expedition to Chile in 1540 which led to the foundation of Santiago. Meanwhile, the Spaniards in the Caribbean had begun to explore the Colombian hinterland. In 1536 Gonzalo Jiménez de Quesada reached the plain of Bogota after hacking his way through forests and swamps, and was rewarded by the discovery of gold and emeralds in large quantities.

Quesada was one of the fortunate *conquistadores*; many were less so, yet if they found nothing of value to themselves they helped to fill in blank spaces in the map of the New World. In 1513 Ponce de Leon traced most of the coastline of Florida in an unsuccessful bid to find the Fountain of Youth. Even more rewarding geographically was Hernando de Soto's fruitless search for the Seven Cities of Cibola, which took him from Florida to the Appalachians and west to the Mississippi. The same quest was extended by Francisco Vasquez de Coronado in 1540 to Arizona, New Mexico, Texas, Oklahoma, and Kansas. In South America the cause of discovery was served by the legend of El Dorado, the Gilded Man, whose variable location eventually became fixed in the mysterious borderland between Venezuela and Guiana. Because of him, Francisco de Orellana made a remarkable descent of the Amazon in 1539 and Lope de Aguirre surveyed the river systems of the Amazon and Orinoco in 1561. Sir Walter Raleigh was among many others who looked for El Dorado, only to find that he was always further on.

Until about 1550 England's role in exploration was comparatively insignificant. Except for the Cabot voyages no important expeditions left her shores. The basic reason for this apathy was economic prosperity; England exported her cloth to Antwerp and did not need to seek markets further afield. But about 1550 the Antwerp market collapsed and English merchants had to dispose of their cloth elsewhere. Cathay with its gold and spices was a tempting possibility, but how was it to be reached? The old route through the Mediterranean was controlled by the Venetians and the new ones south of the equator by the Portuguese and the Spaniards. The only course open to the English was to find a new route round the north of Asia or the north of America. The north-east passage had an influential advocate in John Dee. In line with medieval Arab geographers he believed that Asia sloped continuously south-east beyond the North Cape so that most of the voyage would take place in temperate waters. It was also likely, he thought, that the inhabitants of the cooler lands along the way would provide 'a good vent for cloth'.

The first attempt to find the north-east passage, made in 1553 by Sir Hugh Willoughby, ended in failure, as did Stephen Burrough's

17 Battle with a polar bear during one of Barents' three voyages in search of a north-east passage to India

18 Martin Frobisher, by
C. de Passe

expedition three years later. A side effect of Willoughby's voyage, however, was the establishment by his second in command, Richard Chancellor, of an overland trade route from the White Sea to Moscow. Though Anglo-Russian trade in this period never amounted to much, it did provide England with timber, hemp, and cordage useful to her shipbuilding programme. Contact with Russia also opened up the possibility of an overland route to the Far East through Persia. The pioneer in this direction was Anthony Jenkinson, who got as far as Bokhara in 1558 and Kasvin in 1562. Persia, however, proved to be little more than a cul-de-sac, and trade with it ceased after the Turks had invaded the country in 1579. A year later the search for the north-east passage was resumed by the Muscovy Company. It could take encouragement from the opinion of no less an authority than the great geographer, Mercator. 'The voyage to Cathay by the east', he declared, 'is doubtless very easy and short, and I have oftentimes marvelled that being so happily begun it hath been left off.' But Arthur Pet and Charles Jackman, who tried to follow this route in 1580, failed to get beyond the Kara Sea because of ice and fog. Thereafter the search was taken up by the Dutchman, Willem

Barents. In the course of three voyages between 1594 and 1596, he discovered Spitsbergen, explored the west coast of Novaya Zemlya, and reached the mouth of the Ob, but his ship was eventually crushed in the ice, forcing him and his men to winter far in the Arctic Circle. Barents did not survive the experience for long and with him expired Dutch exploration in this area.

Although the first attempts to find a north-east passage had been disappointing, Englishmen did not give up the idea of reaching Cathay. In 1566 Sir Humphrey Gilbert wrote a tract called *A Discourse of a Discoverie for a New Passage to Cataia*, in which he listed arguments based on authority, reason, and experience in favour of the existence beyond Labrador of a strait running south-west into the Pacific. This route, he asserted, would enable the English to reach the Far East sooner than the Portuguese and the Spaniards and to undersell them. Gilbert also suggested the setting up of staples in America to which England might send her 'needy people'. As yet he envisaged settlement simply as a trading convenience or social prophylactic, not as a source of territorial power and wealth for the promoters. The upshot of this publicity was Martin Frobisher's voyage to the coast of Baffin Island in 1576. He came back claiming that he had found the north-west passage and brought home an Eskimo whom he passed off as a Cathayan, and pieces of black ore alleged to contain gold. Everyone was jubilant, none more so than Michael Lok who promptly set up the Cathay Company. But it was doomed from the start, for Frobisher had not found the passage, only an inlet leading nowhere. As for the quantities of black ore which he collected on two subsequent voyages, they turned out to be utterly worthless. The Cathay Company collapsed and Lok ended up in a debtors' prison. Frobisher's failure dampened enthusiasm for the north-west passage, but did not extinguish it. Between 1585 and 1587 John Davis led three expeditions to the waters between Greenland and the North American coast. 'I have been in 73°', he reported, 'finding the sea all open, and forty leagues between land and land', wherefore, he concluded, 'the passage is most probable, the execution easy.' This was too optimistic; Davis had not found the passage and his progress beyond Sanderson's Hope was frustrated by ice.

Ironically enough it was by way of the Mediterranean and the Middle East that the Elizabethans first made contact with India,

Burma, and the Malay peninsula. In 1578 two London merchants hit on the idea of reviving the old Levant trade which had flourished in the fifteenth century. Their envoy signed an agreement with the Turkish sultan and the Levant Company was formed with depots in various parts of the Ottoman Empire. At the same time a small party of Englishmen led by John Newbery and Ralph Fitch crossed Turkish territory, reaching the Persian Gulf and ultimately India. After presenting letters of credence from their queen to the moghul, they parted company. Newbery perished on the way home, but Fitch pressed on as far as Bengal, Burma, and Malacca and got back to England safely after an absence of nine years to find that his relatives had given him up for dead and divided his estate. His return in 1591 coincided with the first English expedition to the East Indies by sea via the Cape. This did not prove an easy voyage: only James Lancaster got through. Yet within a few years the East India Company had been established and had begun to build up a profitable trade. Logically this should have put an end to the search for the north-west passage, yet several more attempts were made to find it in the early seventeenth century, the most famous being Henry Hudson's fateful expedition of 1610. The only practical result of these voyages was the foundation of the Hudson's Bay Company under Charles II.

The vast expansion of geographical knowledge which accrued from the great discoveries was reflected in Renaissance cartography. From the middle of the fifteenth century manuscript charts were produced showing the progress of discovery. In 1492 Martin Behaim of Nürnberg attempted to bring geographical knowledge up to date in the earliest known terrestrial globe. The oldest map to show Columbus's discoveries and to record Vasco da Gama's voyage to India is the great world map of Juan de la Cosa which is dated 1500. Two years later another fine world map, known as the 'Cantino chart', appeared in Portugal. Its portrayal of Africa is remarkably accurate, India is given its correct peninsular shape, and there is only one Malay peninsula. The culminating point of early sixteenth-century cartography was the work of Diogo Ribeiro, who drew several charts based on the *Padron Real*, the official record of discoveries kept in the Casa de Contratación in Seville. The most informative is the one dated 1529, now in the Vatican: it covers the whole globe between the Poles, shows the East Indies in its eastern and western margins, reduces the Mediterranean to roughly the right proportions, but retains the Ptolemaic exaggeration of the breadth of Asia.

By comparison with manuscript charts, printed maps of the late fifteenth and early sixteenth centuries were slow to assimilate new information and remained far longer under the Ptolemaic spell. They showed a truncated India and two Malay peninsulas as late as the 1540s. The Contarini map of 1506 was the first printed map to show any of the recent discoveries. Another step forward was the publication in 1513 of the first modern atlas, an edition of Ptolemy containing twenty new maps. It held the field for more than a quarter of a century, but important single maps like the Ramusio map (1534) and the Cabot map (1544) were also published. If Italy was the principal centre of cartography in the middle of the sixteenth century, primacy passed to the Low Countries in the second half of the century. Gerard Mercator's famous world map on the projection that bears his name appeared in 1569 and a year later Abraham Ortelius published his *Theatrum Orbis Terrarum*, marking the emancipation of printed cartography from Ptolemy. Here at last was

19 Vissche's engraving of the sixteenth-century galleon
Ark Royal

an atlas devised on scientific principles. It showed Scandinavia, Greenland, and the Arctic regions more accurately than ever before and displayed a thorough knowledge of the East Indies. But it was not entirely free from errors: it showed the Straits of Anian between North America and Asia, made South America look almost rectangular, and included an enormous southern continent.

Terra Australis was the most obstinate of the myths which had coloured geographical knowledge since ancient times. It derived mainly from the theory that the world would topple over if the weight of Europe and Asia was not balanced in the Southern Hemisphere by that of another land mass. Renaissance cartographers also disliked empty oceanic spaces, so that as they depicted Africa, Asia, and America with increasing precision they also filled in the southern part of the world with a huge unknown continent reaching at least as far north in places as the tropic of Capricorn. In the Dauphin map of 1546, for instance, we see it rising up in a broad peninsula to the East Indies. One of the original aims of Drake's famous circumnavigation of the world in 1577 was apparently to find *Terra Australis*, but this plan was not carried out. Instead Drake followed the west coast of America as far north as California after he had gone through the Magellan Strait and then crossed the Pacific to the Moluccas.

No serious attempt was made to probe the mystery of the southern continent until the Dutch took to extensive ocean-voyaging in the last decade of the sixteenth century. Cape York peninsula was sighted by Willem Janszoon in 1606, but he assumed that it was part of New Guinea, and the Spaniard, Torres, who passed through the Strait that bears his name in the same year, also failed to appreciate the nature of his discovery. In 1615 Jacob Le Maire and Willem Corneliszoon Schouten demonstrated that *Terra Australis* did not reach up to the Magellan Strait (as shown in the maps of Mercator and Ortelius) by sailing round Cape Horn. Meanwhile Dutch Indiamen found that sailing conditions in the southern Indian Ocean were better than further north and took to following a course east from the Cape and then northward in a great loop to Java. This led to Dirk Hartogszoon's chance discovery in 1616 of the coast of western Australia, but the relationship between this coast and Cape York peninsula was not immediately recognized. In fact the insular

20 Drake's fleet at San Domingo, which he captured
from the Spaniards in 1585

character of Australia was not revealed until 1642 when Abel Tasman
sailed right round it without sighting it, although he discovered
Tasmania and New Zealand in the process. Two years later he
established the connection between Cape York and west Australia,
but what he saw of the country was so uninviting that exploration
of the area languished until 1770, when Captain Cook discovered
and surveyed the east coast of Australia and passed through Torres
Strait. By so doing he established the real shape of the southern
continent and completed the great cycle of discovery begun by
Henry the Navigator three and a half centuries before.

Europe and the Wider World to the Fifteenth Century

ANTHONY BRYER

The Greek Era

ALEXANDER OF MACEDON (356–323 B.C.) was the first European ruler to make his influence felt on civilizations outside the European, the Semitic, the Greek, and the Persian. His name was legendary. High on the north wall of St Mark's Cathedral in Venice a bas-relief depicts the apotheosis of Alexander the Great. He is shown in the attitude of a Persian king, his chariot drawn by griffins which he feeds on raw meat impaled on his lance. Marco Polo knew the tale and, as a Venetian, probably knew the relief as well. In the thirteenth and fourteenth centuries a number of popular *Romances of Alexander* circulated Frankish Europe. They were paralleled in the Levant by an earlier imaginary biography of Alexander, which found its way from Greek into Armenian, Persian, Syriac, and Ethiopian versions. When, in the thirteenth century, Polo reached the Badakhshan Mountains on the northern confines of Persia, he found

> an extensive kingdom, being in length full twelve days' journey, and it is governed by princes in hereditary succession, who are all descended from Alexander, by the daughter of Darius, King of the Persians. All these have borne the title in the Saracenic tongue of Zulkarnen, being equivalent to Alexander.[1]

These Muslims who claimed that their rulers were descended from Alexander 'the horned one',

> asserted that not long since there were still found in this province horses of the breed of Alexander's celebrated Bucephalus, which were foaled with a particular mark on the forehead.[2]

Bucephalus was as celebrated among the Venetians as he was in remote Badakhshan.

Marco Polo shows no surprise at finding the common heritage of memories of the Macedonian conqueror in Persia; for until he reached the eastern borders of Bactria he was travelling through lands

---

[1] *The Travels of Marco Polo.*   [2] *Ibid.*

21 Bas-relief on the north wall of St Mark's Cathedral in
Venice, showing Alexander the Great in the attitude of a
Persian king

already familiar to him in European legend. Alexander and his
successors had, in the fourth century before Christ, been the first to
break through the conventional bounds of Europe on a significant
and enduring scale. For centuries thereafter the rulers of Persia,
Afghanistan, and of north-western India had prided themselves on
an imperfectly interpreted and laboriously maintained Hellenistic
outlook. In the middle of the third century before Christ, the Great
Asoka, Buddhist emperor of India, erected graven pillars which
record his diplomatic relations with other powers. The rulers of
Syria, Egypt, Cyrene, Macedonia and, perhaps, Epiros are mentioned. To what extent Asoka had alliances, or even contacts, with
the eastern Mediterranean, we do not know. But he felt that it was
part of his world and shared with the Ptolemies of Egypt and the
Attalids of Anatolian Pergamum something of the common experience of the Macedonian Empire of a century before. The massive
ruins of Balkh (Bactra) and the vast city of Ay Khanum (possibly
Alexandria-by-the-Oxus), which has been discovered recently, testify
to a part-Hellenistic and part-native civilization which flourished

beneath the Hindu Kush. Most of the exhibits in the Archaeological Museum at Kabul would not look out of place either in museums of the Hellenistic Mediterranean or of Buddhist India, for the two cultures had curiously deep roots in Afghanistan. The area's role as a link between the eastern Mediterranean and India persisted long after the supposed destruction of Greek Bactria in 130 B.C. For instance, it has been discovered that when Pompeii was buried in the volcanic eruption of A.D. 79 a householder had set up an ivory statuette of Lakshmi, Indian goddess of good fortune. Hellenistic art forms clearly influenced the conventional iconography of the Buddha, but the precise extent is much debated. In turn, the legend of the Buddha entered Christian tradition. By then contacts had become obscured. Byzantines attributed the tale of SS Barlaam and Joasaph (the Buddha) to St John of Damascus, but it probably reached the West through Arabic versions and the Georgian *Balavariani*. Orthodox monastic names must share the same initial as secular names, so when Byzantine emperors called John took the cowl, they habitually and appropriately assumed the monastic name of Joasaph, unconsciously imitating the abdication of the Prince Buddha from his secular rule.

But Alexander the Great had not established a bridge between

22 Fifteenth-century painting showing Alexander's fleet
in Asia endangered by a tidal wave

Europe and Asia. He looked towards central Asia in the same way as Asoka was to claim relations with the Levantine kingdoms. They recognized the definite unity, geographical and cultural, of the borderlands of the two continents. But their concern hardly extended beyond the boundaries of Macedonian conquest. It is true that this community of interest was slight at the best of times, but it existed until the fifteenth century A.D. and can stand comparison with concepts of 'Europe' or 'Asia'. It is worth identifying the links and examining the history of the borderlands as a whole. For Alexander had merely explored a middle ground, lured by an already traditional Greco-Persian rivalry. The victories of Marathon and Salamis in the fifth century B.C. had not saved 'Europe' from Oriental and barbarian invasion any more than the famous defence of Constantinople against the Arabs in A.D. 717 preserved Western Christendom from the hosts of Islam. Rather they brought the eastern Mediterranean, and the Greeks in particular, into a long and only rarely hostile contact with successive high civilizations of Persia from Cyrus to the Ilkhans. The pattern was already set. Western Europe was only included in it in the first four centuries of the Christian era, when the Roman Empire created a political unity in the Mediterranean, thereby inheriting the Greek rivalry with Persia, and in the thirteenth and fourteenth centuries when Mongol contacts with Europe led to an Italian commercial interest in Asia and to Roman Catholic hopes of evangelizing the East.

The Roman Era

The first Roman experience of Eastern contact was long remembered but never repeated on the same terms. Heraclius was the last emperor to consider (and reject) the possibility of establishing his capital in the West. But at the battle of Nineveh in 627 and the subsequent downfall of the Sassanians, he decisively closed the ancient period of Greco-Persian rivalry. Byzantium increasingly set her face to the East and within a few decades Islam and the Orthodox and Monophysite Churches shared the Levant and central Asia between them, as remote from western Europe as the Macedonian Empire had once been.

But the few centuries of Roman domination in the Levant had

been highly significant. Roman motives were partly imperial; through acquiring Egypt, Syria, and the Anatolian kingdoms the empire had been led, willy-nilly, into the politics of the Middle East and found itself face to face with its only major rival – the Sassanian Empire of Persia. The Romans were out of their depth east of their great border fortresses such as Dara, and even in the caravan cities like Palmyra which fringed the desert. Shapur placarded his astonishing triumph over Valerian in 260 in rock carvings all over Persia. Roman prestige in the East never recovered from the loss of their emperor to the Sassanians, and Persian supremacy seemed only to be confirmed when in 363 Julian was brought to his own mysterious death encamped before them. But Levantine merchants, assured of an insatiable luxury market in the West, took aggressive advantage of the situation. They established commercial routes later to be exploited by Arabs, Italians, and, eventually, the Portuguese.

Basically there were three routes. Their outlets were in Alexandria, Berytus (Beirut), and on the Black Sea. From Alexandria traders would travel to the customs stations at the head of the Red Sea (Berenice and Leuke Kome) or near Aden (Eudaemon Arabia, Muza). Until the late sixth century A.D., these were the most remote postings for imperial officials. From the market on Socotra island the winter monsoon took shipping down the East African coast to Nikon and, later in the Middle Ages, further south to Kilwa. Summer monsoons brought merchants to southern India and Ceylon. It seems that most traders preferred crossing peninsular India to circumnavigating it. They landed on the Malabar coast near Cranganore (where St Thomas began his legendary evangelization) and moved inland to the markets of Coimbatore, where three kingdoms met and where at least eleven hoards of first-century Roman coins have come to light. At Arikamedu (Pondicherry) they reached the Bay of Bengal. Here excavations have revealed substantial quantities of Roman glass, Arretine ware, coins, and a carved gem depicting the Emperor Augustus.

Traders from Beirut and the emporia of Damascus and Palmyra operated caravan services to the head of the Persian Gulf (Chandax, later Basra). After the fall of the Nabatean kingdom the caravan centres moved south to Mecca and Medina. By the time of Mehemmed's *hegira* from one city to the other in 622 they were sharing a high proportion of the overland trade. Significantly, the Prophet himself began his career as a successful camel contractor. From the Persian Gulf – Basra at its head and Hormuz at its southern end – ships crept round the coast to the mouths of the Indus, or ventured out on the changing monsoons.

The southern routes were part land and part sea; they could be easily controlled by Levantine entrepreneurs who handled the western markets. The northern route was almost entirely overland. It was always less secure and less frequented because it depended upon the political stability of central Asia. But its potential profits were enormous. Its western clearing-house was Constantinople, through the Euxine controlled-entry ports of Trebizond and in the Tauric Chersonese, through which came furs, slaves, and amber from the steppes. At Tabriz, or further south at Ctesiphon or, later, Baghdad, caravans would branch north-east. In classical times the route effectively came to an end at Balkh (Bactra), Tashkurgan, Begram, and Taxila. Under the so-called *Pax Mongolica* of the thirteenth and fourteenth centuries, Samarkand and its associated markets were as far as most Persian traders penetrated. But both in

23 Mecca, from a sixteenth-century Persian tile picture

55

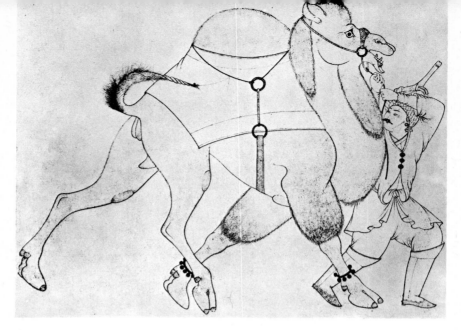

24 Sixteenth-century line drawing of a camel and its driver

the classical and late medieval periods there was a thin, but significant, trickle of merchants who braved the overland route and headed onwards to northern China. It was always a question of 'commercial drift' rather than a regular route to Europe, but its possibilities were to attract a notable succession of Italian merchant adventurers and missionaries. But it was the Romans who first reached China.

In the first two centuries after Christ, the Han dynasty was perfecting an imperial administration and official culture which was to be the basis of all future Chinese government. In retrospect, medieval Chinese historians regarded the Han dynasty with something of the same feeling as Westerners were to have for the Roman Empire. Like the age of the Antonines in the second century A.D., a glow of apparent contentment and good order was attributed to it. It is all the more intriguing, therefore, to find that representatives of the Han and the Antonines actually met in China. A famous passage in the Han Annals describes the arrival of an embassy from 'An-tun', or the Antonine Marcus Aurelius (161–80). The Romans

make coins of gold and silver. . . . They traffic by sea with (Parthia) and (India), the profit of which trade is tenfold. They are honest in their transactions and there are no double prices. . . . Their budget is based on a well-filled treasury. . . . Their kings always desired to send embassies to China, but the (Parthians) wished to carry on trade with them in Chinese silks, and it is for this reason that they were cut off from communication. This lasted till (A.D. 166) when the king of (Rome), An-tun, sent an embassy which, from the frontier of (Annam), offered ivory, rhinoceros horns, and tortoiseshell. From that time dates the intercourse with this country.[3]

It seems almost certain that the 'embassy' was in fact the expedition of a party of Roman merchant adventurers, who, like the elder Polos in later times, were seeking the sources of the merchandise of the central Asian middlemen. Significantly, the Chinese chronicler scornfully listed the gifts the Romans brought with them, interpreted them as 'tribute', and commented on their inadequacy. The episode has a curiously familiar ring about it. In the Han dynasty one can already glimpse a pattern which was to be repeated in most future contacts with the West. Already the Middle Kingdom's superiority complex was excluding all concern with foreign lands except in so far as they recognized the unattainable qualities of Chinese culture.

From the beginning the lure was silk. The Romans had very hazy notions of what silk was, or how it was made, but desired it greatly. Until the sixth century A.D. the Chinese possessed a world monopoly of silk manufacture. In fact most seems to have reached the West not through the so-called 'Silk Road' overland, but by sea via southern India. There is no doubt that the arrival of the second-century Roman 'embassy' in Han China was an isolated incident. But a scattering of Roman and copies of Roman goods even found their way into the tombs of contemporary kings of Korea. In the sixth century came an important development. Procopius describes how during the reign of Justin II (565–78) two Nestorian monks arrived in Constantinople with the secrets of silk-worm cultivation and its eggs smuggled in hollow staves. Whatever the truth of this tale, it is certain that Byzantium became the chief supplier of silk thereafter, so far as western Europe was concerned. It was an imperial monopoly with silk-looms and dyeworks actually incorporated in a quarter of the rambling Sacred Palace in Constantinople. The monopoly was only broken in the twelfth century when silk farms were established in Norman Sicily and southern Italy. China never ceased to supply the finest and most sought-after silk, tradi-

[3] Sir Mortimer Wheeler, *Rome Beyond the Imperial Frontiers*.

tionally sold for its weight in gold, but the prosperity of the late medieval 'Silk Road' has been much exaggerated.

The earliest, and most persistently important item which came to Europe from the markets of southern India and Ceylon was pepper. Its sources lay in the 'Golden Chersonese' of Malaya and the East Indies. Pliny first commented on the popularity of pepper in western Europe:

> It is quite surprising that the use of pepper has come so much into fashion, seeing that, in other substances which we use, it is sometimes their sweetness and sometimes their appearance that has attracted our notice; whereas pepper has nothing in it that can plead as a recommendation to either fruit or berry, its only desirable quality being a certain pungency; and yet it is for this that we import it all the way from India! Who was the first to make trial of it as an article of food? And who, I wonder, was the man that was not content to prepare himself by hunger alone for the satisfaction of a greedy appetite?[4]

Pepper dominated the Oriental trade for centuries. Roman senators debated its exorbitant cost as a drain on the economy, but passed on the taste for pepper to their enemies. Alaric the Goth demanded 3,000 lb of it as part of his settlement with the Romans in 408. Pepper was almost the last exotic commodity which the abbeys of Merovingian Gaul were able to obtain from the East when Mediterranean trade became perilous in the sixth and seventh centuries; for it is a feature of luxury trade, with its ratio of high cost to low volume, that it persists in times of disorder even after comparatively local commerce in staples such as grain has dried up. Pepper offered very high returns to the many hands through which it passed on its long journey west. Later in the Middle Ages the prosperity of Malacca and Trebizond and huge Genoese and Sriwijayan merchant fortunes were partly to be derived from pepper. As late as 1592 Frobisher was to make £102,000 from the windfall of a single pepper ship which sailed into his hands off the Azores.

In the wake of pepper came a host of other spices and drugs. They are mentioned in the two handbooks to Oriental trade which the periods of Roman and late medieval Italian contacts with the East produced: *The Periplus of the Erythrean Sea* (a matter-of-fact navigational and commercial guide to the Indian Ocean written by a first-century Greek) and *La Pratica della Mercatura* (a list of markets,

[4] Pliny, *Natural History*.

commodities, tariffs, and trading conditions compiled by Pegolotti in the 1340s). They are basically spices, drugs, and purgatives which figured in all pharmacopoeia until the nineteenth century but which are often unfamiliar in the West today. Thirteenth-century apothecaries of Padua and eighteenth-century Sorbonne physicians were perfectly aware of their qualities and they deserve to be listed briefly again. From the Russian steppes came corn, amber, hides, wax, and honey. From Syria myrrh, damask, manna, scammony, galbanum, and brocades. From Persia came spike, nard, incense, aloes, quicksilver, mastic, galbanum, camphor, musc, borax, 'camels' hay', maramati, nacheti, carpets, and brocades. From Arabia incense, saffron, gum arabic, hyssop, and thapsia. Somalia offered frankincense and myrrh; Kilwa sent gold, incense, and slaves. The markets of southern India brought paper, cane sugar, indigo, wormwood, madder, ginger, lac, cassia, cardamum, cinnamon, saffron, galangal, white beet, amber, cotton, carpets, and pepper. The rulers of Taprobane (Ceylon), who loved Byzantine gold, sent zedoary, coral, aphrodisiacs, and pearls. A high proportion of pearls known in classical and medieval Europe seem to have come from Ceylon – they were habitually used as an international currency by medieval Italian merchants working the Oriental routes. From Tibet came silk and powdered rhubarb, the most drastic purgative known in medieval

25   Marco Polo visits the pepper-growing district of Malabar

26 Catalonian merchants (probably silk merchants)
travelling home from the East. From the *Atlas Catalan* of 1375

Italy, where it commanded impressively high prices. From China
came zedoary, galangal, cardamum, rhubarb and, of course, silk –
raw, dressed, and gauze. Much of this was sent down to join the
East Indian trade to southern India and Ceylon: pepper, brazil-wood,
zedoary, 'dragons' blood' (made from the sap of the palm tree),
cinnabar, coral, cinnamon, mace, nutmeg, balm and balsamon,
turbit, cloves (the Zanzibar clove industry is very recent), cardamum,
and asafoetida.

These expensive and easily transportable goods seem to have been
largely paid for in specie by Roman and medieval Europe. By the
time they reached Rome their price could be astronomical. Pliny
remarked as early as the first century A.D. that 'in no year does India
absorb less than 50,000,000 sesterces'. We have no global figures,
but there is no doubt that the immense and increasingly mounting
drain of precious metal from the Mediterranean to the East contributed to the economic breakdown of the later Roman Empire. Only
Byzantium, with her own remarkably plentiful gold supplies, was
able to keep up with the cost and pay her civil servants in coined
money. Her gold standard remained more or less stable from the
sixth century until 1071. The *dirhems* of the Califate were eventually
linked to it and it was not really replaced as the medium for Levantine
trade until the Venetian ducat and Florentine florin were introduced

ΕΡΕΤΙΚΙ

ΝΕCΤΟΡΙΟC

27   The heresiarch Nestorios creeping away from the
Council of Ephesos (431) in disgrace. From a wallpainting
in the church of St Sozomenos at Galata in Cyprus.

to feed the Eastern demand for fine gold in the thirteenth century.
One wonders how far such quantities of European gold were useful
to Eastern merchants. A few Oriental imports to Frankish Europe
survive – like the *pallium* which the monks of Durham used for the
shroud of the much-travelled relics of St Cuthbert in 1104, which is
in fact a state robe of silk and gold brocade from the Abbasid Califate.
But evidence for European exports is derived almost entirely from
caches of precious metals. The Indian passion for gold hoarding
seems to have begun with Roman and Byzantine *solidi*.

Roman contacts with the outside world were important because of
their scale. But they were almost entirely military and commercial,
and the commerce was managed by Levantines at the European end
– the merchants of the great Hellenistic cities of the eastern Mediterranean. The imperial government was wary of Persia and remarkably
cautious in exploring the lands even of its closer and more barbaric
neighbours. After the unexpected disaster there in the first century
A.D., the Baltic and northern Germany were largely left to what
Roman pedlars could make from their local rulers, who sought a
certain prestige in acquiring Roman wares. North Africa, it is true,
was an essential, intensely farmed, and densely populated part of the
empire. But it had little contact with the rest of the continent and
looked almost exclusively to the Mediterranean. Expeditions over

61

the desert to the south were largely confined to punishing the Garamantes or Atlas tribesmen and leaving them, chastened, where they were. The Roman mausoleum at Germa, in the Fezzan, remains, like the supposed 'Temple of Augustus' at Muziris (Cranganore, southern India), marked on the Peutinger Table,[5] an isolated curiosity. Augustus had problems enough in Romanizing his own eastern provinces. Ancyra (Ankara) had originally been settled by Latin colonists, but it is doubtful whether more than a handful of its inhabitants, from Augustus' reign to the present day, have been able to understand a word of the autobiography which he caused to be inscribed on stone there – the longest and least read Latin inscription in the world.

But Roman Levantine contacts with the East left one tangible heritage: the work of the second-century Alexandrian Greek, Ptolemy. Over a number of years Ptolemy collated the sightings of a host of travellers, to make a remarkably accurate description of the known world. His maps lose coherence with Scotland to the north-west and the islands of Japan to the east; they are confined by the equator to the south. But they were superior to any other compilations (even the Chinese, which concentrated on China) until they were overtaken by the discoveries of sixteenth-century travellers. The earliest printed atlas (Bologna, dated 1462 but probably about 1477) followed Ptolemy exactly and it was another century before all the outlines inherited from him were finally revised. In other words the best European knowledge of the geography of the outside world remained more or less static from the first to the fifteenth centuries A.D. If anything it shrank. Ptolemy's work was never entirely lost to the medieval West; Frederick II (1197–1250) had a copy, and one of the best versions is the tenth-century copy now in the Monastery of Vatopedi on Mount Athos. But it went out of what popular circulation it may once have had and entered an underground route. His *Geography* went through Syriac, Arabic, and Persian translations until it re-emerged (its authorship sometimes unrecognized) in Greek in Byzantium in the fourteenth century. Instead of Ptolemy's empirical, Aristotelian, view of the world, Byzantines preferred to follow the views of such pundits as Cosmas Indicopleustes ('The India Sailor'). Cosmas's extensive travels in the Indian Ocean served to prove to him that the world looked something like a gigantic cabin

[5] This is the copy of a Roman map, made in 1265 by a monk from Colmar. It is now kept in Vienna.

trunk – Ptolemy, by contrast, had little doubt that it was a globe. Cosmas drew a mountain (the earth) rising from a sea which covered the floor of his trunk. The sun and the moon circled the peak of the mountain, and so were mutually hidden from each other, neatly solving the problem of night and day. The curved roof of the trunk, which was studded with stars, served for heaven.

Cosmas's cosmology may have been shaky, but he was a shrewd commercial observer. He attributed the prosperity of imperial trade in the Indian Ocean to two causes – the Byzantine gold coinage and Christianity. Certainly the sixth century saw a revival of Eastern trade even greater than those of the fourth and first centuries, which was marvellously assisted by the apparently inexhaustible gold supply of Byzantium, and in which western Europe hardly participated. But with the mention of Christianity Cosmas introduces a link more pervasive, and more elusive, than Alexander's Macedonian Empire or Rome's greed for silk and pepper had ever been. The Christianity of which Cosmas was writing was the Orthodoxy of the empire, but the Christianity shared by the Levant and central Asia was heterodox. From the eighth to the fifteenth centuries Christians could be found in high positions from Paris to Peking, but they were very different Christians.

28 Armenian Cathedral of the Holy Cross on Agthamar Island, Lake Van, in Vaspurkan, built by King Gagik Artzruni between 915 and 921

63

The Eastern Christian Churches

Oriental Christianity which, after all, embraced the very first Christians, had deep roots, Semitic and local. It was especially attractive to the urban proletariat of the Levant, already protagonists of the One God and addicted to Oriental mystery cults. Constantine the Great's adoption of Christianity as an official cult of the state from 313 onwards was astonishing and somewhat perverse. But there was no going back and the faith's consequent interpretation by the Hellenistic intelligentsia as the newly respectable imperial religion eventually alienated the Levantine Christians from the whole apparatus of Roman rule without dissociating them from their primitive faith. For Constantine and his Byzantine successors Orthodoxy ('correct-thinking') was an essential element of imperial theory. Submission to empire and acceptance of Orthodoxy were indistinguishable. For instance, Byzantium sought to bring the Slavs into the empire by evangelizing them, but the Serbs, Bulgars, and Russians learned to set up their own autocephalous Churches, which became instead symbols of the national consciousness of the Slav peoples, enabling them to enjoy the benefits of being within the orbit of Byzantium without being subject to Constantinople. Byzantium's

29   A Muslim caravan from Cairo to Mecca

over-insistence that her subjects should not only be Orthodox, but Greek Orthodox, meant that her policy eventually failed. But Orthodoxy remained, even in the later Middle Ages, the essential test of entry into the Byzantine world, and the distinction between civilization and barbarism.

For the lively and emergent local cultures of the Levant which the late Roman Empire allowed to find clear identities and a certain confidence, Orthodoxy, when it came, too often meant the hectoring Greek bishops of the towns. These were now simply associated with the already intolerable imperial tax-collectors and a clerical class who had a vested interest in maintaining an official Greek, whose administrative jargon only they could manipulate. To the Syrian Christian, say, the alliance was unholy. His resentment found expression in dogmatic differences.

The definition of the tenets of Islam, so early in its history, and the swift conquests of the Muslims in the first hundred years of their faith, came as no surprise. Already, as their only means of demonstrating their political dissociation from the Greeks of Byzantium, the Egyptian Copts, the Syrian Monophysites, the Armenians and Georgians, had adopted, or been forced to adopt, 'heterodox' doctrines. Later other such groups – the Paulicians of Tephrike and the Bogomils in the Balkans – were to seek a way out of the domination of Constantinople through religious dissent. Basically the Monophysite Christians of the Levant believed in the supremacy of the Godhead of Christ. No tricky Greek definition allayed their suspicion that the Oneness of God was being compromised. Inevitably, Mehemmed gained his first followers by declaring the One God as the central tenet of Islam. The first califs, successors of the Prophet, found in Egypt, Syria, and Persia a Christian population so alienated by the demands of the Byzantine bureaucracy and Greek theology that they opened their gates to the invaders from the Arabian desert. The Prophet died in 632, five years after Heraclius crushed the Sassanians at Nineveh. Damascus fell to the Arabs in 635, Jerusalem in 637, Mesopotamia in 638, Persia by 639, Egypt in 640, Spain from 711, and Afghanistan in the 730s. The Arabs were at first reluctant to allow their new subjects the benefits of their faith, for, sensing their cultural inferiority to the peoples they overran, they were intent on keeping exclusive their one claim to supremacy – Islam. But they had to take over existing administrative systems and within a century the nobility of Persia and clerks of Syria and Egypt were also demanding inclusion within the new faith. For many Monophysites, Jews, and followers of local pagan cults of the One God, it was no great step.

The Monophysite antagonism to the clerks and prelates of Byzantium led to curious results. The Patriarch Nestorios was condemned in 431 in the Third General Council at Ephesus for the heretical notion that the divine and human persons of Christ could be distinguished. It hardly matters that certainly Nestorios and probably most of his followers were not in fact 'Nestorian'. But the condemnation was a signal for the Levantine Christians to assert their independence. The achievement of the Nestorian Church was vast and little recognized. By 774 the Nestorians set up a monument in China hopefully recording their triumph over Buddhism. The Malabar coast of India was evangelized. By the thirteenth century the Nestorian Patriarch in Persia, invested in an ass's skin cloak and with state parasol, could claim no fewer than 230 dioceses from Syria to Ceylon and Peking. Significantly, they lay along the old trade routes. Ignored by Rome and Constantinople alike, the Nestorian and other Levantine Churches represented what might now be called a 'Third World'. Crusaders were always incredulous to find such Christians already living around the Holy Land.

Byzantium had failed to bring the Levantine Christians into her world. But her long relationship with the Califate kept her in touch with central Asia. The political and commercial disintegration of the Roman Mediterranean world had been effectively accomplished long before the Arab conquests. Byzantium was drawn into the Islamic orbit remarkably quickly. It was never an entirely happy relationship, but there were many times when each felt closer to the other than did the Constantinople emperors to the embryo barbarian kingdoms of the West – unreliable Celtic and Alemann tribesmen, as the Byzantines termed them. In the early tenth century Nicholas Mystikos, Patriarch of Constantinople and pupil of Photios (in whose reign the first ecclesiastical differences with the West became apparent) put the situation to the emir of Crete like this:

> Two sovereignties – that of the Saracens and that of the Romans [i.e. the Byzantines] – surpass all sovereignty on earth, like the two great lights in the firmament. For this one reason, if for no other, they ought

30 Mehemmed at the siege of Banu-Nadir, from a
Mongolian manuscript of the fourteenth century

to be partners and brethren. We ought not, because we are separated
in our ways of life, our customs, and our worship, to be altogether
divided; nor ought we to deprive ourselves of communication with one
another. . . . This is the way we ought to think and act, even if no other
necessity of our affairs compelled us to it.[6]

The Frankish kingdoms were, save in the special case of Umay-
yad Spain, almost entirely deprived of this experience. There are
scattered hints of contact, it is true. But one of the most substantial,
the Frankish report that Charlemagne entered into diplomatic
relations with Harunu'l-Rashid, is not mentioned in any Oriental
source. Probably an isolated party of travelling merchants claimed to
be an official embassy in order to net bigger profits. But in these years
califate and empire, partners in the old Macedonian Middle Kingdom,
got the measure of each other in realistic fashion. Of necessity the
Arabs had to inherit and adapt a Byzantinized bureaucracy in Syria
and Egypt. As always, the clerical class survived. The greatest Greek
theologian of the period, and last Father of the Church, St John of
Damascus (died 749) was a high official in the Muslim civil service.
St John was a great defender of intercession through icons. The
origins and real nature of Byzantine iconoclasm are greatly disputed
and, in some ways, obscure. But it is a fact that Leo III's first Iconoclast Decree in 726 had been preceded by a similar edict issued in
723 by Calif Yazid. A cautious historian has said that 'It is asking too

[6] Sir E. Barker (ed.), *Social and Political Thought in Byzantium.*

much of human credulity to suppose that the two steps were wholly independent of one another.' Islam's debt to Semitic and early Christian teaching is apparent; to examine the influence of Islam upon Orthodoxy is to enter ill-charted and tricky waters. But it is surely to be sought in many local cults which survived, sometimes until modern times, in the twilight area between the two official faiths.

One of Byzantium's main problems in creating a uniform state was that there were not enough of the dominant people, the Greeks, to go round. The califate felt this problem earlier and more acutely. The first Arab conquerors were comparatively few in number. Persia, as always, engrossed her invaders. It is a land of small-town aristocracies, guardians and exploiters of the complex *qanat* irrigation systems, source of their wealth and political authority. As in Arabia, the central plateau of Persia was the preserve of nomads, who were more or less uncontrollable. From the desert came political anarchy. The califate could do remarkably little to change the old Sassanian system here. And like the Orthodox emperors, the Sunni califs were troubled by local heresies which often had national or separatist overtones. Greeks and Arabs found the problems of ruling the East unchanging.

The 'live and let live' attitude reached by the empire and califate in the ninth and tenth centuries is demonstrated most vividly by the heroic poetry of the peoples who lived on the borders of the two great states. The Byzantine epic *Digenis Akrites*, describes the exploits of an imperial border baron. His mother's family boasted their genealogy thus:

> We from the Eastern theme, of noble Romans;
> Our father is descended from the Kinnamades;
> Our mother a Doukas, of Constantine's family;
> Twelve generals our cousins and uncles.

But Digenis's father

> Was an Emir of breed, exceeding rich . . .
> My father died while I was still a baby;
> My mother gave me to my Arab kinsmen,
> Who brought me up in faith of Mahommed.[7]

The part-Greek and part-'Saracen' border baron of the epic represents what must have been a common accommodation of faiths and

---

[7] John Mavrogordato, *Digenes Akrites*.

68

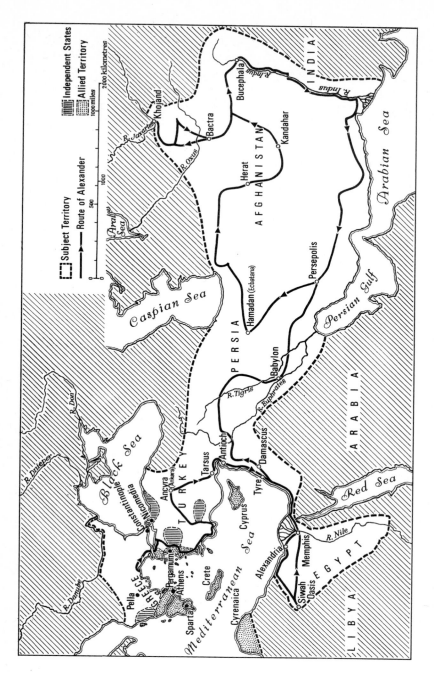

MAP 2   Alexander the Great's Empire

interests along the frontiers, where Baghdad and Constantinople were equally remote. With rather more spirit the Armenian oral epic, *David* (or *The Daredevils*) *of Sassoun*, describes the rivalry of the sultans of Egypt and the kinglets of the Armenian mountains in superhuman terms. In neither work, nor in later Turkish poetic descriptions of the conquest and settlement of Asia Minor, is the meeting of Christian and Muslim presented as a clash of faiths, but rather as a series of chivalrous encounters between fabulous and equally heroic neighbours.

Armenia, the high eastern plateau of Asia Minor, played a crucial part in Byzantine-Abbasid relations. Long the threshold of conflict, its rulers learned how to play off one great neighbour against the other from earliest times. Armenia was the social catalyst of Byzantium, giving hardy mountaineers to its armies, great generals such as Kourkouas or Tzimiskes, and even emperors, such as Basil I, founder of a dynasty and descended, perhaps, from the Artzrunis of Vaspurkan. But Armenia had a very different social system from either of its bureaucratic neighbours. Its steep valleys encourage a local separatism; its society was aristocratic. A complex feudal system developed reaching its fullest extent in eighteenth-century Georgia, for the links between the two Caucasian peoples are close. Its parallels with classic Western feudalism are striking, but its basis was social, not political. Armenian chronicles read like animated genealogies, reaching back to grandiose ancestors – Sennacherib or King David.

By contrast, feudalism came late to Byzantium and in rather different form to the califate. While Western rulers were struggling to create a centralized government over their feudatories from the twelfth century, the process was reversed in the East. Here centralized bureaucracies were becoming increasingly feudalized from the eleventh century, although the results were never so thorough-going or extensive as they had been in the Frankish kingdoms. In the East the process coincided with, and was partly precipitated by, the Seljuk encounter with the relatively stable califate and empire in 1043–81. Once again the battleground was Armenia. This time she virtually lost her political independence, but not before she had helped influence the social and political systems of both conquerors and conquered.

The Turkish Move from Central Asia

Since they had first emerged from across the Oxus in the late seventh century, the Seljuks (originally a group of nomadic Turks under a chief named Seljuk) had been a potential embarrassment to the califate. Their rulers were not converted to Islam until the tenth century; it is within the bounds of possibility that some Seljuks were converted at the same time as the Christians they conquered in Asia Minor in the eleventh century. The Baghdad Califate employed them, somewhat gingerly, as border mercenaries. From the reign of Calif al-Mustansir (1036–94), with his Armenian vizier, the government increasingly abandoned the old system of letting out state lands against prepayment of the appropriate taxes (*daman*), and for Seljuk benefit began to extend one of granting fiefs (*iqta*), whereby the untaxed income of an estate was left to its occupant. Almost precisely the same development was beginning to occur in Byzantium. From the mid eleventh century some state domain and functions were being surrendered to the care (*pronoia*) of a landowner for his lifetime. In the twelfth century a few grants were made in return for military service, the fief-holder retaining taxes which would have gone to the state in the past. By the thirteenth century some became hereditary fiefs. The process had begun in the eleventh century to satisfy the demands of a so-called 'military aristocracy',

31 Turkoman painting, *c.* 1510, depicting a garden, with two ladies bathing, spied on by a young man

71

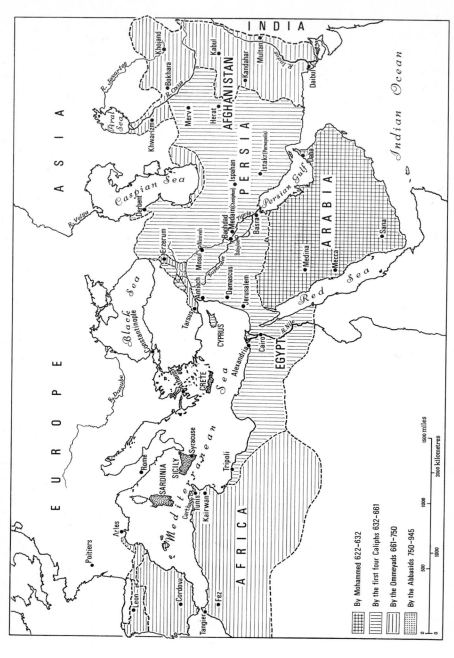

MAP 3 The Conquests of Islam

By Mohammed 622–632

By the first four Caliphs 632–661

By the Ommeyads 661–750

By the Abbasids 750–945

represented by some twenty great families, Byzantium's first hereditary aristocracy, which emerged at this time. Most were Anatolian, a high proportion were Armenian in origin, and almost all were warlords. This development coincided with the pre-Ottoman Turkish conquest of Anatolia and of much of what was left of the Abbasid Califate, a process which led to a profound change in family structure and government in the heart of the middle lands which lay between Frankish Europe and central Asia.

The eleventh-century Seljuks retained the social system but not the economy of their, now very distant, nomadic past. Byzantine chroniclers who recorded the invasions did not term the Seljuks 'barbarians'; indeed to some extent they restored law and order and a settled administration to a harassed land. The first raiders entered Byzantine territory in the 1040s, but their first triumph was the virtual capture of the Baghdad Califate in 1058, when al-Mustansir crowned the Seljuk leader Tüghrul as 'Sultan of the Eastern and Western Worlds'.

Byzantium had prepared for the loss of the central plateau of Asia Minor by a major political blunder. The long reign of Basil II (976–1025), which left the empire victorious in the Balkans and the East but fatally exhausted, ended with the outright annexation of the Armenian kingdoms. This merely turned useful buffer States into increasingly reluctant vassals. The Seljuk threat came in Armenia. Mathew of Edessa, an Armenian chronicler, explained what happened as follows:

> Armenia was surrendered to the blood-drinking Turks by the impotent, effeminate, ignoble race of Greeks. The Greeks deposed our true rulers, scattered our defences, and sent eunuchs to protect us. Like cowardly shepherds they thought only of themselves when the wolf came. So the Turks broke through and in one year they reached the gates of Constantinople.

An exaggeration, of course, but the fate of Byzantine Anatolia was decided in 1071 at the battle of Mantzikert, fought in Armenia. Many Armenian leaders welcomed the Seljuks almost with relief and some regained their old local authority under the new régime.

The Seljuks were not particularly numerous. They conquered the non-Greek central plateau of Asia Minor quite casually, and eventually left Byzantium only its Greek core, transforming a multilingual empire into what looked very like a Greek national state. Byzantium thought that she could assimilate the Seljuks, as she had incorporated other invaders in the past. But her Anatolian subject peoples soon gave their loyalty to the Konya Sultanate of Rûm instead.

The Seljuks were followed by other Turkic peoples, particularly Turkoman, who arrived in clans. Settlement was a long-drawn-out business. There were annual battles for summer grazing land and the process was not completed in some areas until long after the fall of Byzantium herself. For instance, a branch of the Chepni Turkomans who started settling Paphlagonia in the late twelfth century, reached central Pontos in the fourteenth century, eastern Pontos in the eighteenth century, and are still moving into valleys abandoned by Greeks there in the Exchange of Populations of 1922–3.

Each group looked to a common ancestor as a unifying factor. In some cases the settlers added the extensive Armenian and Caucasian genealogies of the mountain leaders of eastern Asia Minor to their own tribal explanations of their origins. At one time the Danishmend emirs, rivals to the Seljuks, were not too proud to claim Armenian ancestry. The great Armenian-Anatolian families of eleventh-century Byzantium (such as the Taronites-Tornikes) have been partially examined, but the families who became Turkicized in turn have been little investigated. Their role was probably highly important. For instance the Gabras dynasty of Greco-Anatolian warlords from Pontos seem to have retained their position under several régimes. The eleventh-century Theodore Gabras, Duke of Chaldia, was canonized locally for his heroic stand against the Seljuk invaders. In the twelfth century the Gabrades became virtually autonomous and hereditary rulers of Chaldia and began to compromise with the Seljuks. Manuel I (1143–80) had an indifferent general called Michael Gabras in Constantinople but the Constantine Gabras whom he sent as ambassador to Sultan Kilij-Arslan I defected to the Seljuks (Sultan Masud's Gabras minister had been captured by Manuel in 1146). It was a Gabras who negotiated with Saladin on behalf of the Seljuk government in 1180. He seems to have been a Muslim, but the John Gabras whom Sultan Ala al-Din Kay-Kubadh I sent as his ambassador to Pope Gregory IX and Emperor Frederick II in 1234–6 was Christian. The family survived

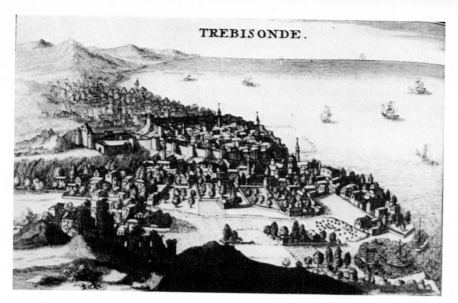

32 Trebizond in 1701

in high places in the subsequent Anatolian emirates, in the Crimea, and in the Greek Empire of Trebizond (where a Gabras was appointed as governor of the Greco-Turkish port of Sinope in 1254–66). There were other families, less easy to trace under Turkish names. Evrenos, last Greek governor of Proussa (which became the early Ottoman capital of Bursa), for instance, took service among his conquerors. His grandson led Ottoman armies into Macedonia and the Morea and the family held the military fief of Yenidje Vardar until the nineteenth century.

On a small scale one might take the Oflu of eastern Turkey as an example of the far-reaching social changes which began in the eleventh century. The Of Valley had a Laz Caucasian people who had been Hellenized by the Byzantine Empire since the sixth century. After 1071 it was cut off from Byzantine Constantinople, but it was not incorporated into the Ottoman Empire until the sixteenth century. The Oflu number about 40,000 today, scattered in part all over Turkey. Some retain Greek as their first language, but all are noted for their fanatical devotion to Islam. They explain this paradox by a common ancestor, who seems to be wholly mythical but unites all Oflu in a bond of mutual kinship. He is said to be a Bishop

Alexander of Of, who apostatized to Islam and, taking his flock with him, became İskender Pasha. Some Oflu family names are recognizable in thirteenth-century Greek charters, but they are neither Turkish nor Greek. From the period of administrative breakdown in the late eleventh century, until the abolition of their feudal privileges in 1839, the Oflu were led by local families whose authority derived from a supposed network of kinship, rather than any political office.

On a larger scale, the events of the eleventh century eventually gave rise to extended ruling families on a national, and even international scale. In eastern Anatolia there had always been such dynasties – for example the Bagratids, whose members ruled parts of Armenia and Georgia from the first to the nineteenth centuries. What is intriguing is to find that the same family networks arose, for the first time, among the Greeks as well as the Turks. It is not surprising to find that the Ottomans remained to the end a great extended dynasty, not an ethnic unit. But the emergence of such families as the Greek Kantakouzenoi, which, by the fourteenth century, had ramifications in most ruling houses from the Adriatic to the Caspian, is more significant. Michael VIII Palaiologos, reconqueror of Constantinople from the Latins in 1261, had conventional family alliances in western Europe, but he was also father-in-law of a Mongol Ilkhan of Persia. The family network of this Greek family, which first emerged in the eleventh century, stretched ultimately from Spain to China. Politically its extent was never exploited, nor was there any question that it could ever have been, but it is more important than any of the Polos' wanderings. On a lesser scale the Greeks reacted to the Turkish settlement system. A fourteenth-century bishop invented a common ancestor (St Eugenios, the patron saint) for one Pontic Greek valley, the Matzouka, at a time when a Turkoman clan was settling the neighbouring Philabonites Valley.

Thus it was that, when Mehemmed II took Constantinople in 1453, he had through his ancestry as good a claim to the Byzantine throne as had most ruling Greek families. The final transference of Constantinople from Byzantine to Ottoman hands in 1453 masks a more fundamental change of social structure and administration which had been going on in the Greek and Turkish borderlands

33 Mongol troops crossing a river on ice

between Europe and Asia since the eleventh century. The ancient unity of the Near East survived as long as the eastern Mediterranean still looked towards the Levant. To this, the Crusader states founded after the First Crusade of 1099 were largely an irrelevance and always alien. Only in the Morea and Cicilian Armenia did the already outdated legalistic Frankish concept of feudalism take more than shallow roots. But in 1258 Hulagu Khan took Baghdad and as a consequence three Italian Powers, Rome, Genoa, and Venice, were by the end of the thirteenth century drawn into the Middle East. For two centuries the Mongol Empire gave western Europe a final glimpse of a wider world which stretched as far as China.

The Rise of the Mongols

Ala-ad-Din Ata-Malik Juvaini, Persian biographer of his conqueror Chingis Khan (1206–27) gives a somewhat jaundiced description of the rise of the Mongols, which contrasts strongly with the heroic tales of their own *Secret History*.

Before the appearance of Chingis Khan the Mongols had no chief or ruler. Each tribe lived separately; there was constant fighting between them. Some of them regarded robbery and violence, immorality and debauchery as deeds of manliness and excellence. Their clothing was of the skins of dogs and mice, and their food was the flesh of those animals and other dead things; their wine was mares' milk and their dessert the fruit of a tree shaped like a pine. . . . The sign of a great emir amongst them was that his stirrups were of iron; from which one can form a picture of their other luxuries. And they continued in this indigence, privation, and misfortune until the banner of Chingis Khan's fortune was raised and they issued forth from the straits of hardship into the amplitude of well-being, from a prison into a garden, from the desert of poverty into a palace of delight. . . . And so it has come to pass that the present world is the paradise of that people; for all the merchandise that is brought from the West is borne unto them, and that which is bound in the farthest East is untied in their houses. . . .[8]

The Mongol expansion from their early grazing lands in the mountains south and east of Lake Baikal during the early thirteenth century was certainly impressive. After sacking Peking in 1215, Chingis Khan turned west; within seven years his lieutenants reached the Black Sea and twenty years later the Golden Horde established a Tatar suzerainty over Russia which was to last for more than two centuries. In 1238 the Assassins of Syria sent to implore Henry III of England to save Islam from the new enemies of civilization, and in the same year a glut of herrings was recorded at Yarmouth because their German buyers had stayed at home for fear of the Mongols.

What Juvaini was describing, however, were the great changes wrought on the Mongols by the lands which they conquered. To a significant extent Persian and Chinese forms of government survived to the west and to the east. Even by the middle of the thirteenth century the Mongol Empire had ceased to be a unity. Kubilai Khan's dynasty was never on good terms with the Persian Ilkhanids, who in turn opposed their cousins on the Volga, the Golden Horde. The *Pax Mongolica* was more often a *Bellum Mongolicum* than not. But all Mongol rulers clung to a certain tribal unity and prided themselves upon their Chingiskhanid ancestry – even Timur (1336–1405, Marlowe's Tamburlaine), whose status as a member of the dynasty is doubtful. The Mongol rulers of the urban civilization of China, central Asia, and Persia would leave their palaces periodically

[8] Juvaini, *History of the World-Conqueror* (trs. J. A. Boyle).   78

to return to tented encampments at Karakorum for *kiriltays*, dynastic discussions followed by formidable drinking-bouts. For Westerners penetrating the East, the unity of the Mongol Empire retained in such meetings was adequate enough to open up a whole new world to their astonished eyes in the thirteenth century.

The most spectacular, but ultimately the least important, contacts with the East were made by Rome. Tales of Prester John prompted hopes of Catholic evangelization. In 1245 Pope Innocent IV decided to find out about this sudden new empire, so strange and ruthless that it fitted no known category. Two years before a Mongol 'ambassador' had appeared, but he turned out to be a renegade Englishman. The Pope sent John of Plano Carpini through the devastated lands of the Russians, Cumans, Kanglis, 'Bisermis', and others to Kara Kitay and High Tatary. The friar arrived at Kara-korum barefoot to be present at the election of Guyuk as Supreme Khan at the *kiriltay* of 1246. Outside the election tent he joined

34   Detail from a map of 1558 showing Prester John on his throne

Duke Yaroslav of Suzdal in Russia, several chiefs of the Kitayans and Solangi, two sons of the King of Georgia, the ambassador of the Calif of Baghdad (himself a Sultan), more than ten other Saracen Sultans and more than 4,000 envoys bringing tribute.[9]

On 22 July 1246:

Leaving there we rode all together for three or four leagues to another place, where on a pleasant plain near a river among the mountains another tent had been set up, which is called by them the Golden Orda; it was here that Guyuk was to be enthroned. . . . This tent was supported by columns covered with gold plates and fastened to other wooden beams with nails of gold, and the roof above and the sides on the interior were of brocade. . . . A vast crowd assembled . . . saying prayers and genuflecting towards the south. . . . After they had done this for a considerable time, they returned to the tent and placed Guyuk on the imperial throne, and the chiefs knelt before him and after them all the people, with the exception of us who were not subject to them. Then they started drinking and, as is their custom, they drank without stopping until the evening.[10]

Pope Innocent IV's suggestion that Guyuk be baptized led to an amazed response from the Supreme Khan. He wrote to the Pope:

How do you know that the words you speak are with God's sanction? From the rising of the sun to its setting, all lands have been made subject to me. Who could do this against the will of God?[11]

Guyuk ordered Innocent to submit in person and explain himself, concluding ominously:

If you do not observe God's command, and if you ignore my command, I shall know you as my enemy. Likewise I shall make you understand. If you do otherwise, God knows what I know.[12]

The encounter of 1246 has been described at length because all of the quite numerous succeeding embassies from the West to the Mongols followed the same pattern. Friar John told the Pope outright that 'it is the intention of the Tatars to bring the whole world into subjection', as it undoubtedly was. Each side was pursuing totally different aims. Except for the more practical exchanges between the Ilkhans and such Western rulers as Louis IX and Edward I over a plan (which never materialized) for joint action against the Turks, the correspondence between successive popes and

[9] Christopher Dawson, *Mongol Mission.*   [10] *Ibid.*   [11] *Ibid.*   [12] *Ibid.*

35 Mongol archer on horseback

khans was blind. Probably many of these missives were never really understood in the West until those that survive in the Vatican and the French State Archives were edited in modern times, for the contemporary Latin translations which accompanied them were usually grossly inaccurate and often represent no more than wishful thinking. Western kings and evangelist popes continued to believe the Mongol rulers and their subjects to be likely converts to Catholicism, until Timur's Muslim zeal disabused them. At least the Persian Ilkhans had potential as saviours of the pathetic Frankish outposts in the Holy Land, until Acre fell in 1291. The khans continued to look upon the scruffy friars who turned up at their courts as absurd, but inadequate, ambassadors bearing the submission of Frankish barbarians. But Catholic missionary zeal was unabated and Franciscans, in particular, sent notable men into Tatary. By 1307 Friar John of Monte Corvino was appointed first archbishop of Khanbalik (Peking), and the succession continued throughout the fourteenth century. Probably converts were counted in hundreds, rather than thousands, for most Christians of the Mongol Empire clung to their Nestorian faith, but the Mongol Mission became a Catholic obsession. Among scholars the detailed reports brought back by the missionaries led to a Western familiarity with central Asia. When, as late as 1373–4, the Franciscan William Woodford was

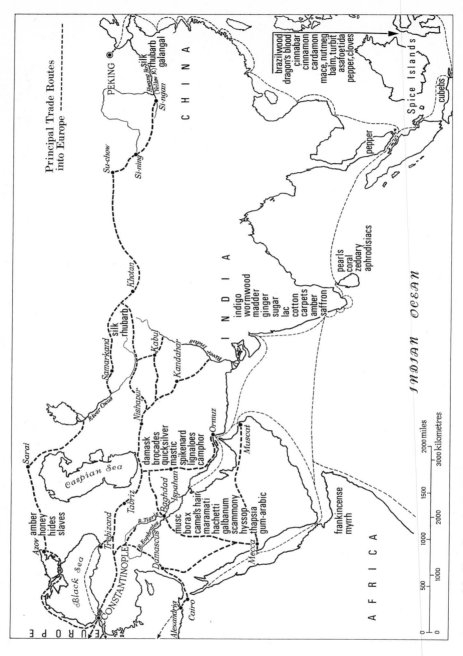

MAP 4 Medieval trade in Asia

lecturing at Oxford on the first part of St Matthew's Gospel, he was able casually to mention, in explaining the text 'et cum jejunasset quadraginta diebus' (4:2), that a member of his community had found that in Tatary men were indeed able to go without food for forty days.

The so-called *Pax Mongolica* reunited not the Catholic mission lands, but the old Nestorian Church of central Asia, which achieved its last flourishing in the thirteenth and fourteenth centuries before it was all but suppressed by Timur. Once again the oldest of the 'heretical' Churches counted its diocese from the Black to the Yellow Seas and counted faithful in some very high places – including members of the Chingiskhanid dynasty itself. The khans recognized the usefulness of the Nestorians as clerks and thought them particularly suited as ambassadors to the Christians of Europe. They did not realize that the Christians of Europe were rather different Christians, but nor, for that matter, did at least one Pope. The most remarkable of these ambassadors was a hermit who retired to a cave above the Huang Ho River, called Rabban Sauma. He was in his fifties when, in 1278, one of his disciples persuaded him to go on pilgrimage to Jerusalem. They undertook the immense journey under the protection of Kubilai Khan's passport. Neither, however, reached the Holy Land. In Persia Rabban Sauma's disciple was elected as the Nestorian Patriarch Mar Yaballahah III, while in 1287 the Ilkhan Arghun named Sauma himself as Mongol ambassador to the Western kings. He saw Andronikos II Palaiologos of Constantinople, Philip the Fair of France, Edward I of England, the leaders of Genoa, and Pope Nicholas IV. From the elderly Uighur ascetic from China, who gave them Communion according to the Nestorian rite, the Western rulers heard a first-hand account of Kubilai Khan.

But in the West any real knowledge or understanding of central Asia was confined to merchants in Genoa and Italy and to the missionary Orders. Travellers who did not return from Tatary with fantastic tales were suspect. Marco Polo was asked to recant his obviously unrealistic stories of travel even on his death-bed. With the shrinking. of genuine contacts with the East, popular knowledge and interest declined. When in the mid-fifteenth century Johann Schiltberger, a Bavarian mercenary in Sultan Bayezid's army who was captured by Timur's Mongols at the battle of Ankara in 1402,

came to write an account of many years' wandering in the East, he had to include in it a number of fictitious stories. The now rare travellers from the East could get away with anything; indeed they were almost obliged to be outrageous. As late as May 1461 Friar Lodovico da Bologna, charlatan 'Patriarch of Antioch', who had done a little Oriental travelling, paraded a circus of Eastern ambassadors throughout Europe. The envoy of Prester John himself, among them, was received in all solemnity at the courts of Charles VII of France and Philip the Good of Burgundy. He was a Mr Hanse, a 'merveilleusement grand clercq'. His special and appropriate accompaniment was a profound knowledge of astrology. It is very unlikely that Mr Hanse would have been taken seriously in the two previous centuries.

In the Far East, scene of so many Roman missionary journeys, China remained almost sublimely indifferent to the presence of Europe. There was no appeal or challenge to learn more about the West. True, Mongol conquests in Persia and Russia led to a remote concern for the more distant subjects of the empire, but it was a very perfunctory interest. *The Secret History of the Mongols*, for instance, has the laconic entry: 'They destroyed the towns of Ejil, Jayah, and Meget' to describe the Mongol conquests of Russia and in the Caucasus – and two of the names mentioned are not towns at all. Geographers had a slightly wider interest in the West than official annalists, and a fourteenth-century Sino-Korean world map,

36 [*opposite*] Marco Polo and his two uncles leaving Venice for their travels to the East

37 Kubilai Khan (1216–94)

which has yet to be adequately studied, is said to have over 100 place-names in its European section and thirty-five for Africa. Chinese of the Mongol Yuan dynasty usually copied extracts from an earlier Sung compilation, Chao Ju-kua's *Description of the Barbarians*, on the rare occasions on which they wished to claim knowledge of Europe. Westerners were scarcely mentioned in Chinese annals and Marco Polo never. The lack of interest in the West was almost total. There were a few tall stories in circulation about 'Ferengistan' on Mandevillian lines. Most of them are summed up in the first, and longest, reference to medieval European travellers in the Chinese annals. It is less matter-of-fact and demonstratively less reliable than the Han annalist's description of Marcus Aurelius' 'embassy' of A.D. 166. Five years before Marco Polo claimed that Kubilai Khan 'was delighted by our arrival, for he had never seen a Latin before', the Mongol ruler of China received an earlier European 'embassy'. The entry in the annals is dated 6 June 1261:

These people came and presented garments made from vegetable fabrics and other presents. These envoys had travelled three years from their country to Shang tu. They reported that their country is in the Far West beyond the Uighurs. In their country is constant daylight and no night. It is evening there when the field mice come out of their holes. If someone dies there, then Heaven is invoked and it might even happen that the person is restored to life. Flies and mosquitoes are born from wood. The women are very beautiful and the men usually have blue eyes and fair hair. There are two oceans on the route from there, one which takes one month to cross, the other a whole year. Their ships are so big they can hold between 50 and 100 men. These people presented a wine beaker [to Kubilai Khan] made from the egg-shell of a sea-bird. If one poured wine into it the wine became warm immediately.[13]

It would be difficult to find such garbled ideas about China in thirteenth-century Western chronicles. Simon de Saint-Quentin, and Vincent de Beauvais who followed him, give patchy, but remarkably accurate, accounts of the Mongol Empire. But it was the merchants of Genoa and Venice who had the most practical information of conditions in central Asia, for the Mongol capture of Baghdad in 1258 led to the reopening of the old overland routes to Europe on a substantial scale for almost two centuries.

The Expansion of Venice and Genoa

The Italian cities were well prepared for the situation. Venice, then nominally a Byzantine city, had cleared the Adriatic of pirates by 1000. She had obtained her first trading concessions in Constantinople eight years before. The inefficient Byzantine credit and fixed interest system had prevented Greek merchants from taking full advantage of the capital's position as an entrepôt. Venice, with her more flexible economy, was swift to take advantage of the self-imposed Byzantine disabilities. Her establishment in the Levant passed through three stages: first the setting up of more or less temporary quarters for transhibernating merchants, then permanent communes, and finally a claim in running the host country. By 1123, in the *Pactum Warmundum*, Venice was claiming regal rights in her quarters in the Latin kingdom of Jerusalem. As families emigrated and settled permanently in the Levant from Venice, the Republic became an experienced colonist. Her consequent demands for political authority in the countries through which she traded in the East reached their most extreme when, in 1204, she came near to taking over her host country in Byzantium altogether. While a Latin puppet government was set up in Constantinople from 1204 to 1261, Venice founded a much more lasting and substantial overseas empire in the debris of the Fourth Crusade. Genoa followed when by 1261 Michael VIII effectively traded her support in his recapture of Constantinople for

[13] Sir Mortimer Wheeler, *op. cit.*

the franchise of the Black Sea. From 1261 until the fall of her great
Crimean emporium at Kaffa to Mehemmed II in 1475, Genoa
created a colonial empire in the Euxine. Her colonies fringed the sea,
reflecting those of the Greeks which had been set up there in the
same places and for much the same reasons in the seventh and sixth
centuries B.C. Meanwhile, Venice concentrated on the eastern
Mediterranean. Her colonial empire there was larger and lasted
longer than Genoa's Euxine stations. Crete, under Venetian control
from 1204 until the fall of Candia in 1669, was the greatest prize.
It was the granary of Venice. Crimean corn fed Genoa in the
fourteenth century as it had once fed the Athenian and Byzantine
Empires. But these commercial ventures differed from earlier trading
ventures in the Levant, because they were what amounted to genuine
Western colonial movements as well – the first of modern times.
Some characteristics of the movement may even have influenced later
and more mature patterns of colonization in the Americas.

The mechanics of trade with the Eastern outlets were established
even before the arrival of the Mongols, for the bulk of it was always
local. In Venice, for instance, a sub-committee of the Senate reviewed

38   The reception of Venetian merchants in Cairo

39 Painting attributed to Paolo Veronese of Persian
merchants at the Court of Venice

confidential reports from their agents (*bailis*) in the Levant in
February. These advised on local trading conditions, tariff changes,
arrival of merchandise, and so on. The number and size of municipal
ships which were to be sent on each Levantine route was then fixed.
Private shipping is less well documented. In May the municipal
ships were auctioned at the *incanti* in lots (so many shares per ship).
The convoys left Venice in mid-July, slowly proceeding past the
Venetian stations in Dalmatia. At Methone-Corone the Alexandrian
and Cretan ships turned south-east. The Aegean ships mostly
stopped at Negroponte (Euboia). The reduced convoy reached
Constantinople, sending on only three or four ships round the Black
Sea (largely a Genoese preserve), where the principal Venetian
stations were at Tana on the Sea of Azov, and Trebizond. At each
port there was an official trading period (*muda*), usually fixed at the
end of September to mid-October. At first many merchants waited
at the foreign stations for the spring caravans, returning for the
summer fleet. Later Italians spent their whole lives in the Levantine
colonies.

The Genoese and Venetian stations were usually sovereign areas, often walled. They would be commanded by a *consul* or *baili*, advised by a council of burgesses. His staff would include secretaries, a chaplain-notary, a small armed guard, and warehousemen. His duties were to hold a court, negotiate with local rulers, maintain a caravanserai and dock facilities, and act as an intelligence agent.

After 1258 Venetian and Genoese trade in the Levant and Euxine began to extend beyond local markets. The routes to Persia and, eventually, Ceylon, China, and the East Indies, lay open once more. True, only a handful of Italians, such as the Polos, travelled much further east than Tabriz, the final Italian outpost, to investigate the sources of their trade. But its extent and range was formidable, reaching its height in the early fourteenth century. The western European demand for spices, drugs, and Oriental luxuries seemed insatiable. After the Black Death precipitated a domestic servant crisis in the late fourteenth century, thousands of Circassian and other slaves were also shipped to Italian households. Missionary friar and Italian merchant arrived in a number of Near Eastern cities together. On the quays of Trebizond Provençals and Krim Tatars jostled with Mingrelians and Uighurs.

A number of factors combined to close the commercial outlets to the East in the fifteenth century. While Venice and Genoa were entering a series of costly disputes, the Ottomans were establishing themselves in the vital Straits between the Black Sea and the Aegean. In his long, devastating reign Timur reunited once more the disparate parts of the old Mongol Empire and conquered Delhi. In October 1405 Ruy Gonzales Clavijo, ambassador of King Henry III of Castile, attended the last great Mongol *kiriltay* outside Samarkand. Tribute bearers from Russia, India, and central Asia assembled. On a plain outside the city the wondering townspeople of Samarkand watched the tribes coming in.

As soon as the camp of His Highness had been pitched all these folk of the Horde exactly knew where each had its place. . . . Thus in the course of the next three or four days we saw near twenty thousand tents pitched in regular streets to encircle the royal camp, and daily more clans came in from the outlying districts.[14]

The Spaniards were taken to the presence of the tired, lame conqueror, then in his seventieth year:

[14] *Ruy Gonzales Clavijo, his embassy from Henry III of Castille to Tamberlaine the Great at Samarkand 1403–1406* (trs. Guy le Strange).

> We found Timur and he was seated under what might be called a portal, which was before the entrance of a most beautiful palace. . . . He was sitting . . . upon a raised dais before which there was a fountain that threw up a column of water into the air backwards, and in the basin of the fountain there were floating red apples.[15]

The clan councils were accompanied by gargantuan feastings which the ambassadors had to attend. Clavijo suffered diplomatic agonies because he was teetotal.

> It is the custom of the Tatars to drink their wine before eating, and they are wont to partake of it then so copiously and quaffing it at such frequent intervals that the men soon get very drunk. No feast we were told is considered a real festival unless the guests have drunk themselves sot. . . . To any who would not drink, he would be told that it must be held a despite he thus offers to his highness Timur.[16]

The Fifteenth Century

Two months after Clavijo left the *kiriltay* at Samarkand, Timur died and the Mongol Empire swiftly disintegrated among his successors. It was the end of an era which had begun when Friar John of Plano Carpini attended the first great *kiriltay* of 1246. The European window on the East opened then was effectively closed in 1405. The fifteenth-century Italian economic depression, the Ottoman conquest of the old outlets from 1453, and changing interests in Europe, put an end to Western concern with Asia. By the time Albuquerque reached Diu in 1509 and established the new sea road to India, the old overland route was long abandoned. There were still a few men, usually scholars or Crusaders – such as Bessarion, Philip the Good of Burgundy, and Pope Pius II (who was both) – who had a lively interest in the fate of the separated Christians of Asia. But Pius' Crusade ended in fiasco, as had earlier attempts to stem the Ottoman tide at Nicopolis and Varna.

But, curiously, it was in the middle decades of the century that scholars such as Pius, John of Segovia, Nicholas of Cusa, and Jean Germain reached what has been called 'the moment of vision' in the long muddled history of Christian views of Islam. Christian theologians never really came to grips with Islam, but it was not until the 1450s that the faith, and the threat it posed, was fully explored in a realistic manner by Western scholars. Islam was seen at last, not as

[15] *Ibid.*   [16] *Ibid.*

a barbaric parody of Christianity, nor as the manifestation of the armed Anti-Christ, nor even as a new mission field, but on its own terms. It was agreed at last that neither conquest nor persuasion could bring the Muslims into Christendom. It had hardly occurred to the Byzantines to do either, but now that Frankish Europe had reached its conclusion about the faith, it began to lose interest in it. The Muslims of Spain could only be expelled, not assimilated. Despite all the discoveries of the sixteenth century, most Westerners knew less about Islam in 1600 than they had in 1450.

Although the Ottoman Empire, with its part-Christian bureaucracy, was combining once more the old borderlands between Europe and Asia, there were some final European adventures in the East. Ludovico de Varthema preceded Sir Richard Burton in disguise to Mecca by several centuries.

> In 1503, on the 8th day of April, the caravan was set in order to go to Mecca. I was desirous of beholding various scenes and not knowing how to go about it, formed a great friendship with the captain of the Mamelukes of the caravan, who was a Christian renegade, so that he clothed me like a Mameluke and gave me a good horse, and placed me in company with the other Mamelukes.[17]

[17] *Travelers in Disguise* (trs. John Winter Jones).

40   Timur (1335–1405)

41 View of Venice; from Hartmann Schedel, *Liber Chronicarum*, 1493

The trick worked and the first known European Christian witnessed the pilgrimages to Mecca and Medina.

Apart from an earlier awareness of the empires of Ghana and Mali, the final 'discovery' of medieval Europe was Ethiopia. In 1520 a Portuguese embassy arrived at Arkiko, to seek the centuries-old medieval myth figure of Prester John. King Lebna Dengel confirmed all their hopes. From behind the barrier of Islam came at last a missive from a genuine, although admittedly eccentric, Christian potentate. But it was too late, for in 1516 the Ottomans had already conquered Egypt and all the old emporia, from Kaffa and Pera to Beirut and Alexandria, were finally closed.

Western Europe was looking elsewhere. When Columbus left Spain to discover a sea route to the East Indies and to Cathay, land of the Great Khan, he still had a copy of Marco Polo to guide him. But what he found was, in the words of Maximos Trivolis in a homily on St Gregory dated forty years later, 'a great land called Cuba, whose confines are unknown to those that inhabit it'. It was left to a Byzantine to tell the Russians of the discovery of America and point to the momentous change in western European outlook: 'And today there is over there a new world, an entire new human society.'

92

The Middle East (1453-1574)

V. J. PARRY

The Ottoman State

ON 29 MAY 1453 Constantinople fell to the Ottoman Turks. To set this event in a true perspective it is essential to understand the basic character of the Ottoman state. One fact about it – the most significant of all – must be realized at once: that it was *not* the creation of a nomadic horde pouring out of the Eastern lands to overrun, in a vast wave of rapine and destruction, much of the Muslim world and also no small portion of Christendom.

Two main factors had brought the Ottoman Turks to greatness. Of these factors one – a potent dynamic force – was the spirit of *jihad*, of war against the infidel on behalf of Islam. To the Muslims the world was divided into the *Dar al-Islam* (the 'Abode of Islam'), the regions owing allegiance to the Muslim faith, and the *Dar al-Harb* (the 'Abode of War'), the territories outside the domination of Islam. The notion of *jihad* assumed concrete form in the *ghaza* (whence the Italian word *razzia*), the raid directed against the *Dar al-Harb*, and above all into the lands of Christendom. The expansion of the Ottoman state can be viewed as the continuing movement, north-westward from Asia Minor, of a frontier of *ghazi* warriors – soldiers of the faith, to whom the *jihad* was not a mere occasion for war and plunder, but the *raison d'être* of their whole existence.

The other factor was more complex in character. To the men of the *ghaza* had been given the dynamic strength required to extend the limits of the *Dar al-Islam* – but not the capacities needed to maintain an empire. A force was at hand, able to transform the achievement of the *ghazis* into the durable fabric of Muslim rule. It can be designated as 'High Islam': all the experience and practice, political, administrative, economic, and financial, elaborated over long centuries in the heartlands of the Muslim world. Behind the advancing frontier came the sultan and the apparatus of government, consolidating the conquests made and developing in them the essentials of a viable régime.

93

It was about the year A.D. 1300 that the Ottoman state was born in north-west Asia Minor. At first it grew slowly, absorbing Brusa, Nikaea, and Nikomedia in the years 1326–37. Not until 1354 did the Ottomans win a firm base on the soil of Europe – at Gallipoli. There followed a swift and astonishing subjugation of the Balkans, carried out between 1354 and 1402. Needing large resources, human and material, Turkish and Muslim, in order to ensure the continuance of their hold, in the Balkans, over subject peoples non-Muslim, non-Turkish, and far more numerous than themselves, the Ottomans had now to extend their domination in Asia Minor. The attempt was made in the reign of Bayezid I (1389–1403). It brought them into conflict with the great soldier from Samarkand, Timur. At the battle of Ankara in 1402 Timur crushed the forces of Bayezid I. This grave reverse led to the dislocation of the Ottoman state.

The years 1402–53 witnessed the restoration of Ottoman control over the territories which had recognized Sultan Bayezid as their suzerain. These years also saw the Ottomans victorious against the last 'Crusade' from Europe – the last sustained effort to throw the Muslims out of the Balkan lands and to save Constantinople from the danger now threatening it. The Hungarians, with some aid from the other states of Christendom, set in motion a vigorous offensive down the Danube. It was broken at Varna in November 1444 and at the second battle of Kosovo in October 1448. Constantinople was to fall less than five years after the second battle of Kosovo. The presence of the Ottomans in Europe had been, hitherto and in a real sense, provisional. Now, in 1453, it was – and was seen to be – lasting.

Constantinople would become Istanbul, a capital which united the Balkan and the Asiatic territories under Ottoman rule as Adrianople and Brusa had not been able to do. The young Sultan Mehemmed II (1451–81) built a new fortress at Rumeli Hisar in 1452 – opposite the fortress of Anadolu Hisar constructed in the time of Sultan Mehemmed I (1413–21). These castles gave the Ottomans control of the Bosphorus. Some years later, in 1463–4, Mehemmed II built forts on either side of the Hellespont. He also fortified the island of Tenedos. A defence system was thus created for the protection of Istanbul and – an advantage not heretofore in the secure possession of the Ottomans – for the maintenance of safe communication across the narrow waters separating Asia Minor from the Balkans lands.

The Constantinople of 1453 was not the splendid capital of former times, the God-guarded metropolis of the Byzantine Empire in its Golden Age. It was now a ghost of its imperial self, much of it depopulated, its streets vacant and forlorn. Sultan Mehemmed began at once a process of reconstruction which would change Byzantine Constantinople into Ottoman Istanbul. It was a vast labour of renewal continuing far into the future and demanding an immense expenditure of state revenue over the long years of its prosecution. Mehemmed II invited the inhabitants who had fled in 1453 to return to their homes. Of the captives acquired during the siege he settled his own share in one of the suburbs of Istanbul. He also drafted into the new capital of his empire merchants, craftsmen, and artisans from the towns which he reduced to obedience in the course of his numerous campaigns – as, for example, from Trebizond in 1461 and from Kaffa in 1475. Mehemmed tried, moreover, to encourage the immigration of Jews from Europe. It was a sound endeavour, which the sultans who came after him continued to foster,

42   View of Constantinople; from Braun and Hohenberg,
Civitates Orbis Terrarum, 1572

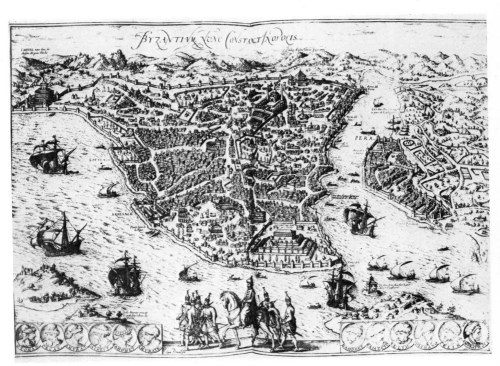

and with success. A large number of Jews, above all from Spain, found a refuge at Istanbul and elsewhere in the Ottoman lands during the fifteenth and sixteenth centuries. Mehemmed II assigned some prisoners-of-war to farms located in villages not far from Istanbul. On these released captives he imposed, though under favourable terms, the burden of meeting in some degree the food requirements of the imperial palace and of the capital. To enrich the economic and social life of Istanbul the sultan began, in 1455–6, the construction of a great bazaar (*bedestan*), embracing a number of subordinate markets, each representing a different trade. In 1463–70, he built the great mosque known after him as *Fatih*, the Mosque of the Conqueror. Round it stood a complex of colleges, libraries, hospitals, and charitable establishments. And it was not Mehemmed alone who strove to meet the varied needs of his people. The viziers and the great dignitaries, the soldiers and the men of religion imitated, within the means available to them, the august example of their master. After 100 years of this embellishment Istanbul, towards the end of the reign of Sultan Süleyman, stood forth once more as the proud capital of a great empire, exhibiting now within itself all that was most characteristic of Ottoman civilization in the time of its refulgence.

The conquest of Constantinople established Mehemmed II as a *ghazi* of unrivalled fame. It gave him the vast prestige essential to the achievement of his main purpose – to bring the Balkans and Asia Minor under more effective Ottoman control. Yet he was not a *jihan-gir*, a world-conqueror cast in the mould of Timur. It is true that, seeking to round off the territories of the empire, he did indeed take over regions thus far not dependent on the house of Osman – but much of his endeavour was in fact to eliminate or else reduce to closer obedience the autonomies, protectorates, and enclaves within or adjacent to the Ottoman frontiers.

Mehemmed II carried out two campaigns against the Morea in 1458 and 1460, making an end of Byzantine rule there. All that remained of an independent Serbia was annexed in 1459. Bosnia fell to the sultan in 1463. A long conflict with Venice (1463–79) gave the Ottomans Negroponte in 1470 and much of northern Albania, including Skutari, in 1478–9.

A similar consolidation was achieved in Asia Minor. The campaign

of 1461 saw the end of Kastamuni, a Turkish state long hostile to the Ottomans. It saw, too, the reduction of Trebizond, where a Byzantine régime, distinct from that of Constantinople, existed since the time of the Fourth Crusade in 1204. Karaman, of which the chief centre was Konya, had been a dangerous foe to the house of Osman. Now, in the years after 1464, it was absorbed into the Ottoman Empire – but Karamanid resistance would continue for some while yet in the fastnesses of the Taurus Mountains. The problem of Karaman was even at this late hour a most serious one. Venice, at war with the Ottomans, sought to engage on her side the Ak Koyunlu or White Sheep Turkomans, dominant in eastern Asia Minor and over much of Persia. A line of communication might be fashioned between the Signoria and Uzun Hasan, the *beg* of the Ak Koyunlu, through the wild terrain where the Karamanids still held out against the forces of the Ottoman sultan – a terrain situated close to the harbours on the southern shore of Asia Minor. In 1472 a Venetian fleet was operating in the waters of the Aegean Sea. Uzun Hasan, in the same year, moved into Karaman. The crucial moment came in 1473. At the battle of Otluk Beli Mehemmed II was able to drive the Ak Koyunlu from the field. It was a success won only through hard fighting and yet decisive in its consequences, for it effectively broke the Venetian-Ak Koyunlu *entente*.

44 Persian battle scene
of the late fifteenth
century

The labour of consolidation was also visible elsewhere. Mehemmed II made the Black Sea into an Ottoman lake. He took Galata from the Genoese in 1453 and Sinope from them in 1461. Ottoman influence was strengthened in the lands north of the Lower Danube. A vigorous campaign in 1462 brought Wallachia to obedience. Moldavia, led by an astute *vaivoda*, Stefan (1457–1504), defended itself more stubbornly. At Racova in 1475 Stefan defeated the *ghazi begs* of the Danube line – only to meet with a serious reverse at Valea Alba in the following year. It is true that Moldavia had to recognize the sultan as its overlord. None the less, it retained a certain freedom of action arising from its character of a border state poised between two more powerful neighbours, the Ottoman Empire and Poland. On the northern shore of the Black Sea in 1475 Mehemmed II seized the Genoese emporium of Kaffa – an event which foreshadowed the future dependence on the Ottoman sultan of the Tatar khan of the Crimea.

Sultan Mehemmed strove also to define the laws and institutions of the Ottoman state. He issued two sets of regulations (*kanun-name*), the first bringing together customs of earlier date and the second describing the offices of government, with their particular grades, procedures, and salaries. A wide range of individual decrees concerned the mines of the empire, the coinage, customs dues, and taxation. He also gave an official sanction to matters which affected the imperial house, defining, for example, the status of the princes of the blood and confirming the 'law of fratricide', under which a new sultan had to kill his brothers and their male children. He laboured also to augment the personnel of his slave household – a household which constituted in large degree the central régime of state. At the same time he sought to extend the fief system established in the provinces of the empire. His reign witnessed, too, a marked advance in the field of war. Mehemmed was eager to make full use of cannon and fire-arms. He maintained a corps of artillery which served him well in his frequent campaigns. The arquebus now gained ground amongst the sultan's troops, and especially amongst the Janissaries. It is not excessive to describe these years as an era of revolution in the Ottoman practice of war. At all the levels of government, therefore, the reign of Mehemmed II was one of notable change. To examine that reign with care is to behold the delineation of Ottoman rule in its 'classic' form – to see the shaping and the raising of a great empire to the threshold of its Golden Age.

Egypt and Syria

No prospect so favourable confronted the Muslim state centred on Cairo and Damascus. The Mamluk sultanate of Egypt and Syria, a famous example of a slave régime, had been established in the year A.D. 1250. Most of the human material needed to sustain it was drawn, during the thirteenth and fourteenth centuries, from amongst the heathen Turks inhabiting the steppe lands north of the Caspian Sea and the Aral Sea, from the region known as the Dasht-i Kipçak. This material was taken to towns in or adjacent to the Crimea, to Kaffa, for example, sold to the slave merchants and carried thence, through the Bosphorus and the Dardanelles, to the shores of Syria and Egypt. The word *mamluk* means in Arabic 'possessed' or 'owned'. A young slave purchased for the sultan would become a Muslim and receive a long training as a soldier. He had, through the years of his slavedom, no remuneration and no equipment personal

45 Slave market in Constantinople

to himself. After a rigorous preparation for his future career he was freed and at once acquired the status and privileges granted to a full member of the dominant warrior caste. As soon as he was granted his liberty, the *mamluk* – now a horseman highly skilled in the art of war – would be given a fief yielding revenues adequate to maintain him as an effective soldier. Also available to him were donatives paid at special times, for example before a great campaign or on the accession of a sultan. He enjoyed other emoluments, too, including fodder for his animals, a meat ration each day and, twice a year, a sum of money for the buying of horses and camels. The system, with its thorough training in the practice of arms and equitation and its careful heed for the welfare of its members, produced in the first 100 years and more of the régime one of the best cavalry élites that the Muslim world was to know.

To become a *mamluk* a man had to be of non-Muslim birth, to be born outside the territories of Islam, and to be a slave. The children of the *mamluk* soldiers, being born Muslim, free, and inside the lands of the sultanate, did not belong to the warrior caste. Out of the time of slavedom came the skills of the competent soldier – and also the basic loyalties which determined in large measure the conduct of each *mamluk* throughout his active career. These loyalties were twofold and enduring: first, to the master (sultan or, below him, *amir*) who bought, trained, and freed him; and second, to the comrades – his *khushdashiya* or brethren-in-arms – who had been, with him, slaves to the same master and had shared with him his actual training and release. The *mamluks* of a given lord would act together, even to the extent, if circumstances were favourable, of raising to the throne their master or one of themselves.

A new sultan was chosen, as a rule, from amongst the more important *amirs*, the *mamluks* who had risen to high appointment in the service of the state. The successful candidate for the throne would have the support of his *khushdashiya* – and also of his own *mamluks* (*julban* or *mushtarawat*), a group in general not numerous, since the resources normally available to an *amir* did not suffice for a lavish recruitment and training of slaves. Each sultan strove during the first years of his reign to enlarge rapidly the number of his *julban*, hoping thus to strengthen his control over the régime. And it was on his *khushdashiya* and his *julban* that he conferred exalted

46   Child tribute taken from the Balkans

rank and office in Egypt and Syria. Against him stood, more often than not, the *mamluks* whom he inherited from earlier sultans (*karanisa*), and in particular the *mamluks* of his immediate predecessor, whom he would seek to remove from their appointments in favour of his own men. One of the main resources of an able sultan was the balancing of one group amongst the *karanisa* against the other and of the *karanisa* against the *mushtarawat* dependent on himself.

The régime, in the thirteenth and the fourteenth centuries, had functioned well. It became thereafter less efficient. One factor of great significance was a change in the direction of recruitment. North of the Black Sea the Mongol state known as the 'Altun Ordu' (the 'Golden Horde') had long maintained an ordered rule under which the slave traffic from the Dasht-i Kipçak was able to continue and flourish. The effects of the Black Death and the campaigns of Timur in southern Russia contributed greatly to bring about the collapse of the Altun Ordu and the disruption of the old trade routes. A new source of human material had to be found, if the Mamluk system in Egypt and Syria was to survive. It was indeed found – and in the Caucasus, where a number of non-Muslim peoples lived amongst the mountains. From about 1400 onward the Jarakisa (the Circassians) replaced the Turks as the main ethnic element in the régime. Their dominance was, however, to have serious disadvantages. It was not uncommon for the Jarakisa to remain in contact with their former homeland in the Caucasus. Nepotism was rife among them. Their relatives came to Egypt and Syria, often rising there to high office without undergoing the arduous years of instruction as a slave soldier. Discipline was now less good than before, the training in arms less rigorous and effective. The rivalries dividing the Mamluks – *julban* and *karanisa* – tended to become more envenomed. Not infrequently the conduct of the *julban* belonging to the sultan on the throne deteriorated into unbridled licence. Ibn Taghribirdi notes in his chronicle that when Sultan Aynal (1453–61) was ill the common people prayed for his death out of hatred for his *julban*.

The long survival of the Mamluk régime can be attributed to several factors of importance. Of these factors not the least significant was the existence in Egypt and Syria of a powerful bureaucratic class drawn from the local population and representing, with its elaborate apparatus of *diwans* and procedures, a late and highly

47 The fall of
Constantinople (1453),
from a painting by
Tintoretto

developed embodiment of the traditional methods of Muslim rule.
It was this bureaucracy which controlled all the normal business of
administration and finance, thus ensuring a stability that the Mamluks, dedicated to the arts of war, had not the capacity to achieve.

One other factor conducive to survival deserves mention here:
the régime during most of its life encountered few serious threats
from outside. To the west in North Africa, to the south in Nubia,
and to the south-east in Arabia no strong foe arose to challenge the
sultanate. At sea in the Mediterranean there is little to record beyond
occasional hostilities with Cyprus of the Lusignans and with Rhodes
under the Knights of St John. It is true that in the years before 1291
the Mamluks carried out a series of major campaigns which led to the
eviction of the Latins from Syria. There was, too, in the same area a
conflict with the Mongol Ilkhans of Persia until 1303. A moment of
critical danger occurred also in 1400–1, when the forces of Timur
seized Aleppo and Damascus. The peril was short-lived, for Timur
chose to move not on Cairo, but against the Ottomans under Bayezid I.

The extension of Ottoman control eastward in the time of Mehemmed II meant that a power of the first magnitude stood now beyond
the Mamluk frontier in Syria. Friction grew rapidly between the
two states, each of them eager to establish a dominant influence in the

48 Sultan Mehemmed II, established by the conquest of Constantinople as a *ghazi* of unrivalled fame

ill-defined zones along the border. At the extreme west of the frontier was the region of Cilicia, with the towns of Adana and Tarsus. Here, too, was one of the few important breaks in the vast barrier of the Taurus Mountains – the Cilician Gates, a pass of the greatest significance in relation to trade and also to the needs of war. This area owned allegiance to the Ramadan-oghlu, princes of Turkoman origin, from the nomadic Turkish tribes present in the region. To the east of Cilicia was the district of Malatya, where the River Euphrates cuts through the mountains and flows down from the plateau of Asia Minor into the plains of Syria – again a major route through the Taurus range and of high importance for war and for trade. The neighbouring region of Albistan was also under princes of Turkoman descent, the house of Dhu'l-Kadr. Albistan, like Cilicia, filled the role of a border state poised precariously between rival powers far stronger than itself. Still further to the east were the Kurds, obedient to their own *begs*, but refractory to all forms of organized control from outside.

After 1465 there was a rapid increase of tension along the frontier. On the death, in that year, of the Dhu'l-Kadr chieftain Arslan Beg his brothers, Budak and Shahsuwar, entered into conflict over the succession. The Mamluk sultan, Khushkadam (1461–7), raised

Budak to the throne. In 1467 Shahsuwar – with aid from the Ottoman sultan, Mehemmed II (himself married to a princess of Dhu'l-Kadr) – drove out Budak, only to be captured later and executed at Cairo in 1472 on the order of the sultan, Ka'it Bay (1468–96). Budak Beg ruled thereafter as a vassal of the Mamluks. Not until 1480 was Mehemmed II free to intervene once more. He now set in command of Albistan his own nominee from the house of Dhu'l-Kadr, a prince named 'Ala al-Dawla.

On the death of Sultan Mehemmed in 1481 his sons Bayezid and Jem fought for the Ottoman throne. Jem, defeated in the field, fled into Syria, intent on seeking assistance from the sultan at Cairo, Ka'it Bay. At this time Karaman, the Turkish state which Mehemmed II had taken over in Asia Minor during the years after 1464, was still restless under Ottoman rule. Kasim Beg, of the dispossessed house of Karaman, returning from exile at the Ak Koyunlu court in Persia, tried to evict the Ottomans from his ancestral lands. The attempt ended in failure. Kasim, like Jem, found a refuge with the Mamluks. The two princes entered into an alliance, gathered fresh troops in Syria, with the approval of Ka'it Bay, and marched into Karaman. An attack on Konya in the summer of 1482 was of no avail. Jem, despairing of success, escaped to the Knights of St John at Rhodes. The whole affair deepened the mistrust existing between Istanbul and Cairo. There were irritations, too, of a different nature. The Turkoman tribes on the frontier, the Warsak and the Torghud, raided into Karaman and molested the caravan traffic passing, through Cilicia, to and from the Ottoman territories – incursions that Istanbul ascribed to encouragement received from Cairo.

The friction along the border flared out into open warfare in 1485. An Ottoman force marched now from Karaman into Cilicia and occupied Adana and Tarsus. A Mamluk counter-offensive was soon in progress and the Ottomans, having the worst of the fighting, withdrew northward into Asia Minor. At Istanbul it was resolved to make careful preparation for a new and more vigorous campaign. The Grand Vizier, Da'ud Pasha, overran Cilicia in 1487 and then ordered punitive measures to be taken against the Turkomans in the area. A still larger mobilization of troops, Mamluk as well as Ottoman, occurred in 1488. Near Adana, in August, the Mamluks again won the advantage over the Ottomans, who retired from

Cilicia in some confusion. 'Ala al-Dawla, the prince of Albistan, hitherto loyal to the Ottomans, now transferred his allegiance to the Mamluk side. With his co-operation they thrust far into Asia Minor in 1490. After a fruitless siege of Kayseri the Mamluk army retreated into Syria on the approach of a powerful Ottoman relief force.

Ka'it Bay, the Mamluk sultan, felt disinclined to continue a war which, for him, had attained its objective – the retention of Cilicia. The Ottoman sultan, Bayezid II (1481–1512), was mindful of the uncertainties prevailing along the Danube and the Sava – uncertainties arising from the death, in April 1490, of the Hungarian king, Matthias Corvinus. Moreover, the conflict had been a most expensive one for the participants. A peace was made, therefore, in 1491. Cilicia remained to the Mamluks, but the revenues of Adana and Tarsus would be assigned henceforth to the sanctuaries of Mecca and Medina.

The war ended for the Ottomans in disappointment and frustration. And yet the final result was deceptive. Jem, the brother of Sultan Bayezid II, after his flight to Rhodes in 1482, was transferred to Europe. He was to be held there until his death in 1495 – a dangerous pawn in the hands of the Christians. As long as Jem was alive, the Ottomans sought to avoid a major conflict in the east. Bayezid II had used only a portion of his forces in the war against the Mamluks. Ka'it Bay, however, was obliged to muster the maximum strength available to him – and this to achieve no more than a negative success, for the situation on the frontier was, for the Mamluks, no more favourable in 1491 than it had been in 1485. The war underlined the fact that the issue between the Ottomans and the Mamluks was above all a political one. It raised also a question which had as yet no answer – what would happen if, perhaps in the not remote future, the Ottomans found themselves free to confront the Mamluks with all the strength of their war machine?

The Mamluks had good reason to be apprehensive. This warrior caste lived, in Egypt and Syria, almost as a garrison in an alien land, set over, but not of, the populations subject to its rule. It would have, in a time of mortal danger, no real resource beyond its own skill in war – and that skill was now less efficient than it had been before the rise of the Jarakisa. Moreover, the prospective foe was formidable indeed. The Ottomans had known no extensive intervals of peace.

49 Matthias Corvinus, King of Hungary 1458–90

Their excellence in war was fashioned and tempered in a long series of great campaigns. In Cilicia, between 1485 and 1491, the troops of the imperial household – the mounted regiments of the sultan, the Janissaries, and the various technical corps, such as artillerists and engineers, had been given but a limited role. Would the Mamluks be able to match these élite soldiers if the uncertain peace broke down into a new and more perilous confrontation? Even in relation to the actual conduct of war the outlook was becoming more and more unfavourable for the Mamluks. Amongst the Ottomans cannon and fire-arms had been introduced long since on a considerable and increasing scale – the reign of Bayezid II was to see indeed a marked advance in the employment of the new weapons. The Janissaries constituted a powerful force of infantry, a large number of them using the arquebus; the Ottoman artillery was an effective instrument of war. No such readiness to welcome the advent of gunpowder and cannon was discernible among the Mamluks. This cavalry élite, proficient within its own frame of reference, opposed to the new circumstances of warfare a mind conditioned against the need for change. The Mamluk system, though still able to produce horsemen endowed with high expertise, was in fact obsolescent.

The Ottomans and Asia Minor

It was not only on the frontier with Syria that complications of a grave nature beset the Ottomans. There was danger threatening in Asia Minor. Uzun Hasan, the chieftain of the Ak Koyunlu, the White Sheep Turkomans, rose to prominence in the region of Diyarbekir. In 1467–9 he broke the control which a rival confederation, the Kara Koyunlu or Black Sheep Turkomans, held over much of Persia, Adharbayjan, and the adjacent lands. Once he had reduced to obedience the territories of the Kara Koyunlu, Uzun Hasan sought to extend his influence westward, an ambition that brought him into conflict with the Ottoman sultan, Mehemmed II. At the battle of Otluk Beli in 1473 the Ottomans crushed the forces of the Ak Koyunlu. Uzun Hasan died in 1478, leaving the throne to his son, Ya'kub Beg (1478–90). It was an old tradition among the Turks that power rested not in the hands of one man, but in all the princes of the ruling house. This attitude had the serious disadvantage that when the tide of success slowed down, quarrels tended to break out with great violence. The death of Ya'kub Beg in 1490 let loose dynastic discords so bitter as to ruin the cohesion of the régime. As the domination of the Ak Koyunlu crumbled into fragments,

50   Battle between Black and White Sheep Turkomans

there came into being a power vacuum in the lands under their control. Only one force was available and strong enough to fill that vacuum – the Safawiya.

Shaykh Safi al-Din (1252–1334) had founded a religious Order known after him as the Safawiya. The main seat of the Order was to be at Ardabil, near the Caspian Sea. It was a region long since associated with the Shi‘a, the most famous of Muslim heterodoxies, the adherents of which claimed the califate for one or other amongst the descendants of ‘Ali, the son-in-law of the Prophet Muhammad. The Safawiya began to disseminate a religious propaganda which made of Ardabil a noted centre of pilgrimage. This propaganda, from the time of Shaykh Khoja ‘Ali (1392–1429), assumed an extreme Shi‘i character. Shaykh Junayd (1447–60), seeking to add political influence to his religious prestige, strove to transform the Safawiya into a powerful instrument for war; and with such success that he had to flee before the wrath of Jihan Shah, the lord of the Kara Koyunlu, then dominant in Persia.

Junayd, driven into exile, found now in Asia Minor a rich field for the propaganda of his Order. The nomad tribes – the Turkomans –

located in this area constituted for the Ottomans a great problem. The government at Istanbul, wishing to protect the settled lands from encroachment and depredation, sought to bring the tribesmen under more effective control. The nomads, hostile to all the devices of organized rule, viewed the imperial government with suspicion. There was distrust, too, of another kind. The Ottoman régime exemplified the orthodox form of Muslim belief. A 'popular' version of Islam flourished, however, among the tribes: a faith far removed from the religion visible in the great urban centres of the empire, hybrid in character, embracing shamanistic ideas surviving from earlier centuries of nomadic life and also elements deriving from the Shi'a. Of this 'popular' Islam the most vivid embodiment was to be seen in the dervish *tarikas*, some of which had a vast influence over the tribesmen.

The problem of how to control the nomads – excluding the resort to force needed in times of particular stress – was in large degree an administrative one. To that problem a new and dangerous dimension was added with the rise of the Safawiya. Shaykh Junayd, during the years of his exile after 1448, carried the extreme Shi'i beliefs of the Order through much of Asia Minor. The Safawid propaganda made rapid progress in the regions of Siwas, Karaman, Albistan, Cilicia, Tekke, and Kastamuni; and the successors of Junayd, Shaykh Haydar (1460–88) and Sultan 'Ali (1488–94), acting through their agents (*khalifa*), enlarged the hold thus gained over the tribesmen. When, after the death of Ya'kub Beg in 1490, the domination of the Ak Koyunlu began to disintegrate, Shaykh Isma'il, following Sultan 'Ali as the head of the Order, called the Turkomans to his side in 1499 and with their aid routed the princes of the Ak Koyunlu house at the battles of Shurur (1501) and Hamadan (1503). These campaigns marked the emergence, in Persia and Adharbayjan, of a Safawid régime destined to survive until the year 1722.

To the people of Persia the rule of the Safawids was no less alien than the dominations which had preceded it. The Safawid régime was the creation of men Turkish in origin: it was but the latest in a series of Turkish ascendancies. After 1503 a new warrior caste enjoyed the rewards of conquest, a caste Turkoman still, like the Ak Koyunlu before them, yet owing allegiance to a lord who was not only the shah of Persia, but also the shaykh of a great *tarika*, a figure held to be invested with more than human attributes. The actual business of government did not fall to the victorious tribesmen, ignorant of such mysteries. All the routine of administration and finance, of religion, law, and education remained in the hands of the Persian *'ulema*, the men learned in the Shi'i faith, and of the bureaucratic class, also of Persian descent.

The Turkomans who moved eastward to answer the call of Isma'il constituted the warrior class in the new state, retaining still, in Persia, the tribal and nomadic mode of life known to them in Asia Minor and providing in time of war the armed strength required to defend the Safawid cause. To their chieftains went the offices of power and profit appropriate to their élite status, the appointments as *wali* or governor of a province for instance. The continuance among the warrior caste of tribal divisions and identities was unavoidable, given the particular antecedents of the régime. It was also not without danger for the Safawid state. On the death in 1524 of Shah Isma'il, his son Tahmasp, a minor, ascended the throne. The earlier years of his reign stand out as a time of intrigue and faction, with the Turkoman *begs* in violent conflict for the control of the young shah. The feuds continued till the reign of Shah 'Abbas (1587–1629),

52   Shah Isma'il Safawi, from a woodengraving by Melchior Lorich, 1557

54 Fifteenth-century Persian miniature depicting a lady reclining under a tree, and surrounded by attendants

53 Persian miniature of about 1485 showing Sultan Husayn Mirza in a garden with attendants, maidens and musicians

the greatest of the Safawids, who at last reduced the warring factions to obedience. His reforms, indeed, gave to the Safawid régime 100 years of further life.

To the Ottomans the appearance on their eastern frontier of a new and powerful state was a matter of serious concern. The armies which had raised Isma'il to the throne of Persia came from Asia Minor: among the Turkomans who fought for him can be numbered, for example, the Rumlu (the men from Rum – here, the region round Siwas), the Karamanlu, the Tekkelü, and the Shamlu (the warriors from Sham, which is Syria). For the Ottoman administration it was a laborious task to restrain the Turkomans, even under normal circumstances. Now, the allegiance of the tribes was being diverted to a religious and political master located outside Ottoman territory and beyond their control. Should the Safawid propaganda continue unchecked, it might well undermine Ottoman rule over much of Asia Minor. Nor was this subversion the full extent of the danger. The religious teaching of the Safawiya had been successful above all in those areas where the Mamluks and the Ottomans came into conflict. To halt the growth of Safawid influence among the tribesmen, the Ottomans would have to intervene in the lands along the Syrian border. Their intervention might impel the Mamluks to seek an *entente* with the Safawids. The mere prospect of such an alignment sufficed to transform a difficult situation into one of almost incalculable menace.

Two factors hastened the onset of the crisis: a conflict between the sons of Sultan Bayezid II over the succession to the Ottoman throne and the outbreak of a great Shi'i rebellion in Asia Minor. The customary 'law of fratricide' reflected the urgent need which the Ottomans had felt, during the growth of their state, to avoid at all costs the risk of dynastic dissension and to maintain a united front against their foes. No sultan ventured to name his heir. To do so would mean, of deliberate volition, to mark all his other sons for execution. It was Allah, therefore, who made the choice. The princes had to find their own salvation. As the father grew old and the moment of his death became less remote, the psychological pressure on the sons rose to intense proportions, driving them to prepare, with the utmost skill at their command, for the evil and inescapable hour when the sultan would die.

Selim I

Of the sons of Bayezid II the eldest, Korkud, had not the resources, personal and material, to make an effective bid for the throne. The main contention was to lie between Ahmed, the *sanjak beg*, or governor, of Amasya, and Selim, the *sanjak beg* of Trebizond. Ahmed, it was true, had won the assistance of a strong faction among the high dignitaries at Istanbul. Selim, however, was able to gain an advantage still more precious. He led the men of his province on a series of raids into the Safawid lands. These incursions brought him fame as a soldier and with it the abiding esteem of the Janissaries.

Selim was not the man to wait for the hour of decision. He preferred to choose the time himself. Of his father Bayezid he asked, and received, for his own son Süleyman an appointment as *sanjak beg* of Kaffa in the Crimea. He also reached a close understanding with Mengli Giray, the khan of the Krim Tatars. In 1511 Selim crossed the Black Sea with the forces of Trebizond, landed at Kaffa and, drawing into his service a large number of Tatar horsemen, rode southward over the Danube. This daring move was carried out without the consent of the sultan. Selim now demanded of his father a province in Europe, stating that he wanted to make *jihad* on the Christians. Bayezid, reluctant to take extreme measures against his son and worried about the situation in Asia Minor, yielded to Selim and assigned to him the government of Semendria.

Meanwhile, a great revolt, Shiʿi and pro-Safawid in character, had broken out in the region of Tekke and was sweeping far and wide through Anatolia. The Grand Vizier, ʿAli Pasha, received orders to crush the rebellion and was given for this purpose a large contingent of Janissaries and other troops from the imperial household. Selim, fearing that ʿAli Pasha, if he were successful, might use the powerful forces at his command to raise Ahmed to the throne, marched on Adrianople (Edirne), where Bayezid II was in residence with his court. The sultan now had no choice but to oppose his son. The Janissaries, though much inclined towards Selim, remained true to their lord and master, Bayezid. At the battle of Çorlu, fought in August 1511, their discipline and their skilful use of the arquebus routed the Tatar horsemen assailing them. Selim, with his army broken, fled to the Crimea.

The revolt in Asia Minor had been crushed, meanwhile, in a great

55 Selim I, conqueror
of Egypt and Syria

encounter near Kayseri (June 1511), but in the course of the fighting
both the rebel chieftain, Shah Kuli, and the Grand Vizier, 'Ali Pasha,
lost their lives. Ahmed, assuming command of the troops engaged
in the campaign, resolved to lead them to Istanbul, hoping that with
the aid of the high dignitaries committed to his cause, he might be
able to cross the water and gain the throne. It was an attempt doomed
to failure. In September 1511 the Janissaries made a violent demonstration against the officials known to favour him. The warning was
clear and definite. The Janissaries would not have Ahmed as sultan.
With his partisans silenced, Ahmed took the only road open to him.
In order to strengthen his position he seized most of the Ottoman
territories in Asia Minor. His use of force amounted in fact to overt
rebellion against the central régime of the empire. At Istanbul one
fear was overriding: that Ahmed might seek and obtain the active
assistance of Persia. It was evident that a major campaign would have
to be carried out in Anatolia. Sultan Bayezid was too old for service
in the field. The Janissaries insisted that Selim be called from the
Crimea to deal with Ahmed. Bayezid had to agree, but his acqui-
escence meant in fact his abdication. In April 1512 Selim I (1512–20)
ascended the throne. A rapid thrust in the autumn of the year drove

the forces of Ahmed from western Asia Minor. Selim, in November 1512, ordered the death of five nephews resident at that time in Brusa. The same fate befell Korkud, the eldest son of Bayezid II. Near Yenisehir, in April 1513, Selim met and defeated Ahmed, who was captured in flight and executed at once.

The campaign against Ahmed was transformed, without a break, into a war against Persia. Selim knew that it was essential to make an end of the Safawid threat in Asia Minor. To guard his rear, while he was marching on Tabriz, the sultan gave orders for a series of punitive expeditions throughout the areas where the influence of the Safawiya was strong: expeditions which led to the death or imprisonment of numerous adherents of the Shi'a. In 1514, having left a powerful force to hold the eastern frontier, he advanced via Erzinjan and Erzurum, pushing forward through territories which the foe had despoiled of all sustenance for man and beast alike. At Çaldiran, in August 1514, the sultan inflicted a terrible defeat on the shah, occupied Tabriz for a brief interval of time and then withdrew to winter quarters around Amasya and Ankara. The famous battle of Çaldiran did not foreshadow an Ottoman conquest of Persia. It was, none the less, a decisive victory. Never again did the shah venture to face the Ottomans in a major field battle, and

56 Early sixteenth-century miniature painting of a camel

the mere fact of his refusal to do so indicated that a limit had been set to the extension of Safawid influence inside the Ottoman lands.

The campaigns of 1515 and 1516 in Asia Minor complemented the success won at Çaldiran. Ottoman control was established over Erzinjan and Kamakh. The hour of reckoning had come also for Albistan. As Selim was moving eastward in 1514, he asked 'Ala al-Dawla, of the house of Dhu'l-Kadr, for reinforcements of men and supplies. The prince gave an evasive answer. Moreover, he allowed his Turkomans to harass the Ottoman columns on the march. In June 1515 the Grand Vizier, Sinan Pasha, defeated and slew 'Ala al-Dawla, with four of his sons. Albistan was now entrusted to one of his nephews, Shahsuwar-oghlu 'Ali Beg, who held it until his own disappearance from the scene in 1522. After his death the region was absorbed into the Ottoman Empire.

Ottoman control was extended, too, over Kurdistan. The Safawids had dominated this area since the years 1507–8. Their rule led, however, to much discontent among the Kurdish *begs*, some of whom rose in revolt after Çaldiran. With Ottoman assistance the Kurds defeated the forces of the shah at Koç Hisar in 1516 and drove them from the land. The system of control now imposed on Kurdistan illustrates the political wisdom of the Ottomans. An agreement was made with the Kurdish chieftains, dividing their territories into twenty-four separate governments; five of them autonomous under their own *begs*; eight of them also autonomous, but with a right of supervision reserved to the sultan; and eleven of them assimilated to the provincial régime of the empire. This readiness to take account of local rivalries and particularisms won from most of the Kurds an abiding allegiance to the Ottoman cause.

The events of 1514–16 altered to the disadvantage of Egypt the balance of force existing hitherto along the Taurus frontier. At Cairo, in 1514, the hope must have been strong that Selim I would encounter defeat in his campaign against Persia. The news of Çaldiran came no doubt as a grave disillusionment to the Mamluks: a disillusionment made even more profound when the Ottomans overthrew the Dhu'l-Kadr chieftain, 'Ala al-Dawla, and intervened in the affairs of Kurdistan. On the arrival at Cairo of emissaries from Shah Isma'il, the Mamluk sultan Kansuh al-Ghuri (1500–16) stated that if the Ottomans moved once more against Persia he would appear on the Syrian border with all his forces. This assurance rested on the belief that a military demonstration in northern Syria might be enough to dissuade Selim I from further campaigns in the east; and that such a demonstration involved no real risk of war, so menacing would be the prospect for the Ottomans of a Mamluk-Safawid *entente*.

Selim I regarded the Safawids as a foe more dangerous than the Mamluks. He was therefore eager, if possible, to renew the assault on Persia. His Grand Vizier, Sinan Pasha, was at Kayseri in June 1516 with numerous troops under his command. The vizier, fulfilling the orders that Selim had given to him, now made for Kurdistan. He broke off the advance, however, on receiving in July the fateful news that Kansuh al-Ghuri was marching towards Aleppo. Selim I, at the head of large reinforcements, left Istanbul in June. It was late July when he reached the camp of Sinan Pasha, then in Albistan. At this moment a Mamluk ambassador came to Selim, warning him not to attack the Safawids and asking that Albistan be restored to its former dependence on Egypt. Selim's answer revealed at once how mistaken the Mamluk assessment of the situation was: insistence on such demands, the ambassador was told, would mean war. With all his forces now concentrated for a major campaign, Selim moved into the plain of Malatya. Here on 4 August, having learnt that Kansuh al-Ghuri was seeking assistance from Persia, the Ottoman sultan made the daring and critical resolve to abandon the advance eastward through Kurdistan and to turn south into Syria.

At Marj Dabik near Aleppo on 24 August 1514 Selim met and routed the Mamluks. It was a decisive success. Kansuh al-Ghuri was slain in the course of the battle. The Mamluk sultan had left most of the state treasure and the equipment of war inside Aleppo. The arrogance and indiscipline of his troops during the weeks before Marj Dabik aroused much bitterness in the town. Now, streaming back from the battlefield in disorder, the Mamluks found the gates of Aleppo closed to them. No means was available to them for the defence of Syria. A flight to Egypt alone offered them a chance to continue the war. Syria itself yielded to the Ottomans without resistance. Soon Aleppo, Tripoli, Damascus, and Jerusalem surrendered to the victorious sultan. With Syria under his control Selim had no need now to fear a Safawid-Mamluk alliance.

At Cairo a new sultan, Tuman Bay (1516–17), ascended the throne. Selim, preoccupied still with the war against Persia, was willing to leave the Mamluk régime untouched in Egypt if Tuman Bay and his *amirs* would agree to govern the land in the name of the Ottoman sultan. The Mamluks, however, sent a strong force across the Sinai Desert into Palestine. At the battle of Gaza in December 1516 the Ottoman Grand Vizier, Sinan Pasha, drove them back in confusion. This defiance from Tuman Bay convinced Selim that there was no choice before him but to conquer Egypt. The moment was not unfavourable. In Asia Minor, where the winter was long and harsh, there would be small likelihood of a Persian advance until the summer of 1517. Ample time was in hand, therefore, to complete the work begun at Marj Dabik. On 23 January 1517 the guns of the Ottomans forced the Mamluks from their prepared defences at al-Raydaniya, near Cairo. There followed several days of street fighting before Selim was master of Cairo itself. Tuman Bay, with a remnant of the Mamluk army and with some aid from the Arab tribes, was able to continue the war until April 1517. After a final repulse suffered at Giza on 2 April the Mamluk sultan fled to the region of Buhayra, lying between the Damietta branch of the Nile

57   A court eunuch of the late sixteenth century

58 Persian miniature of the sixteenth century by Bihzad, depicting a prisoner being brought into a mosque

and the Western Desert. Soon he was betrayed to the Ottomans, taken to Cairo and executed there on 14 April.

The conquest of Egypt and Syria gave the Ottoman sultan immense prestige in the eyes of the Muslims. Selim I now became *Khadim al-Haramayn*, the guardian of the two sacred cities, Mecca and Medina. It would be incorrect to infer that he claimed for himself the status of a calif. But, in view of his pre-eminence in the Muslim world, he was held to be, and indeed felt himself to be, responsible for the defence of Islam and of Muslims everywhere. Nor was this the sole effect of the campaigns fought in 1516–17. The subjugation of Egypt and Syria considerably increased the resources available to the Ottomans.

It is true that after 1517 changes did occur in the government of the former Mamluk territories, for instance, the Ottoman 'feudal' system was introduced into Syria. Yet, in general, the old institutions and procedures deriving from the pre-conquest era continued to exist and function, though now with the Ottomans and not the Mamluks in control. The Mamluks as a warrior élite survived the conquest. There was no question of an Ottoman settlement *en masse* in Syria and Egypt. A *pasha* ruled at Cairo with a strong garrison to assist him. The Ottoman establishment was too small, however, to provide of itself an adequate protection for the cultivated lands against the nomads of the desert. A powerful militia would be needed for this purpose – and also to guard Egypt against external danger. The Mamluk class therefore remained in existence. As in earlier times, the main source of recruitment was to be Circassia. The young men brought to Egypt received a thorough training for war in the households of the *begs*.

The measures taken by Selim I for the government of the conquered lands amounted in fact to a vast improvisation. A Mamluk *amir*, Kha'ir Beg, ruled at Cairo until 1522. At Damascus Janberdi al-Ghazali, also a Mamluk *amir*, was *beglerbeg* of Sham (Syria). Selim, returning to Istanbul in 1518, left behind him a situation far from secure. Amongst the Mamluks there was a smouldering discontent, a regret for the independence of former years. In 1520, on the death of Selim, Janberdi al-Ghazali rose in rebellion. His attempt to seize Aleppo ended in failure and he himself was slain in February 1521, resisting the Ottoman forces sent to subdue him. There was trouble, too, at Cairo. Ahmed Pasha, appointed to be *beglerbeg* of Misr (Egypt) in 1523, was of Circassian origin. A bond of ethnic descent existed therefore between himself and the Mamluk militia. Ahmed, gathering the malcontents round him, laid claim to the sultanate of Egypt. A pro-Ottoman junta was able, however, to drive him from Cairo. After a vain effort to organize resistance in the Sharkiya (the region to the east of the Nile Delta) Ahmed was captured and killed in March 1524. This episode caused such concern at Istanbul that no less a personage than the Grand Vizier, Ibrahim Pasha, was now sent to Cairo. He carried out there, in 1525, a series of reforms which established Ottoman rule on a firm basis and which also ensured for Egypt a long interval of peace.

Selim I had solved brilliantly the grave problems confronting him on his accession to the throne. A Venetian who saw the great sultan at Cairo in the hour of his triumph wrote that no man was his equal 'in virtù, iustitia, humanità e grandezza d'animo'. Selim died in 1520, leaving his only son, Süleyman (1520–66) to succeed him. The reign now beginning was to be the most splendid in the annals of the empire: a time of far-reaching and restless endeavour, a Golden Age of Ottoman civilization, which saw, too, the institutions of the Ottoman state exhibited in their most complete and characteristic form.

The Ottoman Empire

The princes of the house of Osman – at least, until the death of Süleyman in 1566 – constitute an unbroken and almost unrivalled sequence of talent, indeed often of genius. Not the least among the factors responsible for this excellence was the care taken over their education. It was the custom for a sultan to send his sons, while still of tender age, to govern a province in Asia Minor. Each son would have with him a tutor and all the apparatus of a small court. He was trained in the accomplishments of a gentleman and of a soldier, but also in the art of wise rule and in the complexities of the administrative machine. It was a long instruction, designed to evoke the best capacities of the individual and to prepare him for the throne. The law of fratricide served also, no doubt, to sharpen in the princes their instinct of self-preservation and to call forth the full deployment of their powers.

Two institutions had a special importance, the slave household and the 'feudal' system. The sultan's household was more than a device created to fulfil the domestic needs of its master and the ceremonial requirements of a splendid court. It was the mechanism which governed the empire, embracing within itself the great offices and departments of state. It included also the troops of the central régime: the Janissaries, the *altı bölük* or six regiments of imperial horse, and the various technical corps. Most of the personnel recruited into the household bore the designation of slave (*ghulam*, pl. *ghulaman, ghilman*; or *kul*, pl. *kullar*) and came from two main sources: from captives taken in war against the Christians, either on land or at sea, and from the *devşirme*, the tribute of children levied on the non-Muslim peoples of the empire, and above all on the Slavs and the Albanians.

The recruits now became Muslim. A large proportion of them would be hired out to estates and villages in Asia Minor, there to undergo some years of physical hardening. On their recall to Istanbul these young men entered the corps of Janissaries and began

59 Christian child
taken for training as a
Janissary

a rigorous training in the arts of war.

The best of the slaves – the most intelligent and the finest in physique – went into the schools of the imperial palace. A remarkable education awaited them there. No effort was spared to transform each *ghulam* into a true Ottoman, well versed in the *mores* and culture of the world around him. Great care was given to his physical well-being. He became proficient as a horseman and a soldier. His years in the palace made him familiar with the means used to govern the empire. And he acquired, too, a profound allegiance to his master, the sultan. It was no mistaken view which led Busbecq, the ambassador of Austria, to write that the Ottomans rejoiced at the finding of a man of talent as over the possession of a precious thing ('tanquam adepti rem pretiosam'), lavish of their time and labour to achieve the unfolding of his faculties.

As the *ghulaman* rose from the lower to the higher grades of instruction, individual slaves would be drafted, at each level, to that form of service which suited their abilities: into the chancery, into the fief system, or into the élite cavalry of the household. To the small number of the *ghilman* who reached the summit of the educa-

123

tional structure was reserved a brilliant future. These slaves went out to appointments as *sanjak beg* (governor of a province) or *beglerbeg* (governor-general over a group of provinces). A slave of this exalted status might even attain the highest office of all, the Grand Vizierate.

Of great importance, too, were the *sipahis*, the 'feudal' horsemen established in most, though not in all, of the regions of the empire. The fiefs fell into two main categories: the *timar*, extending in value to 20,000 *akçes* per annum; and the *zi'amet*, producing 20,000 to 100,000 *akçes* a year. A new *sipahi* received a fief of minimum yield (2,000–3,000 *akçes*), sufficient to maintain him as an effective soldier. He might expect, from time to time and in return for meritorious service, an increase of his *timar* and therefore of his annual revenue. As his fief rose in value, so his obligations became more onerous. He had to bring to war one horseman (*jebelü*) for each 3,000 *akçes* of income assigned to him.

The Ottoman *timar* differed greatly from the fiefs characteristic of feudalism in western Europe. There was no bond of vassalage and no sub-infeudation. Most of the land in the empire belonged to the state. The *sipahi* enjoyed no right of possession over his fief. He was given no more than the usufruct of the lands included within it,

60   Ottoman *sipahi* or feudal horseman

124

61 A prince and his retinue picnicking in the mountains. Persian miniature, *c.* 1540

in other words, the right to take from the peasants living on the soil certain specified taxes due from them to the imperial government.

A *sipahi* could not bequeath his *timar* to his sons. It was, however, normal for them to obtain a fief yielding at first a revenue close to the lower end of the scale, but assessed in relation to the *timar* income of their father. Some of the fiefs went to veteran Janissaries or to *jebelü* warriors distinguished for their valour. Of the *sipahi* class a large proportion was of slave origin – above all, slaves of the sultan and of the high officials of the empire. A *timar* might be granted also to a Muslim volunteer who fought well on campaign. At the same time, a strict prohibition forbade the assignment of fiefs to men of Muslim faith, yet of peasant status. The *sipahis* with their *jebelü* horsemen, equipped with bow, lance, sword, and shield, constituted the main strength of the Ottoman armies in the Golden Age, far outnumbering the troops of the central régime.

The work of Mehemmed II, the rise of the Safawiya, and the conquests of Selim I gave to the lands of the Near and Middle East

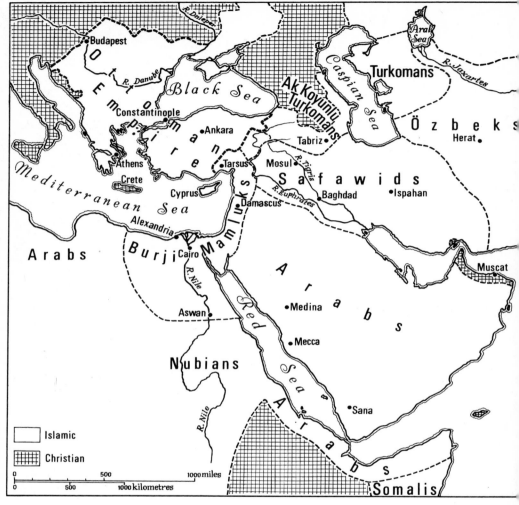

MAP 5   The Middle East in the sixteenth century

a configuration destined to last, without fundamental change, for almost three centuries. This vast reshaping – still incomplete when Selim died – was to be amplified and elaborated during the reign of his son, Süleyman (1520–66), known to his people as *Kanuni*, the Giver of Laws, and to the Christians of his time as *Il Magnifico*, the Magnificent Sultan.

Mehemmed II had established Ottoman influence over the principalities of Wallachia and Moldavia and also over the khanate of the Crimea. The littoral extending from the Lower Danube to the Sea of Azov, with the territories behind it, was a region of high strategic and economic importance. Here the great rivers, the Dnestr, the Bug, and the Dnepr, all of them natural lines of communication, flowed into the Black Sea. Here, too, was the narrow corridor east of the Carpathians, through which armies and trade had moved since unremembered time; and, on its western side, the passes leading across the Carpathian ranges into Transylvania.

In 1484 Bayezid II marched into Moldavia. His main purpose – soon achieved – was to capture Kilya on the Danube and Ak-Kerman on the Dnestr. A rich flow of commerce linked these fortress towns, via Podolia in the Ukraine, with Lwow and Dantzig. The occupation of Kilya and Ak-Kerman ensured to the Ottomans a large revenue in tolls levied on this traffic. It also gave them another advantage of no small importance for the future, a firm hold on the land route to Kaffa. The Krim Tatars had begun to take over a special role in the warfare of the Ottomans, raiding far ahead of the imperial armies and screening their advance. To the Tatar horsemen the Hungarian campaigns of Süleyman offered a welcome chance to win plunder on a scale not often available to them in the lands north of the Crimea. It was along the coast of the Black Sea and then across the Carpathians or through the Dobruja that the Tatars rode to join the Ottomans on the Middle Danube.

Süleyman, in 1538, intervened in the affairs of Moldavia, depriving that state of southern Bessarabia (including Bender) and thus strengthening Ottoman control over this area. The scene had in fact been set for a future confrontation between the Ottomans and the Russians. Indeed, the first foreshadowing of conflict became visible when Ivan IV of Moscow seized Kazan in 1552 and Astrakhan in 1554. An Ottoman attempt to build a canal from the Don to the

Volga failed in 1569–70. There was friction between the Ottomans and the Muscovites on the River Sunzha, north of the Caucasus, in 1583. These events were only brief episodes indicating trouble to come, but even now sufficient to persuade some of the astute minds in the Papal Curia – such as the nuncio Komulović, active at Moscow in 1593–7 – that it was Russia which, in the fullness of time, would bring low the proud might of the Ottoman Empire.

Sultan Süleyman made three campaigns against Persia. Of these campaigns the first, in 1534–5, won Erzurum for the Ottomans and also Iraq, a logical complement to the conquest of Syria and Egypt in 1516–17. The second venture, in 1548–9, brought under Ottoman control the region round Lake Van. A third campaign, in 1554, amounted to little more than a destructive raid into Adharbayjan. It did lead, however, to a peace concluded between the sultan and the shah at Amasya in 1555.

Süleyman had been able to take over much of eastern Asia Minor. The frontier, none the less, was insecure. Feuds and incursions continued unceasingly, the Turkoman *begs* of the border professing loyalty now to Tabriz and now to Istanbul. A further cause of unrest was the religious odium dividing the Ottomans and the Safawids. Each side strove also to win the aid of the local chieftains, Christian as well as Muslim, in Georgia, Shirvan, and Daghistan.

It was most difficult for the Ottomans to achieve a durable advantage over the Safawids. Warfare on the eastern front was expensive in munitions and equipment, in men and in beasts of burden. And it was unwelcome to the Ottoman rank and file. The theatre of war was remote, the winter long and harsh, the campaign season short. Moreover, the terrain was mountainous and wild, with a tribal population well able to defend itself. In addition, the Safawids made use of tactics well suited to their purpose: a 'burnt earth' procedure, leaving the land bare of supplies; a sustained retreat before the advancing foe, thus lengthening his lines of communication; and a continual harassment of his columns. To these tactics there was no simple and effective answer. A basic question now confronted the Ottomans: whether to rest content with the frontier of 1555, despite its uncertainties and frictions, or to go forward and attempt the conquest of Adharbayjan and the Caucasus. To choose the road of conquest meant to undertake the laborious

building of forts to cover the main routes, fords, and defiles. It meant also the raising of numerous troops to man these defences and the organization of repeated 'convoy campaigns' designed to break through to the garrisons with the reinforcements and munitions needed to maintain them. It would mean, in fact, a vast enterprise exorbitant in cost and unsure in outcome.

The Ottomans and the Portuguese

The acquisition of Egypt in 1517 and of Iraq in 1534 brought the Ottomans into contact with the Portuguese. Vasco da Gama had reached Calicut in 1498. The Portuguese, thereafter, set out to win control of the Indian Ocean. Goa, taken in 1510, became their main base in western India. Their efforts to dominate the Red Sea met with little success. Socotra was occupied in 1507, but Aden held out

63   Disembarkation at Arzila, 1471, during the war
against the Turks conducted by Alfonso V of Portugal,
from the Tapiçeria de Pastiana

against a vigorous assault in 1513. None the less, the Portuguese did
enter the Red Sea from time to time, penetrating even to Suez in
1541 and also sending aid to Christian Abyssinia, then in conflict
with the Muslims of Adal and Harrar. They sailed, too, along the
Gulf of Oman to the waters of the Persian Gulf – Hormuz (gar-
risoned in 1515), the Bahrayn, and Muscat being here the chief
centres of their influence.

The advent of the Portuguese disrupted for a while the transit
trade from India through the lands of the Middle East to the
Mediterranean world. Unwilling to lose the revenues accruing to him
from this traffic, the Mamluk sultan Kansuh al-Ghuri – with the
aid of materials and technicians obtained from the Ottoman Empire
– built and sent to India a fleet which overcame a Portuguese squadron
at Chaul in 1508, only to suffer defeat itself near Diu in the following
year. A second fleet sailed from Suez in 1515, bound now for the
Yemen. This campaign, still in progress when Selim I conquered
Syria and Egypt, achieved no success of note.

The Ottoman Grand Vizier Ibrahim Pasha, during the course of

his visit to Cairo in 1525, reorganized the naval administration at Suez and sent a small squadron to the Yemen, though without much positive result. The building in 1535–6 of a Portuguese fortress at Diu in the Muslim state of Gujarat and the rapid growth of tension between the Christians and the Gujaratis, moved the Ottoman government now to vigorous action. Orders went to Süleyman Pasha, the *beglerbeg* of Egypt, bidding him construct a new fleet at Suez. It was a difficult assignment. Egypt had few resources of timber or metal. Almost all the requisite supplies and stores came from the great arsenals of the empire, such as those at Istanbul and Gallipoli, being carried across the sea to Alexandria then along the Nile to Cairo in barges and at last overland on beasts of burden to Suez. In 1538 Süleyman Pasha sailed to India. His siege of Diu ended in failure. He was able, however, to bring Aden under Ottoman control. To counter the *entente* between the Portuguese and Ethiopia the Ottomans began in 1555 to organize a new *beglerbeglik* of Habeṣ (Abyssinia) at Massawa and Suakin on the western shore of the Red Sea.

64 A giraffe, its keeper, and two
other figures, from a Persian
manuscript, *c.* 1360

There was conflict, too, in the Persian Gulf and in the Gulf of
Oman. Baghdad had fallen to Sultan Süleyman in 1534. Ottoman
rule was extended thereafter to include Basra (occupied in 1546) and
also the region of Lahsa (al-Ahsa, al-Hasa) opposite the Bahrayn.
Piri Re'is, setting out from Suez with a large squadron in 1551,
attacked the Portuguese at Muscat and Hormuz and then made for
Basra. A new admiral, Murad Beg, tried in vain to break out of the
Persian Gulf in 1552. Sidi 'Ali Re'is, a seaman with experience of
warfare in the Mediterranean, fought several actions against the
Portuguese in 1554 and, with his fleet much damaged in a storm off
the coast of Makran, found refuge at last in Surat. The Ottomans
also sent an expedition from Lahsa against the Bahrayn in 1559.
The final episodes of note came in the reign of Murad III (1574–95),
when a certain 'Ali Beg, operating from the Yemen, raided Muscat
in the Oman and, later, Malindi and Mombasa on the coast of
East Africa.

It was clear, even before the death of Süleyman in 1566, that the
Portuguese had not the means to achieve an absolute command of
the trade routes crossing the Indian Ocean. The Portuguese were
too few and their resources inadequate to their ambitions. It was

132

impossible for them to obliterate the long-established Muslim interests in western India, impossible for them to drive the Muslims from the sea. Their gradual loss of momentum was due largely to factors inherent in their own situation. And yet it would be a serious mistake to underestimate the effect of the Ottoman resistance. It did much no doubt to restrict the success of the Portuguese. The transit trade, disrupted for a time, began to revive. A rich traffic was flowing once more to Alexandria during the last years of Süleyman. Aleppo was flourishing as a terminus for the caravans from Persia and Iraq. Spices and silks, indeed, came now to Europe via the Cape of Good Hope, but also – as of old and abundantly – through the lands of the Middle East. An equilibrium had been created between the old traffic and the new. Not until the arrival on the scene of nations stronger than the Portuguese – the English and the Dutch – would the balance incline decisively in favour of the route round Africa.

The Ottomans and the Mediterranean

It was almost inevitable that the Ottomans should wish to liquidate for their own benefit the imperium of Venice in the eastern Mediterranean; to seize the islands and the coastal enclaves long under the rule of the Signoria. The war of 1463–79 brought to the Ottomans Negroponte (Euboia) in Greece and Skutari in Albania. A further war in 1499–1503 meant for Venice the loss of Modon and Koron in the Morea, of Lepanto in the Gulf of Corinth, and of Durazzo on the Albanian shore. After yet another conflict in 1537–40 the Signoria yielded the last possessions remaining to her in southern Greece, Napoli di Romania and Monemvasia.

A situation more complex was emerging in the western Mediterranean. The *Reconquista* in Spain against the Muslims did not come to an end with the taking of Granada in 1492. Its momentum carried it across the sea. Oran fell to the Spaniards in 1509 and Bugia in 1510. A question of great importance was now raised: would North Africa come under Christian or remain under Muslim rule? The reaction to this 'Crusade' from Spain was of a most unusual kind. At Algiers – with some help from the Ottomans – a sea captain of genius, Khayr al-Din, known to the Christians as Barbarossa, founded a régime dedicated to 'il corso', piratical raids against the ships and against the coasts of Christendom. By 1529 this corsair state was strong enough to have a more than reasonable chance of survival.

Spain, now ruled by the Emperor Charles V, attempted to dominate the narrow waters of the Mediterranean. Sicily belonged to the crown of Aragon. Spanish arms had conquered Naples in 1501–4. Genoa, possessed of a powerful fleet, moved in 1528 from the orbit of France into alignment with Spain. In the same year the Knights of St John, whom Süleyman had driven from Rhodes in 1522, established a small garrison at Tripoli in North Africa. And in 1530 Charles V assigned to the Order the strategic island of Malta.

Süleyman, as the overlord of Algiers, viewed these events with concern and made now a decision of great consequence. The Ottomans had abundant timber in Asia Minor, ample supplies of labour, and a numerous seafaring population along the coastlands of the Aegean Sea; almost all that was required, in short, for the maintenance of a large fleet. A serious defect, however, was the lack of a high command able to match in resource and skill the sea captains of Venice or Genoa. To make good this need the sultan called Barbarossa from Algiers and in 1534 made him *kapudan*, admiral in charge of all the naval affairs of the empire. Khayr al-Din did not come to Istanbul alone. He brought with him his own technicians and his own lieutenants trained in the endless *razzias* at sea.

In August 1534 the new *kapudan* occupied Tunis. It was a success of brief duration, for in 1535 the Emperor Charles V took the town, reduced the sultan of the Hafsid line to the status of a vassal, and left a strong garrison in the fortress of La Goletta, controlling the harbour of Tunis. Spain, during the Ottoman-Venetian War of 1537–40, sent her fleet to the assistance of the Signoria. At Prevesa in 1538 Khayr al-Din met and repulsed the Christian armada, thus winning for the Ottomans a naval initiative not to be taken from them until the battle of Lepanto in 1571. Charles V tried to capture Algiers itself in 1541, but the expedition ended in failure. The year 1546 saw the death of Khayr al-Din. To the sultan he left a group of able captains, amongst them the famous Torghud 'Ali Re'is, the Dragut of the Christians. In 1551 Torghud 'Ali conquered Tripoli, a notable event which marked the emergence of a second corsair state in North Africa. A Spanish assault on Jerba in the Gulf of

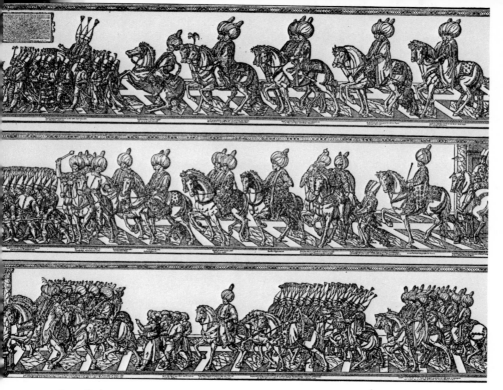

65 Süleyman I riding in triumphal procession, *c.* 1565

Gabes met with disaster in 1560. On the other hand, in 1565, the Ottomans suffered a defeat no less severe in their siege of Malta, the Knights of St John resisting stubbornly until the arrival of reinforcements from Messina.

A new phase began in the confrontation at sea, when the Ottomans resolved to invade Cyprus. The island had been under Venetian rule since 1489. Now, in 1570, Nicosia yielded to the Ottoman *sirdar*, Mustafa Pasha. Famagusta fell in 1571. The further course of the war underlined how fragile was the spirit of co-operation amongst the Christians. A *sacra liga* was formed in 1571 between Pope Pius V, Philip II of Spain, and the Signoria. Venice – as in 1538, when she had also made an alliance with Spain and the Pope – wanted to defend her territories *oltremare*. Spain – now, as formerly – was concerned with the affairs of North Africa. This divergence of interest hindered greatly the prosecution of the war against the Ottomans. One moment of triumph was given, however, to the

Christian league: its forces destroyed the Ottoman fleet at Lepanto in 1571. The victory, greeted with jubilation throughout Europe, was barren of result. To the campaign of 1572 the Ottomans brought an entire new armada, built during the preceding winter, a remarkable deployment of the resources available to them.

Venice, tired of a conflict at once expensive and unfruitful, renounced all claim to Cyprus and made peace with the Ottoman Empire in 1573. The long contention was almost done; only a brief epilogue remained to be written. Spain, in 1573, reasserted her control over Tunis. The Ottomans conquered the town in 1574, and a third corsair state was now in being. To the problems of the sea, unanswered when Süleyman called Khayr al-Din to Istanbul, the march of events had given a solution. North Africa was to remain under Muslim rule. Spain would not dominate the narrow waters between Naples and Tunis. And as for the Signoria, a large proportion of her heritage was now lost beyond recall.

The Ottomans and Europe

Süleyman made seven major campaigns on the Danube. Belgrade, besieged in vain by Mehemmed II in 1456, surrendered to him in 1521. At the battle of Mohács in 1526, the most brilliant of his

66 Late sixteenth-century pen drawing of a seated lady with an old woman leaning on a staff behind her

victories, the sultan broke the power of Hungary. Amongst the dead was the Christian king, Lajos II. The crown descended now to Ferdinand, the Habsburg Archduke of Austria, who had married the sister of Lajos. A 'native' faction among the Hungarian nobles refused to accept dependence on Vienna and chose as their candidate for the throne the *vaivoda* of Transylvania, Zapolya Janos, who sought and obtained the protection of Süleyman. The sultan regarded Hungary as his own realm, won by the sword. But what should he do with it? To maintain a vassal king at Buda was, of all solutions, the most economical and perhaps the most advantageous also. A chain of subordinate principalities would screen the northern frontier of the empire: the khanate of the Crimea, Moldavia, Wallachia, and now Hungary. To the west, between the Sava and the Adriatic shore, Bosnia filled in effect a similar role. After the Ottoman conquest of 1463–4 most of the local magnates embraced Islam, retained their privileged status in Bosnia, and became the most formidable of all the border warriors devoted to the *ghaza*.

Süleyman was not content merely to support Zapolya. He sought to deliver against the Archduke Ferdinand an assault so massive that it would eliminate him as a factor in the Hungarian situation. In 1529 the sultan marched into Austria. Incessant rains and swollen rivers hindered the advance. It was not until 27 September that Süleyman stood before Vienna. No time was left for a sustained siege and the Christians beat back the Ottoman attempts to storm the walls. A growing shortage of supplies and still more the imminence of winter led the sultan, on 14 October, to give the order for retreat. In 1532 he marched once more against Austria. The little fortress of Güns, brilliantly defended by its small garrison, defied for three weeks the full might of the Ottoman army, capitulating only on 28 August. Most of the summer was now gone and the Imperialists had been able to assemble meanwhile a force of veteran soldiers, German, Italian, and Spanish, for the defence of Vienna. The sultan, therefore, abandoned his original purpose and the campaign became in fact a vast raid through Styria and Slavonia. On two occasions now Süleyman had tried to use against Austria the tactics of a *Blitzkrieg*, and twice it was time, distance, and weather, as much as the Christian foe, which had thwarted him.

Zapolya Janos died in 1540, leaving an infant son as heir. The sultan remained true to the child of his dead servant. None the less, he knew that to install the little prince in nominal command at Buda would be to invite disaster. A new solution was required for the Hungarian imbroglio, and the choice that Süleyman made was in favour of permanent conquest. The troops of the Archduke Ferdinand had marched south in 1540 after the death of Zapolya, attacking Buda (though without success) and establishing a garrison in Pest. A war with Austria was therefore unavoidable. The campaigns of 1541 and 1543 brought under direct Ottoman rule the lands along the Danube from Belgrade, through Buda, to Esztergom. To the son of Zapolya was given the office of *vaivoda* that his father held in the time of Lajos II. He was sent now to Lippa, there to govern Transylvania in the name of the sultan. In 1552, as a result of Austrian intervention in the affairs of the young prince, the Ottomans seized Temesvár, a fortress which enabled them to keep a close watch over the territories east of the River Tisza. The war of 1541 ended in 1562, when a peace was negotiated between Süleyman and Ferdinand (now emperor, since the abdication of his brother, Charles V, in 1556). Out of these long hostilities there emerged not one, but three Hungaries: Austrian, in the north and west; Ottoman, between Belgrade and Esztergom; and Transylvanian, beyond the Tisza. This division was to endure, with little change, until the Austrian conquest of the kingdom in the years following the Ottoman siege of Vienna in 1683.

Warfare on the Danube confronted the Ottomans with difficulties of a serious nature. The terrain was distant and it abounded in rivers and marshes; the climate was often adverse and the campaign season limited in duration. Moreover, the frontier soon began to harden. At river crossings and along the main routes Christian and Muslim alike built small forts, *palankas*, of timber and earth, with wooden palisades. And in the midst of these lesser defences stood the major strongholds such as Raab and Komorn for the Imperialists, Buda and Stuhlweissenburg for the Ottomans. The Archduke Ferdinand was unable to launch a great campaign of conquest, yet in the course of time he did find the means to erect a formidable barrier against the Ottoman advance, repairing and improving the fortresses under his control and using as garrison troops mercenaries of German, Walloon, and Italian origin, professional soldiers adept in the latest practice

67 Zapolya Janos, *vaivoda* of Transylvania, supported by Süleyman as vassal King of Hungary

of war. The Ottomans, above all after the death of Zapolya, found themselves committed to an assault on a strong defensive system, to a war of sieges demanding a ruthless expenditure of men, equipment, and munitions. As on the frontier with Persia, so on the Danube line a choice was offered to them, either a warfare of local attrition and of endless raids, Muslim *beg* against Christian marcher lord, or a sustained offensive to liquidate the barrier, regardless of cost, and drive the Habsburgs from Hungary.

The peace of 1562 between the Imperialists and the Ottomans was soon broken. Once more, and for the last time, Süleyman marched to the Danube. He died in his tent before the fortress of Szigetvár in September 1566. The Golden Age of the Ottoman Empire was now almost over. An era of bitter conflict with Persia and Austria was imminent, of fierce revolts in Asia Minor, of intrigue and violence round the throne. The portents of adverse change indeed became visible during the last years of the old sultan. Against them must be set, however, the matchless splendour of his reign. It was an age of notable achievement in the fields of war and statecraft, bringing to fulfilment that long refashioning of the Muslim world which had begun in the time of Mehemmed II. It was also an age

68 The arrival of Süleyman the Magnificent's Ambassador at
Frankfort in 1562, from a contemporary woodcut by Jost Amman

adorned with able administrators like Rustem Pasha, with great
poets like Baki, with the genius of Sinan, the most renowned of
Ottoman architects, and, not least, with the presence of the sultan
himself. To his personal character and abilities the Christians who
saw him bore abundant witness, above all in the noble tribute of the
Venetian Bernardo Navagero, who wrote that Süleyman, if well
informed, did wrong to no man. Nor was his fame less secure
amongst his own people. Let us take leave of him with Baki who,
within the ornate flow of his language, enshrined a genuine sense of

loss, when he said farewell to Süleyman, dead at Szigetvár –

> . . . what has befallen the emperor, the lion of war? . . .
> He laid his face to the ground, graciously, like a fresh rose petal,
> The treasurer of time put him in the coffer, like a jewel. . . .
> The day is born. Will not the lord of the world awake from sleep?
> Does he not show himself from his pavilion, that is like the heavens?
> Our eyes are on the roads, no word has come
> From the place where lies the dust beneath the threshold of his majesty.
> The colour of his cheek has gone, he lies dry-lipped
> Like a fallen rose. . . .[1]

[1] The quotation comes from B. Lewis, *Istanbul and the Civilization of the Ottoman Empire*, pp. 164–5 *passim* (THE CENTERS OF CIVILIZATION SERIES, No. 9), University of Oklahoma Press. Norman, 1963.

Africa in 1500 ROBIN HALLETT

Africa as Known to Europe and to Asia in 1500

TO A WELL-INFORMED CITIZEN of Lisbon or of Venice, of Constantinople or of Baghdad, Africa in the year 1500 was far from being a completely unknown, dark, and mysterious continent. For at least 2,000 years there had been intercourse between the northern and southern shores of the Mediterranean; indeed, during the centuries when the Roman Empire was at the height of its power the entire North African littoral was under European rule. In the seventh and eighth centuries A.D. Arab armies advancing from the east overran an even larger extent of North Africa. The traders who followed the armies developed routes that led across the Sahara to the country Arabs called *Bilad as-Sudan*, 'Land of the Blacks', the great belt of savanna plains that stretches across the continent from the Atlantic to the Red Sea. Long before the expansion of Islam the peoples of Arabia had been familiar with the territories of Ethiopia and the Horn of Africa that lay across the narrow divide of the Red Sea. East Africa, too, was not unknown to Asian peoples: as early as the beginning of the Christian era seafarers of the Indian Ocean, men from Arabia and the Persian Gulf, from India and even from distant Indonesia, visited its shores on trading expeditions. Indeed, Indonesian adventurers went on, in the course of the first millennium A.D., to colonize and draw into the orbit of Indian Ocean trade the vast and previously uninhabited island of Madagascar.

But to the outside world Africa had an aspect not unlike that of the moon. While one large segment was comparatively familiar to observers in parts of Asia and of Europe, more than half of the great land mass – those parts lying to the west and to the south – was completely unknown, wrapped in seemingly impenetrable darkness. Indeed, it was not until the Portuguese voyages of the latter half of the fifteenth century that outsiders and even Africans themselves were able to obtain a notion of the basic shape of the continent. And the Portuguese maritime explorations still left the interior unexplored.

142

For more than three centuries after 1500 the outside world remained completely ignorant of much of the African interior, the vast equatorial regions presenting a particularly provocative blank on European maps. Gradually, however, in the course of the nineteenth century a variety of enterprising outsiders – Arab traders in slaves and ivory, European explorers and missionaries, and finally the agents of the newly established colonial governments – began to penetrate ever deeper inland. By 1900 the map of Africa, though imprecise in many of its minor details was reasonably complete. But the outside world still remained ignorant of many aspects of the great continent. It knew little about the extraordinary variety of forms of political organization and social structure to be found within Africa, and virtually nothing about the great range of ideas concerning man and his place in the universe developed by different African peoples. And when outsiders turned to speculate about the history of Africa they found themselves faced with darkness that seemed as impossible to illuminate as that which once had covered

69   One of the earliest printed maps of Africa, from an edition of Ptolemy's *Geographia* by Henricus Petri (Basle, 1540)

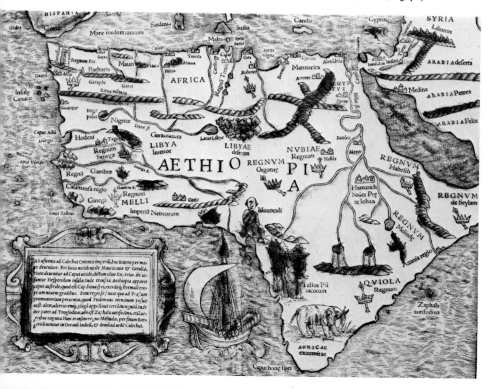

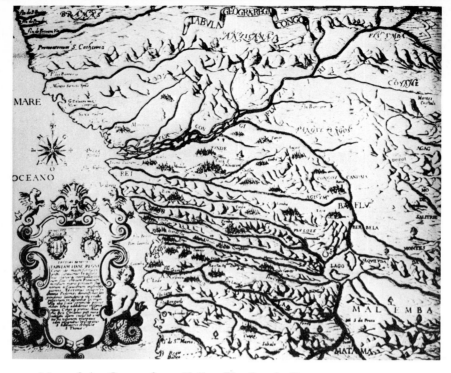

70 Map of the Congo from Felipe Pigafetta's *Regnum
Congo* engraved by de Bry in 1598

the geography of the continent. Africa, European scholars were
accustomed to remark in the first half of the twentieth century, was
the continent whose history only began when it was drawn into the
orbit of European enterprise. History, those who held this view
pointed out, is dependent primarily on written sources; most
African peoples had not acquired the technique of writing when
Europeans first made contact with them; incapable of producing
written records, such societies clearly had no history of their own.
Superficially the argument seemed convincing – indeed it is still
accepted in certain academic circles. In fact it was based on a
number of false premises. One of the most exciting intellectual
developments in recent years has been the growing realization that
African history can be explored no less effectively than the history
of any other continent. As a result of the advances that have been
made in this field it is now possible to know much more about the
complex structure of Africa and its peoples in 1500 than any indi-

vidual living in the world at that time could have done. But before presenting a picture of Africa at the beginning of the great age of European expansion, it is essential to say something about the sources of this knowledge, to see by what means historians and other scholars have succeeded in throwing broad shafts of light into the dark places of the African past.

The Sources of African History

The discipline of historical research is based on the same principles in Africa as in any other part of the world. But whereas in Europe historians devote almost all their attention to an examination of written material, in Africa the historian has to familiarize himself with a variety of other sources. Nevertheless, even in studying African history written material is of the greatest importance. Taking the continent as a whole, the historian has a remarkable range of documents at his disposal.

The earliest written records in Africa – or indeed in the whole world – are represented by the hieroglyphic inscriptions, some of them close on 5,000 years old, that have been found on the monuments of ancient Egypt. Egypt has also preserved, by virtue of the extreme dryness of its climate, a large number of documents written on papyrus whose contents vividly illuminate the social life of the country at many different periods of its past. In the latter half of the first millennium B.C. Greek and later Roman historians and geographers began writing about Africa. The works of the great scholars of Classical antiquity – Herodotus, Strabo, Pliny the Elder, Ptolemy, and others – contain a mass of interesting information about those parts of northern Africa known to the Mediterranean world.

After the Arab conquest of North Africa in the seventh century A.D. historians and geographers in many parts of the Muslim world, from Andalusia (southern Spain) to Baghdad, began collecting information about all those parts of Africa – the Sudanic belt and the east coast as well as North Africa and the Sahara – regularly visited by Muslim traders. Thus, to cite a single example, al-Idrisi, the most famous of Muslim geographers, who compiled his work in the twelfth century while residing at the court of the Norman king, Roger of Sicily, was able to present a fairly detailed account of the

Negro kingdoms to be found immediately south of the Sahara.

Many of the peoples with whom the Muslim traders came into contact adopted the new religion of Islam and with it the technique of writing Arabic. In some centres local Muslim scholars began producing works of history. Timbuktu, for example, the greatest centre of learning in the Western Sudan, was the home of a flourishing school of Muslim historians in the sixteenth and seventeenth centuries. Other Muslim chronicles dating to this period have been found in Bornu (northern Nigeria), Somalia, and Kilwa on the East African coast. A somewhat similar development took place in Ethiopia; Geez, the literary language of the medieval Christian kingdom, was written in a script ultimately derived from the ancient Sabean civilization of south Arabia.

The Arab conquest of North Africa disrupted peaceful intercourse across the Mediterranean for many generations, but by the tenth century European traders were once again doing business in North African ports and medieval archives, especially those of the Italian city-states, contain a certain amount of information about North Africa. It was not, however, until the expansion of Portuguese activities at the beginning of the fifteenth century that Europeans once again began to make a substantial contribution to the outside world's knowledge of Africa. Portuguese chroniclers were primarily concerned to narrate the heroic achievements of their countrymen, but their accounts contain much information about the contemporary African situation. Thus the book which Father Alvarez wrote about his experience on the first Portuguese mission to Ethiopia in the 1520s contains a detailed account of the political organization of the Ethiopian kingdom. During the course of the sixteenth century other European peoples, notably the French, the English, and the Dutch, began to interest themselves in Africa, with the result that the volume of material relating to the continent in European libraries and archives began steadily to increase.

There are many parts of Africa in which, even as late as 1500, the historian can find no contemporary written source to illuminate the past. But this, of course, is no different from the situation which the student of history finds in every part of the world when he pushes back far enough in time. Fortunately, the techniques used for exploring the remoter past in other continents can be applied no less effectively

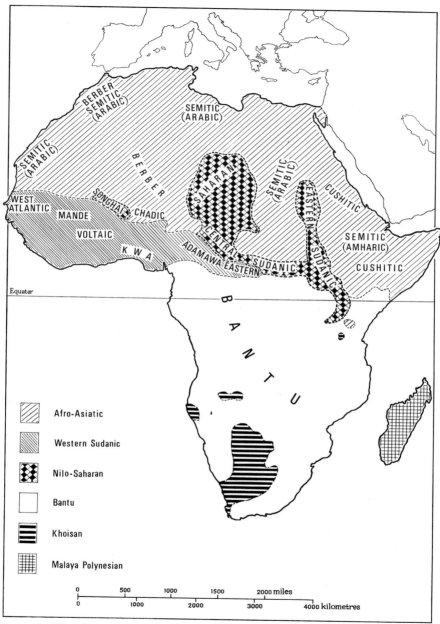

Legend:

- Afro-Asiatic
- Western Sudanic
- Nilo-Saharan
- Bantu
- Khoisan
- Malaya Polynesian

MAP 6   The Languages of Africa

here. Research in a variety of disciplines, including social anthropology, linguistics, and botany, helps to throw new light on the African past, but of all the disciplines it is of course archaeology that has the most to contribute to an exact knowledge of the early historical development of Africa.

Archaeologists have been interested in parts of Africa for more than a century. At first their attention was concentrated on those sites which seemed to present by virtue of their spectacular ruins the greatest prospect of intriguing discoveries. So it was that in the nineteenth century archaeological research in Africa was confined to the splendid remains of ancient Egypt and the cities of Greek or Roman foundation in North Africa. Later archaeologists working in parts of South and East Africa began to find evidence of the existence of early man in sites far older than those known from other continents. Within the last fifteen years archaeologists, aided by the advances in dating techniques made possible by the work of physicists and

71 Antiquities at Zimbabwe, from a plate published in 1892: 1. Vulture's head; 2. Model of the ruins; 3. Oxen; 4. Head of a man; 5. Hunting scene

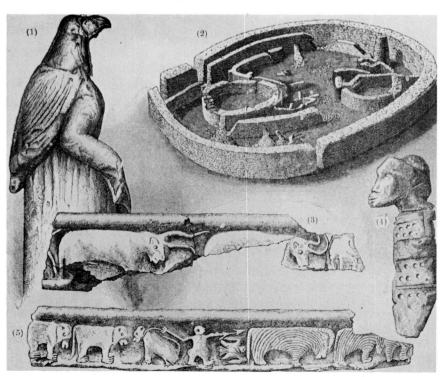

72   Massive round tower at Zimbabwe

chemists, have been able to add much more to our knowledge of the past. The massive stone-walled constructions at Zimbabwe in Rhodesia – to give but one example – have been explored with great thoroughness and the mystery which for so long surrounded this strange site has now been completely resolved. But though not a year passes without some advance in the field of African archaeology, there are still vast parts of the continent that remain completely unexplored. Archaeologists working in sub-Saharan Africa may not discover treasures comparable to those found in other parts of the world, but by using the latest techniques to examine comparatively simple artefacts – beads, iron implements, pieces of pottery, and so on – they should be able to reveal many things about the African past that were completely unknown before.

The prime task of social anthropologists working in Africa has been to examine contemporary African societies, to study their social and political institutions, and to examine their systems of ideas. Most societies possess a store of historical knowledge preserved not in written documents but in the memories of the older men and women and handed down from generation to generation, to which the term 'oral tradition' has been applied. Oral tradition varies from people to people. Some groups preserve memories only of the recent past, others have records of kings and other great men going back over 500 or 600 years.

The detailed studies made by anthropologists of African societies have revealed how complicated a form of social organization even the most 'primitive' society possesses. These studies have shown too how subtle has been the range of thought and how highly developed the skills and techniques of peoples whom Europeans have tended to dismiss or denigrate by using such terms as 'backward' or 'savage'.

One of the most important historical documents possessed by any people is its language. More languages are spoken in African than in any other continent; by studying the connections between them linguistic scholars can point to developments of great historical significance which throw light on the movements of peoples and their relations one with another. Xosa, for example, one of the main languages of South Africa, is basically a Bantu language but one that incorporates many words from the entirely different languages of the Bushmen; it presents an enduring monument to the intercourse that took place about 500 years ago between the invading Bantu agriculturists of Negroid stock and the autochthonous Bushmen hunters.

Africa contains many other monuments to its past. Every species of cultivated plant or domesticated animal has behind it a record of development and diffusion from one area to another. The techniques of the hunter, the farmer, the blacksmith, and the woodcarver have been evolved as the result of centuries of experimentation and borrowing. All these different aspects of human activity are of interest to the historian, but in studying them he must turn for assistance to scholars in other disciplines, including botany, zoology, agriculture, and art history, where special methods have been developed for studying such matters.

Africa in its Geographical Setting

Africa is the second largest continent. Its area, 11 million square miles, is about three-quarters the size of Asia, one and a half times that of North or South America, and three times that of Europe. The sheer bulk of the African land mass is a factor of great historical significance. It has meant that various parts of the continent have been so far removed one from another that no direct contact has been possible between them until quite modern times. In 1500 people living in West Africa knew absolutely nothing of the southern and eastern parts of the continent. Intercourse between regions was further restricted by the fact that over Africa as a whole population density has been – at least during the last 2,000 years – very much lower than in the other continents of the Old World. This meant that in many parts of Africa, and especially in the southern half, people found themselves with plenty of room in which to expand. When population increases in a confined area, as happened in the Nile Valley in the fourth millennium B.C., local communities are forced to devise new forms of social organization to cope with the resultant strains. But when disputes over agricultural and pastoral land can easily be resolved by one party moving away to find new territory for itself, the need to develop more elaborate forms of organization does not arise and a relatively simple social structure is preserved for generation after generation. Such was the experience of many African peoples.

Set in a world map, Africa's most striking feature is its relative

73   Ships exploring the west coast of Africa, from Juan de la Cosa's map, c. 1500

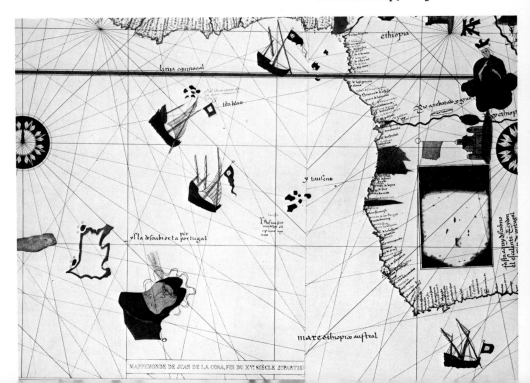

isolation from other continents. The degree of isolation obviously varies from region to region. North Africa has a record of intercourse with southern Europe and western Asia reaching back over thousands of years. North-east Africa has been connected as intimately with Arabia across the narrow divide of the Red Sea as England with the other lands of western Europe. The coast washed by the Indian Ocean has been regularly visited by Asian merchants taking advantage of the monsoon winds from at least as early as the last centuries of the first millennium B.C. But the long western side of Africa faced the vast and lonely stretches of the Atlantic, the medieval world's 'Sea of Darkness', an ocean whose waters were traversed by no ships – if the vague and doubtful story of a circumnavigation of Africa by the ancient Egyptians be discounted – until the pioneering voyages of the Portuguese in the fifteenth century. Africa's isolation was obviously much less marked than that of the Americas or Australia, but clearly many parts of the continent experienced no direct contact with the rest of the world until the coming of Europeans.

In its natural features Africa appears to present a much greater

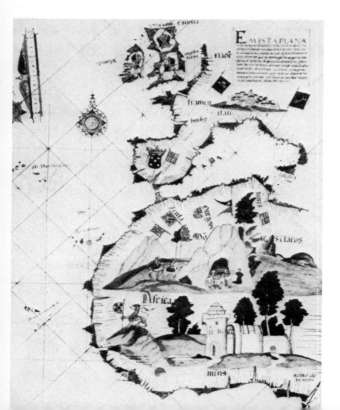

74   A mid sixteenth-century map by Lazaro Luis, including a painting of the important Portuguese castle of Elmina

152

regularity of pattern than Asia, Europe, and the Americas. The continent seems less highly compartmentalized. There are no great mountain ranges comparable to the Alps, the Himalayas, or the Andes to divide region from region, no massive peninsulas and few offshore islands of the kind found in Europe and Asia capable of providing for those who inhabit them natural frontiers well designed to encourage the development of a spirit of national unity. Across wide stretches of the continent there lie broad belts of territory, superficially characterized by the uniformity of their landscapes – the Sahara, the savanna plains, the equatorial forest. But while the geography of Africa undoubtedly does present a greater regularity than that of other continents, it would be a mistake to exaggerate either the uniformity of its landscapes or the absence of natural frontiers. The Sahara, for example, is often thought of as a monotonous waste of sand-dunes; in fact it is a highly complex area which includes among its natural features mountains almost as high as the Alps, and many parts of the continent – the mountains and plains of Morocco, the fertile valley of the Lower Nile, the Ethiopian plateau, the Interlacustrine area of East Africa, the high veld of South Africa – stand out by virtue of their individuality.

The Evolution of Man in Africa

Man has been defined as a creature capable of making tools in a set and regular pattern. It was this tool-making capacity that distinguished the earliest men from the higher primates and enabled them to acquire an increasing mastery over their environment. Thus the emergence of the technique of tool-making represents the first and fundamental act in human history. Recent archaeological discoveries make it virtually certain that this momentous development took place not in Europe or in Asia but in Africa.

One of the most exciting archaeological sites in the world is Olduvai Gorge in northern Tanzania. Here in 1959 Dr Louis Leakey discovered the remains of a hominid he names *Homo Zinjanthropus* in close association with very primitive stone implements. This earliest known tool-maker probably lived about 2 million years ago. Other discoveries made in East and South Africa support the hypothesis that this part of the continent was indeed the cradle of mankind and that it was from here that men gradually spread into northern Africa, Asia, Europe, and the Americas.

This infinitely slow expansion and dispersion of the human population during Palaeolithic times was accompanied by changes in the physical type and by the development of improved tool-making techniques designed to cope more effectively with the varied environments in which man was to be found. By 10,000 B.C. Africa probably contained the four main physical types presented by its modern population. In the north people of Caucasoid stock, brown-skinned, with straight hair, narrow lips, and thin noses, appear to have moved in from western Asia. In parts of the Sahara and in the northern savanna a dark-skinned, frizzy-haired, thick-lipped, broad-nosed Negroid stock had emerged. Small groups of people of Pygmy stock, characterized by their short stature, may already have moved into the equatorial rain-forest, while Bushmanoid groups, ancestral to the modern Bushmen, dominated eastern and southern Africa. In the past 12,000 years there have been many shifts in the distribution of the peoples possessing these broad physical characteristics: Caucasoid groups pressing westwards across North Africa and infringing on the Negroid populations to their south, Negroid groups moving into the areas occupied by the Pygmies and the Bushmen, annihilating, absorbing, or expelling the older population.

At a very remote period early forms of the languages of modern Africa must have been in existence. But over the millennia a remarkable proliferation has taken place. Today more than 700 different languages are spoken in Africa in comparison with about fifty languages in Europe. A brief study of African languages provides one of the most effective means of appreciating the diversity of cultures to be found in the continent. Linguistic scholars have grouped African languages into a number of linguistic stocks, most stocks possessing several subdivisions. Two languages belonging to the same subdivision may differ from one another in much the same way as English does from French. Between languages of the same stock but of different subdivisions the contrast is much more substantial, while languages belonging to different linguistic stocks are as remote one from another in their grammatical structure and system of word-formation as English is from Chinese.

Languages are never static. Not only do they experience internal

75 The castle and fort of Elmina, founded by the Portuguese in 1482 by order of John II

changes in grammar and vocabulary but their distribution is liable to expand or contract even to vanishing point. Arabic, for example, must have been virtually unknown in Africa in A.D. 500; by 1500 it had become the lingua franca of many parts of the continent. Punic, on the other hand, the language spoken by the Carthaginians in the first millennium B.C., disappeared completely during the first centuries of the Christian era. (See Map 6, page 147.)

Another aspect of human evolution is represented in Africa as in other continents by the development of many different systems of thought. 'Religion' is too narrow a term to describe such systems, for they embraced both the natural and the supernatural order and represented the attempts made by different peoples to explain the natural phenomena which surrounded them and to devise a series of rules designed to ensure the survival and well-being of particular social units. To lump all these systems together as 'paganism' and to deride their tenets as 'superstition', as most outsiders have done during recent centuries, is to ignore their remarkable variety and to overlook their subtlety and penetration.

Closely associated with these intellectual developments was the emergence of new forms of political and social organization. The hunting bands of the modern Pygmies and Bushmen provide an example of the simplest known form of human society. Confined today to a few isolated areas, these bands of nomadic hunters, forced by their limited technology to devote most of their time to the search for food, must once have represented the commonest form of social organization in the continent. Improved methods of food production resulting from developments in agriculture, pastoralism, and fishing, enabled many African peoples to lead a more secure life whether in compact villages, scattered homesteads, or cattle-camps. These communities were held together largely by the ties of kinship. In political terms they were independent one of another but inter-marriage, local trade, and common participation in certain religious ceremonies might lead to the maintenance of strong links between the communities of a particular neighbourhood. As late as 1500 the majority of Africans lived in these small, largely self-sufficient, self-governing communities.

The emergence of more elaborate forms of political organization involved the establishment of some form of political authority over a number of previously independent communities. If one terms this form of organization a 'state', then it is clear that most Africans lived in what can be described as 'stateless' societies. Two factors appear to have been of major significance in the emergence of states. The gradual improvement of methods of production made it possible to support groups of specialists – administrators, priests, and warriors – whose skills enabled them to secure a dominant position within their society. At the same time, growing pressure of population in certain areas led to increasing conflict between neighbouring groups and so to the establishment of one group in a position of political superiority. The earliest states to be created in Africa emerged in the valley of the Lower Nile 5,000 years ago; they came together towards the end of the fourth millennium B.C. to form the kingdom of ancient Egypt. By A.D. 1500 states were to be found in many parts of north-east, north-west, and West Africa and in certain areas of Central Africa. But as the blank spaces on Map 7 indicate much of the continent was still unaffected by the development of this more elaborate form of political organization.

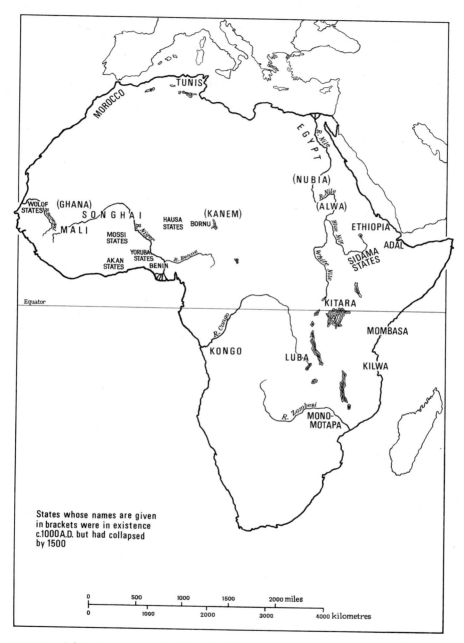

MAP 7   Africa in 1500; the Principal States

76   The market at Cape Corso, one of the earliest
European settlements in Africa

The broad themes of human evolution are the same in every continent. But every continent has been affected in its development by the nature of its own unique environment. To consider the effects of the environment on human development in Africa helps one to gain a clearer realization of the opportunities and of the limitations with which its peoples have been faced in the course of their history.

The Natural Environment and its Effect on Human Development in Africa

In Palaeolithic times, when hunting and food gathering were the only means known to man of obtaining a livelihood, the savanna plains of Africa with their warm climate and their teeming wild life provided an ideal environment for human development. But once the use of food-producing techniques based on agriculture and the domestication of animals became general throughout the Old World. Africa could be seen to possess disadvantages of a kind not encountered in Europe and Asia.

Over large parts of the continent outside the equatorial regions the rainfall was sparse or highly irregular, thus limiting the possibilities of agriculture and increasing the dangers of drought and famine. Though there were some areas of great fertility – the Nile Valley, the Ethiopian Highlands, the area round Lake Victoria, and certain parts of West Africa – these were exceptional. Over much of the continent the soil was poor and deficient in hu.nus. The tropical regions produced a superabundance of pests and disease-bearing parasites that preyed on man, his crops, and his cattle. Large parts of the savanna were infested with the tsetse-fly, whose sting is fatal to cattle. Malaria spread by the anopheles mosquito produced a high rate of infant mortality and other afflictions, such as the many forms of worm infestation, had the effect of lowering the vitality of those who suffered from them. The combined assaults of famine and disease would seem to have kept the rate of population growth at a lower level in Africa than in other continents.

The agricultural revolution of Neolithic times was based on the development of the cultivation of wheat and barley. These cereals could not be grown in warm, damp climates, and millet and sorghum, the domesticated cereals indigenous to tropical Africa, have a less abundant yield than the cereals of temperate lands. The food crops that provide today the staple diet for most of the peoples of sub-Saharan Africa – yams, bananas, maize, and cassava (manioc) – were all introduced from other continents; yams and bananas were brought from South East Asia in the first millennium A.D.; maize and cassava from South America after 1500. Before the introduction of these staples most sub-Saharan African peoples were forced to depend on hunting and the gathering of wild foodstuffs, a time-consuming process and one that never allowed for the accumulation of a surplus sufficient to support a wide range of specialists – crafts-men, administrators, priests, and warriors – engaged in non-productive activities.

With the development of external trade Africa could be seen to possess relatively little to offer to other continents. In Classical times Egypt and parts of North Africa were among the main grain-producing areas of the Mediterranean world. The Arab conquest of North Africa disrupted this trans-Mediterranean trade. In 1500 Africa was exporting relatively little in the form of agricultural raw materials and foodstuffs. Crops such as cotton, coffee, cocoa, groundnuts, tobacco, sisal, and sugar that today provide the basic exports of many African countries represent a development of the nineteenth and early twentieth centuries, made possible by the introduction of domesticated plants from other parts of the world.

For the outside world in 1500 gold was the most important of African exports. The earliest gold-mining took place in the Nubian Desert in the third millennium B.C.; but these mines which at one time contributed great wealth to Egypt had been exhausted by 1500. In their place rich supplies of easily workable gold were being exploited in parts of West Africa (see Map 8)[1] and on the Rhodesian plateau. West African gold was exported across the Sahara and, at the very end of the fifteenth century, from the new Portuguese post at Elmina on the Gold Coast. Rhodesian gold was carried to the Muslim city-states of the East African coast. The wealth derived from gold contributed greatly to the development of the West African states of Ghana, Mali, and Songhai and of the kingdom of Monomotapa on the Rhodesian plateau.

Slaves provided tropical Africa's second major export. In Classical times there had been little traffic in Negro slaves, but the Arab conquests of the seventh and eighth centuries and the expansion of Muslim trade led to the development of a considerable commerce in human merchandise. Some slaves were sent across the Sahara, others down the Nile to Egypt or from Ethiopia across the Red Sea to Arabia, while a few were exported from East African ports. It is impossible to provide an estimate of the annual average export, but it was certainly very much smaller than the figure of 100,000 slaves a year being sent across the Atlantic by European slave dealers in the early nineteenth century. Before 1500 the Portuguese had started to bring Negro slaves to Portugal and to the recently annexed Atlantic islands such as São Tomé. But it was not, of course, until plantation colonies had been established in the New World that the Atlantic slave trade began to assume increasingly formidable proportions and to represent the most vigorous form of commerce conducted in any part of the continent.

Ivory was the third major product that the outside world received from Africa. Most African ivory was relatively soft and easily workable; it was in great demand in India and some pieces must have

[1] See page 163.

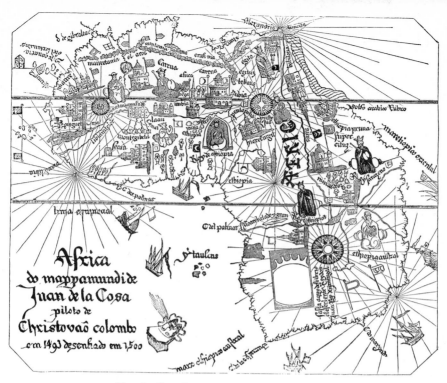

77　Facsimile of a map of Africa which belonged to Juan de
la Cosa, pilot of Christopher Columbus

found their way to Europe. East Africa was the major producer of
ivory. Africa's other exports consisted for the most part of luxury
goods such as tortoise-shell, rhinoceros horn, animal skins, and
ostrich feathers, all produced in very modest quantities. Egypt,
commercially by far the most advanced country in the continent,
owed much of its prosperity to the transit trade in Eastern spices.
Its near monopoly was eventually undermined by the Portuguese
discovery of a sea route to the Indies.

To this external commerce should be added a limited amount of
internal trade – the exchange of salt, iron, copper, beads, and certain
forms of cloth. But all this was on a very small scale when compared
with the vigorous inter-regional trade of Europe where the exchange
of commodities in bulk – oil, wine, wool, and corn – could be traced
back to the first millennium B.C. Like Europe and Asia, Africa
possessed in cities such as Alexandria, Timbuktu, and Kilwa urban

161

centres whose prosperity was largely dependent on trade. But cities were rarer than in the other continents of the Old World. In 1500 the vast majority of Africans – indeed the entire population of certain regions – lived in small, self-sufficient, rural communities.

Today, with the advance in modern science and technology, it is possible to take a more sanguine view of Africa's resources. New mining techniques make possible the exploitation of mineral resources completely unknown before. Turbulent rivers can be harnessed to produce hydroelectric power. Disease can be checked and pests eliminated by a wide range of new methods. And poor soils can be enriched by chemical fertilizers. In 1500 developments such as these lay completely beyond the range of possibility. To Europeans and to Asians, no less than to Africans, most parts of the continent presented a harsh and difficult environment in which mere survival was something of an achievement. If one is seeking to explain the relative backwardness of Africa when set against parts of Europe and of Asia, one will find the answer not in any pseudo-scientific arguments about 'racial inferiority' but in the nature of the physical environment and in the relative isolation of many parts of the continent from the main centres of technological development.

Continental Interactions and Contrasts

None of the continents of the Old World have developed in complete isolation. Each has influenced its neighbours to some degree. In this constant process of interaction lies one of the major themes of the history of Europe, of Asia, and of Africa.

Archaeological evidence makes it abundantly clear that in Palaeolithic times Africa was at the centre of human development, giving more to other continents than it received from them. In Neolithic times this situation was reversed: over the past 10,000 years Africa has been powerfully affected by innovations brought in from the outside. Up to A.D. 1500 the impact of Asia had clearly been vastly greater than that of Europe. From western Asia there had come, in about 5000 B.C., the new techniques of cereal cultivation and of rearing domesticated animals. Introduced first into the north-eastern corner of the continent, these revolutionary new methods of food production gradually spread throughout Africa. From western

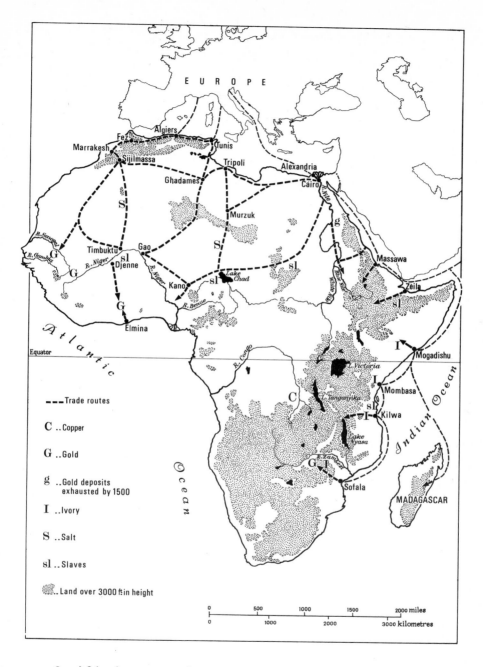

MAP 8   Africa in 1500: trade routes, cities and principal trade goods

78 An early seventeenth-century engraving of a group of
Hottentots

Asia, too, there came in the first millennium B.C. the new techniques
of iron-working which were dispersed along a variety of routes deep
into the heart of the continent. In the first millennium A.D. Africa
received further stimulants from Asia. The camel, introduced from
Arabia, gave to certain Saharan peoples a means of overcoming the
difficulties of movement in the most formidable desert in the world.
At the same time the banana and the Asian yam, brought by Indonesian seafarers to the coast of East Africa, gradually spread across the
tropical regions of the continent. To peoples previously dependent
on hunting and gathering these new plants provided the opportunity
of leading a more secure and settled life. For both yams and bananas
could easily be produced in bulk.

To these innovations that transformed the economy, the population pattern, and hence the political structure of much of Africa,
must be added the new ideas introduced by Asian immigrants. In
the first millennium B.C. small groups of Semitic-speaking peoples,
the Phoenicians and the South Arabians, exerted a powerful influence on limited areas of North Africa and Ethiopia. Far more profound, however, were the consequences of the great outpouring of
Muslim Arabs that began in the seventh century. By 1500 the greater
part of northern Africa could be described as *Dar al-Islam*, the lives
of the peoples of this vast area being moulded by that complex of

164

ideas and techniques implied in the term 'Muslim culture'.

While Asia had made these massive contributions to Africa's development, Europe had offered relatively little. North Africa had indeed been under European rule – the Macedonian Greeks in Egypt, the Romans over the whole stretch of North Africa – for several centuries, but neither the Greeks nor the Romans had made a permanent and enduring impression on the region, while Christianity, the religion particularly associated with Europe, had suffered a catastrophic decline in North Africa after the Arab conquest. In 1500 the great age of Europe's impact on Africa still lay in the future.

If one sets Europe and Africa against one another at this time when their lines of development were just beginning to converge, certain obvious contrasts present themselves. On the one hand, a relatively compact continent whose various parts are so disposed as to facilitate intercourse across narrow stretches of sea or along easily navigable rivers; on the other, a massive land mass whose sheer bulk restricts intercourse between regions or renders it impossible. In Europe conditions of climate, rainfall, and soil favourable to the development of agricultural economies; in Africa wide areas faced with the constant threat of drought and afflicted by a multitude of pests and parasites, many of a kind not found in temperate lands. To these fundamental differences resulting from the facts of geography must be added sharp contrasts in the nature and distribution of the population. In Europe many areas possessed a relatively dense population by the standards of the time; over most of Africa the population was very much thinner on the ground. Yet, in spite of its modest population, Africa contained a much greater diversity of peoples, differing from one another in physical appearance, in language, and in other aspects of their culture. In part, of course, this greater diversity could be accounted for by the larger size of the continent. But there were a number of fairly compact areas – the Ethiopian Highlands, the Chad Basin, the Interlacustrine districts of East Africa – where a wider range of ethnic groups was to be found than in any area of comparable size in Europe.

These contrasts endure to this day. In many other respects the contrasts between the two continents were less sharp in the fifteenth century than they are in the twentieth. In 1500 the vast majority of the population of both continents lived in largely self-contained village communities. But whereas in Europe almost every village had by then been placed under the control of some external political authority, in Africa a very large number of villages still formed independent political units. All over Europe the visits of royal officials, feudal lords, wandering priests, or itinerant traders were breaking down the isolation of rural communities and facilitating the circulation of new techniques and new ideas in a way that was not possible in most of Africa. Europeans, in other words, found themselves far more exposed to the galvanising process of change.

One must beware of indulging in too many generalizations. The names men have given to the continents are convenient short-hand expressions covering lands and peoples of great diversity. To gain a deeper appreciation of the nature of African societies in 1500 one must turn from continental generalities to a study of the historical development of particular countries and regions.

North-east Africa

Egypt

During the later Middle Ages Egypt was not only the most powerful of Muslim states but also one of the most highly developed countries in the world. Christian visitors to Cairo marvelled at the city's size and opulence. No less amazing were those other monuments, utterly different in style from the ornate elegance of Muslim mosques and palaces, the three great Pyramids of Giza, memorials to a civilization so remote that hardly any record of its history, beyond the stones themselves, appeared to have survived.

Today, after more than a century of archaeological research, we can trace the history of Egypt in some detail over a long period of time. We know now that about 8,000 years ago the population was confined to hunting bands living well away from the jungle-choked swamps of the Nile Valley. Some time before 5000 B.C. immigrants from Palestine arrived bringing with them revolutionary new techniques of food production represented by the regular sowing of grain crops and the rearing of domestic animals. More abundant supplies of food made possible a rapid increase in the population. Gradually, men began to move down into the river valleys. There, after clearing the jungle, they found the soil, constantly enriched by silt spread by the Nile floods, so fertile that they could produce crops in an abundance never known before.

The pressures exerted by an ever-increasing population forced these early Egyptians to devise more elaborate forms of political organization. By 3500 B.C. the Nile Valley contained a number of small states that were united in about 3000 B.C. to form a single kingdom. For 2,500 years this kingdom survived as an independent state, experiencing over this vast span of time many changes of dynasty, some periods of complete breakdown and anarchy, others of exceptional stability and prosperity. By the third millennium B.C. Egypt had achieved a level of development most other parts of Africa were not to know until the twentieth century. But after this great leap forward, in which the country's own natural resources were exploited to the utmost, Egypt lacked the means to progress any further. Moreover, as other great powers began to emerge in the eastern Mediterranean, it became apparent that Egypt, with its relatively compact settled area, was extremely vulnerable to foreign invasion. Thus from the sixth century B.C. onwards the Egyptians had to suffer the painful experience of conquest and occupation by foreigners – Persians, Macedonian Greeks, Romans, Byzantine Greeks, Arabs, and Turks.

79   The city of Cairo (with the Pyramids to the right of the picture), c. 1600

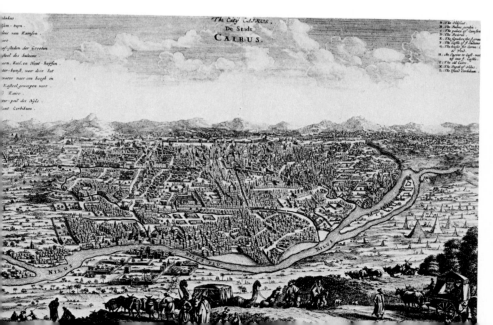

80 The Pyramids –
relics of one of the
most ancient world
civilizations

It may be said of the Egyptians that they have lived longer than any people anywhere in the world under that elaborate form of political organization we call the 'state'. Moreover, from the earliest times state government in Egypt has tended to be of an absolutist, even of a totalitarian kind. Inevitably, the country has known great contrasts in the quality of its rulers. In general she suffered most when reduced to the status of an easily exploitable province of an international empire. This was her fate under the Persians, the Romans, the Byzantine Greeks, and the Arabs. The Ptolemies, on the other hand – a Macedonian Greek dynasty founded by one of the generals of Alexander the Great – ruled Egypt as an independent state; so too did the later Muslim dynasties, some of which were established by soldiers of Turkish origin. Under the most efficient of these foreign rulers Egypt recovered something of the prosperity she had known under the ablest Pharaohs, her wealth being further enhanced by the development of a vigorous trade with European and Asian lands.

Despite the heavy weight of tradition, Egypt has never been immune to change. In A.D. 1500 most Egyptians were Arabic-speaking Muslims. In A.D. 500 Christianity was the religion of the majority and Greek or Coptic their language. In 500 B.C. the people of the Nile spoke the language and worshipped the gods of ancient Egypt. But these vast changes had taken place gradually. It required a period of several centuries after the Arab conquest of Egypt in A.D. 640 for Islam and the Arabic language to be accepted by the majority of Egyptians.

81 Columns at Meroe in the Sudan, once part of the ancient land of Kush

The Sudan

South of Egypt lies the vast stretch of country that today forms the Republic of the Sudan. The modern Sudan contains many different peoples: a settled peasantry, sometimes known as Nubians, in the Nile Valley immediately south of Egypt; Beja nomads in the Red Sea hills; Arab pastoralists in Kordofan and Darfur; Nuer and Dinka cattle-herders among the swamps of the Bahr al-Ghazal; and a great variety of Negroid peoples living in small agricultural communities in the areas of higher rainfall.

Today Islam and the Arabic language occupy a dominant position in the culture of the Sudan. This was not so in 1500 when the Arabs could still be regarded as recent immigrants in many parts of the country. The Arab movement into the Sudan had begun in the eighth century A.D. at a time when the Nile Valley south of Egypt was dominated by two substantial kingdoms, Nubia and Alwa, both ruled by dynasties that had been converted to Christianity in the sixth century. For more than 600 years these remote Christian kingdoms held out against Muslim pressure. By 1500 they had collapsed, to be replaced by petty Muslim principalities, but even at this late date there were still a few traces of Christianity left.

Some of the Arabs who settled in the Sudan were traders, but the majority were Bedouin who moved south from Egypt with their herds of camels. Those who reached the savanna of Kordofan were forced to turn from camels, which cannot survive in areas of higher rainfall, to cattle. Some of these Arab pastoralists moved westwards to Darfur and the country around Lake Chad.

Medieval Egypt exercised relatively little direct influence on the lands beyond its southern frontiers. In ancient Egyptian times the situation was different. About 1500 B.C. the Pharaohs conquered Nubia, known to the Egyptians at that time as the 'land of Kush'. For several centuries Kush remained an Egyptian colony until it achieved sufficient power to break away, forming an independent state that survived for more than 1,000 years (800 B.C.–A.D. 300). Kush was indeed one of the most substantial kingdoms of the ancient world. The ruins of pyramids and temples at such sites as Napata and Meroe testify to the wealth of this earliest of tropical African states; they also indicate the powerful influence exerted by Egypt on its culture. These ruins lie in country that must once have been fertile but is now desert. Much of Kush's wealth is known to have come from cattle. Overgrazing in areas of low rainfall easily leads to soil erosion. This, it has been suggested, was the basic cause for the gradual impoverishment of Kush, the sapping of its economic foundations, the eroding of its political power.

Ethiopia

In the fourth century A.D. Kush was shattered by an invasion from Axum, the state from which the medieval kingdom of Ethiopia was later to develop. The history of Axum is closely associated with that of south Arabia where a group of substantial states began to emerge at the beginning of the first millennium B.C. About 500 B.C. colonists from south Arabia moved across the Red Sea and founded settlements in the north-eastern highlands of Ethiopia. The immigrants, who spoke a Semitic language, possessed a more highly developed technology than the Cushitic-speaking peoples they found occupying the highlands. In time they came to dominate their Cushitic neighbours and to establish the kingdom known from its capital as Axum. At the beginning of the Christian era Axum eclipsed the parent states in south Arabia; it developed a vigorous foreign trade, with ivory as its major export, and maintained commercial relations with India and with Egypt. In the fourth century A.D. the rulers of Axum were converted to Christianity, establishing particularly close relations with the Coptic Church of Egypt and following the Copts

82   Stone obelisks at Axum

in accepting certain doctrines that other Christian Churches regarded as heretical.

Axum collapsed in the latter half of the first millennium A.D. but Christianity survived and with it the prestige of the Semitic-speaking aristocracy. Gradually these Christian Semites pushed deeper into the interior, converting the pagan Cushites to the new religion and inducing them to adopt a Semitic language. From this blending of Semites and Cushites emerged the Amhara, the dominant people of modern Ethiopia. By the twelfth century a powerful kingdom had been re-created on the Ethiopian plateau, a kingdom that was brought to the height of its power by a dynasty claiming descent from a highly exalted ancestor, King Solomon of Biblical fame. Neighbouring peoples were reduced to vassal status – and the ruler of Ethiopia assumed the grandiose title of 'King of Kings'. In medieval Ethiopia there was no fixed capital; instead the monarchs maintained an elaborate court in the midst of a great tented camp and spent their time touring their dominions, supervising provincial governors, intimidating vassal kings, and warring with the Muslim States on

their southern borders. Christianity flourished and innumerable churches and monasteries, some richly decorated and exhibiting striking styles of architecture, testified to the wealth and power of the Ethiopian Church.

Yet this was a Church that had developed in almost complete isolation from the rest of Christendom. It was not until the twelfth century that garbled rumours reached Europe hinting of the existence of a great Christian monarch, known as Prester John, whose kingdom lay beyond the ring of hostile Muslim States. To the rulers of Portugal, engaged in an unremitting struggle with the 'infidel Moors', Prester John, who was said to be also at war with the Muslims, seemed a Heaven-sent ally. During the fifteenth century tenuous contacts were established between Europe and Ethiopia and a passionate desire to develop a close relationship with this mysterious Christian kingdom became one of the principles of Portuguese policy.

The Horn

The Horn of Africa is for the most part a harsh and arid country where agriculture can only be practised in a few favoured districts and where pastoralism, the raising of cattle or of camels, provides a meagre livelihood for the mass of the population. The dominant peoples of the Horn, the Somali, the Danakil, and the Galla, are all speakers of Cushitic languages. Very little is known at present of their early history, but it is clear that in 1500 they were much less widely dispersed than they are today. The Galla, later to move on to the Ethiopian plateau, were probably confined to the Ethiopian Rift Valley, while Somali expansion had not yet reached the northern province of modern Kenya.

Today the vast majority of the people of the Horn are Muslims. Their conversion to Islam represents a long process that began in about the tenth century when Muslim merchants from Arabia and the Persian Gulf established trading settlements along the coast – settlements that developed into towns such as Zeila and Mogadishu. From the coast some traders penetrated into the interior along the line of the Rift Valley, seeking supplies of ivory and slaves. In time they too established settlements that became the focal points round which little states could be formed. Thus by the thirteenth century there had come into existence a string of petty Muslim sultanates along the southern edge of the Ethiopian plateau. Much of their history is a record of wars with their powerful northern neighbour,

84   Yekuno Amlāk, King of Ethiopia, 1270–85, waited upon by Muslim ambassadors and slaves (from late eighteenth-century Ethiopic manuscript)

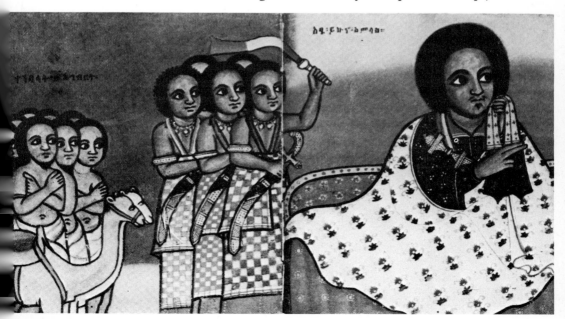

the Christian kingdom of Ethiopia. In these wars the Ethiopians seemed gradually to be gaining the upper hand, but the sixteenth century was to bring a devastating Somali assault on the Ethiopian kingdom followed by a massive Galla migration from the arid plains to the fertile highlands; these events created an entirely new situation in Ethiopia and the Horn.

North-west Africa

Barbary

To sixteenth-century Europeans all of North Africa west of Egypt was known as 'Barbary', a term derived from *barbari*, the word used by the Romans to describe the native population of the area. These people later came to be known to Europeans, through an Arabic variation of the Latin *barbari*, as 'Berbers'. Thus the term 'Barbary'

85   Early map of north-eastern Africa, showing towns, mountains, harbours and rivers, and also latitudes and longitudes according to Ptolemy

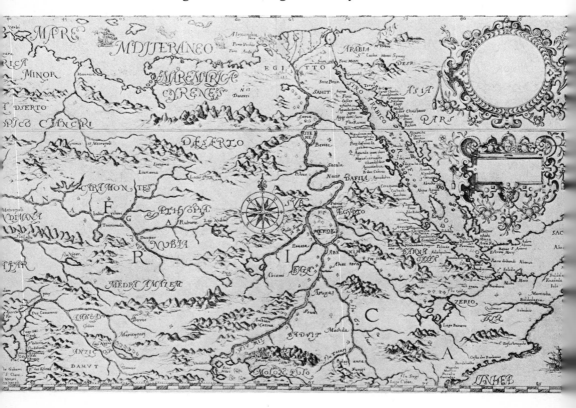

serves to stress the fact that the majority of the population of North Africa are of Berber origin.

The history of Barbary as usually told is a record of invasions, of a long procession of outsiders – Phoenicians, Romans, Vandals, Byzantine Greeks, Arabs, and others – attempting to colonize and dominate the area. Foreign invaders have indeed found it relatively easy to occupy the coast and the fertile plains of Tunisia and Morocco, but they have never succeeded in permanently subjugating the Berber communities living in the lonely upland valleys of the Atlas and its outlying massifs.

Nevertheless, though only a limited part of Barbary has been brought under direct foreign rule, outsiders have made an immense contribution to the development of the area. Most of Barbary's towns and cities are of foreign foundation. The earliest urban settlements were established by the Phoenicians, commercially minded seafarers from Tyre who set up a string of trading posts along the North African coast early in the first millennium A.D. Carthage, the most important of the Phoenician settlements, became the metropolis of a great empire. After the Romans had taken over the Carthaginian Empire, many of the old Phoenician cities experienced a period of great prosperity, while new towns were established in the interior by the Roman authorities. The Arab invaders who overran North Africa in the seventh century also encouraged urbanization; Kairouan, Tunis, and Fez, three of the most splendid cities of medieval Barbary, were all Arab foundations.

Economic development also owed much to alien initiative. The Phoenicians drew coastal districts into the commercial world of the Mediterranean and encouraged agriculture in the hinterland of Carthage. The Romans ensured a long period of peace, built roads, and devised ingenious means for conserving water, with the result that Africa Proconsularis (Tunisia and eastern Algeria) became one of the most prosperous provinces in their Empire. The Arab invasion destroyed the commercial links with countries on the northern shores of the Mediterranean but created new ties with Egypt and Syria, with Andalusia (that part of southern Spain conquered by the Muslims in the eighth century), and with the Negro kingdoms beyond the Sahara. Disastrously for Barbary, there occurred a second Arab invasion in the eleventh century when a horde of Bedouin nomads

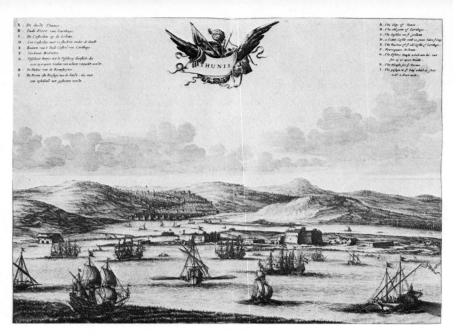

86   The city of Tunis, *c.* 1600

who had been expelled from Egypt moved into the region. 'They pulled down houses', a contemporary historian wrote of the Bedouin, 'when they wanted stones on which to rest their cooking-pots'. As the result of their depredations large parts of eastern Barbary, rendered fertile by 1,000 years of careful farming, were transformed into desolate steppe.

The Bedouin impact was not entirely negative, for it assisted a process that had been going on for centuries, the penetration of Barbary by alien religions and alien languages. Punic, the language of the Carthaginians, disappeared during the centuries of Roman rule to be replaced by Latin. The new religion of Christianity found many devoted supporters in the African provinces of Rome, while some of the greatest figures of the early Church, men such as Tertullian and St Augustine, were in fact Romanized Berbers. But the North African Church was torn by bitter schisms and proved unable to withstand the impact of Islam. By 1200 there was hardly a single Christian congregation left in North Africa. Slowly the entire Berber population was converted to the religion of the Prophet, while Arabic became established as the language of the towns and later,

87 The city of Algiers, *c.* 1600

after the Bedouin migrations, of the fertile plains and of the northern fringes of the desert.

The Berbers never accepted these alien influences passively. Foreign conquerors were faced with the constant threat of revolt or of raids by hostile groups living beyond the frontiers. Resistance was often paralysed by the fact that even the smallest Berber communities were frequently divided by bitter internal feuds. But there were occasions when the Berbers overcame these weaknesses and showed themselves capable of producing substantial states of their own. The two greatest medieval dynasties, the eleventh-century Almoravids and the twelfth-century Almohads, which ruled in North Africa and in Spain, were both of Berber origin.

Under the Almohads parts of Barbary were more highly developed than much of western Europe. But with the Christian reconquest in the thirteenth century of most of Andalusia, whose rich culture had proved a powerful stimulant for Muslim North Africa, and with the devastation caused by the Bedouin migrations, Barbary's fortunes declined. In 1415 the Portuguese captured the Moroccan town of Ceuta and later occupied other coastal districts of Morocco.

177

In 1492 the Spaniards took Granada, the last Muslim stronghold in Spain. By 1500 the balance of power in the western Mediterranean seemed to have swung decisively in favour of Christian Europe.

The Sahara

Seven thousand years ago many parts of the Sahara were less desolate than they are today. Recently discovered rock paintings and engravings show that men were once able to hunt elephants and giraffe and later to pasture herds of cattle in areas that are now almost devoid of vegetation. The change that has taken place has been due in part to a decline in the actual rainfall. But overgrazing accompanied by soil erosion has also been a powerful factor, making for the destruction of natural resources.

The cattle-herders shown on the rock paintings must have moved into the Sahara from further east about 5,000 or 6,000 years ago. As these pastoralists spread westwards, they must have encountered small groups of hunting peoples, probably of Negroid stock. By the beginning of the Christian era the northern Sahara appears to have been occupied by light-skinned peoples of Caucasoid stock, the ancestors of the Tuareg and other Berber-speaking groups, the central and southern Sahara by dark-skinned people akin to the modern Tebu and to some of the ethnic groups of the Western Sudan.

In the first centuries of the Christian era a revolutionary development took place in the Sahara: the introduction from further east of the camel. Being capable of travelling long distances without water the camel was far better adapted to desert conditions than the horse and the ox, both of which had previously been used by Saharan peoples for transport purposes. The spread of the use of the camel eventually made possible a great expansion in Saharan trade. A certain amount of trade had been carried on in the Sahara in the pre-cameline era: West African gold reached the coast of Morocco in the fifth century B.C., and salt from Saharan mines was probably being carried to the salt-starved peoples of the Western Sudan. But it was not until after the Arab conquest that conditions became ripe for a vigorous expansion of the trans-Saharan trade. The Muslim merchants who followed in the wake of the Arab armies possessed capital, commercial experience, and contacts with a wider market. From the Saharan nomads the merchants learnt of the wealth in gold and in slaves offered by the countries beyond the desert. Gradually, using the nomads with their camels as guides and carriers, a trans-Saharan caravan trade came into existence. By A.D. 1000 the desert was spanned by a number of well-trodden routes (see Map 8)[2] and the profits provided by the trans-Saharan trade were making an important contribution to the economic development of Barbary and of the Western Sudan.

By the fifteenth century well-informed businessmen in southern Europe were aware that the gold they occasionally obtained in North Africa came from beyond the mysterious Sahara. Clearly North African Muslims would never allow their Christian rivals to do business on the trans-Saharan routes. But might it not prove possible to tap 'the golden trade of the Moors' from another direction by sailing down the unexplored coast of western Africa? A determination to test this hypothesis provided one of the driving forces behind Portuguese expansion in the fifteenth century. After more than half a century of effort Portuguese enterprise received its reward. On that stretch of the West African littoral that came to be known as the Gold Coast the seamen of Portugal found to their joy that they were in direct contact with a gold-producing area richer than any that Europe had ever known before.

[2] See page 163.

88　The city of Tripoli, *c.* 1600

West Africa

In 1500 the most powerful state in West Africa was the empire recently formed by the Songhai, a river people dominating the navigable stretches of the Niger bend with their large canoes and intimidating their neighbours on every side through their possession of a substantial force of cavalry. The expansion of the Songhai Empire had been made at the expense of its neighbour, Mali, whose territory lay astride the Upper Niger. In the fourteenth century Mali too had been a great empire, controlling much of the Niger bend and reducing many peoples, including the Songhai, to vassal status. Mali had been preceded by yet another substantial state, the Empire of Ghana, whose metropolitan provinces lay in southern Mauretania. Ancient Ghana – to be distinguished from the modern West African state of the same name with which it has no historical connection – was at the height of its power in the eleventh century. Much of the territory that it occupied is now desert, and it seems likely that its economic foundations were fatally weakened by the same process of overgrazing and soil erosion that appears to have led to the decline of Kush. By 1250 Ghana, dismembered by the assaults of many enemies, had ceased to exist as an organized state.

To the east of the Songhai Empire, in territory that now forms part of Nigeria, lay a cluster of states formed by the Hausa people. Still further east the more substantial kingdom of Bornu occupied the area west of Lake Chad. Far to the west most of modern Senegal was divided up among a number of states formed by the Wolof and related peoples.

All these states lay in the northern belt of the savanna. Immediately to their south and still within the savanna lived a great variety of ethnic groups, organized for the most part in small, independent village communities. Most of the peoples of the forest were similarly divided. But in some parts of the forest more substantial polities could already be found. Benin in mid-west Nigeria was a highly organized kingdom by 1500; so too were some of the Yoruba states of western Nigeria, and there were considerable chiefdoms to be found among the Akan peoples of modern Ghana. But the great age of state-building in the forest lands of West Africa still lay in the future. Ashanti and Dahomey, destined to become two of the most

89   The city of Benin. By the sixteenth century Benin, in
mid-west Nigeria, was a highly organized state

powerful states of tropical Africa, ·were not founded until the
seventeenth century.

Behind this complex pattern of states and peoples lay a long
history, a history of which at present we know all too little. The
accounts of Arab geographers and of Sudanese chroniclers tell us
something about the states of the northern savanna from about
A.D. 800. For the southern savanna and the forest we possess little
reliable information before the coming of the Portuguese. In time
archaeological research should throw a flood of light on the West
African past; at present West African archaeology is in its early,
pioneering stage. In the meantime a study of the languages and
physical types of the region provides us with some clues about the
broad lines of its historical development.

The great majority of West Africans are people of Negroid stock,
but the region has received a limited admixture of Caucasoid groups
coming from the north. Most West Africans speak languages belonging to the linguistic stock known as Western Sudanic, but this
stock possesses six subdivisions. The differences between these
subdivisions are so substantial that it must have taken thousands of

years for them to have emerged. The profound differences between West African languages stand in sharp contrast to the broad similarity of the Bantu languages spoken over most of Central and Southern Africa. In Bantu Africa the large-scale movement of peoples is a fairly recent historical phenomenon; in West Africa many ethnic groups have probably been settled in the areas they now occupy for a period that may well reach back several thousand years.

To the rule that most West Africans speak Western Sudanic languages there are two important exceptions. The Hausa and many of the smaller groups to their east speak languages that are classified as forming the Chadic subdivision of Afro-Asiatic, while the Kanuri of Bornu and probably also the Songhai speak languages of the stock known as Nilo-Saharan. The Hausa, the Songhai, and the Kanuri all live immediately to the south of the Sahara, and their own traditions confirm that they have been strongly influenced by peoples of Saharan origin.

Two factors appear to have been of major importance in the development of the states of the savanna belt: the impact of Saharan nomads and the growth of trans-Saharan trade. For the nomads of the Sahara the fertile lands to their south had an obvious attraction. The nomads were at once more mobile and more warlike than the agricultural peoples with whom they came into contact and so found it relatively easy to dominate them and compel them to pay regular

90　Bronze plaque showing a Bini warrior bringing in a wounded captive, from Benin

tribute. At the same time the development of caravan traffic across the Sahara brought a great access of wealth to those rulers who could control the commodities sought by North African merchants. Ancient Ghana and later Mali and Songhai all found themselves in a particularly advantageous position, for they dominated the routes that led to the gold-producing areas of the Senegal, the Niger, and the Volta. Part of the gold was used to buy horses from North Africa. A good supply of horses enabled a ruler to equip a cavalry force that could be used on slave-raiding expeditions. Some of the slaves thus obtained were kept for local use, others were sent across the Sahara.

As the trade developed, communities of North African merchants began to settle in the major towns of the Western Sudan. They brought with them their religion of Islam together with a wide range of new techniques and ideas. Many Sudanese rulers accepted the new religion, established diplomatic relations with their fellow sovereigns in North Africa, and even undertook the pilgrimage to Mecca. By 1500 Timbuktu, founded three centuries earlier as an entrepôt where men from the desert could meet the canoemen of the Niger to exchange their wares, had developed into a major centre of Muslim learning. 'Here', noted a Moroccan traveller of the time, 'are great store of doctors, judges, priests, and other learned men.' He spoke in almost equally enthusiastic terms of the company he met in some of the other Sudanese cities that he visited.

Today Islam is widely accepted over most of the Western Sudan; in 1500 it was the religion of a small minority – the ruling classes of some of the savanna states. Elsewhere, people maintained their ancestral forms of belief. Traders from North Africa scornfully lumped all of these non-Muslim peoples together as 'infidels'; like later Christian travellers in the region, they had no appreciation of the complexity of indigenous West African cultures. The Yoruba, for example, had evolved a pantheon as elaborate as that of the ancient Greeks. They had also achieved remarkable skill as craftsmen. The famous Ife heads, naturalistic sculptures in bronze or terracotta that are among the greatest works of art produced in tropical Africa, are thought to have been made about 1300. The manufacture of such wonderful sculptures implies the existence of a wealthy and sophisticated society.

Until the fifteenth century external influences could reach West

Africa only from the north and east. The coming of the Portuguese represented a revolutionary development. Now for the first time West Africa was exposed to powerful new forces of change, whose impact spread inland from the coast. Today the wealth of the region is largely concentrated in its coastal areas; very different was the West Africa with which Europeans became acquainted in the early sixteenth century, when the richest states were to be found in the northern belt of the savanna.

Equatorial and Central Africa

The great block of territory that stretches from modern Cameroun to Rhodesia was almost completely unknown to the outside world in 1500. Arab traders had been doing business at Sofala near the mouth of the Zambezi for centuries and some Muslim merchants had moved up the river to establish direct contact with the gold-mining peoples of the Rhodesian plateau. In the 1480s the Portuguese reached the mouth of the Congo and visited the kingdom of Kongo situated to the south of the river. A decade later, on Vasco da Gama's first voyage, they came to Sofala and in time pushed inland from the coast. But apart from these limited areas of intercourse the vast interior of Central and Equatorial Africa was completely unknown both to Europeans and to Arabs and many districts remained blank on European maps until late in the nineteenth century. Nevertheless, though relatively unaffected by the outside world, this part of Africa had experienced great changes in the centuries before 1500.

The most striking geographical features of the region are the complex system of waterways associated with the River Congo, the dense expanse of the equatorial rain forest, and the savanna plains that border the forest to the north and to the south. In the first millennium B.C. the southern savanna appears to have been populated only by nomadic bands of peoples of Bushmanoid stock, while the forest was the domain of Pygmy hunters. North of the forest lived a variety of Negroid groups among whom were the ancestors of the Bantu-speaking peoples.

'Bantu' is the term applied by linguistic scholars to a group of closely related languages that are spoken today not only over most of Central and Equatorial Africa but in much of East and South

91 Antiquities from Benin:
winged head of a negro in bronze;
bronze panther; carved elephant
tusks

Africa as well. The differences between Bantu languages are much
less marked than those that exist between the languages of other
linguistic stocks, a fact which suggests that the dispersal of Bantu
speakers has been a process of relatively recent occurrence. In our
present state of knowledge scholars can only put forward hypotheses,
derived partly from linguistic, partly from archaeological evidence,
to suggest the way in which this great movement took place. Linguistic evidence indicates that the area of northern Cameroun was
the original home of the Bantu people. Possibly about the beginning
of the Christian era small groups of Bantu farmers and fishermen
may have moved up the Shari and the Logonie rivers, struck overland
to the Ubangui and thus reached the river system of the Congo
Basin. Following first the Ubangui and then the Congo, these groups
passed through the inhospitable rain forest until they came at last
to the almost empty lands of the southern savanna. Here in the south-
eastern part of the ex-Belgian Congo a great expansion of population
took place, made possible by the agricultural techniques that the
Bantu speakers brought with them. Population pressure forced
individual groups to break off from the main Bantu nucleus, some

moving westwards into the southern Congo and Angola, others eastwards into East Africa, yet others southwards across the Zambezi and the Limpopo. The Bantu probably brought with them the technique of iron-working, and discoveries of iron implements in sites that can be dated by the radio-carbon method provide archaeologists with a means of tracing the gradual spread of these iron-workers.

Most of these Bantu groups lived in small, independent communities, but in at least three areas – Katanga, northern Angola, and Rhodesia – substantial indigenous states had come into existence by 1500. A cemetery site recently discovered near Lake Kisale in northern Katanga has produced fine pottery and elaborate copper jewellery dated as early as the eighth century A.D. Clearly this was an area of great political and cultural importance. From Katanga small conquering groups moved into the area of modern Zambia and Rhodesia. One such group was the Rozwi, a clan of the Shona-speaking peoples, who succeeded in establishing their hegemony

92   Map of the Congo, a continuation of the map on p. 174

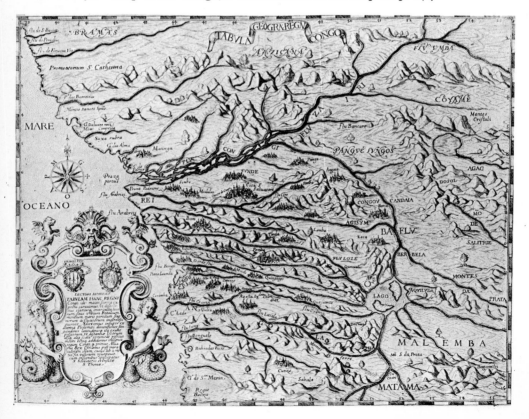

over the smaller chiefdoms of the Rhodesian plateau. In the middle of the fifteenth century a Rozwi ruler embarked on a series of campaigns with such success that his people gave him the title *Mwene Mutapa* ('master pillager'). This title was used by all his successors and in the form 'Monomotapa' came to be applied by the Portuguese to the kingdom as a whole. The Rozwi rulers were responsible at a later date for the construction of the great stone buildings at Zimbabwe, the most spectacular archaeological site in southern Africa.

Quite unconnected with these developments in the eastern part of the region was the process that led in the early fifteenth century to the formation of the kingdom of Kongo. Kongolese traditions tell of the coming of a dominant group from across the River Congo to the north, but of the local pressures that led to these movements we know nothing.

East Africa

The Indian Ocean is a much gentler sea than the Atlantic and the régime of its winds is so disposed as to make it comparatively easy to sail between India and Arabia and the East African coast. From December the monsoon blows from the north-east, in March it swings round to blow from the south-west, thus making it easy for sailors to accomplish the passage between south Arabia or western India and East Africa.

We do not yet know when the first foreign sailors reached East Africa, but a commercial handbook, known as *The Periplus of the Erythrean Sea* and written by a Greek in about A.D. 100, paints a vivid picture of the East African trade at that early period. Merchants from south Arabia dominated the coastal trade and it seems likely that their forefathers had been responsible for introducing the coastal peoples to foreign commerce. According to the *Periplus* these Arabian merchants obtained 'a great quantity of ivory' together with rhinoceros horn and tortoise-shell in exchange for iron implements.

In the course of the first millennium A.D. other seafarers reached East Africa. Some came from the Persian Gulf, others from western India, yet others from the distant lands of South East Asia. This last group was made up of Indonesians who arrived on the East

African coast in their outrigger canoes after they had boldly explored the northern perimeter of the Indian Ocean. In course of time these Indonesians went on to colonize the vast uninhabited island of Madagascar. There is no evidence to show that they ever settled in large numbers on the East African coast, but their coming was an event of profound importance for they brought with them certain plants domesticated in South East Asia but hitherto completely unknown in Africa. We do not know the routes by which the Asian yam and the banana, the two most valuable plants of Indonesian origin, spread across tropical Africa, but it is clear that their introduction immensely improved men's prospects of survival in the hot, moist lands where millet and sorghum, the cereals of tropical African agriculture, could not be grown.

From an early date foreign traders must have developed the habit of residing on the East African coast either in existing villages or, like the Phoenicians in Barbary, in specially established trading settlements. Gradually the more important of these settlements developed into small city-states. At first the Arabs, the most important alien element, may have been sharply distinguished from the local population, but intermarriage and the adoption of the local language soon blurred these differences. The emergence of Swahili as the lingua franca of the coast illustrates the cultural fusion that was taking place. For Swahili – the name is in fact derived from *sahil*, the Arabic word for 'coast' – is a Bantu language which has absorbed a large number of Arabic words.

By A.D. 1000 Islam must have been established in some of the coastal towns. As the new religion spread to the lands of the Indian Ocean, the commercial horizon of East African merchants gradually widened. News travelled quickly along the trade routes of the Islamic world, and people in distant parts of Asia heard of the enticing and exotic products to be obtained from East Africa. Indian or Indonesian middlemen sold African slaves and ivory in Canton in southern China, and in the early fifteenth century fleets of Chinese junks appeared on at least three occasions in East African waters.

Expanding trade brought increased wealth. The local aristocracy of cities such as Kilwa, Mombasa, and Malindi used their profits to erect those 'fair houses of stone' that made such an impression on Vasco da Gama's men and to import Indian cloth and Chinese

93   Muslim ruins at the town of Gedi, in modern Kenya

porcelain. Mosques and palaces were constructed in styles that indicate the work of craftsmen specially brought in from overseas; their ruins still survive as a memorial to this remarkable period. The great age of the East African coast ended when the Portuguese burst into the Indian Ocean, pillaging the cities and disrupting their trade. But much of the distinctive culture of the coast survives to this day, a culture that in its blending of diverse elements may well be described as truly Afro-Asian.

In 1500 the interior of East Africa was completely unknown not only to Europeans but also to the Asian merchants who did business in the coastal towns. Ivory, the major product of East Africa, must still have been obtainable in sufficient quantity from the coastal peoples; in such circumstances there was no incentive to penetrate the interior. Indeed, it was not until the nineteenth century that coastal traders began to make their way inland. This isolation from the literate cultures of the coast means that the historian of the East African interior has no written records to assist him before 1800, but archaeology, linguistics, and the oral traditions of the peoples themselves make it possible to discern the main outlines of the area's development.

There were a number of different elements in the population of the interior in 1500. Bantu-speaking Negroid agriculturists probably already represented the largest group, but in an area with an exceptionally long record of human occupation they could be regarded as relatively recent immigrants, their movement into East Africa from the west being dated to the first centuries of the Christian era. Many millennia earlier there had begun a southward movement of peoples along the line of the Rift Valley, a movement which in its later stages brought Cushitic-speaking Caucasoids on to the Kenya Highlands where stone burial chambers, terraced fields, and legends preserved by the present inhabitants of a vanished race of 'red men' provide evidence of their settlement. Their technology was greatly superior to that of the bands of nomadic hunters, probably akin to the modern Bushmen, who once formed the main element in the population. A few hunting peoples survive to this day; in 1500 they must have been much more numerous, especially in the drier areas such as central Tanzania.

Some time after A.D. 1000 tall, light-skinned, pastoralists, possibly

94   Pictorial chart of Moçambique (1583). This was the chief station of the Portuguese on the east coast of Africa, and port of call for their ships travelling to the East

95   Saharan rock-painting of herdsmen and cattle

akin to the Sidama of south-western Ethiopia, began to enter East
Africa from the north. Some moved on to the Kenya Highlands
where they contributed to the collapse of the earlier culture of the
Cushitic Caucasoids, others reached the country north of Lake
Victoria where they established themselves as a dominant minority
over the Bantu agriculturists and formed in the kingdom of Kitara
the only state one can discern in any part of the interior at this period.
About 1500 Kitara was taken over by yet another group of immigrants, the Nilotes, a Negroid people from the Southern Sudan, the
speakers of languages quite distinct from Bantu. Out of Kitara the
Nilotes created the kingdoms of Bunyoro and Buganda that were to
develop into two of the major states of tropical Africa. If the
inhabitants of Buganda, the Ganda, had not emerged as a distinct
ethnic group by 1500, the same could be said of many other well-
known East African peoples. The legends of the Kikuyu and the
Masai, for example, suggest that neither people were established in

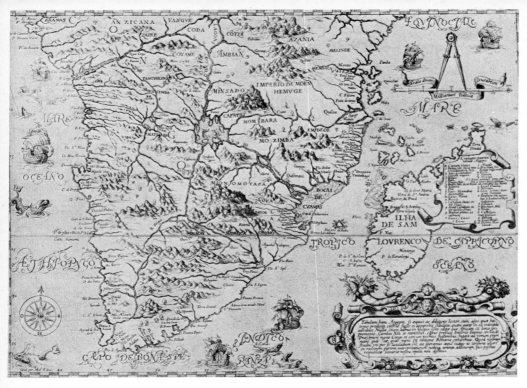

96 Sixteenth-century map of the southern part of Africa,
a continuation of those on pp. 174 and 186

the Kenya Highlands much earlier than 1700. In sharp contrast to
its coastal areas the East African interior was still in 1500 at that
stage of historical development in which a slowly expanding
population spreads out gradually over an almost empty land.

South Africa

There are certain obvious parallels between the East African interior
and South Africa in 1500. At the beginning of the Christian era
South Africa's population appears to have consisted of nomadic
hunters of Bushmen stock. Early in the first millennium A.D. a few
groups of Caucasoid pastoralists entered the region, gradually merging with certain Bushmen bands to form the pastoral Hottentots.
Towards the end of the same millennium Bantu agriculturists from
the north crossed the Limpopo. As the Bantu population increased,

sections broke away and pushed into the country that now forms Natal and the Transvaal.

No part of the continent has undergone such immense changes in the course of the last 400 years as South Africa. Today the most advanced in its technology of all the countries of Africa, in 1500 it was certainly the least developed, remote from the main centres of commercial activity, and appearing to possess no resources likely to interest the foreign entrepreneur. It was the Bantu moving in from the north, and the Europeans arriving in the south, who were to transform this situation.

The Islands

In the eastern Atlantic and in the western Indian Ocean there lie a number of islands or island groups that may be regarded as being more closely attached to Africa than to any other continent. The remoter islands were not drawn into the orbit of history until the age of European expansion: São Tomé, St Helena, Réunion, and Mauritius were all uninhabited when the Portuguese discovered

97 Bushman painting of hunters and eland, from Ndeme Gorge, Drakensberg

193

them. On the other hand, islands nearer the mainland had long been settled by local coastal peoples, the Berber-speaking Guanches in the Canaries, and Bantu-speaking groups in Fernando Po, Zanzibar, and Pemba. Madagascar, which rivals France in area, began to attract first Indonesian and later Bantu African immigrants in the first millennium A.D. By 1500 there were a number of petty states in coastal districts, some of which were in touch with Muslim merchants from other parts of the Indian Ocean. In the interior of the great island the Malagasy peoples, their language clearly of Indonesian origin, their culture and physical appearance a blending of Indonesian and Bantu Negroid elements, were engaged in that pioneering task of taming the primeval wilderness which has confronted man in every part of the globe.

Conclusion

Here in this notion of pioneering lies a major element in the internal dynamics of any continent. The history of Africa, no less than that of Europe, Asia, and the Americas, is concerned with the efforts of a multitude of human societies to found new settlements in unknown areas, tread pathways through the virgin bush, clear the forest, drain

98   Sixteenth-century picture of birds and plants to be found off the coast of Madagascar

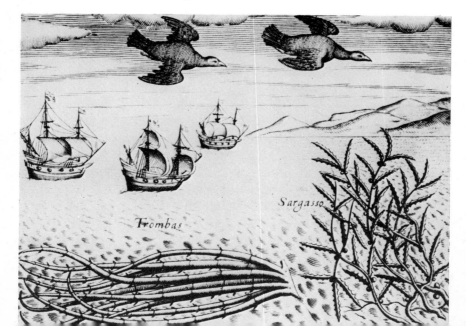

the swamp, terrace the hillside, discover new resources in the environment, absorb innovations – material objects, techniques, ideas – introduced from the outside, and so gradually to construct more elaborate forms of political, social, and economic organization and devise more complex systems of thought.

For Africa as for Asia the caravels of Portugal were the harbingers of a new age. But it would be a mistake to over-estimate the immediate impact of the Portuguese and of the other Europeans who followed them on the destinies of Africa. Strictly limited were the areas directly affected by their coming; not until late in the nineteenth century was the entire continent brought within the range of European influence. The consequences of that later impact are easily visible today not only on the map but also in every city in Africa with its schools and churches, its shops and factories, its lorry-park, airport, and railway station. One needs to remember, however, that in every African country by far the greater part of the population lives not in towns but in villages or scattered homesteads. Here in the countryside change comes more slowly, here a pattern of life manifests itself, some features of which – house styles, farm implements, systems of land tenure, for example – may well have been much the same 400 years ago. Here in the villages lie the solid foundations of the continent's diverse local cultures. These cultures, loosely described as 'traditional', have never been static. Slowly they have absorbed the innovations that have reached them from the outside world. Behind them lie long centuries of anonymous human endeavour.

99   Saharan rock-painting of human figures with body paintings

195

India

India and Muslim Rule 1500–1525

THE OBSERVER WHO LOOKED at a political map of India about
A.D. 1500 would never have guessed that the sub-continent was the
seat of a distinctive civilization and mainly peopled by Hindus. For
the whole country, apart from the area south of the River Kistna
in the extreme south, and the arid region of Rajasthan in the north-
west, was ruled by Muslims. This had been the case for about a
century and a half, and there seemed every prospect of its continuance.
Such a person might excusably have thought that India was firmly
in the hands of Turkish Muslim chiefs, that Hinduism was already
reduced, except in the two areas mentioned, to a matter of temple
worship, village superstition, and the strongholds of a few remote
chiefs. Would not Islam eventually triumph in India as Christianity
had triumphed in Europe twelve centuries before?

But though so large a portion of the Indian map was coloured
green there was no single Muslim empire. In fact the Muslims were
never more disunited. These states were the product of a series of
inroads by Turks and Afghans, augmented by a mercenary trickle
from Arabia and individuals from Persia. They had come as conquering armies and as migratory groups, and they had augmented
their numbers by intermarriage and by conversion. All told they
numbered, perhaps, one-tenth of the population. They formed a
thinly spread aristocratic layer reinforced by a few areas of thicker
settlement or wider conversion. They had split up into clans and
personal groups united only by allegiance to Islam and a desire for
power. In 1500 the collapse of the last north Indian empire was over
100 years in the past, while the leading north Indian state was more
an aristocratic confederation of chiefs than a bureaucratic empire.
Muslim power, though expressed in often brilliant courts and states,
was brittle and superficial while Hindu society, though politically
inept, had a social and ideological strength which made it far
from moribund.

100 Sixteenth-century Moghul miniature painting of a Turkish chief

But with all this turbulence and division, there was an underlying feeling for unity. India had traditionally a unified society and culture, and on occasion short-lived periods of imperial unity. The contrast between actual division and conflict and ideal unity produced an uneasy restless feeling of something impending, something about to happen.

In north India the scene was dominated by the Delhi sultanate of the Afghan Lodis. This was a revival of the Turkish bureaucratic empire which dominated north India and conquered much of the south in the two centuries between 1192 and 1398. But it was under a different leadership and possessed a different structure. The Turkish empire of the Tughluqs had collapsed under the impact of Timur's devastating raid in 1398. He not only overthrew the political structure but left two swathes of destruction and horror on his journey to and from Delhi. For fifty years afterwards the north was divided into warring, and impoverished, lordships, the most powerful and brilliant being the Sharqis of Jaunpur. Then the Afghan Lodis seized power in Delhi and gradually revived the sultanate. By 1500 they had overcome the Sharqis and controlled a dominion from the banks of the Indus to the borders of Bengal. But the old imperial bureaucracy with central control was not there. Instead the land was parcelled out as fiefs to a number of predominantly Afghan chiefs. The sultan was a *primus inter pares* and over these nobles ruled by force of personality, by skill in dividing his foes, and by the exertions of his immediate followers. It was an imposing but unstable realm. When the leader had the requisite qualities it was formidable but could not long survive weakness or dissension. In Sikandar Lodi, who reigned from 1489 to 1517, the sultanate had such a leader, but he, like his father, was more a president of an aristocratic republic than an absolute monarch. The régime did not long survive his son Ibrahim's attempt to convert crowned aristocracy into monarchy.

To the south-east the sultanate was bounded by Bengal, still in the hands of Turkish nobles. This also was a turbulent prey to aristocratic faction but in 1500 it had a strong ruler in Husain Shah who had disbanded the Hindu palace guard and exiled African mercenaries who had been acting as king-makers. The Muslim kings of Bengal were in general tolerant. They patronized the arts and did much to encourage the development of Bengali, and also the conversion of the eastern Bengal peasantry to Islam in reaction to

101   A Turkoman prisoner, from a manuscript of the sixteenth century

Brahmin domination. Delhi feared no threat from Bengal, but to the west and south it faced one of the old sultanate's succession kingdoms, Malwa, and in the north the Hindu stronghold, Rajasthan. Malwa, which had broken away from the empire in 1401 was, like Delhi, a military kingdom, and its strength, within the limits of its actual resources, depended on the capacity of its rulers. It was squeezed between the Hindu and Muslim forces of Rajasthan and Gujarat respectively. Rajasthan was divided among many Rajput clans, each with one or more dynasties to represent it. In the case of the Rajputs, a family dynastic quarrel meant fragmentation, while a foreign threat to independence brought about a temporary coalition of jealous chiefs. The Rajputs had heroically resisted the Turks, some two centuries before, but they never united into a single state. At this time the Rana of Mewar had established a personal ascendancy which made the Rajputs as a whole appear a real threat to the reviving Muslim power in the north.

To the south of Rajasthan, round the Gulf of Cambay and the Kathiawar peninsula, lay the compact and prosperous kingdom of Gujarat. It had seceded from Delhi in 1403 and had been under firm rule for a century. Its fertile soil produced cotton and indigo as well as food crops and the port of Surat dealt with the maritime trade to the Middle East. Gujarat was thus more powerful than its size suggested; it was a stabilizing factor in north-western India. Its ruler for fifty-two years (1459–1511), Mahmud Bigarha, created a legend with his physical peculiarities lively enough to reach Europe, where it gave rise to the couplet

> The King of Cambay's daily food
> Is asp and basilisk and toad.

Adjoining Gujarat was the small hill kingdom of Khandesh, another splinter or succession state from the old Delhi Empire.

Between the rivers Narbada and Kistna, across the Deccan plateau to the coastal plain by the Bay of Bengal, lay a complex of Muslim states which represented the fragments of the once powerful Bahmini kingdom. This kingdom was itself a succession state of the Delhi empire, founded in 1347 when the Tughluq governor Zafar Khan rebelled. Its brilliant but erratic career ended with the murder of the minister, Mahmud Gawan, when it split into the five fragments of Bidar, Berar, Ahmadnagar, Bijapur, and Golkonda. All of these were in effect aristocratic Muslim dictatorships which spent the money they wrested from the Hindu countryside on adorning their courts with poets and buildings and in fighting each other and the Hindus of the south.

From the River Kistna to Cape Comorin at the southern tip of India we find the great exception to the general rule of Muslim dominion. Here lay the Hindu empire of Vijayanagar with its power focused in the great city of that name ('city of victory') close to its northern and Muslim frontier. It had been founded in the middle of the fourteenth century as the Delhi dominion over the south broke up and the Bahminis emerged in the Deccan. Its strength and leadership came from the Telugu country now represented by the state of Andhra, but it extended its power over the Tamil and Kanara regions to form a compact military state. It controlled these areas with governors appointed from the centre and backed by military detachments. The capital city was populous and wealthy and the Telugu form of Hinduism was practised there. Foreign observers were deeply impressed with its magnificence, Portuguese travellers considering it larger than Rome. But it was essentially a Telugu dominion over the Tamils and Kanaras; though a champion of southern Hinduism against Islam in the north, it was as brittle as the Muslim kingdoms themselves, and could not survive a disaster.

Finally, strung along the west coast at Goa and down the narrow coastal plain of Malabar and the wider one of Travancore, was the new power of Portugal and a string of Hindu trading principalities. Nature, by placing tropical forests and tangled mountains between them and the interior, had preserved their independence and given them an important intermediate position in the spice trade between Indonesia, Ceylon, and the Middle East. In Travancore pepper and cardamons were grown as well. The leading prince was the Zamorin of Calicut whose Arab connections caused him to resist the Portuguese when Vasco da Gama arrived in 1497. From 1511, the Portuguese settled on Goa as the capital of their eastern maritime empire. It was rapidly qualifying for the title of 'Golden Goa' with its monopoly of the horse trade to Vijayanagar and control of the spice traffic in the Indian seas.

India had as yet little to do with Europe as a whole despite the Portuguese incursion. The Portuguese had fortified themselves at

102 Huge monolithic statue of Marasimha, the man-lion, incarnation of Vishnu, from Vijayanagar

Goa, had defeated the Turkish fleet in 1508 off Diu, and had established a maritime supremacy in the Indian Ocean. But they had none of the mystique of the Spaniards in Mexico and Peru. They came from a known part of the world with a known religion; they had nothing supernatural about them. They were regarded as one nuisance among many rather than as a grave menace to all Indian life. To the east Indonesia was unsettled with the Madjapahit Empire in decline, and Islamic penetration increasing. China, after her fifteenth-century incursions as far as Ceylon, had retired again into isolation. The Indian states had no fears and no ambitions in this direction but carried on a brisk trade in spices and textiles. To the north-west, it was different. On the Iranian plateau there was much restlessness. The Timurid Empire had long broken up and the monarchies which had succeeded were about to be fused into the Safawid Empire of Shah Ismail. In Turkestan there was much unrest where the Uzbeg power threatened the remaining Timurid chiefs. One such, Babur, had abandoned his attempt to recover his ancestral and coveted Samarkand and had settled down instead as the ruler of Kabul on the southern side of the Hindu Kush. All was fluid, and it did not seem at the time that one chief was more likely to become an empire-builder than any other.

Hinduism

Distinctive Features of Hinduism

Hinduism itself is a vague amorphous thing. There are no sharp outlines throwing definite shadows, no clearly defined pictures. There is no single rule of life, no definable doctrine. It is a world of provisos, of ifs and buts. There is no rule which has not an exception, hardly any exception which cannot be a rule in some part of the country. It has been compared to a sponge, which absorbs many things without ceasing to be itself. But Hinduism not only admits new elements; it makes them part of itself. It might perhaps be more aptly compared to the onion which has many layers but no core. Another layer can always be added to Hindu society which may modify but will not change the essential character of the whole. Following the same analogy, it is difficult to say at this length of

103 Pictorial chart of Goa in 1583, centre of the new power of Portugal in India

time what was the original Hinduism and whether anything would be left if all the accretions of time could be removed. Even if not absorbed, new elements can be carried within the society like a bee in amber, distinct, yet part of the whole. Islam is the big instance of proof against absorption, the Nairs of Malabar and certain groups of the north of separateness in unity.

A second characteristic of Hinduism is the element of social tradition and custom. There is a great deal in Hinduism which does not descend from the Vedas or sacred writings, but is in fact custom handed down. Some of it is tribal custom and some of it habits which grew out of special circumstances and hardened into custom, such as that of the Kulin Brahmins in Bengal who acted as nominal bridegrooms to girls of suitable caste who might otherwise never have married. Custom came to be considered as sacred as Hindu sacred law, but as the reformer Ram Mohan Roy pointed out, there was in fact a clear distinction between the two. Thus suttee, or the burning of widows, the Hindu treatment of widows, and veneration of the cow, can find support or sanction in the Shastras but the seclusion of women is a matter of custom. Custom may on occasion override rule; thus remarriage of widows is forbidden by Hindu law, but permitted by custom among the Jats.

A third feature is that of regulation, rule, and ritual. Society is divided into an intricate pattern of groups, each with their own rule of life, with regulations for every phase of life and every aspect of behaviour, from birth through marriage and the family to death. Relations of group with group are regulated in the same way. And all these regulations, positive and negative, are surrounded with rituals. There is a right and wrong way of doing everything, a ritual for all occasions. The really orthodox Brahmin, like the proverbial Jewish pharisee, would spend most of his time achieving correctness and conformity to rule. Along with rule and ritual goes the idea of ritual purity. Touch – what may or may not be touched, living or inanimate – is an important constituent of this. The horror of pollution matches the passion for correctness. Particular groups, certain foods, species of animals, may not be touched without pollution; it was considered up to less than a century ago that travel abroad or 'over the water' was not permissible because it brought pollution.

But Hinduism does not altogether consist of rule and ritual purity.

Within it are to be found a great variety of religious cults. They are groups which worship particular deities or follow particular teachers regardless of caste. Sects drawn from all castes in the first instance may themselves become castes; caste groups may bodily join a sect. Your membership of a sect, like the cult of Krishna in Bengal, may not affect your caste at all. On the other hand a sect like the Lingayats of the south may grow into a caste. The worship of Jaganath at Puri in Orissa is a cult which brings merit to all irrespective of caste. The same is true of the goddess Kali in Bengal or any other of the great Hindu gods.

A last feature of Hinduism is its philosophy and spiritual discipline. Hindu philosophy has a continuous history of some 3,000 years. It contains a metaphysics on the nature of existence which provides a theoretical basis for the main institutions of Hindu society. Theory is never far from practice, indeed it often takes precedence, in the Hindu mind. Along with philosophy, goes a spiritual science and discipline which again has attained, through the continuous experience of three millennia, a high degree of sophistication. The great aim is Realization, to enable the soul to realize the identity of the divine within with the divine without. To that end paths of discipline or *yoga* are enjoined. There is one set for the householder and others, more rigorous, for the devotee. Detachment from worldly cares may be complete or partial, but detachment there must be.

The Development of Hinduism

We can now return to the problem of how these varied features came to be, and how they have achieved some sort of unity. For this purpose it is necessary to go back to origins. There are facets of Hinduism today which can be traced back with some certainty for 4,000 years. It used to be thought that Indian civilization started with the arrival of Aryan-speaking tribes in the second millennium B.C., driving before them dark-skinned savages. But in the last half-century archaeological excavations have revealed that another civilization preceded the Aryans, a civilization indeed developed by dark-skinned people, but no savages. This is the Indus Valley civilization, or, as it has recently been renamed following the excavation of sites, the Harappan culture. This civilization, it is believed, derived from the small communities of farmers and pastoralists who occupied the

104 Late sixteenth-
century woodcut of a
Portuguese officer
travelling in India

Iranian plateau from the fifth millennium B.C. One branch descended
to the Tigris-Euphrates Valley to commence the riverine civilizations
of Mesopotamia. In the third millennium B.C. another group
descended into the Indus Valley, rapidly built up an intricate city
culture, and flourished for 600 years. The known extent of this
culture is at present marked by Rupar, where the Sutlej debouches
from the hills into the Punjab, Hastinapur on the banks of the
upper Ganges, and the Gulf of Cambay, where harbour works have
been unearthed. But archaeologists have not set a limit to its extent
and are now looking towards the Deccan. We do not know the racial
composition of the Harappans, but can surmise that they were
mainly of the Dravidian race which spread over the unafforested
parts of India at some unknown period and are still the dominant
racial strain in the south. The Harappan cities are notable for their
geometrical planning, their careful drainage systems, their artistic
seals, their evidence of cotton culture, and extensive trade, including
contact with Sargonid Mesopotamia. The first three items left no
traces in Hinduism, but evidence has been steadily accumulating of
a carry-over from Harappa to the Indo-Aryans. The numerous clay
toys discovered include solid-wheel bullock carts of a type identical
with the modern Sindhi cart. If we dismiss cotton culture as only a
possible connection, since the Indo-Aryans could have discovered it
independently, there remains the evidence of religious cultures. The
pipal tree, then as now, was considered sacred; there are clear traces

of the worship of the bull and fertility cults, in line with the Hindu cult of the great god Shiva. Since we know that the Indo-Aryans brought neither of these things with them, the inference is strong that there was borrowing, albeit unacknowledged. It suggests an explanation of many features of popular Hinduism: that they had long been part of the pre-Aryan peoples' outlook and way of life, which gradually worked their way into acceptance by the later conquering race.

For the Indo-Aryans were a conquering race. They were a section of a group of tribes speaking allied or Aryan languages which, about the middle of the second millennium B.C., moved into Asia Minor and south-east Europe in the West, and into Iran and on to the Indus in the East. In the West they appeared as the Mitanni and the Greeks; in the East they carried to Persia their language, Avestic, and to India its relative, Sanskrit. These people are called the 'Indo-Aryans' because they were an Aryan-speaking group of tribes who entered India. *Arya* means 'noble' in Sanskrit, and is used because the original generic term for the whole group of tribes is unknown. The Indo-Aryans were tall and fair-skinned; they had the typical Aryan organization of king, nobles, and freemen. Sometimes the king was dispensed with and they organized themselves in what have been described as aristocratic republics. They were

105 Two European ladies in Jacobean dress in an Indian landscape. The figures have been adapted by a native artist from a European painting

206

pastoralists who counted their wealth in herds and cattle. They had no food inhibitions, they loved sport, specially racing and the chase, gaming and wine (the *soma*). They had a nature religion with gods representing the various aspects of nature such as thunder (Indra), the dawn (Ushas), and fire (Agni). Their hymns to these deities formed the major part of the *Rig-Veda*, which is the earliest Hindu work, composed in the second half of the second millennium B.C. These people came in migratory waves until they spread over the present Punjab, as far perhaps as the Jumna. They pushed aside the Harappans, who were perhaps already in a state of decay. We know nothing of the conflict, but only that conflict there was. There are signs of burning in the cities, and references to battles and stormings of cities in the *Rig-Veda*. The Indo-Aryans had a strong contempt for the local people, stigmatizing them as dark-skinned *dasyas*. We have no evidence from the other side and we know nothing of what the Harappans thought of the Aryans. But it has become increasingly clear that there was a protracted conflict, at first in the form of battles and sieges, and later in that of cultural interchange. It is also clear that if the people of the country lost their physical battles, they by no means lost the whole campaign. The Indo-Aryans never succeeded in exterminating them. Willy-nilly they lived beside them, if only in the relation of master and servant, and willy-nilly there was mutual influence. It was out of this contact between the people of the country, at first warlike but increasingly on the more subtle plane of cultural contact, that real Hinduism was born.

The Hindu Epics and their value as historical sources

The Indo-Aryan world of the Punjab and Sind is pictured in the hymns of the *Rig-Veda*, as already mentioned. The next beam of cultural light is shed on India about the year 1000 B.C. or a little later. It reveals what is often called the 'Epic Age' from the name of its sources, but which Professor A. L. Basham thinks should really be called the later Vedic Age. It lasted from about 1000 to 500 B.C.; for our purposes it is important because it shows a recognizably Hindu society emerging from the Indo-Aryan Vedic society. Hinduism is still in a formative stage, but the main features are there, features which differ widely from those of the preceding period. From this period we find aspects of Indian life and thought which are still prominent and active today. Something had clearly happened to produce a radical transformation of the new Indian society, the most radical in its history with the possible exceptions of the fifth and sixth centuries A.D. in the north. That something was intermixture.

The sources for our light are the two great epics, the *Ramayana* and the *Mahabharata*. The *Ramayana* is the shorter, running to 24,000 couplets, and is largely the work of one author, Valmiki. It is the story of Prince Rama and his wife Sita, who are expelled from Ayodhya in northern India, and wander in the forests until Sita is abducted by the demon king Ravan of Lanka (Ceylon). The siege of Lanka and its destruction by Rama with the aid of the monkey-king Hanuman follow, and then the return of the pair to Ayodhya. The siege of Lanka is still celebrated all over India in the Dasehra ('Ten Day Festival'), and Rama's return by the 'Festival of Lights', or Diwali, in the north, in October–November. Rama has become the ideal of manhood and Sita of womanhood. They are regarded as *avatars* or incarnations of the god Vishnu and his consort Lakshmi and the book itself, replete with comment and reflection as well as action, is something like a bible for north Indian Hindus.

The *Ramayana* has no known historical foundation, but the same cannot be said for its larger partner, the *Mahabharata* or 'Great War'. It is thought that the original poem contained about 8,800 couplets, later increased to 20,000. But with time the work assumed a northern and southern form and was swollen with additions to its present size of 100,000 couplets. Embedded within the work is the *Bhagavad Gita*, or the 'Lord's Song', in form a dialogue between Arjuna, the reluctant warrior in a civil war, and Krishna, his chariot-driver, on the subject of moral duty and non-violence. It is probably much later than the original, but is a foundation work of Hindu ethics, occupying within modern Hindu society something of the place of the New Testament in the West. The Pandavas of Indraprastha on the Jumna (modern Delhi), fight the Kurus of Hastinapur on the Ganges (now a mound in the countryside) at Kurukshetra, about 100 miles north of Delhi and now the seat of a university. Each has allies from all over India and the war, after many speeches and great slaughter, ends inconclusively.

The cores of the two epics together provide a picture of Indian society during the earlier centuries of the first millennium B.C. They give little material for political history but a comparison between them and the *Rig-Veda* shows marked changes. Firstly, it is clear that the Indo-Aryans have moved further into India. The centres of the great conflict were astride the Jumna and Ganges, and there were settlements further east at Kosala (whence Rama came) and Kasi (Banaras). What was to be the heartland of Hinduism had now been occupied. Secondly, there is clear evidence of mixture. It is plain that at least one side was not purely Aryan, for the five Pandava brothers shared one wife, Draupadi. This polyandrous practice is still common among the Mongolian tribes of the Himalayas and the Assamese hill tracts. Further, the efforts of both sides to secure non-Aryan allies show a new freedom from prejudice against intercourse with outsiders. Finally, new gods of non-Aryan origin have come in along with new ideas which cannot all be attributed to Indo-Aryan ingenuity. The invading Indo-Aryans had in fact become Indians. It is possible that the 'Great War' represented a late stage in this process. One side being more pure resisted the other which was more deeply tainted. Perhaps fresh waves of Indo-Aryan tribes had allied with Mongolian hill peoples which both gave rise to the story of

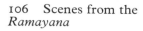

106 Scenes from the
Ramayana

Draupadi and aroused the indignation of Kuruva purists. Be this as it may, it is certain that both sides had already been deeply influenced by indigenous culture.

Developments were not confined to war. Not only had the tribes moved south-eastwards. They had developed agriculture in place of pastoralism; they had built cities, though not on the elaborate plan of the Harappans before them; their tribal groups had grown into little kingdoms, each with a court not unlike that of some rather backward British Indian state in the nineteenth century. It is not unlikely that the 'Great War' is a 'blown-up' version of bickering between two or more of such states. It is certain that each was striving to enlarge its borders, for it is not long after this period that we hear of 'conquerors' and empires. Along with the new policy went the new gods already mentioned. With the exception of Indra, the Vedic nature gods are not mentioned. In their place we find the gods and goddesses of modern India. The great Hindu triad of Brahma, Vishnu, and Shiva, and others like Krishna and Rama now occupy the stage, and animal deities like Hanuman the monkey and the elephant-headed Ganesha, which certainly did not come from the Iranian plateau, have appeared. Along with new gods went new ideas. The earlier worship of the powers of nature, and sacrifices to propitiate and manipulate these powers, had disappeared. Instead abstract ideas had emerged which became the mental substructure of Hinduism. The idea of the incarnation of the divine in human form, known as an *avatar*, unknown to the Indo-Aryans, was by now generally accepted. Rama and Krishna were incarnations of Vishnu, as they still are. Along with this went the idea of reincarnation, that one soul can have many lives. With this was linked the idea of *karma* or the law of moral consequences and *dharma*, the law of moral duty. *Ahimsa*, or non-violence, had also made its appearance. The first three are still basic in modern Hinduism and the last was the inspiration of Mahatma Gandhi. Indian thought had attained its characteristic Hindu form. It would develop with the philosophic treatises, the *Upanishads*, and with the divergent systems of Sankara and Ramanuja, the one a ninth-century thinker the other an eleventh-century philosopher, but it would not fundamentally alter.

A further dividing-line between Vedic and late Vedic India is the development of caste. The four orders of Indo-Aryan society have

107 Trimurti image of
Elephanta

grown into a recognizable system of castes, some of which are mentioned by the Greek observer Megasthenes in the third century B.C.
The features of marriage restriction, of food and touch taboos, are
there, and the idea of ritual purity and the fear of pollution are strong.
All this was foreign to the robust Indo-Aryan tribes of 500 years
before. Here again the system was to grow and to ramify, and to
modify, but not fundamentally to alter its nature. And here again,
in transforming Vedic into Hindu society, we can see the principle of
intermixture at work. Such a change could not have come about
without contact, close and prolonged, with other peoples with other
manners. Many of these must have been the pre-Aryan inhabitants
of the plains. Contact doubtless grew closer as the Indo-Aryans
penetrated further into the interior and they themselves became more
dispersed. But there must also have been close contacts with the
Mongolian hill tribes who stretched out along the foothills of the
Himalayas as far as the Assamese hills. It was from the Sakyas,
probably a mixed tribe in what is now eastern Nepal, that the Buddha
came. This cultural complex was to be further modified as it spread to
the south and met developed peoples it could not overthrow or push
aside. It was to receive fresh infusions of thought and physical
stock from outside. It would be modified at times, and in some

108 Stone frieze depicting 'Nanda's Conversion'

places drastically, but it would not change essentially. It can be said that the changes which can be detected between first-millennium B.C. Hinduism and that of modern times represent additions rather than subtractions. Hindu society possessed a resilience which has enabled it to survive the shocks and strains of two and a half millennia and to absorb every intruding influence except those backed by the steel frame of a world religion.

Hindu Society

Caste

We have noticed the growth of Indian life until, sometime in the early part of the first millennium B.C. it emerged as Hinduism. Hinduism is much more than a religious cult, and even than a social system with intricate rules and regulations. It is a whole way of life, covering all its aspects from the most erudite philosophy to the humblest activities. It actually embodied the medieval European ideal of a society not only controlled but integrated with the religious forces embodied in the Catholic Church. This ideal in Europe came closest to realization in Renaissance Spain and Portugal. The tightly knit religio-social nature of sixteenth-century Portuguese society was one reason why, for all its vigour and charm, it failed to make any serious impact on the Indian society of that time. In considering Hinduism, therefore, we have to take into account not merely ritual or philosophy or art, though it contained all these, but a whole outlook and way of life.

The feature which inevitably strikes the newcomer to India is the caste system. It runs through the whole of Indian society forming a social framework. It therefore seems right to consider it first. It has already been suggested that Hinduism, of which the caste system is an essential part, was the result of contact and friction between the invading Indo-Aryan tribes and the earlier inhabitants. The same principle provides a clue to the origin of caste, which has few, if any, parallels throughout the world. No doubt no single cause can account for it. But we can note certain factors which contributed to its formation. One was the desire to maintain tribal purity through marriage and touch restrictions. Another was colour feeling, very evident in the *Rig-Veda*. Marriages with the dark-skinned, according to Sir H. Risley, were necessary for a time because of a shortage of women in a warrior's world. As soon as possible this was stopped by means of the unique marriage rules of caste. There remains the question of touch and taboo. Professor J. H. Hutton, an authority on the primitive tribes of India, has argued that this comes from the primitive idea that soul stuff or *mana* can be conveyed through touch on the principle of sympathetic magic. Thus the aversion to touch was a two-sided process, and deep-rooted feelings on both sides combined to provide an effective sanction for the complicated rules.

The caste system arose from the four 'orders' of Vedic India. The four orders or *varnas* were originally flexible and only loosely hereditary. They were the Brahmins or priests and literates; the Kshatriyas or warriors; the Vaisyas or merchants and farmers; the Sudras or workers and servants. The castes as they developed were placed within these orders, and it has required great effort, whether of individuals or groups, to cross the line of an order. There are many cases of disputes about placing. Maratha chiefs, for example, would want to be recognized as Kshatriyas in a Rajput caste, and the priests of invading tribes to receive Brahminical status. Within these limits the castes grew and subdivided. They are broadly distinguished on an occupational basis, whether as doctors, writers, cultivators, cowherds, and landless labourers. Beyond the pale, the excluded tribes organized themselves in the same way – such as the weavers, the leather-workers, the scavengers, the toddy-tappers. Along with this occupational bias there goes a tribal undercurrent. Some castes like the Jats, the Gujars, and the Ahirs, are really tribal units recognized *en masse* as a caste, their leaders perhaps being allowed the status of a higher caste. There is also a geographical element in caste, some groups being peculiar to a particular part of the country, while groups of one of the orders, Brahmins for example, in one part of the country will have no dealings with those of another part. Finally, there is a sectarian element, some castes, like the Lingayats of south India and the Dadupanthis of the north, being really religious sects which have become hereditary exclusive communities.

Each caste is a blood-related group, strictly hereditary, and governed by rules of marriage, diet, and touch. Failure to observe the rules led to outcasting, or exclusion. This might be an isolated personal disaster, but if it involved a breach of caste such as marrying without the caste and numbers were involved, it would lead to the formation of a new caste. Ritual pollution by Muslims in times of excitement – such as forcible beef-eating – might have the same effect, if it did not lead to conversion. Lesser breaches could usually be compounded by purification ceremonies and payments to Brahmins. The sanction for all this was public opinion only, for there is no Church organization within Hinduism, no religious hierarchy, and no disciplinary councils. The caste committees, which represented caste opinion, were the only formal arbiters. It might be thought that this lack of direction would leave society in chaos; in fact, where the essentials of Hinduism filled the average man's mental horizon, the system was more effective than legal sanctions would have been, or than excommunication was in medieval Europe. The sanction was effective because the exclusion was total. Within the caste marriage was regulated by its limitation to certain sub-groups. Some of these were in-marrying groups within which you must marry, while some were out-marrying groups within which you must not. In a large caste this was a beneficial and not too difficult arrangement, but in a small or scattered one it might lead to embarrassment and abuse. The rules of the Kulin Brahmins of Bengal were such that one man might have many wives in different villages, some of whom he might never even meet. The caste was further regulated by rules of diet and touch. The high caste man could not take food from a lower caste; hence the custom of employing Brahmin cooks, in whose hands no food could be ritually polluted. The higher castes were vegetarian with various degrees of strictness; but all the four orders joined in venerating the cow and abstaining from its meat. Only some of the outcastes would make no distinctions down to eating carrion. Indeed, one of the ways of raising a caste's status was to change its dietary habits in a Brahminical direction.

Below the regular castes came the outcastes, probably about a quarter of the total Hindu population, or a third of the Hindu caste folk. These performed repellent work such as scavenging, but also ritually impure work such as leather-working (the skin of the sacred cow). They lived (as many still do) in quarters apart from the main village, with inferior wells and temples of their own. They were untouchables because their touch caused ritual pollution; some were even unseeable. They had their own castes, as rigid in their way as those of the Hindus proper. They varied much in their circumstances in different parts of India, from the sturdy Mahars of western India to the despised unapproachables of Malabar.

The leading castes were the Brahmins, the priestly and literate order who had taken precedence over the warriors by the first millennium B.C. They were the hereditary intellectuals of India. Not all were intellectual of course, or all priests. From their ranks in general came scholars, philosophers, administrators, and diplomats.

109   Buddhist stupa at Sanchi

A raja would have his *purohit* or Brahmin spiritual adviser, but he would also almost certainly have a Brahmin minister as well. The Brahmins (from Brahma, God in his creative aspect) were not only hereditary intellectuals; they were the architects of the Hindu system of ideas which justified Hindu society and held it together. They were the repositories of Indian wisdom and religious practice; they were versed in the sacred language of Sanskrit which was the key to this knowledge. In all the rituals and rules of caste people did not, in the main, feel that they were being constrained or victimized. They believed that they were acting according to the divine harmony of life, and this belief came from ideas which the Brahmins had embedded so deeply in their minds that they had become part of their texture.

Concepts and Ethics

The first of these is that of *prana* or breath. It is the concept of spirit pervading all objects, living or inanimate, so that all phenomena, including man, are part of one vast all-pervading being. This is one basis of the worship, for example, in villages of 'rocks and stones and trees'. This idea creates a feeling of kinship with the universe. Next comes the concept of *karma* or the law of moral consequences. Every action has a consequence and every consequence is itself the result of a previous action. Lest this should lead to apathetic fatalism, it is linked with the emotional fact of desire. Desire spurs to action and action brings consequences. But once this reasoning is followed any distance, it becomes clear that consequences cannot be worked out in a single life, if strict justice is to be maintained. Nor could a single life account equitably for all the 'slings and arrows of fortune' to which everyone is subject. Here comes in the next great Indian concept, transmigration of the soul. The soul must go through many lives if all the consequences of its actions are to be rigorously and justly worked out. How then is progress to be made, so as eventually to break the endless chain of death and rebirth? The first answer is by doing one's duty in one's station in life and this brings us to the next concept of *dharma*. The nearest translation of this term is 'moral duty', but this must not be understood in a universal sense. It is the duty of each person as a member of a particular caste. Some moral qualities, like honesty, may extend to all castes, but the para-

110 Palitana, where there are 863 Jain temples on the
five sacred hills

mount duties, the hub of *dharma*, are those peculiar to a caste. Thus
the duty of the merchant is to trade with profit, of the warrior to
fight, and of the king to rule and nourish his subjects. A man is
making progress in life, and may hope for promotion in a future
life, in so far as he conscientously performs his current caste duties.

So, by patience and diligence, one can mount the ladder of society.
But it is a slow business, rung by rung. Cannot the chain be broken
altogether? Here we come to the doctrine of *maya* or illusion.
Broadly speaking it can be said that the one pervading spirit manifests in many forms. But these forms have no ultimate reality; the
soul gains freedom by realizing the oneness of the individual with the
universal soul or self. *Tat tvam asi*, 'thou art that'. This is achieved in
two ways. On the one hand there is the worship of the gods. On the
other there are personal disciplines for the individual. The extreme
form is renunciation of society, the donning of the saffron robe, and
the wandering life of the *sannyasi* or *sadhu*. Less drastic are *margas*
or paths for the individual, the path of knowledge (*dnyana*), the path
or work (*karma*), and the path of devotion (*bhakti*).

217

III The Buddha, sixth-century
relief from the Ajanta caves

Jainism and Buddhism

This is perhaps the place to mention the two main living offshoots
of Hinduism, since, while neither of them were prominent in the
India of 1500, both had influenced Hinduism as it then appeared.
From the seventh to the fifth century B.C. India, while emerging
from the late Vedic into the early historic period, experienced much
intellectual ferment. The Brahmin claims and reliance on spells and
incantations were challenged. One result was the development of the
more lofty, philosophical side of Hinduism. Another was positive
revolt against Brahmin domination leading to the formation of
independent communities. In the sixth century two sages, Mahavira
and Gautama the Buddha or Enlightened One, appeared. Mahavira
(c. 540–467 B.C.) founded the Jain community, which still numbers
over a million members. Until about A.D. 600 they were strong in
north and western India and at times had influence in the south also.
They are still strong in Gujarat both by force of numbers and by virtue of influence on the main Hindu body. Their most characteristic
doctrine is that of *ahimsa* or non-violence, which led them to great
lengths in order to avoid taking even insect life. Jains can still be

218

seen feeding the ants and wearing cloth protectors for their nostrils to avoid inhaling and suffocating insects. Along with the Buddhists, they were responsible for injecting this principle into the main body of Hinduism. The Buddha (*c.* 567–487 B.C.) began by seeking the cause of sorrow, and his enlightenment in a deer park near Banaras began his mission. The secret was cessation of desire and the practice of benevolence. The Buddha gathered disciples and founded a *Sangha* or Church. At first his followers were renunciates, and their mode of life monastic, but society could not be neglected and for it a moral code, the Noble Eightfold Path, was devised. Buddhism developed from an agnostic's prescription for escape from the miseries of life and of rebirth into a religion of salvation with the Buddha as its saviour. In this guise it travelled through central Asia to China and Japan and mingled with Lamaism to produce a unique variation in Tibet, while it survives in its original pattern in Ceylon, Burma, and South East Asia. There was never a Buddhist Age in India but for the millennium from the Emperor Asoka's patronage in the third century B.C. it was a leading religious and social force and contender for the spiritual leadership of India. By 1500 the chief tangible evidence of Buddhism in India was the temple at Gaya in Bihar, and that was largely Hinduized. But its influence continued in its effect on the whole body of Hindu life and thought. Buddhism failed to shake the Brahmin supremacy but it did modify their practice and stimulate their thought. The answer to the Buddhist way of salvation and Noble Eightfold Path was the *Bhagavad Gita*, the doctrine of realization and the *bhakti* cults of devotion. Along with the Jains the Buddhists acclimatized non-violence within Hindu thought. Buddhism also left a rich artistic legacy. Its *stupas* and rock-hewn halls can still be admired today while the frescoes of Ajanta not only give us a picture, more vivid and earlier than the Bayeux Tapestry, of contemporary court life in the early centuries A.D., but reveal the Renaissance heights to which Indian art under its inspiration had risen.

The Social System

In all these conditions, how did these people actually live? Within the caste, the unit was the joint family, a patriarchal arrangement which still persists in spite of the disintegrating tendencies of modern technology and urban life. Sons and grandsons lived under the roof and authority of the father, and daughters under the authority of a mother-in-law. Income was controlled by the head, who in turn was responsible for the maintenance of his dependents. The institution with its great stimulus for a few and repression for the many was, like the caste system, a stabilizing social factor, promoting a highly defensive but unprogressive and disparate society.

In this intricate society women had a defined but subordinate place. Within limits their status was considerable. Their place was defined by Hindu law and largely observed in practice. This authority was the compilation known as the 'laws of Manu', the standard authority for Hindu social practice. As a child, the woman usually received warm affection, though her brothers always came first in the family reckoning. Indeed, she had to pass the early hazard of infanticide, a custom not enjoined by Manu but springing from social pressures in certain communities. Marriage was the turning-point of her life for she did not usually return to the family home and she would be subject to her mother-in-law's authority. As a wife she was the servant of her husband, who was, in Manu's estimation, as a god to her. But the faithful wife, whose model was Sita the wife of the epic hero Rama, was held in high estimation, meriting deep respect. As a mother she received a further promotion; her children venerated her as a *devi* or goddess as she venerated her husband. If she became the head of a joint family, she had great authority over the whole household and particularly over her daughters-in-law. She did not live in seclusion and could take part in public life, for instance as the regent for a minor son. There have been instances of ruling ranis who have been reverenced as the mothers of their people. All this came to an end with the husband's death. Suttee or burning with the husband, in order to tend him in the next world, was permitted but not enjoined. The alternative was hard enough. She was not only in perpetual mourning, but in perpetual penance for causing the husband's death by some bad *karma* in a previous life. Her head was shaven, her clothing was always white, she ate coarse food, spent much time in religious exercises, and became the family drudge. Some preferred to jump into the family well, some fled to the cities, and some went as devotees to holy places.

Hindu society began as a group of nomadic pastoralists and

developed into a body of agriculturists. The *gram* or village was the unit of society, but in time towns were added, where commerce and industry were carried on and the arts practised. There was the market-town for exchange, the holy city like Kasi or Banaras, the royal city or seat of the king's court, the port and the centre of industry. This last often moved with the royal city, for industry under the cottage system was largely dispersed, and it was only the buyers and sellers who needed to congregate. Cities had warehouses rather than factories. The arts, manual and fine, and industries displayed a degree of skill from an early age which again suggests that the contact with the Indus Valley people cannot have been wholly destructive. The Indian industry *par excellence* was then, as now, textiles, both cotton and silk. Next to this came spices, partly the home products of pepper and cardamons from south India, and still more the re-export trade of other spices brought from Indonesia. Then there were dyes like indigo, gems and gold from Golkonda, and gold-dust from the Himalayas. These products gave rise to a flourishing export trade which enriched the south and coastal areas like Gujarat and Bengal elsewhere. India not only supplied herself with cottons, but sent them in an age-long intercourse to Indonesia, the Middle East, and, in the heyday of the Roman Empire, to the Mediterranean world. It was with cotton goods

112   An early Buddha (second–third century A.D.) from Gandhara

221

113 Fresco from Ajanta (sixth century A.D.). *Left*, a dancer with musicians. *Right*, a young prince rides through a gate on an elephant, accompanied by Amazons. *Above*, the prince listens to a white-clad ascetic

that India bought east Indian spices, but the spice trade with the Middle East and Europe was in her hands. Pepper was the commodity most in demand, and we read of Muziris on the Malabar coast where the Greeks came, 'making the water white with foam and returned laden with pepper'. The other form of foreign trade was over the north-western passes to Persia in its periods of imperial stability.

With all this activity, however, India remained an essentially agricultural country. It was generally divided into many states, ruled by rajas who were usually of the warrior castes. The raja would be surrounded by ministers and advisers who were often Brahmins, and by professional priests or pundits who attended to the state ritual and worship. To his court came the chiefs, often related to him, who in turn controlled the countryside by various forms of tenure. On the nature and success of this control depended the stability of society and the strength of the state. The raja was not absolute, though he was subject to much deference. Like others he had a *dharma*, which was to preserve society and promote the welfare of his subjects. Failure to do this absolved his subjects from the duty of obedience, for he then no longer possessed the halo of sanctity. He was further limited by tribal custom which, in later Rajputana, produced many succession disputes and successive breakaway states. Periodically a raja of distinction would build up a personal empire of subordinate states, while twice in 1500 years a bureaucratic empire appeared. In this aristocratic structure the merchants played an active but rather subdued part. Princes wanted their products to adorn their courts and their money to wage their wars. The merchants were important but subordinate. It was not an accident that they supported Buddhism, for the Buddhists challenged the Brahmins, and the Brahmins supported the rajas in their own interest. By implication Buddhism was more democratic than Brahminism, and it was aristocracy which blocked the way to mercantile autonomy.

The Arts and Sciences

In such a closely knit theocratic society it was natural that the arts should be closely linked with religion. At times they attained as high a level as in some periods of Europe and China. Their rapid progress may again be linked with the early stimulus of contact with the Indus Valley folk, and they were further stimulated by outside influences like those from Persia and the Greeks. But Hindu Indian art developed in a highly individual way according to its own genius. Foreign influences, as in the world of thought and religion, led not so much to imitation or even to synthesis as to absorption. Thus Persian influences were absorbed in the early Buddhist style while Greek influences, prominent in the Gandhara style of the Kushans, had joined the great stream of Indian art by the time of the Guptas in the fourth century A.D. Architecture found expression in the temple, the palace, and the fort. Other buildings were mostly of wood as were even palaces until the Christian era. Temple-building went on steadily, reaching its apotheosis in the Temple of the Sun at Konarak in Orissa and in the great towers of the south, standing like sentinels oblivious of time. The pattern remained constant, a shrine for the god, a courtyard for the priests and the worshippers, a reservoir or tank for ablutions. It was the form of the decoration which varied. This feature gave the Hindu sculptor his opportunity so that some temples seem to be almost backgrounds for walls of sculpture, some showing wearisome repetition, but some full of vigour and life. All, even the most crudely sexual, are expressions of Hindu ideas. In the early Christian centuries there was a long period of rock-hewn temples, whose most impressive example is the Kailash Temple at Ellora in central India. The early Buddhist temples were *stupas* or dome-like structures to secrete sacred relics. Later votary chapels developed and halls of worship. Both religions used paintings and it is to this fact that we owe the exquisite Ajanta frescoes. The Buddhists, with their fund of material from the stories of the Buddha's incarnations, revealed both in sculpture and painting many details of daily life. The Hindus were more wedded to their own vast mythology. Both Buddhists and Hindus created a huge literature, but while that of the former (in Pali) is now the heritage of the extra-Indian Buddhists, the Hindu *corpus* is part of the modern Indian world. It is written in Sanskrit, an early form of which was the spoken tongue of the first Indo-Aryans. But by 500 B.C. it had become a

114   Rock-hewn temple at Karli, from a painting by Henry Salt

dead language converted into a sacred monopoly by the Brahmins. It is difficult to tell, from internal evidence, whether a Sanskrit work was written in 300 B.C. or A.D. 300. Along with literature went knowledge of the sciences. The Indians were expert metal-workers. They had an extensive knowledge of medicine which has held its own against the Greek or Yunani systems introduced by the Muslims. In the early Christian centuries they led the world in mathematics. To them we owe the cipher, which makes the decimal system possible. It was borrowed from them by the Arab world in the seventh century, whence it was passed on to western Europe via Spain to supersede, with the Arabic numerals, the clumsy Roman figures and the abacus.

The Historical Link

India emerges into the light of recorded history in the fourth century B.C. From this time literary, epigraphic, and numismatic evidence is available whereas our earlier knowledge is largely a matter of inference from literary and archaeological sources. By the fifth century B.C. north India was organized into a number of kingdoms of whom the best known was Magadha with its capital Pataliputra, near the modern Patna. For a time the Punjab was a Persian satrapy and Indian archers are said to have fought at Marathon. It was this connection which probably prompted Alexander's invasion of India in 325 B.C. though Persia had clearly ceased to control the country. More important, it led to the first Indian empire, for Chandragupta Maurya of Magadha was able to defeat Alexander's eastern successor Seleucus and establish a bureaucratic dominion right across north India. Chandragupta's grandson was Asoka, one of the select band of great world rulers. After a bloody campaign in what is now Orissa, Asoka patronized the rising Buddhist movement and personally preached non-violence. His edicts and his precepts were inscribed on pillars and rock surfaces and make it clear that his rule stretched far to the south. In his time, 273–232 B.C., Ceylon is said to have been converted to Buddhism by Asoka's brother. Perhaps it was the patronage started by him which made the surrounding country a stronghold of Buddhism, its modern name of Bihar being a corruption of the word *vihara*, a Buddhist monastery.

The Mauryan Empire collapsed within fifty years of Asoka's death, leaving, however, the Magadhan kingdom intact. It also left a powerful Buddhist movement which remained strong in the north until the Hun invasions of the fifth century A.D. In Taxila near Rawalpindi in Pakistan some of its monasteries have been uncovered. To this first bureaucratic empire with its organization and its hopeful idealism succeeded the Age of Invasions. These were not like those of the Indo-Aryans, for they did not overwhelm what already existed, and set up, as it were, on their own. They added to Indian life, modifying it rather than overturning it. The first of these invaders were the highly sophisticated Greeks of Bactria, the part of modern Turkestan between the Hindu Kush and the Oxus, at that time in revolt from the Greek Seleucid Empire in Persia. They conquered the Punjab about 175 B.C. and set up a number of states which have left their traces in hoards of beautifully executed coins. They produced one famous king, Menander, prominent in Buddhist literature, and once penetrated as far as Patna. They were minority aristocratic adventurers leading mercenaries and their culture was exotic. Behind them came the Pahlavas or Parthians, who were not so much war bands as migratory tribes, also engaged in taking over Persia. The Greeks deflected them down the Indus Valley whence they passed to Gujarat and western India. After them came the Sakas or Scythians, a nomadic people from central Asia, themselves being pressed by a horde ejected from China, the Yueh-Chi. By the turn of the era they had overrun the Greek kingdoms of the Punjab, founding one of their own at Taxila, and had spread down the Indus into Sind and on to Gujarat. They were settlers rather than raiders and, with the Pahlavas, added a new element to the people of north and west India. In particular they contributed to the formation of the later Maratha and Gujarati peoples. In the first century A.D. the Yueh-Chi themselves, spurred on by others behind them, moved into India as the Kushans, the name of their leading tribe. The Kushans founded an impressive empire, with Peshawar as the capital, extending from Turkestan to the Upper Ganges Valley. This empire lasted a century and a half and fragmented portions remained until the fourth century. All this invasion suggests disruption of life and culture. But in fact this was much less than might have been expected. On their way the various groups acquired a tincture of

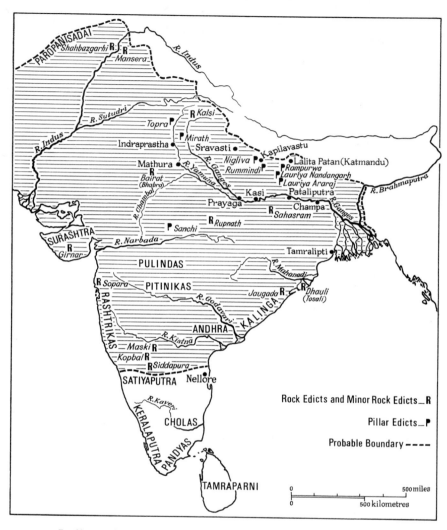

MAP 9   India at the time of Asoka

Rock Edicts and Minor Rock Edicts — R

Pillar Edicts — P

Probable Boundary - - - -

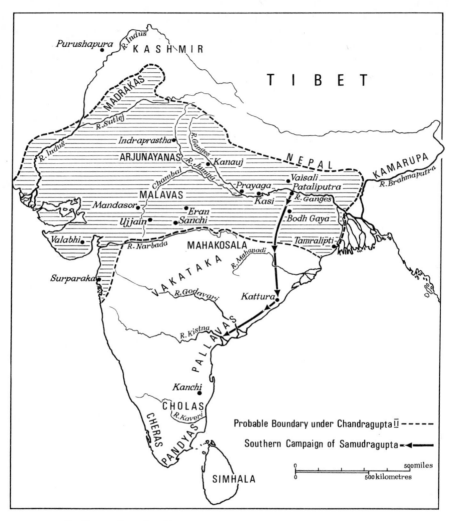

Purushapura
R. Indus
K A S H M I R

T I B E T

MADRAKAS

R. Sutlej

Indraprastha
R. Indus
ARJUNAYANAS
R. Ganges
R. Jumna
Kanauj
N E P A L
KAMARUPA
R. Brahmaputra

Vaisali
Pataliputra
Prayaga
Chambal
MALAVAS
Mandasor
Kasi
R. Ganges

Ujjain
Eran
Sanchi
Bodh Gaya

Valabhi
R. Narbada
MAHAKOSALA
Tamralipti

Surparaka
V A K A T A K A
R. Godavari
R. Mahanadi
Kattura

R. Kistna
P A L L A V A S

Kanchi

CHOLAS
R. Kaveri

CHERAS
PANDYAS

Probable Boundary under Chandragupta II - - - - -

Southern Campaign of Samudragupta ◄━━━━

SIMHALA

0   500 miles
0   500 kilometres

MAP 10   India under the Guptas

Persian culture and on arrival proved susceptible to Indian influences. Society was not so much disrupted as enlarged and enriched. The Kushans adopted Buddhism, and under their great ruler Kanishka promoted a changeover from the old agnostic to the new redemptive version. The Buddha became the incarnate redeemer as well as teacher of mankind. Perhaps as a consequence of these invasions there was a fresh outburst of Indian creativeness under the imperial Guptas in the fourth and fifth centuries. The kingdom of Magadha again expanded to the Indus and western India and its rule seems to have been milder than that of the earlier Mauryas. It is generally agreed that Hindu civilization achieved its peak at this time. Gupta art, and specially sculpture, has never been surpassed in India. The philosophy of the Vedanta reached maturity, though its two greatest masters, Sankara and Ramanuja, lived a little later. Literature also reached a peak with the poet-dramatist Kalidasa, and the same can be said for science.

The Gupta era was followed by a confused and obscure period caused by the invasions of the Huns and associated tribes from about A.D. 450, while another branch was simultaneously threatening western Europe. Unlike previous invaders, they were highly destructive, ending Buddhism as well as Gupta rule in north India. The traces of their firing of the monasteries at Taxila may still be seen. By 600 they had been contained and partly absorbed, and the north had another gleam of brilliance under Harsha of Kanauj. Then the mists close in again until they clear to reveal a new northern and central India, that of the Rajputs. Though the Huns themselves had eventually been defeated their invasions set off the greatest social disruption since the coming of the Indo-Aryans. It appears that waves of nomadic tribes came in and settled, and, carrying no high culture, eventually reconciled themselves to Hinduism, but at a price. They were too numerous and powerful to be treated as outcastes or even as low castes, so that the Brahmins had to reconcile themselves on their side to a new situation. Some groups were accepted wholesale like the Jats, the Brahmins considering them Sudras and the Jats claiming to be Kshatriyas. Others were broken up, the noble families becoming Rajputs (sons of chiefs or kings) and the followers falling into lower castes. So we find in the eighth century new peoples, new names, and a new polity. It was an age of tribal and clan kingdoms which rose and fell with personal prowess or decrepitude in constant succession. The Rajput chiefs were brave and chivalrous, but proud and quarrelsome with no idea of bureaucratic organization. They allowed Hindu life to proceed, while their status as recognized newcomers or promoted chiefs from within tended to make them unduly respectful of Brahmins. Their fights were commonly too local to undermine society but too numerous and frequent to allow it to expand. Philosophy developed and literature flourished, but otherwise society remained static, bathed in an apparently tolerable semi-anarchy. Meanwhile, in the south and west, a series of more stable states had grown up, broadly representing the four main divisions of Dravidian society. It was Rajput India which encountered the Turkish onslaughts from the eleventh century onwards, and which had been largely submerged, except in Rajasthan, by 1500. It was the southern kingdoms which fell briefly before the Turks in the fourteenth century, but which recovered to form the empire of Vijayanagar, in its full flower in 1500. The Rajput bards gave their India a romantic glow; but the Turkish invaders exposed its inner weakness.

115 Fresco forming central disc of a ceiling in one of the Ajanta caves. The design is formed by a large open lotus, surrounded by flying celestial figures bearing flowers

Islam in India

Chronology of the Connection

Islam proved by 1500 to be the one cultural influence to have entered India which not only resisted the creeping tentacles of Hinduism, but proved able to make converts on its own. The political dominion so obvious in 1500 concealed a body, small indeed compared to the main body of Hinduism, but alive, vigorous, and an established part of the Indian community. Other foreign influences and groups survived, but none on so large a scale, and none had succeeded in extending their borders. The experience suggests that entrants to India with a corporate consciousness and a level of culture and ideology comparable to Hinduism could survive but not easily expand. Islam had that something extra which enabled it to do both.

Before considering the reasons for its success the other cultural influences may be briefly noted. First came the Christians in the early centuries, at a time when Buddhism was expanding overland to China, and overseas to Indonesia and South East Asia. They came as individual preachers and merchants from Edessa in Syria to the north-west, through Afghanistan. There are fleeting traces of these people through the centuries, but they were limited to individuals and small groups and never had a firm communal identity. By 1500 they had vanished. Their second approach was to Malabar, in Greek ships as traders and artisans. It is certain that during the first Christian centuries a compact community was formed linked with the Eastern Churches and possessing a recognized status. In 1500 they were Nestorians and perhaps 100,000 strong. They are now known as Syrians. While they preserved their identity, they failed to expand, becoming inlooking like a Hindu caste, and indeed being treated very like one by the Hindus. There were two other bodies of whom much the same could be said. The first were the 'black' Jews of Cochin who trace their arrival as refugees from beleagured Jerusalem in A.D. 68. They were reinforced by 'white' or Spanish Jews in the fifteenth century. Then there were the Parsis, who migrated from Muslim Persia in the seventh century A.D. in order to preserve their Zoroastrian religion. Like the Christians, they survived but did not grow.

Muslims have been in touch with India almost since the beginning of Islam in A.D. 622 (the date of the *Hegira* or flight of the Prophet from Mecca). The Arabs succeeded the Greeks as spice traders on the Malabar coast, and as they became Muslim they carried their faith with them. This was the beginning of a long tradition of Muslim evangelism by trade, which took the faith through Indonesia and the eastern seas to the Philippines. Intermarriage and settlement took place so that by the eighth century a mixed community of Arab descent, known as the Moplahs, was established. It is claimed that Arab contact influenced the thought and practice of southern Hinduism, but the Muslims did not, as a body, penetrate the barrier of jungle and hills which separates Malabar from the Mysore plateau. They influenced the Zamorin of Calicut but never established an independent kingdom.

In the south the Muslims came as traders; in the north, as imperialists. In A.D. 712 the young Arab general Muhammad bin Kasim conquered Sind on behalf of the calif, whose armies had overthrown the Visigoths of Spain the year before. For nearly three centuries this remained the limit of Muslim advance, for the Kutch marshes and Rajput desert proved too strong physically, and the Punjabi Hindus too sturdy to be overthrown. Arab rule was tolerant, and, indeed, soon diluted with Hindu elements.

A great change occurred with the arrival of the Turks on the borders of India from central Asia in the tenth century. They were wild and warlike, of nomadic origin, Muslims with the zeal of recent converts, and only slightly tinctured with the culture of the Persians, whose country of origin they were overrunning. They collected scholars and poets like trophies, so that their courts were brilliant though barbaric. One of their chiefs, Mahmud of Ghazni, commenced a series of raids about the year 1000. By his death in 1025 he had sacked Kanauj on the Ganges, Mathura on the Jumna, and Somnath in Kathiawar. His raids were ferocious and destructive, particularly of Hindu temples. The solid results of this successful fanaticism were two. The Punjab as far as the Sutlej was annexed, and the idea of Muslim ferocity and intolerance firmly implanted in the Hindu mind.

There followed an interlude of nearly two centuries while the Turks were held on the Punjab line. But the insecurity felt can be judged by the sites of the contemporary cities of Delhi, one in a stony wilderness and the other on a rocky eminence well away from

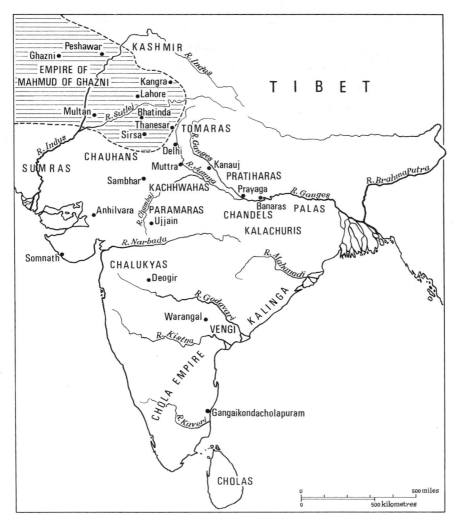

MAP 11   India in 1030

116 Yantra painting with figures of Hindu gods and
goddesses, animals and plants, Gujarat, 1447

the Jumna and its cooling breezes. Clearly security was more important than comfort. The Turkish breakthrough occurred in 1192 when
Muhammad of Ghor defeated a Hindu host at Thaneswar. Delhi
fell the next year and within ten years the Muslim Empire stretched
to the Bay of Bengal. The Turks were less destructive than two centuries before, but they were still fierce enough. They were responsible
for the end of Buddhism in Bihar, burning the monasteries and slay-
ing the monks. They destroyed fewer temples, perhaps because there
were fewer temples to destroy.

For 200 years the Turks of north India were organized under the
sultans of Delhi. They were stern rulers but in general men of great
ability. They began as generals of an army of occupation; their
realm became a refuge for Muslims fleeing from the Mongols of
Chinghis Khan; they developed a bureaucracy and their career
culminated in the conquest of the south. They were still capable of
savagery and intolerance, but they learnt to live on terms with the
Hindus, who, in fact, manned the subordinate parts of the administration. Their rule remained alien and their attitude superior but
they provided a certain rough justice, and as individuals became
progressively acclimatized to the Indian scene. The conquest of the
south, from the raids of Ala-ad-Din's generals to the revolt of the

234

Deccan, occupied the first half of the fourteenth century. In the south itself the Muslim presence was an extended foray rather than a conquest. The south shook the Muslims off and went on its Dravidian Hindu way. The lasting result was the Muslim control of the Deccan, which, in the final form of the Hyderabad state, lasted until 1948. The Delhi sultanate in its Turkish form ended with the invasion of Timur in 1398. There succeeded an age of numerous succession kingdoms leading to the Afghan sultanate which has already been touched upon. The Turkish sultans preserved India from the menace of the Mongols, at that time in their wildest state. They confined the Rajputs to their Rajasthan fastness and they added the Deccan to Islamic rule. Lastly, and perhaps most significantly for the future, they provided a strong administrative umbrella beneath which the Muslims were transformed from being members of an army of occupation into a living and viable community, an integral part of the whole Indian people.

Concepts and Ethics

Islam, as a socio-religious system, presents a striking contrast to Hinduism. It is clear and precise where Hinduism is vague and confused, it is world-accepting where Hinduism is world-rejecting, it has one rule for all where Hinduism has many rules for each. It is a religion which expresses itself in a society, whereas Hinduism is a society which has developed within it one or more religions. To be specific, God to the Muslim is one and supreme, the world his creation and human beings his creatures. He rules by command. There is equality in the sight of God, though not between men and women. The consequences are a hatred of idolatry as raising the creature to the divine level, and of caste as denying equality. The world is a place to be lived in, the believers are a brotherhood who must extend their faith and rule even over those who do not accept it – hence evangelism is promoted. Islam has its taboos (no pork for example) but they are different from those of Hinduism. Muslims specially object to the Hindu attitude to the cow, both because it is a taboo unknown to them and because its worship is to them idolatrous. Islam was a Semitic religion closely connected with Judaism, and it had a Semitic intensity. This quality gave the already civilized Arabs great bursts of energy and feats of achievement. Finally, we must remember that Islam, springing from Arabian tribal conditions, necessarily changed in form as it successively threw its mantle over different societies. It was much influenced by tribalism everywhere, whether of the Arabs themselves, the Afghans, or the Turks, and this we find carried to India where the Muslim Rajputs are a very different sort of Muslim to, say, the East Pakistani. It was also influenced by pre-existing cultures, such as that of the Byzantines, who passed on Greek philosophy to the Baghdad califate, and the Persians who promoted Muslim mysticism.

The main vehicle of Islam in India was thus the Turks, themselves recent converts. Their severity was gradually mellowed by progressive infusions of Persian culture which was to them what the Classical world was to medieval Europe. They were reinforced later by the Afghans whose tribal element was stronger, and response to Persian influence weaker. It was with these influences that the Muslim community of north India grew under the sultanate.

The Process of Conversion

The community began, as we have seen, as an army of occupation with its followers. These in themselves could not have provided more than a thinly spread aristocracy which would have been absorbed. How did it manage to throw down roots into the country? The first answer was the urge to convert. The crudest form was forcible conversion, at the point of the sword or by ritual pollution such as forcing beef into a hapless caste man's mouth. This was done probably a good deal in the first Turkish onrush across the north, and also at times of stress later. But the number thus involved was never large nor could the converts have been enthusiastic; this method did not account for the large community in India by 1500. The more important type was the voluntary, in which class can be distinguished the individual, the group, and the mass conversion. There was a trickle of individuals, often of high caste, all through the Muslim period. Some doubtless came from conviction and others in the hope of high office. Another class was the group or tribal conversion. It might take the form of a caste group conversion, the caste usually having a tribal connection. This happened in the case of certain outcaste groups like the weavers, who became the Muslim *Momins*. Islam, with its brotherhood, its greater range of opportunity, and its association with authority, had obvious attractions for the disinherited Hindu groups. Other group conversions occurred with the martial castes of the north. Clan groups of Rajputs, for example, marched as it were with flags flying and drums beating into the Muslim camp. Just as they had formerly retained pre-Hindu habits, such as meat-eating, when admitted into Hinduism, they now carried their own customs and Hindu ritual into Islam. The same was true of the Jats and other tribes. Then comes the mass conversion, when a whole countryside changes its allegiance. This occurred in east Bengal. Here an animistic people with a lost allegiance to Buddhism had been depressed by a succeeding Brahmin dynasty. Islam came as a relief to these people who over two centuries added it to their animist traditions.

There were two chief agencies in this process apart from the soldier in the heat of the battle. The first were the *mullahs* or *maulanas*, the doctors of Muslim law. They corresponded to the rabbis of Judaism as being authorities of the law which regulated both civil and religious life, and they held a place comparable to the clergy of western Europe. They were not priests but expounders of

117 Portrait of an aged Mullah by Farrukh Beg (*c.* 1610)

118 The cultural impulse of the Indian Muslims came from Persia: this painting depicts 'Mehr Afruz entertaining Rustam in a garden pavilion' from the *Romance of Amir Hamzah*

the law which was sacred, and as such they had great influence. In the matter of conversion, however, they were not prominent, for they thought and spoke more in terms of punishments and rewards than appeals to the heart and conscience.

This latter work was performed by the *sufis* or Muslim devotees. They were an importation from Persia, where they represented a revolt from the legalism of the *maulanas* and the hard transcendentalism of early Islam. They appealed to the heart and fostered a religion of devotion. They settled in centres many of which have become places of pilgrimage and devotion, and are still in the hands of the descendants of the founders. Examples are the shrine of Nizam-ad-Din at Delhi and Salim Shah Chishti at Ajmir. They were organized into four orders, and attracted by their lives and then captivated by their teaching. They carried with them into India the tradition of Persian mysticism and they found answering echoes in Hindu thought. Theirs was a heart religion, a cultivation of the spirit within for ultimate union with God, and the boundary between their ideas and Hindu concepts of the self was sometimes very thin. Thus they fulfilled the double function of spreading Islam throughout the countryside – they 'charmed' while the *maulanas* 'denounced' – and formed a bridge between Hindu and Muslim thought and practice. They had probably much to do with the conversion of eastern Bengal to Islam. *Sufi* activities thus linked with the religious stirrings within Hindu society. In philosophy it was an age of commentators, but in Hindu religious practice the widespread *bhakti* devotional movement was proceeding. It was to be found all over India and preached the way to Realization by loving devotion to a deity, denouncing caste but not the family and teaching brotherhood and spiritual liberation. They had obvious affinities with the *sufis* and it is clear that each group was influenced by the other.

Culture and Social Structure

Behind the government and wars of the Turkish rulers, the forays of the Afghans, the preachings of the *sufis*, the cultural impulse of the Indian Muslims came from Persia. The principal members of the Muslim aristocracy, the Turks and Afghans, have not been noted as torchbearers of cultural light. The Turks, and to a lesser extent the Afghans, however, had been to school with Persia, then the main centre of cultural radiation in the Middle East, and now recovering from the Mongol devastation of the fourteenth century. The Turkish chiefs thus added a veneer of Persian manners and tastes to their tribal customs. The increase of the Persian percentage in this rather perplexing amalgam can be traced through the centuries. Thus a ruler like Mahmud of Ghazni in the eleventh century, while a fierce conqueror, a bigot, and an idol-smasher himself, was proud to attract to his court Persian poets and philosophers (like Albiruni) as well as theologians. In the late seventeenth century the visible Turkish element almost vanished from the Mughals except for their ferocity in the wars of succession. The Afghans were more tardy pupils, but the ensemble was reinforced by Persian migrants such as the Bahmani minister, Mahmud Gawan. We thus find that each Muslim court became a centre of Persian culture transmitted through a Turkish and Afghan lens and reflecting back in addition from the mirror of Hindu life. In time this exotic culture developed a strain of its own with a blend of Persian, Turkish, and Hindu elements, to become a distinctive type of Indo-Persian culture.

During the Turkish Delhi sultanate, these influences were

120 Painting portraying Timur and the first two rulers of the Moghul dynasty, Babur and Humayan

119 Babur receiving gifts on the birth of his eldest son in 1507, by Yaqub of Kashmir, from a manuscript copy of the *Memoirs of Babur*

concentrated in Delhi and radiated, if at all, through the media of the provincial governors. Ibn Batuta has recorded the magnificence of fourteenth-century Delhi, full of mosques, colleges, *sufi* centres, and enlivened by poets, philosophers, and men of letters. With the collapse of Delhi each succession state sought to make its court a smaller replica of the imperial model. It seemed as important for one of these kings to patronize learning and the arts as for an English politician to be interested in sport. The Bahmanis, in particular, had a pronounced foreign bias, entertaining not only the migrant Persian, but people from further west and from Europe itself. The most visible result of these tendencies is to be seen in architecture. From about 1350 in the Deccan and 1400 elsewhere provincial styles of Indo-Muslim architecture grew up round all the succession courts. The fifteenth century was a great age of Muslim embellishment all over India. While Delhi declined until the late fifteenth century, Jaunpur to the east produced a unique style with great propylons over entrance gateways, dominating massive mosques. In central and western India and the Deccan, in places like Ahmadabad, Mandu, Ahmadnagar, Bidar, and Kulbarga, these styles attained great variety and elegance. Though the palaces are ruined, the mosques and the great tombs have survived. Persian influence was strong and Muslim methods of construction, such as the true arch and the dome, predominate. But Hindu influence can also be traced, sometimes to a considerable degree. The pointed arch is often no more than a shaping of the stone beneath a Hindu-style transom; in the detailed work such things as stylized versions of temple bells and elephants' heads and trunks are common.

Each court had its coterie of literary men, poets, historians, wits, and dilettantes besides theologians. They depended on royal patronage in the form of gifts, pensions, and office, and it is relevant to our theme that this patronage was forthcoming. The Muslim flair for history was in evidence, so that the period, confused though it is, has a considerable documentation of contemporary history. In some places, notably in the Bengal and Deccan courts, there was interchange with Hindu *litterateurs*. Indeed, King Husain Shah of Bengal is said to have been the first royal patron of the Bengali language. Along with literature went the taste for painting, chiefly as frescoes on the walls of palaces or as miniatures. Little has survived but the state of the art in the later sixteenth century makes it clear that the Hindu tradition persisted. Music was also cultivated in a secular setting, suspect as it was to the Muslim orthodox. Muslim influence introduced changes into the *corpus* of the Indian classical tradition. Among the smaller arts calligraphy was highly prized by the Muslims and much care was bestowed on the lapidary art and the inset of semi-precious stones in buildings.

Muslim society, as it existed about 1500, consisted first of a large and very active class connected with the governments and armies. They were divided amongst themselves by tribalism (Turks, Afghans, and so on) and by personal rivalries bearing fruit in palace revolutions. But they had an underlying Muslim solidarity which enabled them to keep the Hindus at bay even while fighting amongst themselves. Then came a very small middle class of merchants, professionals, and government agents. Below them came a large class of peasants, artisans, and hangers-on. These were often of low-caste origin, people who had attached themselves to the ruling race like the villagers of east Bengal or the weavers of Banaras, but lacked the opportunity or ability to rise higher. The top class was spread thinly all over the country north of the River Kistna; the others in patches, some large and thick as in east Bengal, the Punjab, and Sind, others small and scattered all over the north. The material condition of the country is difficult to gauge because reports from different parts of the country differ so greatly. The north-west would appear to have been the least prosperous, perhaps because of continued wars after Timur's hammer-blow. In general those areas where trade and industry and cash crops supplemented agriculture were the wealthiest. The north suffered from unsettled conditions on the Iranian plateau. Bengal prospered with its textile trade with the East. Gujarat had its indigo, cotton, and trade with the Middle East. The Deccan kingdoms, for all their aristocratic conflicts, prospered on the proceeds of the cotton which grew largely undisturbed around them. The Hindu south was at this time a legend for prosperity, largely built up by Portuguese reports. It had the spice trade, both primary production and transit from the East, a flourishing textile industry, and also the luxury of a firm government which enabled the profits to accrue. The great temple towers of south India are an evidence of this prosperity for many Hindus, like fifteenth-century English wool

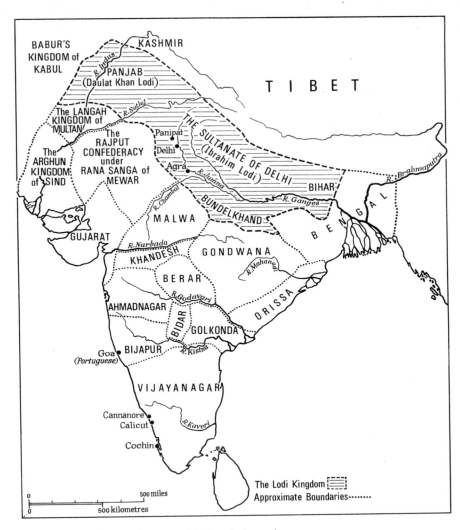

MAP 12   India on the eve of Babur's invasion

121 Late sixteenth-century painting of hunters carrying
a dead lioness

merchants, put much of their money into religious buildings. We
thus have a picture of an India in political turmoil and uncertainty
indeed, but also pulsating with much activity and creative vigour.
Confusion there certainly was, but India was waiting for the genius
who would unify her structure and canalize her energies. The great
achievement of these centuries was that the Muslims were now no
longer aliens in India and their culture a foreign one; they had
become a body in their own right with its own genius and they were
acclimatized as part of the Indian scene.

Nobody with these origins and in these circumstances could live
side by side with Hinduism for so long without feeling its influence.
So it was with Indian Islam, and it is precisely these influences which
have given Islam in India its special characteristics. While the
Muslims remained firm on the one God, idolatry, and caste, they
were influenced by Hindu delight in venerating holy men and the

122   Hunting scene from an Indian Muslim manuscript
of the sixteenth century

shrines of the saints. Caste was repudiated, but there was a strict division of class with a hereditary tinge. Many groups, openly or surreptitiously, retained Hindu customs after conversion. A Hindu spirit of live and let live crept in which, except at moments of great stress, made for the toleration of apathy if not of appreciation. The Hindus on their side were influenced by Islam more than they cared to admit. The *bhaktis* of the fourteenth and fifteenth century commonly denounced caste and promoted both monotheism and brotherhood. In 1500 Guru Nanak, the founder of the modern Sikh community, was doing this very thing. There was a coming together but no actual junction. The two bodies were too firmly rooted and too far apart for that; in social terms the immovable object of caste confronted the irresistible force of monotheism, brotherhood, and missionary zeal. Islam and Brahminism had reached a virtual deadlock, which they have, on the whole, maintained ever since.

The Trading Empires and Island Kingdoms of South East Asia

AILSA ZAINU'DDIN

Introduction

THE ISLAND WORLD of South East Asia straddles the sea route between China and India. For hundreds of years, at this busy cross-roads of world trade, the rhythm of life was controlled by monsoonal and trade winds which brought the sailing-ships and traders from Arabia, India, and China and then, in due season, took traders back to Arabia, India, or China. The busy seaports along the Straits of Malacca provided a meeting-place for traders of many nations, speaking many tongues, practising various religions and social customs.

Stretching along the Equator for 3,000 miles east to west, and about 2,000 miles from 20°N to 10°S are over 20,000 islands. At any given time the count is a bit uncertain as some of them, little more than rocky protuberances, have been known to appear or disappear as the result of volcanic activity. Less than 2,000 of these islands are inhabited, some are only sparsely settled and are poorly endowed with natural resources, but others are richly enough endowed to give a factual basis to the legend of the fabulous wealth of the Orient which lured the men of remote, far-distant Europe to brave unknown perils in search of the shortest route to such treasure.

Along with the Malay peninsula, which is linked to mainland Asia by the narrow Kra isthmus, these islands form the three modern nations of Indonesia, Malaysia, and the Philippines. The boundary-lines drawn between them are, to a large extent, the accident of more recent history. During the period with which we are concerned the whole area was loosely linked through trade while at the same time often divided by local rivalries. Some of those were personal or dynastic. Others arose from trade competition or from the conflicting interests of the agricultural hinterland and the coastal trading ports.

Because these islands are situated on and around the Equator they have very little seasonal variation. Although in the eastern and northern islands there are more clearly marked wet and dry seasons,

246

in the majority of the islands December to February is perhaps wetter and July to August rather hotter than the rest of the year, but there is little difference in the length of day and night or in the temperature throughout the year. The climate is moist and warm, rarely hotter than the high eighties or cooler than 70 °F. At sea-level the coastal areas provide an atmosphere not unlike a constant Turkish bath, relieved at times by a cooler sea breeze.

The wealth of these islands is derived from their fertile soil, which in turn is connected with their volcanic nature. Even today there are more active volcanoes here than in any other area. The island of

123 'A New Chart of the Isles of Java, Sumatra, and Borneo'

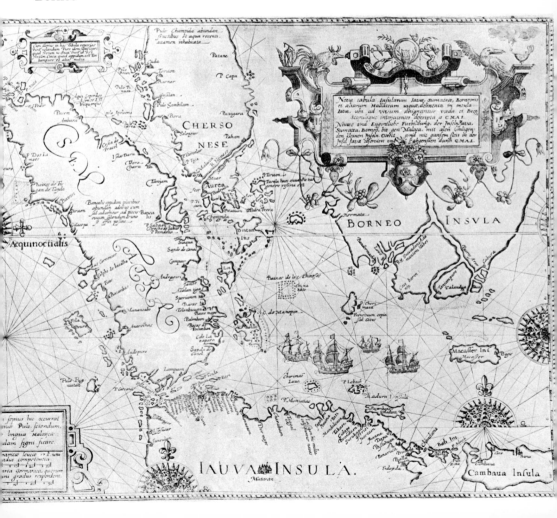

124   A ship from the eighth-century Buddhist sculptures
on the stupa of Borobudur, Java

Sumatra consists of one long mountain chain rising sharply from its
western coast while to the east a series of rivers, rising in these
mountains, runs down to the sea, entering it through mangrove
swamps, which are particularly extensive in the southern part of the
island. The other major islands – Java, Kalimantan (Borneo),
Sulawesi (Celebes), West Irian, Mindanao, and Luzon, as well as
the Malay archipelago – also have this combination of high mountains, main rivers, and, particularly in Kalimantan and West Irian,
extensive coastal mangrove swamps. Ternate, one of the five clove
islands of east Indonesia, is little more than a volcanic peak rising
from the ocean-bed. One of the early European arrivals described
with awe the way in which it threw out fire from its summit.

Most highly prized among the treasures of the Indies were the
spices which grew there and which, at that time, were found nowhere
else in the world – cloves and nutmeg. We are apt to dismiss them
lightly today as optional extras for stewing with apple or sprinkling
on junket, but in the fifteenth century, and indeed back to Roman
times, such spices provided more than flavour for food. They were

valued highly for their medicinal properties. Van Linschoten, a
sixteenth-century Dutch geographer, wrote of them in glowing
terms. Cloves strengthen the heart, liver, and stomach, he claimed.
They aid digestion and relieve fever or headache. Nutmeg and mace
comfort the brain, sharpen the memory, warm and strengthen the
stomach, relieve flatulence, and serve as a general preventive against
'cold diseases' in the head, brain, stomach, and liver. They were
also valued as ingredients in cosmetic preparations, particularly for
'making a sweet breath',[1] and were equally prized as preservatives
of food, combining the functions of the modern canning and
refrigeration industries.

Cloves are native to a group of five small islands off the west coast
of Halmahera in eastern Indonesia. For hundreds of years ships had
voyaged from Java or China in search of the 'nail incense' bartered
for cloth, foodstuffs, or porcelain by the local inhabitants. Nutmeg
and mace, one the inner core and the other the outer husk of the one
fruit, are native to a group of six even smaller islands further east
again in the Banda Sea, south of Ceram. Merchants from Java and

[1] J. H. van Linschoten, *Voyage*, vol. II, pp. 83–4, 86.

Makasar brought rice and coarse cloth to trade for the nutmegs. Both cloves and nutmegs were then brought back along the trade routes, some being sold in Java, some in the ports along the Malacca Straits, some being taken further afield to China, or to India and Arabia, from whence a small proportion found its way overland to the Levant, and thence to Europe, each sale and resale providing a margin of profit to the middleman who derived his livelihood from trade.

Although pepper was not limited to this area, the pepper of Sumatra and Sunda (west Java) drew Chinese traders to the islands, while the white sandalwood, found exclusively in Timor, and used not only for incense, but also medicinally, was highly valued by the Chinese. Records of Chinese contact with the islands of South East Asia go back to the first half of the fourth century A.D.[2] and from these it seems clear that trading relations with India and Arabia were also well established by the early years of the Christian era.

The islands were linked together by the regular ebb and flow of international trade, and the interinsular patterns of local trade. Some settlements on the larger islands were more closely linked with each other by sea routes than by land where mountains and jungle provided an effective barrier to transport. Early European explorers did not at first realize that Kalimantan and Sulawesi were two large islands but believed them to be two island groups.[3]

In Java also the island is divided into several natural regions separated by mountain ranges, so that travel by land is more difficult than by sea. Some of the archaeological discoveries made in Java, in particular the elaborate drainage system of the Dieng plateau monuments, dating from the eighth century A.D., suggest that the Javanese of that period had the engineering ability to undertake work as complex as highways. Even so, travel by water, including inland rivers, seems to have been more common for long distances and for transporting freight than travel by land through tropical jungles with their attendant wild life – tigers, elephants, rhinoceros, orang-outang, wild boars, and pythons.

Nevertheless, we do know that in Java, Sumatra, and Bali, and possibly also in Sulawesi, there developed inland kingdoms based primarily upon agriculture. As far back as written and archaeological evidence can take us, there were terraced ricefields, ploughed by

[2] See W. P. Groeneveldt, *Historical Notes on Indonesia and Malaya Compiled from Chinese Sources.*
[3] See T. Pires, *The Suma Oriental*, vol. I, pp. 224–6 and M. A. P. Meilink-Roelofsz, *Asian Trade and European Influence*, p. 85.

buffaloes, planted out by hand, weeded, and finally harvested delicately, blade by blade, so that the rice spirit would not be offended. A whole complicated system of dikes and terraces was built up to follow the contours of the land and to allow for the constant steady irrigation of the plots of land while the rice seedlings were growing to maturity. Even more intricate and skilful are the wet ricefields of the plains, providing the right balance of earth and water to give the best environment for the growth of the rice.

The development of such irrigation systems, even when they depend on rivers and natural rainfall rather than on artificial water storage as they did in parts of mainland South East Asia, requires a high degree of co-operation between those engaged in agriculture, and would seem to presuppose some degree of centralization and bureaucratic control. That this is not necessarily so can be seen from northern Luzon where there are terraced ricefields without any evidence of centralized government.[4] In Java there did develop various centralized kingdoms, self-sufficient as far as the necessities of life were concerned, linked with the trading network of the area

[4] *See* F.-C. Cole, *The Peoples of Malaysia*, pp. 37, 131.

125   Terraced rice-fields in Java

126 Stupas at Borobudur, a famous Buddhist temple of
enormous size in central Java, which combines elements of
both Indonesian and Hindu artistic traditions in its design
and decoration

as exporters of foodstuffs to less fertile regions and importers of
luxury goods to enhance the splendour of court life. At the height
of their power such kingdoms were able to claim authority over the
cities of the trade routes. In periods of decline they were still an
important element in the power politics of the area.

When we ask the question: 'Why did the Europeans discover
Asia when Asians made no attempt to discover Europe?', we may
seek an explanation in terms of the questing spirit of Europe, and
the technological advances of the Age of Discovery, but we should
also consider the extent to which the Asian world was already
self-sufficient. There was an abundance of rice. The population
explosion of the nineteenth century had not yet upset the balance
between people and productivity. Even in the eastern islands, which
depended upon imported rice, there was a sufficiency of sago. There
was a rich variety of fruits and vegetables, fish and flesh, and the
spices with which to preserve and flavour them. Cotton and silk
could be obtained from India and China; the woollen cloths of
Europe were unsuited to the tropical climate. For the poorer folk
there were local spun cottons or, in the eastern islands, bark cloth,

and, as the early explorers noted, there were many areas where clothes, quite sensibly considering the climate, were reduced to an absolute minimum. Timber for building houses and ships, palm leaves for weaving thatch, matting, or sails, and resin for caulking boats or for illumination were all available. Gold and other metals, along with precious stones, were abundant and were extensively used for tools, weapons, and ornamentation as well as for exchange. Asia had no incentive to discover Europe; even the good Muslim of Asia had no need to travel any further west than to Mecca, the Holy City, while the climate of Europe was too cold to attract those used to tropical warmth. Europeans, on the other hand, were lured east to search for spices and gold, the exotic treasures of the Orient which had no counterpart in Europe itself.

What kind of a world did these first arrivals find when finally they reached Malacca? And how did the local inhabitants view the arrival of this hirsute, travel-worn band of traders from an unknown corner of the world? Most of our evidence is drawn from the accounts of the early arrivals who may not always have fully understood what they were describing. Their accounts were also primarily concerned with the trading world and the trading prospects for fellow Europeans so that we have a clearer picture of the seaports and coastal principalities than we do of the more shadowy inland kingdoms.

Economy and Trade

In the fertile river valleys of the Brantas and Solo, which rise in the mountains of southern Java, then flow north and east until they reach the sea opposite the island of Madura, archaeologists have unearthed the bones of Solo Man, believed to have lived there at least 35,000 years ago. Near the town of Trinul, not far from the River Solo, were found the remains of an even older upright ape man (*Pithecanthropus Erectus*) known as Java Man, older than his 'relative', China Man. It seems likely that these islands were the home of some of the earliest known humans, although we know very little more about them than that they existed.

For hundreds, perhaps thousands, of years, sedentary agriculture has been practised in this region, and over this same period migrants from the south-east corner of the Asian continent found their way to

253

the islands, probably in canoes hollowed out from tree-trunks. In some of the more isolated areas of Indonesia, Malaysia, and the Philippines the descendants of Stone Age and later Bronze Age arrivals still preserve a culture and economy closely resembling that of their remote ancestors, while even in the areas which have had closer and more continuous contact with the outside world, some common elements suggest the existence of an indigenous Malay culture capable of adapting and modifying influences which came from overseas.

Before there is any evidence of contact with either India or China there is evidence of communities with a pattern of agriculture based either on shifting dry cultivation or on irrigated ricefields, and owning domestic animals and locally made metal implements. The coastal and river communities were also skilled in fishing, and the typical Malay house was one built on piles either to raise it above tide level near the shore, or to provide protection against wild animals or enemies. The simplest of these could quite easily be put together in a day to provide shelter for the evening. In areas of more settled agriculture and so of more permanent village settlements elaborate local variations of this style of architecture have been developed, with piles made from tree-trunks, floors from boards rather than split bamboo, and high, sweeping distinctive roofs which served the practical purpose of providing an upward draught which not only rid the houses of cooking smoke but also circulated the air most efficiently. Such houses are found today in Nias off Sumatra, among the Bataks and Karo Bataks of north Sumatra, and among the Toradja of central Sulawesi.

By the late fifteenth century there were, as there still are today, two main kinds of indigenous agriculture practised in the islands of South East Asia. One was sedentary, the other shifting. The former, usually regarded as typical of the area, is represented by the terraced ricefields of Java, Bali, and Lombok; enclaves in central and north Sumatra; Makasar and Menado in Sulawesi; parts of Kalimantan and the mountains of northern Luzon. Even today in modern Indonesia, where this wet-rice cultivation has been extended to its limits, it still occupies only about 11 per cent of the total area of the country.

The shifting agriculture practised throughout the greater part of

127 Traditional Minangkabau house with high, sweeping
roofs which help the circulation of air

South East Asia called for a considerable degree of co-operation
within the tribe or clan. Such agriculture is known by various names
– swidden farming, slash-and-burn, slash-and-dibble, or *ladang*
cultivation – but essentially the technique is the same whether
practised in north Sumatra, the islands of the Philippines, or places
in between, as indeed it still is in many of them today.

The tribe chose a site for agriculture and then felled a large tree,
chopping it in such a way that, as it crashed to the ground, it brought
with it a number of smaller trees and undergrowth, thus clearing as
wide a swathe as possible. The felled trees were then fired. The
action of the fire and the subsequent second burning off after an
interval of several days, released more rapidly the nutrients which,
in the normal cycle of the tropical jungle, decay slowly and thus
enrich the soil.

Having cleared sufficient ground the villagers then planted crops,
using a sharp-pointed instrument (the dibble) and first planting

255

fast-growing shade trees to protect the young plants grown beneath them, then a variety of crops, including rice, thus paralleling the normal variety of plant life to be found in the jungle. Within two or three years at the most, as the yield from this plot decreased, the group moved on and began again the process of clearing jungle, while letting the former area revert to jungle again. Such a method of agriculture is only possible in a sparsely populated area with plenty of land available, nor does it provide much more than subsistence for the villagers. If the cultivated land is not allowed to return to jungle soon enough it can revert to savanna grassland. Unprotected from the tropical sun and without the enrichment provided by the slowly decaying vegetable matter of the steamy jungle, it may produce little else except rank grass.

Such semi-nomadic people were also, of necessity, hunters, not only to protect themselves from the wild animals of the jungle but

128 Marco Polo, who spent five months in Sumatra in 1292, leaving Venice for the Far East

also to provide meat for their diet. Their most distinctive weapon was the blowpipe, skilfully constructed from bamboo and fitted with a poison-tipped dart. Within a range of 50 feet it is very accurate, and particularly deadly to smaller animals, but even at longer range it could be effective, and, because it is noiseless, it does not disturb a grazing herd. Fishing too was often aided by the use of a special drug to stupefy the fish.

Marco Polo, who spent five months in Sumatra in 1292, reported that the Sumatran hill tribes lived 'like beasts', eating every kind of flesh, clean or unclean, including human flesh and because of this he and his company erected fortifications to protect themselves. Nevertheless, these islanders also traded with the strangers.[5]

From early times the jungle products of Sumatra provided important items of trade, gathered by the local people and taken downstream to the coast either by rafts made of bamboo lashed together whose component parts might also be sold on arrival, or in dug-out canoes, or even on the heads of carriers. The Chinese, whose records of trade and tribute from the area go back to the middle of the first century A.D., sought camphor, which they called 'dragon's brain perfume' but which was actually the resin from a particular tree; dragon's blood, another resin, bright red in colour and used for dyeing; and ambergris, or dragon's spittle, which is what they believed this to be. They also sought ivory and rhinoceros horn, the latter valued as an antidote against poison. Marco Polo reported an abundance of highly valued products 'aloe wood, brazil, ebony, spikenard, and many sorts of spice' which were exported from Sumatra to China in the late thirteenth century.[6] Tome Pires, writing over three centuries later, listed the products in which the Portuguese were interested: 'gold in great quantities'; camphor; pepper; silk; benzoin, an aromatic resin; aloes, a bitter medicinal herb; honey and wax; pitch; sulphur; cotton; different kinds of rattan canes; as well as a variety of foodstuffs, including wine and durian 'certainly lovelier and more delicate than all the other fruits'.[7] Perhaps the smell of durian, which even modern enthusiasts liken to bad drains, seemed less offensive in a period when all drains were malodorous.

Sedentary agriculture, associated with wet-rice growing (*sawah*), produced sufficient surplus crops to develop division of labour

[5] *See The Travels of Marco Polo*, pp. 226–7, translated by R. E. Latham.   [6] *Ibid.*, p. 225.
[7] T. Pires, *op. cit.*, vol. I, pp. 136–7.

within the villages, division of classes whereby the villages sustained a largely unproductive aristocratic class, and the development of specialized arts and crafts, not only at village level but also in the *kraton*, the palace-city of the ruler of the kingdom. It also placed a premium upon co-operation and harmony between villagers and between villages as an economic necessity where neighbouring communities depended upon a common water-supply and an interconnected irrigation system.

In these centralized kingdoms the officials of the ruler supervised the collection and marketing of the surplus rice crop and other foods and goods for export. The villagers, whose main connection with the court was through the elected headman or perhaps through an occasional glimpse of the monarch as he went hunting or made ceremonial visits to outlying districts, lived in relative isolation, each village largely a self-contained unit. They owed both duty and tribute to the ruler. In time of war, able-bodied men could be called up to serve as soldiers, or else labour services might be required for the building of temples or shrines, such as the magnificent Borobudur,[8] in central Java, still standing more than 1,000 years later.

Unlike the serf of medieval Europe, the villager was not bound to the soil. He was free to move from one area to another, although such freedom was rarely exercised except in times of natural disaster or warfare, because the strong ties of custom bound him to his birthplace. Within the villages, by the fourteenth century and probably earlier, there was some degree of division of labour. Legislation of the kingdom of Madjapahit (1293–1400?) speaks of ferry-men, butchers, noodle-makers, lime-burners, bleachers and dyers of textiles, and toddy-tappers. The last were the equivalent of the local brewer. They collected the sap from a particular kind of palm tree to ferment it into a palm wine powerful enough to be the downfall of many an unsuspecting European when first he made its acquaintance.

Dependent in part upon this agricultural hinterland both for trade goods and in some cases also for foodstuffs, were the trading ports of the coastal regions, particularly those on either side of the Straits of Malacca and along the north Java coast. Tome Pires, in his *Suma Oriental*, lists eighteen kingdoms and eleven 'lands' along the coastline of Sumatra; two kingdoms – Sunda (west Java) and

[8] F. A. Wagner, *Indonesia, The Art of an Island Group*, pp. 92, 95, 97, 99, 114–16.

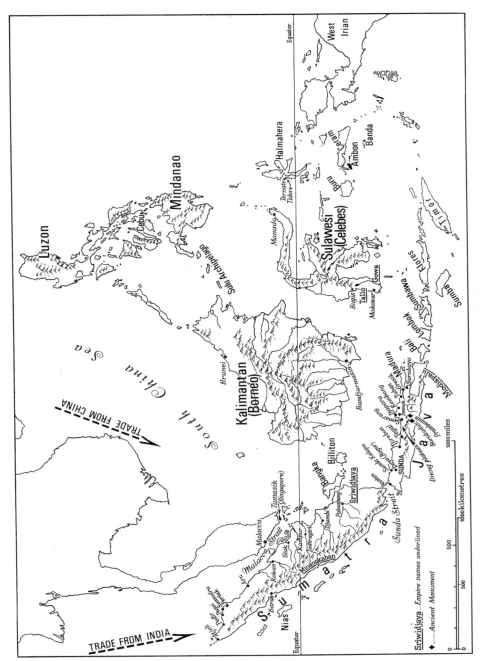

MAP 13   The trading Empires and Island Kingdoms of South East Asia

129   Malacca, described in the sixteenth century as 'from below the wind to above the wind . . . famous as a very great city'

Java – in Java, with six ports in the former and another eighteen in the latter; and at least twenty other ports of varying sizes stretching from Bali to the islands of Sulu and Luzon; with several others along the coast of Kalimantan and the shores of mainland Burma, Thailand, and Malaya.[9] They included the entrepôt of Malacca, whose chronicler in the *Malay Annals*, described it as 'from below the wind to above the wind . . . famous as a very great city'.[10] From all accounts it was at least as large as any comparable European city of the time, possibly larger. Tome Pires listed sixty-one different 'nations' trading there,[11] gave the strength of the army as 100,000 men-at-arms,[12] and spoke of the Gujarat population as numbering 1,000 residents and 4,000–5,000 transients,[13] concluding that it was 'a city for merchandise, fitter than any other in the world.[14]

Prior to the rise of Malacca there had been other great trading cities along the shores of the Malacca Straits. From the ninth to the twelfth

⁹ T. Pires, *op. cit.*, vol. I, pp. 135–6, 166, *passim*.
¹⁰ D. F. Lach and C. Flaumenhaft (eds), *Asia on the Eve of Europe's Expansion*, p. 86.
¹¹ T. Pires, *op. cit.*, vol. II, p. 268.   ¹² *Ibid.*, p. 279.
¹³ *Ibid.*, pp. 254–5.   ¹⁴ *Ibid.*, p. 286.

centuries the kingdom of Sriwidjaya, centred at modern Palembang, had exacted tribute from a large area of Sumatra, Java, Malaya, and southern Kalimantan. Far enough south to control both the Straits of Malacca and of Sunda, it was renowned as far afield as China and India.

By the late thirteenth century its power had declined. Marco Polo, when he passed that way, made no mention of it at all. New rivals had arisen to the north, and the power of the inland kingdom of Madjapahit outrivalled it in the south. These coastal kingdoms depended for their wealth upon the trade which they could attract and the port dues and other levies which they could claim from foreign traders. Sometimes the ruler and members of his bureaucracy were also involved in trade for which they provided the capital. Usually one port was the main entrepôt for a particular area, maintaining a lead over its rivals, demanding tributes from its subordinates, and controlling, to the best of its ability, the pirate states which grew up on the fringes of each sphere of influence.

It should perhaps be pointed out that the distinction between piracy and legitimate trade was a very fine one. Magellan's fleet, for example, only hesitated to capture a rival ship when the odds seemed to be in the rival's favour. D'Albuquerque's conquest of Malacca was basically an act of piracy – accepted when it proved to be successful! For that matter the distinction between the royal compulsion exercised over passing ships to call at a given port and pay dues for so doing was not so very different in principle from straight-out plunder on the high seas.

In the last resort the relative power of these harbour-principalities depended less on the alliances they made, or the rejection of vassaldom, but on the volume of trade, and hence the amount of wealth, which could be attracted to their harbour. Malacca in 1500 was at the height of her power and attracted traders 'because the King of Malacca dealt kindly and reasonably with them',[15] lowering the duties on merchandise and giving foreign merchants some degree of jurisdiction over matters which concerned them, particularly trade matters.

In the east the five clove and six nutmeg islands formed a similar pattern of trade, though on a smaller scale. The inhabitants of the smaller islands, with no port large enough for the junks and trading

[15] *Ibid.*, p. 246.

ships, brought their crops in canoes to the central ports, Ternate in the clove islands, Banda in the nutmeg islands. In some cases they also brought trading goods from further east, including bird of paradise plumes from West Irian which were highly valued as ornamentation by the Arabs. The larger islands supplied foodstuffs to the port areas. The staple diet of the area was sago although imported rice came from Java.

International trade repeated this pattern on a larger scale. To the trading ports of north Java, Sumatra and, above all, Malacca, came junks from China, with raw silk, porcelain, sugar, ginger, musk, some metal goods, and lacquer-work as their main cargo. There they met merchants travelling on Indian ships, particularly the traders from Gujarat, Coromandel, and Bengal, but also Arabs who had transhipped at Indian ports, Persians, and others from west Asia. The Indian traders brought cotton cloth, both coarse and fine, tapestries, wall-hangings, and various preserves and condiments; from Arabia and Persia came rosewater, dates, opium, incense, and carpets. They traded with each other and with the merchants of the archipelago who in their turn made the voyage to India, to Arabia, or to southern China. Much of this trade was in goods of small bulk and high value – 'splendid and trifling'[16] objects whose rarity made the profit on them tremendous, but the trade itself was more than small-scale peddling of luxury items. Foodstuffs, particularly rice, were bulky items with not very much margin of profit. Perhaps for that reason, as well as because of Malacca's dependence on food imports, no import duties were charged on foodstuffs and only the customary gifts were required of ships' captains. Elephants were shipped from Sumatra to India, an equivalent of today's heavy machinery, for they were used to do the work of cranes in shifting cargo, as well as for transport, both on ceremonial occasions and during warfare. They were also used in Malacca to shift cargo from ships to the warehouses rented out to merchants.

The 'thin gold thread of trade'[17] stretched tenuously across the ocean, and, in many of the larger ports, settlements of foreigners were established, each with a small nucleus of fairly permanent immigrants and a large number of temporary residents waiting for the next favourable wind to take them further on or else back to their home country, trading from port to port as they went, utilizing differences

[16] J. C. Vanheur, *Indonesian Trade and Society.*   [17] *Ibid.*

130 Javanese ships, from an engraving by de Bry. The one in the foreground has slaves rowing below deck, and carries soldiers above

in exchange rates and scarcity of goods in different areas to profit by their trade. Silk from China was valued for its rarity by the nobility of South East Asia; cotton from India was valued for its rarity by the Chinese nobility. So the whole complex and interrelated movement of trade linked the island world of South East Asia with the Asian mainland and bound together the otherwise isolated island groups.

Social and Ethical Systems

Two elements have shaped the social and ethical systems of South East Asia. One is *adat* or customary law and tradition, the other is religion, and as both have interacted it is not always easy to distinguish elements of *adat* from elements of religion in some areas. The period which we are considering, round about 1500, was something of a watershed in the history of religion in the area as Islam, represented by merchants from the first century of its existence,

263

began to spread as the predominant religion, at least along the coastal areas, in the inland kingdoms of Sumatra and Java.

The arrival of European Christians seems to have accelerated this process, except in the northern islands of the Philippines. Elsewhere Islam replaced or amalgamated with the older Hindu-Buddhist religious beliefs, except in Bali, where Hindu-Buddhists from Java sought refuge, and except in the areas which retained an even older religious tradition, a blend of animism, or spirit worship, and ancestor worship.

This was the original religion of the Malay settlers in the archipelago and peninsula. All things, animate and inanimate, had their own life spirit, or *semangat*. In a person the *semangat* dwelt especially in the head. The early Europeans warned their fellows that to touch a person's head was a grave insult likely to lead to the death of the offender. Even today it might well lead to trouble, for, just as the Christian religion retains its Christmas trees and Easter eggs from a pagan past, so many of these earlier beliefs still survive. Harvest ceremonies widely practised even in Muslim and Christian areas go back to this earlier animist belief that the rice spirit must be placated if the fields are to yield a good harvest.

In some areas animism was associated either with ritual cannibalism

131   Chinese merchants in the sixteenth century

or with head-hunting. There was in fact a world of difference between this kind of cannibalism, associated with the acquisition of the *semangat* of one's enemy, the literal enactment of a sacramental meal, and the cannibalism proposed and only narrowly averted by the Dutch crew of Captain Bontekoe's ship, burnt in mid-ocean in 1619. The men took to the sea in a lifeboat and were almost driven by lack of food to eat the boys had they not, on the last day of the crew's ultimatum to the captain, sighted land.[18]

It was likely, although not inevitable, that, along with the exchange of goods at cities on the trade routes, there should also be an exchange of ideas. This depended to some extent upon the size of the cultural gap between traders and islanders. There was no communication at all in the 'silent trade' practised between some Chinese merchants and the more primitive islanders of Kalimantan and the Philippines. The Chinese would beat gongs to announce their arrival. The islanders would bring goods for barter, leave them on the shore and then retire. The Chinese would put alongside them the goods they offered in return and, if the islanders were satisfied, they would take these goods and withdraw leaving the Chinese to collect the island products and, in their turn, withdraw. Here, when the gap between levels of culture was considerable, there was little influence either way, especially as the culturally superior power lacked any missionary zeal.

Indeed, Chinese influence throughout the island area seems to have been remarkably small considering the long period of contact. This may perhaps be because the majority of Chinese merchants came from southern China, which itself was part of the Outer rather than the Middle Kingdom, while the merchants were not members of the cultured classes, the traditional transmitters of Chinese civilization and learning. Nor were foreign traders or even ambassadors and tribute-bearers encouraged to visit China itself or to stay long if they did. The Chinese seem to have had little interest in the barbarian world apart from the trade products it offered and the tribute it paid. One exception to this, the seven voyages of Cheng Ho (1405–33), established Chinese suzerainty in South East Asia. Cheng Ho voyaged as far afield as the coast of Africa and the Red Sea. If these voyages had been followed up with merchant colonies supported from the mainland, the colonialism of Europe could well

[18] W. Y. Bontekoe, *Memorable Description of the East Indies Voyage 1618–25*, pp. 52–4.

have been forestalled by that of China. Instead, after the death of Cheng Ho, strong civil service pressure on the Ming court led the Chinese Empire to withdraw from southern expansion, although, as previously, Chinese merchants continued to trade, and sometimes to settle in South East Asia.[19]

Indian influence seems to have been much greater. It was seen most strongly in the rise of Hindu-Buddhist kingdoms in the archipelago and the spread of these two religions at least at court level. The two were never as clearly distinguished in South East Asia as they were on the Indian sub-continent, and they blended with elements of the older animist beliefs.

Colonial historians, over-estimating the power and influence of the colonist, and seeing in early Sumatran and Javanese history a parallel to later colonial empires, have described the spread of Indian influence as if the initiative came entirely from the Indian side. Early Indian nationalist historians tended to accept much the same interpretation, although for rather different reasons. They spoke of 'Greater India' in which Indian adventurers either seized power and carved out kingdoms for themselves, or else married into royal families as the road to power. It could equally well be argued that Indonesian rulers themselves took the initiative in inviting Brahmin priests to their courts. They were then in a better position to make treaties with other Hindu-Buddhist powers in India or elsewhere in the archipelago. We can trace the extent of such Indian influence by the spread of Sanskrit writing, the prerogative of the Brahmin priest, throughout the archipelago, as far east as Sulawesi and as far north as parts of the Philippines. Tome Pires mentions on several occasions the Hindu-Buddhist areas where wives flung themselves on the funeral pyre of their aristocratic husband.

For the ruler the concept of god-king was an important one in Hindu-Buddhist teaching and one which must have encouraged the island rulers to embrace the new faith. On the ruler rested the responsibility of maintaining the cosmic order and the balance and harmony which marked a truly prosperous kingdom. He did this by fulfilling the rituals and ceremonies prescribed. The *kraton* or palace of the ruler was not only the centre of government but also of religious rites. It was the cultural centre of the kingdom and within its walls was a miniature city made up of the ruler's family, usually quite an

[19] C. P. Fitzgerald, *A Concise History of East Asia*, pp. 75–8. 266

extensive one because polygamy was very often practised by ruler
and nobility; the priests, both Hindu and Buddhist, as well as those
coming from an older tradition, who guarded the family shrines of the
ancestors; the royal attendants, court officials, and bureaucrats; and
the court craftsmen – the makers of the semi-sacred *kris* or ceremonial sword with its wickedly curved blade and gold inlay; the
makers of the wax-impregnated, hand-designed cotton *batik* cloths
with designs worn exclusively by the royal family and incorporating
not only the stylized patterns and imagery of Hindu-Buddhist art
but also the older symbols associated with the rice cycle; and the court
musicians, who played the *gamelan* in accompaniment to court
dances and *wajang* or shadow puppet plays.

Although many of the Hindu-Buddhist stories and legends were
woven into the court dances and *wajang*, as well as into the court
literature, some scholars believe that the *wajang* were pre-Hindu
and were linked with an invocation of the ancestral spirits. Certainly
the *wajang*, even in modern Indonesia, is more than a performance or

132 *Wajang-golek* dolls

entertainment. For its Javanese audience it has a semi-religious connotation and plays an important role in moral education.

Islam had been known in South East Asia since the first century of its establishment. There is evidence of a settlement of Arab traders at Baros, the camphor port on the north-west coast of Sumatra, as early as A.D. 674, not quite sixty years after the flight from Mecca to Medina, which marks for Muslims the beginning of the Islamic calendar, but it was another 600 years before there was any record of Muslim kingdoms, the first of which was established on Sumatra's north-east coast. During the eleventh and twelfth centuries Islamic kingdoms were already being established in parts of India, and in 1292 Marco Polo reported that 'owing to contact with Saracen merchants' the city of Ferlec (Perlak) in north-west Sumatra was already Muslim, in contrast to the 'nasty and brutish'[20] villagers of the surrounding areas.

The *ummat Islam*, the Islamic community, was born in the trading cities of Arabia, and then spread along the trade routes to India and Sumatra. With the conversion in the early fifteenth century of the ruler of Malacca, himself a fugitive from Hindu-Buddhist Palembang, the spread of Islam received a new impetus. By 1500 there were

[20] Marco Polo, *op. cit.*, pp. 225, 227.

Muslim harbour-principalities not only along the east coast of Sumatra, but also at Demak on the north Java coast; in Brunei, north Kalimantan; Buru, west of the Banda islands; Ternate and Tidore, in the clove islands; and Sulu and Mindanao in the Philippines. It was also at about this time that the Sumatran inland kingdom of Minangkabau became Muslim. Within the following century Islam also became firmly established in west Java, south Kalimantan, Makasar (in south Sulawesi), and along the rest of the north Java coast, from whence, by the early seventeenth century it finally penetrated to inland east and central Java.

The spread of Islam was facilitated by the development of the *sufi* mystical brotherhoods among Muslim traders. Each *sufi* group usually took with it its own religious functionary as leader of the mystical rites, although Islam, in contrast with Hindu-Buddhism and Christianity, has no separate priesthood. The development of Muslim mysticism made it easier for this new religion to blend with the mystical elements of older Hindu-Buddhist and animist beliefs, specially in Java, where they seem to have been stronger. At the same time, for the harbour-principalities, engaged in a struggle for power against the older inland states, the new faith served as a rallying-point. Where the older Hindu-Buddhist belief was linked to a hierarchical settled agricultural society, the Islamic religion gave more responsibility to the individual believer. It was not left to a god-king and priestly caste to take the responsibility for the salvation

134   Javanese *wajang* puppets

of the kingdom but it was the individual as such who had to accept and act upon the Five Pillars of Islam – the affirmation of faith in One God and Mehemmed as His Prophet; prayer performed at five specific times each day and publicly each Friday; the giving of alms to the poor; the observation of the month-long fast of Ramadan; and, for those who could afford to do so, the pilgrimage to Mecca.

Islam was just as much a rallying-point among Muslim traders, faced, during the sixteenth century, with the new challenge of Christianity as represented by the arrival of traders and missionaries from Portugal and Spain. With the conquest of Malacca by the Portuguese in 1511, rival trading centres attracted Muslim traders – Atjeh (1515–1641); Banten (1526–1687); Makasar (1540–1667); and Bandjarmasin (about 1677).

As in contemporary Europe, the religion of the state or principality was determined by the religion of the ruler. The *Malay Annals*, commissioned by Sultan Ala'u'd-din Ri'ayat Shah of Malacca, records the miraculous conversion of his predecessor, and adds that, not only did the king and his chiefs embrace Islam but that every citizen of Malacca, whatever his status, 'was commanded by the king to do likewise'.[21]

Conversions to Christianity were made, not among Muslims, but among some animist tribes. Indeed, Magellan's conversion of the King of Zzubu (Cebu) and mass baptism of 800 of his subjects was followed by a request from the queen to give her a wooden image of the Virgin and Child, which later explorers discovered being used in traditional rain-making ceremonies so that it had quite literally been 'put in the place of the idols'. The mass baptism ceremony was preceded by the statement that they should not become Christians simply from fear or to please the new arrivals, although 'those who became Christians would be more loved and better treated than the others' and furthermore, on the instructions of his king, if they did become Christians Magellan 'would leave them the arms which the Christians use'. When these arms proved ineffective against a neighbouring rival in the battle in which Magellan himself was killed, the King of Cebu was less impressed by this new form of magic and was prepared to plot against the rest of the crew.[22]

Over against these religious influences, to some extent modified by them but also in other ways hostile to them, stood the local *adat*, the

[21] *Malay Annals*, pp. 53–4.
[22] *The First Voyage Round the World by Magellan*, pp. 88, 93, 103.

135 Wax-impregnated, hand-designed, cotton *batik*
material, with *Parang Kusumo* (fish variation) pattern

customary law and tradition of the different regions. Although such
adat varied from group to group, there were some common elements
occurring in varying forms. One of these is represented by the Dayak
long-house, where one village lives under the roof of a long-house
raised on piles. This resembles the *barangay* group of the Philippines, which, in some cases, traced their ancestry back to a single
ship arriving from overseas. The *adat* house of Minangkabau with its
unswept, buffalo-horn roofs, is the home of the descendants of a
common ancestress. Quite widespread, too, is the common sleeping-
house for all unmarried men of a village, adolescents as yet unmarried,
divorcees or widowers, and strangers.

The pile house was also typical in communities found throughout
the area. In fishing villages the piles served to raise the houses above
flood-tide level. Further inland the houses on piles served as protection against wild animals and provided for a greater circulation of air
than at ground-level. In some river areas the pile house became, by a
fairly simple process of evolution, a houseboat among a village of
houseboats. Perhaps the evolution was in fact the other way round.

The status of women seems to have been higher in the *adat* of

271

various districts than that traditionally accorded to women by certain of the higher religions. The *adat* of Minangkabau, in conflict with the patrilineal emphasis of Islam, has remained matrilineal in inheritance, so that the daughter inherits from her mother rather than the son from his father, and this pattern is repeated in the *adat* of Negri Sembilan, on the Malay peninsula, which was colonized by Minangkabau settlers probably some time during the fourteenth or fifteenth century. In Minangkabau the husband is an outsider who visits his wife and who lives with her in her family home but who obtains no rights of his own there. He retains higher status as the son in his mother's family. In Java, descent from the female line was of considerable importance in establishing the legitimacy of a ruler's claim, and throughout the archipelago marriage alliances between rulers made daughters, particularly beautiful ones, a valuable asset. At a lower level of society women sellers in the streets of Malacca and waterways of Brunei are mentioned by early European arrivals. The dowry and rights of women in marriage were also preserved, which was a counterbalance to the widespread practice of polygamy. At the same time, particularly in east Indonesia and the Philippines, early European visitors warned of the jealousy exhibited by some rulers concerning their wives, who were kept secluded from strangers. These were Muslim rulers, so it is hard to know whether this was a matter arising from earlier *adat*, from religion, or simply because of the reputation of the new arrivals. Certainly, there was potential conflict inevitable between the upholders of the *adat* and the traditional aristocracy, and the supporters of the new religion, forming a new élite.

One final point to be considered when looking at the social system which developed in this area is the question of language.[23] With the exception of the languages of north Halmahera and Papua, all the languages of the area belong to the Malayo-Polynesian group. Malay, the language of the peninsula and of the adjoining coastal area of Sumatra, is also the language of coastal Kalimantan, penetrating inland along some of the river systems. Small enclaves round the perimeter speak the language of south Sulawesi, a tribute to the activity of the Buginese pirates and settlers. Only inland are the languages of Kalimantan predominant.

The languages of Java and Bali have been influenced by Hindu-

[23] *See* D. G. E. Hall, *Atlas of South-East Asia*, pp. 28–9.

Buddhist traditions. Tome Pires reported that the Malays were a haughty race, but that they had learnt this haughtiness from the Javanese, adding 'and that it may be known there is no greater pride than in Java, there are two languages, one for the nobles and the other for the people' in which even the names of common objects differ.[24] By the seventeenth century at least four levels of language had developed, one reserved for addressing the sultan, and the same is true of the Sundanese language of west Java and of the Bali-Sasak languages.

Malay was the lingua franca for the whole archipelago and peninsula. It could be understood from Persia to the Philippines. For this again the kingdoms of Sriwidjaya and Malacca, both centred on the area to which this language was native, were largely responsible. Tome Pires commented that, often, in Malacca itself eighty-four languages were spoken, every one distinct, and that in the archipelago from Singapore to Maluku (the Moluccas) there were at least forty known languages. This Malay lingua franca has become the national language of modern Indonesia as well as of Malaysia.

[24] T. Pires, *op. cit.*, vol. I, p. 199.

136   Manilla in 1616

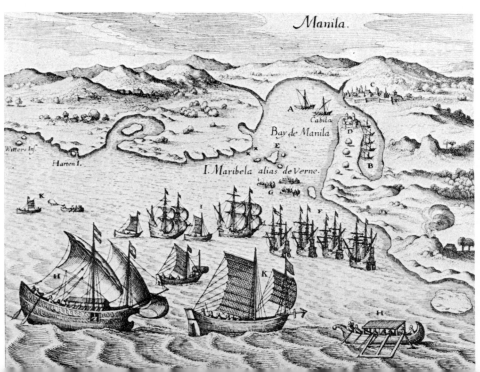

In Indonesia particularly, this national language has been a strong uniting factor, more so than in Malaya, with its large immigrant groups from China and India, or the Philippines, which were on the periphery of trade. In neither Indonesia nor Malaya has it been superseded by any of the immigrant tongues.

Political Organization

There seem to have been three main types of political organization in South East Asia round about 1500 – the villages, the smallest political unit and a common pattern of organization throughout the whole archipelago and peninsula; the inland kingdoms, already in the process of disintegration; and the harbour principalities, often owing some sort of allegiance to a larger kingdom or empire, although as the power of the harbour-principality waxed and that of the empires waned, such allegiance became increasingly a nominal one.

The tribe or village was the basic unit, linked either with shifting or sedentary agriculture on the one hand, or with fishing on the other. Even when princedoms or wider kingdoms came into being, these seem to have been superimposed upon the villages, which retained their essential identity in much the same way as the villages of rural Europe have done. A number of villages might belong to the same *adat* or language group, or might owe allegiance to the one ruler, or belong to a loose confederation of villages, yet each retained its own essential homogeneity.

137 Part of the Hindu temple complex at Prambanan in Java

Within the village the chief functionary was the village head, either elected from among the elders and members of the leading families or else appointed by hereditary right. The leading families were usually those who could claim descent from the founding fathers of the village, or, in the case of Minangkabau (central west Sumatra), from the common ancestress. Village government has traditionally been based on consensus of opinion and consultation aimed at reaching a complete unanimity before action is taken. Many village activities were based on *gotong royong* or mutual co-operation, all working together for the good of each, in which, for some major undertaking such as building a house or bringing in the harvest, villagers would work together, knowing that, in due course, they could call upon such assistance for their own house-building or harvesting.

Among the semi-nomadic tribal groups of the mountain regions of Sumatra, Kalimantan, and parts of the Philippines there was often inter-tribal war. In some places villages might be fenced with sharp stakes and concealed in the forest. The early Europeans recorded that on some islands they were greeted with hostility and suspicion, while in other places, perhaps those accustomed to foreign traders, they were welcomed and encouraged to trade. Magellan, in his search for the Spice islands, was anxious to avoid the main trade routes for fear of being captured by the Portuguese and he met with a mixed reception as he attempted to find his way among the islands of the Philippines. His attempt to intervene between two rival tribes was the cause of his death. His musketeers and cross-bowmen were driven back by islanders armed with arrows, javelins, fire-hardened spears, lances pointed with iron, and even stones and mud. When, to terrify them, Magellan ordered their houses to be fired, it had the reverse effect and 'rendered them more ferocious'. They aimed poisoned arrows at the unprotected legs of the Spaniards, wounding Magellan, the majority of whose men then 'took to precipitate flight'.[25] In later encounters superior technology enabled the new-comers to establish strongholds; but the tenacious life of the village managed to survive, particularly in those areas whose products were of little interest to the foreign traders and who were thus left un-molested to pursue their subsistence level of existence.

We have evidence of the existence of powerful and wealthy inland kingdoms from as far back as the seventh century A.D. From the

[25] Magellan, *op. cit.*, pp. 99–102.

seventh to the ninth centuries there were at least two powerful dynasties, one Hindu, the other Buddhist, situated in central Java. During this period the Hindu temples of the Dieng plateau and of Prambanan were built, while the neighbouring Sailendra dynasty was responsible for the erection of the Buddhist shrine of Borobodur, which represents the Buddhist cosmos, and in its open galleries has a carved pictorial representation of the life of the Buddha.

With the rise of the trading empire of Sriwidjaya, centred at Palembang, and also ruled by a member of the Sailendra dynasty, the inland kingdoms seem to have declined. The new centre of Buddhist civilization in the archipelago was now Sriwidjaya, famous enough to attract religious scholars from India, China, and even Tibet. The decline of the Sriwidjaya Empire in the thirteenth century coincided with the rise of the east Javanese kingdom of Madjapahit, most renowned of all the Javanese kingdoms. We are fortunate to have preserved from this time a panegyric by the court poet, Prapantja. This was one of the treasures taken to Bali and later to Lombok by the Hindu-Buddhist rulers fleeing there after the disintegration of Madjapahit and the coming of Islam to inland Java.

Madjapahit reached the height of its power under the young ruler Hajam Wuruk and his *Patih* Gadjah Mada, the Keeper of the Realm, in the second half of the fourteenth century, and from the *Nagarakertagama*,[26] the panegyric of Prapantja, we glimpse some of the splendour of life in the *kraton*, the royal palace, the sacred city of the kingdom where the *pusaka* or emblems of state were preserved. The *kraton* existed only as long as did the dynasty which founded it. Should another succeed or conquer it, the city would be abandoned and a new *kraton* would be established.

The *kraton* was an inner walled city within the capital itself and here the ruler lived in seclusion, emerging to take part in the ceremonials by which he, as god-king, preserved the order of the kingdom, and occasionally going on royal progress to different parts of the kingdom or setting off on a hunting expedition. To the *kraton* city came the headmen of the villages to pay tribute, and, as the fame of Madjapahit spread, ambassadors arrived from other islands to pay their homage.

According to Javanese belief a dynasty cannot be expected to last longer than ten *windhu*, or eighty years, without declining into dis-

---

[26] *See* Th. Pigeaud, *Java in the Fourteenth Century*, vol. III.

138 Mid sixteenth-century ship by Holbein, *c.* 1532.
Superiority of ships and arms gave the Europeans an
advantage over their rivals in the trade of South East Asia

order. Then they look for the coming of a Just King (*Ratu Adil*) who
will again bring order and peace to the kingdom, establishing a new
dynasty, although one which sees itself as a restoration of the old
and stresses its continuity with the past. When the first Europeans
arrived the fame of Madjapahit was still widespread although its
power had begun to diminish. Tome Pires reported, with that surprise often expressed by the arrogant when they meet arrogance
greater than their own, that 'these kings of Java have a fantastic idea:
they say that their nobility has no equal'.[27] Van Linschoten speaks of
their 'fretful and obstinate nature'.[28] Certainly they had an awareness
of belonging to a great cultural tradition. Riding richly caparisoned
horses, and lavishly adorned, the Javanese nobles were renowned as
great hunters and horsemen. Their stirrups and saddles were inlaid
with gold, as were their *kris*, the semi-sacred sword worn by every
male from twelve to eighty years of age at the back of the girdle about
their waists. (The Malays wore theirs in front.)

The inland kingdom was still Hindu-Buddhist and in constant
conflict with the coastal principalities which previously had been
subject to its authority. The port of Tuban, a fortified city, was

[27] T. Pires, *op. cit.*, vol. I, p. 174.   [28] Van Linschoten, *op. cit.*, p. 114.

closest to the *kraton* and still allied with the inland kingdom, linked to it by roads through populated country. As in other Hindu countries, the wives and concubines of the ruler burned themselves alive upon his death, although in some cases among the nobility they died by the *kris*, while among the poorer folk death by drowning or cremation was practised on the death of the husband.

Less is known about the inland kingdom of Padjadjaran in Sunda, although Pires records that it too was 'heathen' (Hindu-Buddhist) with a form of government similar to that of Java. Dayo, the royal city, was two days' journey from the port of Sunda Kelapa, present-day Djakarta, which even then was a port of some renown, well governed and with written laws for the regulation of trade. The king's house at Dayo was reported as having '330 wooden pillars as thick as a wine-cask and five fathoms high, and beautiful timber-work on top of the pillars'. Pires describes the Sundanese as 'chivalrous, seafaring warriors' who traded with Malacca, while the ports of southern Sumatra across the Sunda strait traded in the Sundanese ports.[29]

Even less is known of Minangkabau, the inland kingdom of Sumatra, famed for its gold-mines. 'Without doubt the most important part of the whole island is here,' wrote Pires.[30] Its product was

[29] T. Pires, *op. cit.*, vol. I, pp. 167–8.   [30] *Ibid.*, p. 164.

139   Minangkabu girls
in traditional horn
headdress

shipped through Indragiri to Malacca or through the west coast ports of Priaman, Tiku, and Baros, where Gujarat ships still traded direct. In the fourteenth century it was ruled over by Adityawarman, who had been educated at the court of Madjapahit. By the end of the fourteenth century it had established the colony of Negri Sembilan in Malaya. By the early sixteenth century it was said that a triumvirate of rajas, reputedly in constant conflict with each other, ruled the kingdom. These may in fact have been the rulers of the three *luhak* or districts into which the Minangkabau heartlands are divided. Later they were known as 'Ruler of the Universe', 'Ruler of the *Adat*', and 'Ruler of the Religious Law', with the first ruler the senior member of the trio. It was rumoured when Pires wrote, that one of these was already converted to Islam while the other two still remained heathen. Their power rested primarily upon their control of the gold mined in the kingdom. Pires reported that no one who was Muslim might visit the mines; two centuries later William Dampier, who was very anxious to visit the mines himself, reported that no one who was *not* Muslim might visit them.[31]

Minangkabau legend tells of a conflict between Minangkabau and Madjapahit in which the latter, although more powerful, was defeated by Minangkabau guile. The Javanese issued a challenge to a buffalo fight the outcome of which should determine the issue of sovereignty, and they brought with them a magnificent champion buffalo. The Minangkabau asked for seven days' grace to find a match to such a splendid animal, but used that time to pen up a sturdy buffalo-calf, and allow him no milk, while his horns were meanwhile tipped with steel. On the day of the contest, while the Javanese buffalo was looking round for his opponent, the famished calf made straight for the bull in a vain search for nourishment and his steel-tipped horns struck the larger animal a fatal blow. From this, they say, is derived the name 'Minangkabau' (*menang kerbau* – 'victorious buffalo') and legend links the name with the traditional roof of *adat* house and rice barn, curved upwards like buffalo horns, and the traditional head-dress of the Minangkabau women.

The inland kingdoms were considerably strengthened by the spread of Hindu-Buddhist ideas of kingship. In Madjapahit an elaborate hereditary bureaucracy was established. Outlying districts were ruled by members of the royal family, who were expected

[31] W. Dampier, *Voyages and Discoveries*, p. 93.

to make an annual visit of homage to the *kraton*. The ruler and his people were like lion and jungle; the lion must protect the jungle, which, in turn, is his protection.

Various explanations have been put forward for the decline of Madjapahit. Warfare against rivals was expensive and disruptive to the agriculture on which the kingdom's wealth depended. A hereditary bureaucracy is not necessarily a strong one. There was a tendency for such a loose-knit kingdom, linked by the personal fealty of subordinate officials, themselves of royal blood, to disintegrate. The ruler's family, because of the practice of polygamy, was a large one, and rivalry often developed between the children of different wives. This was intensified by the practice of contracting marriage alliances with other powerful princes, which could lead to rivalry instead of alliance. Outlying areas might neglect to send tribute, secure in the knowledge that some time must necessarily elapse before such neglect could be effectively punished. If it were not effectively punished one more step was taken towards disintegration. With the revival of trade in the fourteenth century, Madjapahit, peripheral to the main centres of trade, was at a disadvantage, particularly after the rise of Thailand and Malacca on the mainland and China's renewed interest in South East Asia under the Ming dynasty. In particular, the decline of Madjapahit was linked with the rise of Islamic trading principalities along the Javanese north coast.

The harbour-principalities enumerated by Pires included wealthy, and rival, entrepôts such as Pasai in Sumatra, Malacca on the peninsula, or Demak in Java; independent lesser rivals who sometimes traded in these larger ports but also maintained their own foreign trade; ports which owed some sort of allegiance to the great entrepôts or, as in the case of Tuban, to the inland kingdom; and ports on the periphery who plundered from their wealthier rivals rather than trading on their own account.

The rise of Malacca demonstrates all four stages. It was founded originally by a band of pirate marauders who came from Palembang by way of Tumasik (Singapore). Their leader was a prince of Sriwidjaya, fleeing after an unsuccessful revolt against the sovereignty of Madjapahit. Originally a vassal state of Thailand, Malacca grew in importance until it had outrivalled its north Sumatran rivals, and entered into trade negotiations with the ruler of Madjapahit to trade with Malacca as well as with Pasai. He also entered into a marriage alliance with Pasai, one condition of which, according to Pires, was that the king of Malacca should 'turn Moor'[32] – a more prosaic account of his conversion to Islam than that given in the *Malay Annals*. With the rise of Malacca some of the rich Muslim merchants who had settled in Pasai now moved there. (This was rather similar to the early Dutch attempts to attract Chinese merchants to Batavia from their rival, Bantam, although in the Dutch case this was finally achieved by blockading Bantam, rather than by treaties and the lowering of dues.) By the end of the fifteenth century Malacca had vassal states of its own, Rokan and Kampar on the Sumatran coast opposite, and could call upon various of the smaller pirate states in the channel to provide men-at-arms when need arose. At much the same time the ruler had renounced his allegiance to Thailand on the one hand and Madjapahit on the other, claiming that he was a vassal of the more distant Chinese emperor to whom both the others owed at least nominal allegiance. Intermittent conflict with Thailand then developed and trade between the two ceased.

To the north of Malacca the kingdom of Atjeh, northernmost of the Sumatran harbour-principalities, still carried on independent

[32] T. Pires, *op. cit.*, vol. II, pp. 239, 242.

140   Malacca, captured by the Portuguese in 1511. From here they dominated trade with the Far East until ousted by the Dutch

trade with Indian and Chinese merchants, as did some of the other rival northern and west coast ports. Between Atjeh and Malacca were the pirate states of Aru and Arcat, trading mainly in slaves and gaining a livelihood by plunder from passing merchantmen. To the south, along the north Javanese coast, other harbour-principalities had arisen, the most powerful of which, Demak, claimed tribute from both Palembang and Djambi in south Sumatra. Demak, in its turn, was a rebel against the overlordship of inland Madjapahit, to whose royal family the ruler of Demak was related. In many cases the rulers of the other north Javanese principalities were at best only one or two generations removed from ancestors who had taken control of the settlement either by force of arms or by virtue of wealth gained through trade, and had then consolidated their position by intermarrying with the Javanese nobility or by marriage alliances between themselves. With the exception of Tuban, the rulers of these ports were Muslim, and here again the ruler could contract several marriage alliances personally as limited polygamy was permissible to Muslims. Gresik, 'the little jewel of Java in trading ports', was still divided between Patih Jusuf, a wealthy Malay from Malacca, and Zeynall, 'a knight' who, apart from occasional truces at harvest-time or on the arrival of the trading junks, spent the rest of the time in conflict for control of the city,[33] similar to the struggle between nobles and merchants in fourteenth-century Florence.

Beyond the northern seaports of Sunda and Java were the pirate raiders of Bali, Sumbawa, and Lombok. The same pattern emerged in the Sulu islands between Kalimantan and the larger Philippine islands, while Buginese sailors, whose homeland was in southern Sulawesi, were known through the entire length of the archipelago for their prowess and had settlements in south Kalimantan and on the Malay peninsula.

The same rivalry between harbour-principalities occurred between Ternate and Tidore in the clove islands. Their rulers were related through marriage, and at the same time rivals for the suzerainty of the surrounding islands, whose inhabitants could be called upon for assistance in the warfare between the two. Here the ruler of the harbour-principality seems to have set up his government over a number of village groups who paid tribute in crops and services in return for protection.

[33] T. Pires, *op. cit.*, vol. I, pp. 193–5.

141   The inhabitants of New Guinea according to a
European engraving of 1603

When Magellan's crew met the king of Tidore in 1521 he was
described as a man of handsome presence, who gave audience to
them in his royal vessel, shaded by the symbol of sovereignty, a silk
umbrella. Before him was his son, bearing the royal sceptre, and
four men, two bearing gold fingerbowls, and the other two gilt
caskets containing betel nut, attended him. The king wore a shirt of
fine white cloth with gold-embroidered sleeves, over a sarong. Round
his head was a silken veil and over it a garland of flowers. He was
anxious to welcome the Europeans as potential allies in his struggle
against his more powerful rival, the king of Ternate.

The ruling class in both Tidore and Ternate by the early sixteenth
century was Muslim, although the villagers were 'Gentiles'. In
contrast to their rulers they were naked, except for a bark cloth
round the loins, material described by Pigafetta, Magellan's narrator,
as 'like a vein of raw silk with filaments enlaced within it so that it
appears as if it was woven'. In fact it was beaten after having been
soaked in water to soften the bark. Their main diet was sago made
into a kind of bread which, according to Francis Drake, would keep

for up to ten years. He described it as 'tasting in the mouth like sowre curds, but melteth like sugar'.[34] The villagers watched over their own clove trees, harvested the crop, and took it to the coast where the actual trading was controlled by the king and the small Muslim ruling class.

It is clear from the history of the rise of Malacca and from accounts of some of the pirate states, that one central relationship within this political structure was that of retainer and lord. In Malacca the descendants of those who had accompanied the first ruler became the hereditary class from which the state officials were drawn. High and low needed each other in the struggle for power, and the greater the number of a man's retainers the greater his prestige, while, as his prestige rose, so did theirs.

We learn from the *Malay Annals* about the kind of relationship which was supposed to exist between the ruler and his followers.

[34] Hakluyt, *Voyages and Discoveries*, p. 218.

142   Ferdinand Magellan, from a painting in the National Library, Madrid

FERDIN · MAGELLANVS · SVPERATI
ANTARTIC ̃   FRETI · ANGV
TIIS ·   CLARISS

The ruler must never put his subject to shame. However grave his offence a subject must 'never be bound or hanged or disgraced with evil words', while, on the other hand, the first duty of subject to ruler is never to be disloyal or treacherous even if the ruler should be an unjust one. The ruler should take counsel with his ministers and be careful not to lay hands 'wrongfully upon the goods of others'.[35] *Adat* thus restricted the relations of the two and could be appealed to by either should the other overstep the bounds.

A Muslim ruler was 'the shadow of God upon earth',[36] and along with his nobles and retainers, he also respected his Muslim teachers. During the Portuguese attack on Malacca the sultan mounted his elephant Jituji, and went out to see what was happening, taking with him not only two court officials but also his religious teacher 'because he was studying the doctrine of the Unity of God with him'. The king went forward to the bridge among a hail of bullets, whereupon the religious teacher 'clasping the pannier with both hands cried out to Sultan Ahmad Shah, "Sultan, this is no place to study the Unity of God, let us go home!"' Whereupon 'Sultan Ahmad smiled and returned to the palace',[37] from which, at the next attack, he was to be driven as a refugee, carrying with him as much of the royal treasure as could be assembled together, and accompanied by his faithful retainers.

The style of life of the harbour-principality courts was influenced by that of the inland kingdom of Madjapahit but also Malacca, while in Sumatra and Malaya they seem also to have been influenced by the Indian Muslim courts. The *Malay Annals* record the court ceremonial and regulations which grew up there. For such matters as the installation of chiefs, the number of drums, clarinets, and trumpets, the type of transport – elephant, horseback, or foot – the colour of the robes of honour and the number of bearers for these, were all carefully worked out according to precedent and in relation to status. The same applied to the receipt of letters from foreign rulers. A letter from Pasai to Malacca was received with full cere-monial – trumpet, kettledrums, two white umbrellas (the prerogative of rulers, as yellow was for members of the royal family), and an elephant. A letter from any other state was accorded no more than a big drum, clarinet, and yellow umbrella.[38]

Most important of the court officials was the *bendahara* or principal

[35] *Malay Annals*, pp. 26–7, 49.　　[36] *Ibid.*, p. 12.　　[37] *Ibid.*, pp. 167–8.
[38] Lach and Flaumenhaft, *op. cit.*, pp. 84–6.

minister, treasurer, chief justice, and also master of ceremonies at royal festivities. Next came the *tumenggung*, something like a minister of war and justice, who was receiver of the import and export duties, and then the *laksamana* or admiral of the fleet, the leading war-chief. For the traders the most important officials were the four *shahbandar*, each chosen to represent the merchants of different groups of nations. Most senior in rank was the *shahbandar* for the Gujarati, a second represented the other Indian traders – Klings and Bengali – as well as those from Pegu (Burma) and Pasai (north Sumatra), a third represented the interests of all other traders of the archipelago from south Sumatra to the Philippines, while the fourth acted for the Chinese.[39] The power and wealth of an individual *shahbandar* were considerable but, as the position was not hereditary, the *shahbandar*, in the last resort, depended for his position upon the favour of the ruler and his officials.

When a foreign trading ship arrived in port the captain would report to his appropriate *shahbandar*, who would provide him with warehouse space and an elephant to transport the goods from ship to warehouse. Customs duties and gifts to the ruler, the *bendahara*, the *tumenggung*, and to the *shahbandar* himself were first negotiated, after which the captain and merchants on board could transfer their goods to the appropriate warehouse and begin selling. For food-stuffs, on which no duty was paid but only gifts made, the market was a brisk one as Malacca depended almost entirely on imported food. Javanese merchants set up their stalls for produce and did a busy trade, 'for in Malacca they prize garlic and onions more than musk, benzoin, and other precious things'.[40] At the height of its power, Malacca's government seems to have been designed to provide a quick turn-round, which in its turn encouraged foreign merchants to come and so further enriched the ruler and his officials.

The lesser ports and principalities were in their turn influenced by Malacca. The *Malay Annals* gives a brief sketch of Sultan Husain, ruler of the pirate state Aru (Haru), who, in his cups, used to sing the praises of his war-chiefs, particularly his favourite, Din. The sultan married a daughter of the sultan of Malacca, whose vassal he was, and when he returned to Aru he reported to his mother that the two things which most impressed him were the silence and the magnificence of the service at the royal banquet. 'Not a floorboard

[39] Meilink-Roelofsz, *op. cit.*, pp. 41–5.
[40] T. Pires, *op. cit.*, vol. II, p. 287.

creaked, and lo! and behold, there were the dishes! And dishes mind you, that were four times the size of ours . . . every plate, bowl and tray . . . of silver, gold or gold alloy!'[41]

The harbour ports of north Java were more strongly influenced by the inland court of Madjapahit. As with the Sumatran principalities, the Javanese rulers were almost all interrelated by marriage but at the same time in constant conflict with each other. Further north the sultan of Brunei also lived in splendour, and in his court the ceremonial had developed to such an extent that no commoner or foreigner could speak directly with him, but had to speak through an intermediary, who then spoke to the sultan through a speaking-tube.

When Magellan's crew arrived at Brunei the king's ship came to meet them, ornamented with gold, with a blue and white flag tufted with peacock feathers at the mast, and bearing ceremonial gifts including the inevitable betel nut, ceremonially presented as a gesture of welcome but also used widely by all classes of people. Six days later – business was obviously more leisurely there than at Malacca – the return visit was arranged, and the Spaniards, once ashore, were obliged to wait for about two hours until the silk-caparisoned elephants arrived to take them to present their gifts. When they were ushered into the royal presence they found the king

[41] *Malay Annals*, pp. 185–7.

143 Three sorts of fishing boat used in Goa and Cochin, from an engraving by de Bry

seated on a brocade-curtained dais at the end of a hall in which were the king's guards – 300 men with naked daggers in their hands. At the end of the audience the brocade curtains were closed and the men returned to the governor's house where a repast of more than thirty different dishes was served, and although the platters were wooden and the dishes of china, the spoons with which they ate were of gold. That night they slept on cotton-filled, silk-covered mattresses, with Cambay cotton sheets, in contrast to the palm leaf and matting which the king of Cebu had provided for them and his officials.

Strung along the trade routes, replacing the former authority of inland Madjapahit, the rising city-states of South East Asia rivalled in splendour the city-states of contemporary Italy, and, like the Italian city-states, they were both complementary to each other and at the same time rivals. As Tome Pires pointed out, the wealth of Malacca and that of Cambay (Gujarat) depended on each other, while 'whoever is lord of Malacca has his hand on the throat of Venice'.[42] It was, in his opinion, a city of 'such importance and profit that it seems to me it has no equal in the world'.[43]

The Arrival of the First Europeans

It was to this varied, self-contained world of trade and agriculture, rich in forest products and mineral wealth, that the first Europeans made their way at the end of the fifteenth century. The *Malay Annals* describe their arrival from the fortress stronghold which they had established in Goa, and the astonishment of the people of Malacca who came thronging to see the newcomers, to touch their beards, examine their headgear, or grasp their hands. The commander was warmly welcomed by the *bendahara*, who 'adopted him as his son and gave him robes of honour, as befitted his rank'. The general conclusion of the people of Malacca was perhaps less favourable. 'These', they said, 'are white Bengalees!'[44] Tome Pires, writing a few years later, spoke of the Bengalees as 'sleek, handsome black men, more sharpwitted than the men of any other known race', adding that 'all the merchants are false' and that 'when they want to insult a man they call him a Bengalee'.[45]

When, in 1511, the great port of Malacca fell into the hands of Portugal, the repercussions were felt throughout the whole archi-

[42] T. Pires, *op. cit.*, vol. II, p. 287.   [43] *Ibid.*, p. 285.
[44] *Malay Annals*, p. 157.   [45] T. Pires, *op. cit.*, vol. I, pp. 88, 93.

144 A tombstone in North Sulawesi which incorporates
into its design a Portuguese (or Spanish) trader

pelago. Once the Portuguese had established their fort, built from
the stones of the magnificent mosque which had previously dominated
Malacca, they proved stronger than the armada sent from Demak
and the north Javanese ports, and were fortunate enough to intercept
the north Sumatran ship which was negotiating a similar attack by
the fleets of Sumatra. They maintained control until blockaded into
submission by the Dutch in 1641.

Initially, the new traders, by providing additional competition,
raised prices throughout the archipelago. Pires claims that the people
of Banda received better quality goods from the Portuguese than
they had from the Javanese. Later the effect of the attempted
monopoly of the spice trade was to disrupt the old trade routes,
particularly during the drop in navigation which followed the
capture of Malacca. The more leisurely trading of the Javanese,

289

'selling here, selling there, making money in each place in such a way that the time draws out', moving from Malacca along the north Java coast, trading Malaccan goods for Javanese merchandise to sell in Sumbawa, and Sumbawa cloth to sell in Banda and Maluku, did not suit the Portuguese. They preferred to go via Kalimantan and Buton (south Sulawesi), making their way quickly to the main object of their trade, the spices of east Indonesia, because ahead of them lay the long voyage round the Cape of Good Hope and back to Portugal.

The newcomers may have disrupted but they did not entirely destroy the old way of life. They had a greater initial impact on the ports than on the inland kingdoms, although their arrival seems to have hastened the final collapse of Madjapahit. In several places along the route their support for one side in a local struggle tipped the balance of power between rivals, and enabled them to extend their own power through the area. They also divided the lands on either side of the Straits of Malacca, formerly one interrelated area.

The Spanish settlement in the Philippines and their ruthless proselytizing effectively prevented the spread of Islam any further north than Sulu and Mindanao but did not manage to eradicate it in these southern islands. The Portuguese seem on the whole to have stimulated the extension of Islam and the development of the Islamic principalities such as Atjeh, Bandjermasin, Makasar, and Banten, which reached the height of their power in the seventeenth century, just as the second group of Europeans, the Dutch and English, were making their way east in rivalry to the Portuguese.

The early Europeans made it a matter of policy to encourage the settlement of Chinese merchants in the ports with which they traded. There had been small settlements prior to this, but it was with the coming of the Europeans that the overseas Chinese began to increase in number and to act as middlemen, gradually ousting the Javanese from trade along north Java.

In the long run the advantage lay with the European traders whose ships and arms were superior technologically to those of their rivals, and whose single-minded concern with trade and monopoly was backed by support from the new nation states of Europe which they represented. They established armed fortresses rather than harbour-principalities and retained their control by force of arms and naval supremacy. In the even longer run, Dutch rule in Indonesia for example was to prove more ephemeral than that of Sriwidjaya whose trading empire is believed to have lasted for a period of about 300 years, and barely longer than Madjapahit. As an empire (1870–1942) it did not outlive its allotted span of ten *windhu*. When the colonial period ended the older society was found to have had a greater resilience and survival power than its conquerors had expected. The economic relationships between agricultural and trading areas, the social influence of *adat* and of Hindu-Buddhism and Islam, and the political loyalty of subjects to traditional rulers have remained constant underneath the tide of colonialism. They are still factors in the life of the area today.

Viet-Nam

RALPH SMITH

ALTHOUGH PORTUGUESE AND SPANIARDS were active in the south China Sea for much of the sixteenth century, few Europeans appear to have visited Viet-Nam before about 1600. The importance of the fifteenth and sixteenth centuries in the history of Viet-Nam, therefore, has nothing to do with European discovery and the present section will not need to mention European visitors again. But the period was one of great significance for the internal development of the country, its culture, and its institutions. It was also important for its external relations with the great Chinese Empire to the north, and with the very much smaller kingdom of Champa on the south.

Dai-Viet, Champa, and China

The name 'Viet-Nam' is a relatively modern one, having been used only in the nineteenth and twentieth centuries. In earlier periods, that is from the eleventh century onwards, the Vietnamese referred to themselves as 'Dai-Viet', and were known to the Chinese as 'An-Nam'. In the sixteenth century, the kingdom of Dai-Viet stretched from the present border with China southward to a point a little south of the present Binh-Dinh in central Viet-Nam. It did not include the area round Saigon, nor the Lower Mekong Delta, which were under Cambodian rule until their conquest by the Vietnamese in the period 1680–1760. Moreover, much of the present central Viet-Nam had only been added to Dai-Viet since about 1300. One of the most important themes in Vietnamese history has been a gradual southward expansion of both political control and ethnic settlement, to include areas that were formerly non-Vietnamese. The most important conquest before 1600 was that of the kingdom of Champa which flourished in the coastal regions of the present central Viet-Nam from the eighth to the fifteenth centuries. Cham temples of that period can still be seen in the vicinity of Vietnamese towns like Da-Nang and Nha-Trang. Their architecture shows evidence of a strong Indian influence, and Champa was indeed a Hindu kingdom, unlike Dai-Viet which drew its cultural inspiration from China. Thus the southward expansion of the Vietnamese represented also a small expansion of the Chinese cultural world into South East Asia. From the eleventh to the fifteenth centuries there was continual conflict between the Vietnamese and the Chams, and slowly the latter began to lose ground. They lost a large slice of territory to Dai-Viet in 1071, and parted with another under a marriage agreement between the royal families of the two kingdoms in 1306. In the fourteenth century there was a short-lived Cham recovery: in the 1370s the Cham king, Che Bong Nga, took advantage of internal conflicts in Dai-Viet to the extent of attacking and sacking Hanoi on two or three occasions. But in the following century the Vietnamese were once more in the ascendant and the Cham capital of Vijaya (near the present Binh-Dinh) was sacked in 1446 and again in 1471. In the latter year the Vietnamese annexed yet another slice of Cham territory, including Vijaya itself, and thus reduced the southern state to a small region round Nha-Trang. It was finally extinguished altogether towards the end of the seventeenth century, when the Vietnamese march towards the south was resumed.

In speaking of Viet-Nam before 1600, therefore, we are concerned only with the territory north of the present Binh-Dinh. And even then, we must remember that the more recently conquered areas in the south were held down by military colonies, only gradually transformed into villages under regular civil administration; there were also, in the far south, some penal settlements where criminals were sent into perpetual exile. The thoroughly Vietnamese part of the country was thus limited to the areas of Tongking (the Red River Delta) and northern Annam (Thanh-Hoa, Nghe-An, Ha-Tinh, and perhaps Quang-Binh).

This was the area which had been conquered by Han China in 111 B.C., and the relationship between Dai-Viet and China was always conditioned by the fact that the Chinese had been rulers of the country for 1,000 years between that year and about A.D. 900. There had been a number of Vietnamese revolts, of which the most notable was that of the famous Trung sisters in A.D. 40, which was remarkably similar in some ways to the revolt of Boadicea in first-century Roman Britain; another serious revolt was led by Ly Bon in the sixth century. But each time the aftermath was not only suppression, but the imposition of even firmer Chinese rule. Only when the T'ang Empire broke up in the early tenth century did the Vietnamese succeed in separating themselves both from northern China and from the states which grew up in southern China at that time. One of these states attacked the Vietnamese in 938, but its army was repulsed and it is from that date that the Vietnamese usually count their independence from Chinese rule. The Sung dynasty attempted to reconquer Dai-Viet in 981, and again in 1075–7; but on both occasions their armies were driven back. In the eleventh century Dai-Viet found an increasing measure of internal stability under the Ly dynasty, which lasted from 1009 to 1225. This was followed by a second major dynasty, the Tran, ruling from 1225 until 1400. A more persistent effort to recover control of Dai-Viet was made in the years 1281–8 by the new Mongol dynasty of Kubilai Khan, but it too was foiled under the leadership of one of the most celebrated of all Vietnamese heroes, Tran Hung Dao.

For another century and more Dai-Viet was safe from the Chinese. But a new and more successful attack was launched in 1407 and for a while the country fell once more under the Chinese yoke. The Ming conquest and its aftermath may be said to have marked the beginning of a new phase in Vietnamese history, and it is therefore worth looking at the circumstances in a little more detail. In 1400 the Tran dynasty was overthrown by the powerful general Ho Quy Ly, who founded a new dynasty and placed his own small son on the throne. The conflict preceding this event had been to some extent a regional one, and indeed marked the beginning of a long series of regional struggles within the country lasting till the end of the eighteenth century. The Tran dynasty had its political roots in the Tongking Delta region, the long-established centre of Vietnamese political and social life. Ho Quy Ly on the other hand, was a native of Thanh-Hoa, which had earlier been a 'frontier' area on the south but was now beginning to play a more active part in the country's politics: Quy Ly himself belonged to a family which had married into the imperial clan. But although he was able to overthrow the Tran, he was not able to prevent them from appealing to the Ming Emperor of China, who promptly sent an army to conquer Dai-Viet. Ho Quy Ly was defeated and killed, and from 1407 to 1427 Dai-

145   Map of Viet-Nam in 1650

Viet became once again a Chinese province. But whilst Tongking submitted peacefully to its fate, Thanh-Hoa was less easily subdued, and in 1418 a new leader emerged in that region: Le Loi, who proclaimed himself 'pacifying prince' and swore to drive out the Chinese. He conducted a campaign of guerrilla warfare which had several features in common with that adopted in the twentieth century by the Viet-Minh against the French, not the least of them being that he took control of the countryside first, leaving the capital of Hanoi to be taken last. His final success came in 1427, when he forced the withdrawal of the Ming Army and the restoration of the Tran. The following year he seized the throne and founded a new dynasty of his own. The proclamation issued on this occasion reflects very well the traditional Vietnamese attitude towards China:[1]

> Our Dai-Viet is a country where prosperity abounds, where civilization reigns supreme. Mountains, rivers, frontiers, and customs: in all these things the South [Dai-Viet] is distinct from the North [China]. Trieu, Dinh, Ly, and Tran created our nation, whilst Han, T'ang, Sung, and Yuan rules over theirs. Over the centuries, we have been sometimes strong and sometimes weak, but never yet have we been lacking in heroes. Of that let our history be the proof.

The Chinese did not again conquer Dai-Viet, although they made one more unsuccessful attempt during yet another period of internal Vietnamese strife in 1788. One of the most remarkable features of Vietnamese history has been the capacity of this relatively small country to maintain its independence against the armies of a northern neighbour many times its size and with far greater wealth.

To speak of 'independence', however, is to risk misunderstanding the realities of the situation. The world that was dominated by traditional China knew nothing of Western concepts of sovereignty and law and all China's immediate neighbours, however 'independent', recognized the formal superiority of the Middle Kingdom. Thus the Vietnamese, whilst they were able to avoid becoming a Chinese province, accepted the obligation to send tribute to the Chinese capital every few years; and when a king of Dai-Viet died they sought investiture for his successor by Chinese ambassadors. This tributary relationship was especially strong in the fifteenth century, after 1428, and although it lost some of its vigour as the Ming dynasty declined, it was revived and possibly strengthened under the Ch'ing.

---

[1] *Bulletin de l'École Francaise d'Extreme-Orient*, XLVI (1952), pp. 279–96.

The Chinese Cultural Influence

Nor was Dai-Viet culturally independent of China. A thousand years of Chinese rule inevitably left their mark on the institutions, religion, and cultural life of the country, and even after the Chinese had ceased to be their masters the Vietnamese continued to look for inspiration to China, and to imitate when it suited them to do so. The essential link between the two countries was that of language. The Vietnamese language is of obscure origin, but it has features in common with both Thai and Cambodian, and it survived the Chinese period as something more than a mere dialect of Chinese. Nevertheless, because educated Vietnamese had for so long tended to learn Chinese in addition to their own language, they began to use Chinese-style characters for their own language (known as *nom* characters) and so linked it to the cultural world that was dominated by the Middle Kingdom. Moreover, they used Chinese as their language of ritual and administration (much as medieval Europeans used Latin) right down to the nineteenth century. It was only in the late nineteenth and twentieth centuries, with the general adoption of a Roman script for Vietnamese (under French influence) that the two languages began to diverge. Thus the Vietnamese scholar of the fifteenth and sixteenth centuries was a man who knew Chinese and had studied the Confucian classics, and perhaps other Chinese texts, and he might well also be a graduate of Confucian examinations modelled on those established in China under the T'ang. Consequently he would be in touch with what was happening in China and would seek to persuade the Vietnamese emperor to follow Chinese models. Even in the eighteenth and nineteenth centuries, when the Vietnamese were writing poetry increasingly often in *nom* rather than in Chinese, they still drew many of their themes from China and made frequent allusions to Chinese mythology.

Another important aspect of Chinese influence was religious. The Vietnamese adopted not only Confucian ideas about society and government, but also the veneration of ancestral spirits on which they were based. Ancestor worship was the pivot of traditional religion in Dai-Viet just as it was in China. As a result the clan became the central institution of Vietnamese society, since it was within the clan (or extended family) that the ancestors were worshipped. The Confucian monarchy and bureaucracy could exist over

297

and above the clan system, being sanctioned by principles which did not conflict with it: loyalty to the ruler was just as much enjoined as filial piety. But no other religious community could develop into anything like an all-embracing, nation-wide 'Church'. Outside ancestral religion and Confucian ethics there was room only for small sects, which in their internal structure very often resembled the clan itself, with a 'genealogy' of masters in place of clan chiefs. Thus, although many Vietnamese espoused Buddhism at one time or another, they did so within a framework of small sects rather than of a single Buddhist *sangha* of the kind that exists in Burma or Siam. In this respect Dai-Viet had far more in common with China than with her South East Asian neighbours. Indeed, down to the thirteenth or fourteenth century a number of sects originally founded in China flourished in Dai-Viet, notably three sects of the Zen (or Chan) school of Buddhism. The Ly and Tran periods were the Golden Age of Vietnamese Buddhism. In the fifteenth and sixteenth centuries, although the religion by no means died out, it became less important after losing its former prominence in the life of the court. During that period, Buddhism grew weaker as Confucianism grew stronger. At one point, in 1461, there was even a decree forbidding the establishment of new Buddhist temples, but it is unlikely to have been effective for very long. By the eighteenth century, the imperial court was once again patronizing Buddhist sects.

Internal Political Development

It would be a mistake, however, to see Dai-Viet in the fifteenth and sixteenth centuries as no more than a smaller version of Ming China. That the Vietnamese did not succeed in reproducing Chinese institutions in their entirety can be seen from an examination of the internal politics of Dai-Viet in the two centuries following the recovery of independence in 1428. Important institutional developments took place during that period, but they somehow failed to establish Dai-Viet permanently as a stable and unified kingdom held together by Confucian harmony.[2]

Under the Tran (that is, before 1400) the pattern of government had been essentially oligarchic. In some periods the oligarchy was

[2] The paragraphs which follow owe much to the recent reinterpretation of Vietnamese history in this period by John K. Whitmore, *The Development of Le Government in Fifteenth-century Viet-Nam*, unpublished thesis, Cornell University, 1968.

limited entirely to members of the imperial clan, and for several generations the Tran emperors followed the practice of abdicating in the prime of life in order to ensure a smooth transition of power to their sons when they eventually died. Later on, the oligarchy was widened to include powerful court families whose daughters married into the imperial clan. Such was Ho Quy Ly, whose seizure of power at the end of the Tran period has already been mentioned. Neither rule by the imperial clan nor an oligarchy of 'imperial counsellors', however, really corresponded to the Chinese ideal of government through a bureaucracy of scholars selected by an examination of their mastery of Confucian texts. This is not to say that such a bureaucracy did not exist before 1400: it did in fact gradually develop during the two centuries before that date, as an examination system developed. But the scholar-officials of that time held a much more lowly position in the state than in Sung and Ming China. It was not until the middle of the fifteenth century that the scholars began to challenge the power of the less educated oligarchy, the 'counsellors'. In the meantime, of course, both the Tran dynasty and Ho Quy Ly had been swept aside by the Ming, and they in turn had been driven out by Le Loi. The latter (as the Emperor Le Thai-To) created an oligarchy of his own followers, those who had assisted him in the ten years of war against the Ming, and although he himself died in 1433 the followers retained their influence under his successors.

Thus about 1450 power lay with what might be called the Thanh-Hoa faction (most of them being natives of that area), who were predominantly military men. But they were now being challenged by a new generation of scholars which had emerged from the examinations of 1442 and 1448: men who were not willing to accept the subordinate position of the older scholar-officials. Moreover, the scholars were mostly natives of Tongking, so that once again there was a conflict between men of two different regions. The conflict came to a head in 1459, when the throne was seized by a young Le prince who favoured the Tongkingese. His victory was short-lived: within a year he himself had been overthrown by the Thanh-Hoa faction, who placed on the throne Prince Tu-Thanh, better known as the Emperor Le Thanh-Tong (1460–97). This could well have been the prelude to a long and bloody civil war, but Le

Thanh-Tong was a remarkably able man and during the first decade of his reign he was able to bridge the gulf between the rival factions and to create a situation of peace and stability. As a result, the scholars were able to flourish and to make of Dai-Viet a more Confucian state than it had ever been before, without the complete alienation of the counsellors. In 1463 the examination system was established on a regular triennial basis, and the next few years saw the introduction of a whole series of administrative reforms. In 1483 a new code of laws was compiled, and about the same period the dynastic history of Dai-Viet was rewritten by the scholar Ngo Si Lien. Literary activity became an integral part of the life of the court, and the latter part of Thanh-Tong's reign (the Hong-Duc period, 1470–97) was a sort of Golden Age of Confucianism in Dai-Viet. It was also in this period (1471) that the Vietnamese achieved their final decisive victory over Champa and annexed Vijaya. In many respects one might compare the achievements of Le Thanh-Tong with those of the first Ming emperor of China, who reigned from 1368 to 1398 and whose example may indeed have given the Vietnamese ruler some of his inspiration.[3]

Unlike the Ming, however, the Le were unable to give to their country a lasting unity and stability. In China the troubles which followed the death of Ming T'ai-tsu soon gave way to a new order in the Yung-Lo period. In Dai-Viet, after the death of Le Thanh-Tong, the old conflicts re-emerged and his successors were unable to contain them as he himself had done; his son was able to hold the country together for a while, but he died in 1504. By this time both the Tongking and the Thanh-Hoa parties had their respective links through marriage with the imperial clan. In the succession conflict of 1504 two princes in turn were placed on the throne, the first the nominee of the Thanh-Hoa group, the second the nominee of the Tongkingese. The second of them reigned for a few years, then in 1509 the Thanh-Hoa men found a new leader in a minor scion of the Le clan, who marched upon Hanoi and seized the throne for himself. But the conflict was bound in the end to weaken the Le themselves, and in 1516 there were two successive attempts to depose the dynasty altogether; each was lead by a different member of the Thanh-Hoa faction, but neither was successful. Simultaneously, there was a revolt in Tongking led by a politically minded monk who

[3] See China, pp. 306 et seq., on the Ming period.

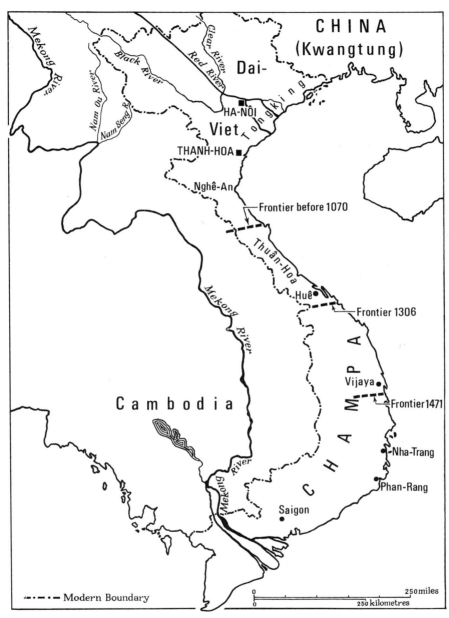

MAP 14   Viet-Nam before the seventeenth century

claimed descent from the Tran, and for a few years the country dissolved into chaos. The dynasty was rescued by a new military leader, a Tongkingese named Mac Dang Dung. But he had his own ambitions, and in 1527 he himself seized the throne and established the Mac dynasty (1527–92). He had probably over-estimated his own strength, however, for he was unable to secure the allegiance of the two leading Thanh-Hoa clans, the Nguyen and the Trinh. In 1534 the Nguyen took action to restore the Le dynasty at Thanh-Hoa, and as a result the kingdom actually became divided into two political units. Inevitably a civil war ensued. The Chinese sent an army to the Vietnamese borders in 1541, but when the Mac submitted they decided not to intervene. The war became a simple trial of strength between the various factions within Dai-Viet.

In this time of trouble it is likely that much of Le Thanh-Tong's work was undone. The powerful clans of Mac, Trinh, and Nguyen did not share the scholar-officials' concern for learning and administrative propriety, and in the midst of war it was not easy for an imperial court to develop the standards and values achieved in the Hong-Duc period. Interestingly, the most important literary figure of the sixteenth century was a man who, though he began life as an official, chose to retire from the court and become a Taoist hermit. This was Nguyen Binh Khiem, who lived from 1491 to 1585 and spent the last forty years of his life in his 'refuge of the White Cloud', refusing to join either of the contending factions although occasionally willing to offer advice to their generals. Something of the Confucian administrative system may have survived, but on the whole the country seems to have slipped back into the situation where power depended on strength rather than on scholastic attainment.

In 1592–3 the Thanh-Hoa men finally defeated the Mac, whose survivors fled to Cao-Bang near the Chinese border; they were allowed to stay there until 1673, as rulers of a small principality under Chinese protection. The Le returned to Hanoi. But by this time they had lost everything but the throne and its purely ritual functions: power lay with the Trinh and the Nguyen. These two clans, moreover, were now at loggerheads with one another. If either one of them had been able to eliminate the other, it is probable that it would have taken the throne and established yet another dynasty;

but they were too evenly matched. By 1593 the Nguyen had a separate power-base in the far south. When the Trinh had attempted to destroy their rivals once and for all in 1558, the Nguyen leader had eluded the blow by persuading the Le emperor to make him governor of Thuan-Hoa, one of the areas formerly belonging to the Chams. He was followed thither by a number of Thanh-Hoa families, and the move in fact marks an important stage in the 'Vietnamization' of the conquered territories. The price of this retreat, however, was that the Trinh now dominated the Le court, and from about 1570 one may say that the Le had ceased to count for anything at all in political struggles. After the Le, together with the Trinh, returned to Hanoi in 1593, the Nguyen leader was persuaded to go to the northern capital to pay his respects. For a few years he lived at Hanoi, playing his part in the final subjection of Tongking. But in 1600 he learnt just in time of a new plot to eliminate him by implicating him in a revolt, and so he again withdrew to the south, and became ruler of an almost separate principality in what is now central Viet-Nam.

This new division into two political units once again led to civil war, in the period 1620–73, but this time neither side was strong enough to destroy the other. Despite their numerical inferiority the Nguyen were able to resist a whole series of attacks from the north, and after 1673 the Trinh accepted the impossibility of defeating them. For another century after that, Dai-Viet remained virtually two states, both owing allegiance to the Le dynasty but actually ruled by the Trinh and the Nguyen respectively. During the seventeenth and eighteenth centuries, the scholars again gradually came to the fore, and Confucian civilization reasserted itself. But then in the last quarter of the eighteenth century, new conflicts led to further civil war, and Confucianism proved once again incapable of holding the country together. Only in 1802 was the area we now call Viet-Nam united under a single ruler.

China

C. A. CURWEN

IN 1508 KING MANOEL OF PORTUGAL sent six ships to Malacca to obtain permission from the sultan to trade. The leader of the expedition, Diogo Lopes de Sequiro, was also instructed to make inquiries about the Chinese, whose ships were often found in those waters.

> You shall ask after the Chijns, and from what part they come, and from how far, and at what times they come to Malacca . . . and the merchandise that they bring, and how many of their ships come each year, and regarding the form and type of their ships . . . and if they are wealthy merchants, and if they are weak men, or warriors, and if they have arms or artillery, and what clothes they wear, and if they are men of large build . . . if they are Christians or heathens, if their country is a great one, and if they have more than one king amongst them, and if any Moors live amongst them or any other people that are not of their law or faith; and, if they are not Christians, in what do they believe and what do they adore, and what customs they observe, and towards what part does their country extend, and with whom do they confine.[1]

It was not that Europe was entirely ignorant of China. Although her civilization had grown up in relative isolation from Europe, far away at the other end of the Euro-Asian land mass, there had always been tenuous contacts between them through indirect commerce, notably in silk; through travellers' tales; and by the transmission of ideas and techniques by means which remain largely unexplained.

That China was vast, wealthy, and highly civilized the Venetian Marco Polo had already told his credulous contemporaries.[2] His account of China in the thirteenth century, which earned him the nickname of 'Il Milione' because of his apparent exaggerations, has nevertheless been confirmed to a great extent, at least as far as the magnificence and wealth of Chinese cities is concerned. But the defeat of the Mangols reduced the unprecedented possibilities for contact between East and West which existed during their empire, when religious and dipolmatic motives were added to purely com-

---

[1] Quoted in Donald F. Lach, *China in the Eyes of Europe*, p. 731.
[2] *See The Travels of Marco Polo*, trs. R. E. Latham.

mercial relations. China remained once more remote from Europe until the early part of the sixteenth century, when the ambition of the Portuguese to control the rich spice trade from south India and the Malay archipelago brought them into direct contact with Chinese traders and then with China.

King Manoel's questions were not motivated by intellectual curiosity, but by his interest in commerce and perhaps by religious zeal. They could not be answered at once, and Portuguese adventurers were soon to discover that China was by no means easy to penetrate. The immediate concern of King Manoel and Lopes, however, was to find out whether China was to be a rival in the Indian Ocean, whether the Arab enemy had an ally in China, hence his question whether 'any Moors live amongst them'.

The earliest Portuguese visitors were hardly equipped to know it at the time, but in fact China's preoccupations lay elsewhere. She had entered one of her periods of prosperity and stability, during which she tended to be inward-looking, turning to the past for models and for inspiration. In reality, movement had not stopped, but China's state seemed very like stagnation in contrast with that

146   Chinese drawing of an archer of Kubilai Khan's period

of Europe, where a turmoil of transformation in every realm of human activity had been taking place.

Resentment against the Mongols, who had broken the continuity of their tradition, left the Chinese unappreciative of the links which their conquerors had given them with the world. Disdain cut China off from the stimulus of foreign ideas. Scholarship became introspective, examining again and again the orthodox tradition and not concerning itself with new thoughts. Instead of dynamic change which might have saved China from being overwhelmed by the aggressive energy of the West, there was complacent satisfaction with traditional values, and no thought that progress might be desirable.

The Founding of the Ming Dynasty

The rapid turnover of emperors after the death of Kubilai Khan (there were eight in the period 1307–33), was a symptom of the decline of Mongol authority in China. At the top there were violent struggles for the succession between imperial princes; throughout the country maladministration and oppression coincided with natural disasters to produce a highly combustible atmosphere. In 1329, according to official figures, more than 7,600,000 people out of a total population of some 45 million, were starving. Popular risings became increasingly frequent, extensive, and violent. In 1351 the Yellow River burst its banks and the conscription of 170,000 men to repair the dikes led to futher discontent. But the risings were sporadic and uncoordinated, their leaders frequently in direct rivalry with one another. Some claimed to be descendants of the imperial house of the Sung dynasty (960–1279), which the Mongols had destroyed, others owed their support to secret societies inspired by millenarian Buddhism or popular Taoism. When the Mongol rulers made the mistake of reviving nationality laws and discrimination against Chinese, the revolt ceased to be purely social and economic and became a national struggle for the expulsion of the foreign overlords.

Eventually one rebel leader gained ascendancy over the others. He was Chu Yuan-chang (1328–98), an orphan of peasant origin who had become a monk in order to save himself from starvation. He had acquired a rudimentary education and perhaps in his travels as a religious mendicant had made contact with a secret society. By 1355

147 Chu Yuan-chang, founder of the Ming Dynasty

he was at the head of a rebel army of several thousand men. He was undoubtedly a capable and energetic man, and since he increasingly fought the Mongols rather than the rich, more and more gentry threw in their lot with him. In 1356 his troops captured Nanking, the economic and strategic centre of the Lower Yangtze Valley, the richest part of the country. This enabled him to dominate his rivals and in 1368 he captured Peking, which had been under nomad rule for 430 years. The Mongol ruler and his court rode away to the north. Chu Yuan-chang then proclaimed himself emperor and founder of a new dynasty, the Ming (Brilliant), which was to last until 1643. He made his capital at Nanking.

For a long time, even after the beginning of the sixteenth century, Europeans could not answer with any precision King Manoel's question, 'towards what part does their country [China] extend, and with whom do they confine'. In many places there was no very clear demarcation of frontiers and it was not always easy to determine where China's administration ended and where independently governed tributary states began. Mongol power had not been utterly destroyed, and along her northern frontier China remained for decades menaced by nomadic tribes and federations. Chu Yuanchang incorporated south Manchuria (or Liaotung) into his empire mainly for protection against Japan. Korea, which had been under Mongol domination, tacitly acknowledged Ming suzerainty in 1370. But there was a strong pro-Mongol faction there and China did not feel secure until a new Korean dynasty (the Yi dynasty, 1392–1910) entered into regular tributary relations with her. She no longer had control over Turkestan, which had broken up into small states after the collapse of the Mongol empire. But this was no longer of great military or economic importance because the route to the West was blocked by Arab and Turkish control over the Near East and central Asia. China's immediate neighbour in the north-west was now the state of Hami, populated by Uighurs. Tibet was not under effective Chinese administration, but, in theory, was a Ming vassal. Yunnan and Kueichow were brought under complete Chinese control; beyond were Burma, Siam, Laotien, and Champa (later Viet-Nam).[3]

[3] *See* Albert Herrmann, *Historical and Commercial Atlas of China* and T. R. Tregear, *A Geography of China*.

148 Chinese sold as slaves by the Mongols after their conquest by Genghis Khan

Restoration of the Economy

Years of civil war and the heritage of Mongol maladministration presented Chu Yuan-chang with enormous social and economic problems, which he tackled with vigour. There was also rivalry amongst his close companions, mostly men of plebeian origin like himself, and between them and the ex-officials, Confucians, gentry, and military commanders who had joined him in the fight against the Mongols. If nearly 17 per cent of the population were starving in 1329, it is not difficult to imagine the state of the economy after forty more years of civil strife. In some parts, where the destruction of war had been greatest, whole areas of once cultivated land now lay deserted; elsewhere destitute people crowded into regions where there was not enough land to support them. Nor was nature kind to the new régime. From 1368 to 1376 famine, drought, floods, and locusts added to existing problems. In the cities and towns where trade had once flourished an economic depression left merchants and artisans destitute and discontented. There was a dangerously large number of vagabonds in the country, and perhaps it was only weariness and the general desire for peace and stability which prevented new explosions.

Chu Yuan-chang, the ex-rebel, had been a peasant himself; no one knew better that the ruler is a boat and the people the water, which supports it but can also overturn it. He was careful to see that at least some of those demands which had led peasants to support him and other rebel leaders, were satisfied by the régime which he established. 'Mindful of the encroachments upon the meek by powerful interests during the Yuan [Mongol] period,' wrote the official historian of the Ming, 'he legislated on behalf of the poor and curbed the influence of the rich.' Some of his first measures were directed against wealthy landlords, and over 14,000 in south-east China were forced to give up their land and go to live in Nanking. Landless peasants were resettled on a very large scale and exempted from taxation for three years; for others there was a general reduction of taxes. If peasants put abandoned land to the plough they were given permanent ownership of it, so that, by 1374 nearly 14 million acres of fallow land are said to have been put into cultivation.

One means which Chu Yuan-chang employed for restoring agricultural production, which at the same time helped to consolidate

frontier defence, was the establishment of military and civil agricultural colonies. He ruled that in the border regions 30 per cent of the strength of each garrison be employed in military duties and 70 per cent should work on land allocated by the state. In the interior the ratio was 20 to 80. Of the civil colonies, some consisted of settlements of vagabonds and criminals; but there were also merchants' agricultural colonies. These arose because the government ruled that if a merchant delivered a certain amount of grain to the frontier garrisons, he would receive in return a permit to buy and sell a certain amount of salt, the trade in which was a profitable government monopoly. In order to benefit by this privilege without the necessity for transporting grain all the way to the frontier, merchants settled landless peasants in the border regions to produce it for them on the spot. The land occupied by civil and military agricultural colonies in the early Ming period represented about 10 per cent of all cultivated land.

In order to regularize landownership and labour service and prevent the rich from evading taxation, a recurring tendency in every dynasty, new population and land registers were drawn up early in the Ming period. In China the strength and wealth of the state, the court,

310

150 A six-oar tax boat used on the Yangtze and Han rivers (*T'ien-kung k'ai-wu*)

六槳稅紅

the government, and the army depended primarily on acquiring by taxation as much of the produce of the agricultural land as possible without causing unrest. In the early part of the dynasty land taxes were collected according to a complicated system inherited from the past which took into consideration both the quality of the land and the quantity of its produce. Taxes were collected twice a year, in the autumn and the early spring, by which time the main autumn harvest would be in store. Some of the land tax was collected in silver and silk, but the bulk was in grain, and this had to be transported to the capital at Nanking, and later to Peking; a huge fleet of 2,000 boats was maintained for the purpose.

We do not know what proportion of the rural population was made up of peasants who owned their own land, but we may be sure that the overwhelming majority consisted of small peasant proprietors, tenant farmers, and agricultural labourers. Most of them lived at a bare subsistence level, even when the harvest was good. Bad years brought famine, destitution, suicide, and the sale of children; at best peasants would run into debt, with interest rates of 20 per cent per month or more. The position of large sectors of the rural population was 'like that of a man standing permanently up to the neck in water, so that even a ripple is sufficient to drown him'.[4]

[4] R. H. Tawney, *Land and Labour in China*, p. 77.

On the other hand, even a slight improvement in rural conditions might produce a remarkable effect. Indeed, this is what happened in the early Ming period. Although government policy did not entirely live up to its promise to legislate on behalf of the poor and curb the influence of the rich, it did lay the foundations for a restoration of the economy.

The government also devoted much attention to water conservancy, irrigation, drainage, and river transport, on which so much of China's prosperity and unity depended. There was, too, a considerable advance in agricultural methods. The most important innovation had been made earlier, during the tenth century, when a new strain of rice from Champa had been introduced into Fukien Province. By Ming times this kind of rice was widely grown throughout China. It had several advantages: it was resistant to drought and could be cultivated in poorly watered land; it was also more productive than native Chinese strains and, because it ripened quickly, it was possible in many places to grow two rice crops on the same land, or else to sow to wheat or rape (for oil) after the main harvest. With better knowledge of fertilizers, used in accordance with the characteristics

151　A water-wheel of
the Ming period
(*T'ien-kung k'ai-wu*)

of the soil, the use of bone-ash to counteract acidity, and the introduction of new crops, the former system of fallow cultivation was
gradually abandoned and a tremendous increase in productivity
achieved. New methods of irrigation were introduced, including
windmills for water-raising, and water-mills with the triple function
of pumping, hulling, and milling.

The restoration and advance of the rural economy in the later
fourteenth century was soon reflected in a 60 per cent increase in
revenue from the land tax during the last fifteen years of Chu Yuan-
chang's reign. In the long term it is shown by the immense increase in
China's population in the following centuries.[5]

Handicraft Production and Commerce

As one would expect in a predominantly agrarian country in which a
state depended almost entirely upon revenue from the land, farming
was looked upon as the 'fundamental occupation'. Trade, on the
other hand, was regarded by the élite as a parasitic and disreputable

[5] *See* Ping-ti Ho, *Studies on the Population of China, 1368–1953.*

152   Hand-weeding in
a rice-field (*T'ien-kung
k'ai-wu*)

313

pursuit, which fed upon the farmers and was therefore in competition with the state, which led to usury and encouraged luxury and dissipation. Artisans were hardly better thought of. Of course, China could not do without either, and in spite of social and institutional sanctions against the commercial classes trade and handicraft industries flourished. 'As for the merchants,' Marco Polo had written of a city in south China in the late thirteenth century, 'they are so many and so rich and handle such quantities of merchandise that no one could give a true account of the matter, it is so utterly beyond reckoning'.[6]

The total volume of trade was undoubtedly increased by the incorporation of China into the vast Mongol Empire. But foreign trade was controlled by privileged Muslim merchants from central Asian states which were allied with the Mongol rulers, and the régime came to depend on them to a great extent for the collection of taxes in China. They were thus able to dominate domestic as well as foreign trade and accumulate great wealth, most of which went to their own countries.

Handicraft production was stimulated by this increase in trade; but Mongol rule was very oppressive, the whole population being categorized and registered, as commoners, scholars, miners, doctors, and so on. Artisans were registered and virtually enslaved under a system of forced labour service. Workshops under state management produced iron and steel, luxury articles of gold, silver, and jade; there were brick-kilns and tanneries, and separate factories for bows, arrows, bowstrings, armour, and saddles. This organization and specialization, oppressive as it was, probably contributed to the development of productive techniques.

In the early years of the Ming dynasty control by foreign merchants over Chinese trade was rapidly removed. Artisans remained an hereditary caste and were not allowed to change their occupation; they were still obliged to perform services for the state, but only for three months every three years. By 1505 even this corvée was transformed into a tax; free production was more economical than forced labour where sabotage was possible. Under the system of free production the products of handicraft industries came on to the open market, where previously they had gone into government stores. This in turn raised the quality of home handicraft products once agricultural

[6] See *The Travels of Marco Polo*, p. 188.

153 Shaping (*below*) and polishing (*above*) clay-ware with a potter's wheel (*T'ien-kung k'ai-wu*)

production had been restored, and stimulated the manufacture in the countryside of goods specifically for the market.[7]

The region where agricultural and handicraft development was most marked was in the lower valley and delta of the Yangtze. From about the thirteenth century on, this had become the key economic area of China, giving sufficient economic power to those who controlled it to enable them to dominate the whole country. Its naturally fertile lands were intersected by a complex network of waterways. By access to the Yangtze and to the Grand Canal it was linked with the far interior and with the north. The population had been swollen by immigration from north China during periods of 'barbarian' rule, and there was marked urban development. Nanking and its surrounding prefecture boasted a population of over a million, that of Suchow over 2 million.

The two cities were the centre of the silk-weaving and dyeing industries; their products were sold throughout the country and even transported abroad in large quantities. Cotton had been introduced from Bengal in the twelfth century, and by Ming times the

[7] For further information *see* Franz Schurmann and Orville Schell (eds), *China Readings I, Imperial China*, pp. 65–74.

cotton cloth of Sung-chiang 'clothed the whole empire'. For the army alone 50 to 60 million bolts were needed every year. The government encouraged the growth of cotton, and the weaving of cotton cloth became the peasants' main subsidiary occupation. In the south-west one out of every ten families had its own loom; a new cotton-gin was invented so that 'one man could do the work of four or eight men'.

At Ching-te-chen in Kiangsi, where the imperial kilns were situated, high-grade white porcelain which was harder than steel had been developed. Examples soon found their way to Europe, but the secret of 'china' or 'china-ware' did not, and the technique remained a mystery until a German alchemist accidentally dis-covered the technique in 1708. At Ching-te-chen a private porcelain industry began to develop and the light of the kilns 'lit up the sky, so that one could not sleep at night. Men spoke of it as a town of per-petual lightening.'

154 Silk manufacture: separating single cocoons from double- and multiple-worm cocoons (*T'ien-kung k'ai-wu*)

155 Cotton gin for separating fibres from seeds (*T'ien-kung k'ai-wu*)

156 Cylinder wheel used in irrigation works (*T'ien-kung k'ai-wu*)

There was also a marked development in building, to which the Imperial Palace in Peking is a lasting monument; in the making of firearms and glass; and in the techniques of salt-evaporation.

In southern and central China the transportation of goods was relatively easy because of the proliferation of waterways. The north was less well served; there and in the mountainous regions, which occupy a large part of the country, goods had to be carried in cumbersome ox-carts, horse-carts, and on wheelbarrows or on the backs of men. When the capital was moved from Nanking to Peking, the Grand Canal had to be repaired and kept in service. Every year nearly 300,000 tons of rice was carried, in boat-loads of from 11 to 17 tons, from the south-east up to Peking. For the purposes of government communications there was a nation-wide state postal service, with post-stations every 30 or 40 miles, which could transmit imperial edicts at the speed of 200 miles in twenty-four hours.

Ming Politics and Administration

In 1398 Chu Yuan-chang died and was succeeded by his grandson, a boy of sixteen. The rivalries which had been fermenting immediately came to the surface. The main threat to the authority of the new emperor came from the princes who controlled the border regions and had built up considerable military power during Chinese campaigns against the Mongols; some of them had achieved a degree of regional autonomy incompatible with strong central government. When the young emperor and his advisers began to take strong measures against these men, dispossessing some of the less powerful, his uncle, the prince of Yen, raised a rebellion in order to save himself from a similar fate and win the throne. He had been responsible for the defence of the northern frontier, which was the most vulnerable, and commanded an army of over 100,000 men. Civil war lasted from 1399 to 1402. Then Nanking was captured by the rebel army, and its palaces burned to the ground. The emperor vanished, but his supporters were massacred. The victor declared himself emperor, with the reign title 'Yung Lo'.

In 1421 he moved his capital from Nanking to Peking, which was his own power-base, and from which the empire was better able to look to the defence of its northern borders against its inveterate nomad enemies. The economic base, however, remained in the south, and for the rest of the dynasty Nanking remained as a kind of subsidiary capital, of greater economic and cultural importance than Peking. The Yung Lo emperor rebuilt Peking, and much of his city, including the magnificent Imperial Palace, still survives. The walls were 40 feet high, forming a square more than 14 miles round. The palace, called 'The Forbidden City', was in the middle, surrounded by a moat and wall within which there were pavilions and halls, lakes and an artificial hill.

Although there had been this short period of civil war during which imperial authority had been challenged, most Chinese would probably have been surprised at King Manoel's question as to whether 'they have more than one king amongst them'. The emperor was 'the Son of Heaven'; there could only be one. In him was invested ultimate power, which was virtually free from legal and constitutional restraints. Secluded in his vast palace and endowed with the charisma of an earthly legate of heaven, he could chose to reign in a more or less despotic manner. Only three of the Ming emperors opted for the traditional Confucian virtues of emperorship and ruled in a moderate and benevolent way, trusting their officials and receptive to their suggestions. The others, except those who were weak, or frivolous, or misfits, tended to rule as despots, following the example of the founder of the dynasty.

In their isolation the emperors of the Ming, like many others before them, came to depend on the palace eunuchs, the only male

157 Blue and white pilgrim bottle, Ming, early fifteenth century

attendants permitted to live within the Forbidden City. In other periods the eunuchs had often become very powerful and influential, but in the Ming dynasty many emperors came completely under their sway. Chu Yuan-chang had been conscious of the danger involved and had limited their number to 100, but by the end of the fifteenth century there were nearer 10,000, and more than 70,000 by the end of the dynasty.

Their ties with the emperor were personal; they were his intimate servants and companions, the playmates of his childhood, and they were often privy to his secrets. Being mostly of plebeian origin and uneducated, they owed no particular loyalty to Confucian doctrine and had no desire to preach to the emperor. They had no ties with great families, no heirs to plot for, no duty to public opinion, and no future apart from imperial favour. Factional divisions within the bureaucracy played into their hands and they became a dominant force in the life of the country, supervising the state monopolies and foreign trade. They had a military arm in the emperor's personal corps of bodyguards and sometimes achieved high rank in the military hierarchy. They staffed the emperor's secret service and could terrorize officials.

Compared with the eunuchs and with the civil service, the nobility which was more or less limited to members of the imperial family, had little influence. One of the emperor's sons was nominated heir apparent and resided in the Imperial Palace. Others were given territorial titles and were expected to live on their estates without administrative or judicial functions. They had little part to play and emperors took care to curb their ambitions.

The country was divided into two large metropolitan areas and thirteen provinces, which were further subdivided into prefectures, sub-prefectures, and districts. The administration of this huge empire was the responsibility of what was undoubtedly the most effective organized government in the world at that time. The body of salaried officials numbered between 10,000 and 15,000, divided into nine grades and eighteen degrees.

Officials were nearly all recruited through the competitive examination system. Once appointed to a post, an official would remain in it for a maximum of nine years, under the constant surveillance of his superiors; his promotion depended upon an elaborate method of credit rating. The highest rewards were honorific titles, but he was not immune from the death sentence.

By contemporary European standards the Chinese bureaucracy was enormous, but considering the vast territory and teeming population which it controlled, it was quite small. The officials did not, however, administer the country unaided, but were assisted by functionaries performing clerical and other tasks, numbering about 100,000. Unlike the officials, these men had no exalted prestige and, as a rule, no means of improving their status within the bureaucracy. Their role was nevertheless a very important one: officials were not permitted to hold office in their own home regions and were transferred fairly rapidly from one post to another; they had little chance to get to know their administrative district, so they came to rely heavily on the local knowledge and experience of the lesser functionaries, and sometimes came completely under their influence.

There was no strict demarcation between administrative authority and policy-making. Policy clearly emanated from the emperor, but a great deal depended upon his character and ability. He might choose to accept suggestions, which all officials had the right to make, but could, if he wished, compel his government to follow his whims. He might accept the proposals of his ministries and of the Grand Secretariat, through which most suggestions seem to have been channelled in practice, but nothing prevented him from drafting his own edicts. There might be discussion in court, but more often policy would be worked out in private discussion between the emperor and his trusted ministers.

The top echelons of government exercised control over the administrative, censorial, and military hierarchies. The system of government was not an invention of the Ming, but was a deliberate effort to return to models which had been established before the invasion of China by 'barbarians', especially to the governmental structure of the T'ang dynasty (618–906). This, in turn, was founded on principles which had been sanctioned by tradition. But under Chu Yuan-chang and his successors it evolved into a more centralized and more highly sophisticated system which was to survive without fundamental changes until the twentieth century.

The first Ming emperor abolished the Secretariat, which had been in charge of chief councillors (or prime ministers) because he feared that too much power could be concentrated in their hands. This left, at the top of the bureaucracy, six administrative nerve-centres, the ministries, responsible for personnel, revenue, rites, war, justice, and works. Thus, a heavy burden of administrative and coordinating routine fell upon the emperor himself, and not all had Chu Yuan-chang's energy – it is said that he dealt with 1,600 documents on 3,391 separate matters in one ten-day period. Consequently, a new secretariat evolved, called the 'Grand Secretariat', which by the 1420s had already acquired a great deal of executive power. Its members attended and advised the emperor, passed on to him documents which were submitted from all government agencies, and drafted replies and decisions for him.

Outside the capital, by the middle of the fifteenth century, the administration of the thirteen provinces was under the control of officials who eventually came to be called Provincial Governors. The Chinese term means literally 'to tour and soothe', because Chu

158 Blue and white vase with unglazed base, Ming, late fifteenth century

Yuan-chang once sent the heir apparent to do exactly this in a certain troubled region. Technically, throughout the dynasty they were delegates from the central government. Later there were also 'supreme commanders', civil officials whose territorial supervision covered more than one province.

The routine business of provincial administration was carried on by the Provincial Administrator's office, which supervised the activities of subordinate divisions called 'Circuits', under Circuit Intendants, some with territorial and some with functional jurisdiction. Each territorial Circuit Intendant was responsible for several prefectures, divided into sub-prefectures and districts; but their function was supervisory rather than executive. The basic unit of administration was the district (*hsien*), and this was the only level at which ordinary people came into contact to any extent with actual government. Each of the 1,171 districts was administered by a District Magistrate, with a deputy and an assistant. The District Magistrate was commonly called the 'father and mother official', a title which reflected not only the benevolent concern which was expected of him, but also the extent and variety of his responsibilities. He assessed and collected the taxes, imposed labour service, cared for the aged and poor, performed official sacrifices and ceremonies, kept the peace, and administered justice. All this, in theory at least, in an administrative district which in Ming times had an average population of 50,000. As long as they paid their taxes, did not shirk *corvée* labour services, and did not rebel, most of the rural population had little contact with the government even at the lowest level. Between the District Magistrates and the mass of peasants in the countless villages and hamlets scattered over the whole country, was interposed an intermediary system which regulated much of the day-to-day life of the countryside. Part of this system was concerned with the collection of taxes and the levy of *corvée* service, the other with security and self-policing.

For these purposes the rural population was divided, in theory, into sets (*pao*) of 110 neighbouring households. The heads of the ten most prosperous families were nominated elders of the community and they acted, in rotation, as intermediaries between the district government and the people. The remaining households were divided into groups of ten (*chia*), each with a group head. The members of these groups, and indeed the whole community, could be held responsible for the good behaviour of the others, and it was the duty of the group and community elders to report infractions of the law and see that the taxes were paid. Thus the rural communities themselves were expected to maintain public order and the government had no need to establish local police forces. The management of local affairs, the settlement of disputes, and the maintenance of certain communal services, such as the temple, school, and granary, were handled by the community organization in accordance with a kind of charter of community government drawn up in each locality on an imperially prescribed pattern. The text included an imperial exhortation to everyone to observe private and public morality, and was read out and sworn to in monthly assemblies.

It would be wrong to suppose that this system represented a kind of democratic self-government. Its purpose was imperial control and extraction of revenue. Village leaders were appointed by the District Magistrate, not elected by the people. But it would be equally wrong to exaggerate the sinister aspects of the *pao-chia* system and see it only as an elaborate network for mutual spying. In a way it was an attempt by the government to bring under its own control the natural social organs of the village communities. In times of rural peace and relative prosperity the system functioned smoothly, but it was ineffective when social stability was threatened and broke down completely in face of real unrest.

The second branch of the central administration was the Censorate, a uniquely Chinese institution which also traced its ancestry back as far as the third century B.C. Its function was to keep a watching eye on all government activities from outside the normal administration, and to impeach, punish, or censure government personnel for violation of the customary norms of conduct, whether public or private. The Censorate also initiated and transmitted proposals for reform of policy or procedure, which might involve criticizing the conduct or decision of any official, and even of the emperor himself. It was, as the Jesuit missionary Matteo Ricci wrote at the end of the sixteenth century, 'the keeper of the public conscience'. Censorial officials were often called 'the eyes and ears of the emperor'. It was a highly organized attempt by the government to police itself, to keep to an ideal, and was an essential buttress of the Confucian state system. But its record was uneven; it was part of the government apparatus and was vulnerable to the same factional interests and equally, if not more, dependent upon individual qualities.

The judiciary did not have an independent status within the administration. In each district the magistrate was judge; he was also prosecutor, coroner, and chief of police. Chinese law was traditionally penal and administrative; civil law was extremely rudimentary and no provision was made for guaranteeing the rights of individuals. In a country where social harmony, regulated by ethics and virtue, was the ideal, arbitration and compromise were the traditional means of settling disputes. To appeal to law was a desperate last resort; it revealed a lack of virtue and was considered by the government to reflect unfavourably on the leaders of the community involved. Punishments were severe, and the use of torture a matter of course. But when the Portuguese began to send back reports of what they learned about the judicial system of China, it was not this which struck them – such things were common in Europe too – but the fact that the Chinese took 'all possible pains to avoid condemning anyone to death', and that all such sentences had to be confirmed by the emperor himself.

The élite who governed China were servants of the emperor; but they were also heirs to a tradition which had its own principles and loyalties, which no emperor could afford to ignore. The officials who administered the empire were drawn from the ranks of the gentry, the class which played a dominant role in the economic, cultural, and political life of the countryside.

But if the word 'gentry' implies privilege based uniquely upon the accident of birth or on wealth, then it is inadequate to describe the local élite of China. It is true that most of them were landlords, who increased their holdings at the expense of the free peasantry, especially in times of natural disaster. Many of the gentry were also usurers, into whose debt peasants living at a subsistence level could easily fall. But the status of the Chinese gentry depended upon the attainment of a degree in the competitive examinations, and was consequently not self-perpetuating. Landowning and wealth did not of themselves give gentry status, but they did make its acquisition possible, since it was very difficult for a poor man to find leisure and opportunity to reach the required educational standard. It was often possible to purchase the lowest degree for a relatively small sum of money, especially when the government was in financial straits; but the status which went with a purchased degree did not give much prestige or the assurance of high office.

The Chinese gentry was a cohesive but unorganized social class. As the rural élite they acted as a customary arm of government control, functioning as the link between officialdom and the common people, who did not have access to their rulers. They fulfilled an important function as the community leaders, directing and providing public services which the government did not. They contributed to and supervised the operation of schools, temples, charities, and public works. They were often the tax-collectors, but were themselves exempt from many taxes and from *corvée* service. Their connections with officialdom gave them extra-legal privileges and opportunities for acquiring wealth.

Once a year all districts were visited by inspectors sent by the provincial government, who certified all men of adequate academic standard and good character, and gave them the title of 'Bachelor'. This was renewable every three years to allow of no falling off, but it gave the candidates the right to sit the provincial examinations, also held every three years.

Success in the provincial examination gave a man the title *chü-jen*, meaning 'recommended men', which endowed him with more privileges, including that of sitting the triennial metropolitan examination. This was an arduous test, but the reward was great. Those who passed were examined once more, for classification purposes, by the emperor himself. Graduates were called *chin-shih* ('presented scholars') and were guaranteed appointment to office, after which, if they did not make too many mistakes, they could rise to the highest dignities of the state. During the 276 years of the Ming dynasty there were only 24,874 *chin-shih*.

Since the children of an official had better opportunities than anyone else for acquiring the kind of education needed, the civil service did become to a great extent self-perpetuating – a strong, semi-autonomous power-block within the Chinese state system.

Success in the examinations was the only way to office, to prestige, and to respectable wealth, untainted by commerce. There was no limit on the age of a candidate or the number of times he could try his luck, and the examinations became the overwhelming and all-absorbing preoccupation of the entire literati. This is vividly described in the eighteenth century Chinese novel *Ju-lin wai-shih* (The Scholars) by Wu Ching-tzu, which is set in Ming times. One of the characters in the novel is Chou Chin, Commissioner for Education in Kwangtung Province, who himself had not been able to pass the prefectural examination until after he was sixty. Supervising an examination he,

. . . sat in the hall and watched the candidates crowding in. There were young and old, handsome and homely, smart and shabby men among them. The last candidate to enter was thin and sallow, had a grizzled beard and was wearing an old felt hat. Kwangtung has a warm climate; still, this was the twelfth month, and yet this candidate had on a linen gown only, so he was shivering with cold as he took his paper and went into his cell. Chou Chin made a mental note of this before sealing up their doors. During the first interval, from his seat at the head of the hall he watched this candidate in the linen gown come up to hand in his paper. The man's clothes were so threadbare that a few more holes had appeared since he went into the cell.

159 Winnowing by tossing (*T'ien-kung k'ai-wu*)

Commissioner Chou looked at his own garments – his magnificent crimson robe and gilt belt – then he referred to the register of names, and asked, 'You are Fan Chin, aren't you?'

Kneeling, Fan Chin answered, 'Yes, Your Excellency.'

'How old are you this year?'

'I gave my age as thirty. Actually, I am fifty-four.'

'How many times have you taken the examination?'

'I went in for it when I was twenty, and I have taken it over twenty times since then.'

'How is it you have never passed?'

'My essays are too poor,' replied Fan Chin, 'so none of the honourable examiners will pass me.'

Fan Chin kowtowed and left.

It was still early, and no other candidates were coming to hand in their papers, so Commissioner Chou picked up Fan Chin's essay and read it through. But he was disappointed, 'Whatever is the fellow driving at in his essay?' he wondered. 'I see now why he never passed.'[8]

But having already decided to reward Fan Chin for his perseverance, when Chou Chin reads the essay for the third time he finds that every word is a pearl, and when the results of the examination are published Fan Chin's name is first on the list.

[8] Wu Ching-tzu, *The Scholars*, trs. Yang Hsien-yi and Gladys Yang, pp. 65–6.

'In what do they believe?'

The subject-matter of the examinations and the main ideological restraint upon despotism was the Confucian philosophy. Confucius (552–479 B.C.) thought of himself primarily as a teacher, a transmitter of the ancient cultural heritage, rather than a thinker or an originator. But in transmitting what he believed was the ancient tradition, ancient ideas and institutions, he of course interpreted them according to his own concepts. He evidently believed that the aim of government must be to ensure the happiness and welfare of the whole people. This should not, indeed it could not, be done by rigid and arbitrary laws, but by following 'The Way', the moral code, sanctioned by natural law and handed down by the sages of the past. For Confucius, the right to rule depended not on birth, but on character, education, and the ability to act as an example and radiate harmony.

> If one tries to guide the people by means of rules and keep order by means of punishment, the people will merely seek to avoid the penalties without having any sense of moral obligation. But if one leads them with virtue, and depends on *li* [the rules of propriety] to maintain order, the people will then feel their moral obligation to correct themselves.

The ruler should be served by men of the same kind, trained by widely diffused education for the business of government.[9]

But it was soon clear that moral qualities like righteousness and sincerity, and 'good customs' were not enough, and in the course of time the Confucianism which became the orthodoxy of the bureaucracy became tinged with ideas to which Confucius himself would have been hostile. The political philosophy associated with the first Chinese Empire, founded in 221 B.C., was that of the Legalists (or Realists).[10] They had none of Confucius's confidence in the power of virtue and example, nor did they subscribe to the view that the welfare of the people is the aim of government. For them, human nature was essentially evil, and the only way to achieve their aim – the welfare of the ruler and of the state – was by codified laws and regulations, by regimentation, by punishments and rewards. Some such ideas were clearly necessary in order to hold subsequent

[9] For Confucianism *see* Arthur Waley, *The Analects of Confucius* and H. G. Creel, *Confucius, The Man and The Myth.*
[10] Legalism is discussed in Arthur Waley, *Three Ways of Thought in Ancient China.*

empires together, so Confucian bureaucrats adapted their moralistic scruples to an inevitable measure of Machiavellian legalism.

Partly as a result of Confucian emphasis upon the power of moral suasion, Chinese officials in imperial times were, so to speak, amateurs in office. They were not supposed to restrict their personalities by specialization, because their duty was to manage people. For this, worldly wisdom, poise, a knowledge of history and of literature, and perhaps the rudiments of certain subjects such as water-conservancy, was enough. These accomplishments could be acquired in the first instance by being thoroughly conversant with the Confucian classics, and with the mountains of commentary about them.

During the Ming dynasty, as in most other periods of Chinese history, Confucianism was the official ideology. Even when emperors behaved in an un-Confucian way they tended to justify their behaviour by appealing to Confucian doctrine, just as rulers in the Christian West invariably paid lip-service to Christian dogma. But they did not merely employ Confucian morality as a cynical means of sugaring the astringent pill of autocracy. They too were heirs to the

160 Single-wheel cart drawn by mules or horses (*T'ien-kung k'ai-wu*)

329

Confucian tradition, and to a great extent prisoners of an all-pervading ideology. The language of government was the language of Confucianism; it dominated learning to the exclusion of all other philosophies. It was the orthodoxy of the emperor as well as his officials, and was the content of his education and that of his children. Its emphasis on filial loyalty as the first duty of everyone might not be in the interests of those emperors who had despotic tendencies; but no emperor could do without the bureaucracy, and the bureaucracy and Confucianism were mutually dependent.

Confucianism was perpetuated in a system of schools, from local schools in the countryside to the National University in the capital, which the Ming government, like previous régimes, had established and supported. Students were subsidized; private schools and academies were also encouraged. Orthodoxy was maintained by prescribing the texts and commentaries on the classics which were to be used. The state also singled out for praise men and women whose behaviour was a model of Confucian virtue and punished violations of the accepted code, even when private.

The Ming rulers encouraged scholarly work, particularly in the

161 Single-wheel cart,
pushed by one man
(*T'ien-kung k'ai-wu*)

Confucian tradition, but the period was not noted for great contributions to Chinese thought. Preoccupation with restoration after the Mongol interlude and a penchant for formal organization, led rather to rigid standardization and the confirmation of orthodoxy. The only really important philosopher was Wang Yang-ming (1472–1529), who developed neo-Confucian idealism and brought Confucian teaching nearer to Buddhism, giving it more stress on meditation and intuitive knowledge. He was also a famous general.

Confucianism, with its rationalistic character, did not provide the solace, the explanation of the inexplicable, that men seek in religion; but during the Ming dynasty, as in other periods, there was no single, centralized religious organization. The only strong challenge to Confucianism came from Buddhism and Taoism. These were the only religions with their own canon, priesthood, temples, theology, and rituals.

Buddhism was introduced into China from India in the first and second centuries A.D., and had, in the chaotic centuries which followed, a profound influence upon Chinese thought, both popular and élite, and upon Chinese culture from linguistics to literature, from sculpture to music. It even influenced Confucianism, to which it seemed so hostile. Buddhism also became an economic force in China, until the monasteries were suppressed by a jealous state.

By Ming times Buddhism was well adapted to polytheistic Chinese society, both from a theological point of view and in its relations with secular authority. But especially in its millenarian variants, it had often inspired rebellious movements. Indeed, Chu Yuan-chang himself had been a monk, and was probably associated with a secret society which had Buddhist connections.

Such rebellious currents were also associated with Taoism (pronounced *dowism*), the origins of which, like those of Confucianism, can be traced at least as far back as the fifth century B.C. These two great streams of Chinese thought, essentially hostile and yet sometimes interpenetrating, remained equally powerful until the modern world brought about fundamental changes in China. Confucianism diluted with legalism formed the basis of accepted political thought; Taoism, in contrast, was more a philosophy of protest, an inspiration to the rebel and escapist, to the imagination of the artist and to the silent observer of nature. Taoism denounced the established moral concept of the Confucians and preached naturalism, denounced knowledge and education – at least the Confucian variety – and urged men to forget self and enter a state of oneness with nature. Taoists looked back on a Golden Age of primitive collectivism in which the individual could be free, and spurned the hierarchical paternalism of the Confucian ideal. By the admixture of other elements, and partly in response to the challenge of Buddhism, a Taoist religion developed and flourished as a powerful force in popular culture; but philosophical Taoism never lost its intellectual appeal.[11]

The founder of the Ming was well aware of the potential danger of organized Buddhism and Taoism as subversive forces and of the danger of trying to suppress them. Control and neutralization were brought about by incorporating them into the state apparatus and by supervising their activities at all levels. The size of their religious communities was limited, and measures were taken to prevent all but genuinely religious persons from taking refuge under monks' habits.

Scholarship and the Arts

The period of tranquillity under the Ming rulers, if not very conducive to innovation in the realm of thought, did at least provide the opportunity for a mass of scholarly work. In the Yung Lo reign an enormous encyclopaedia was commissioned and 2,000 scholars worked for four years to complete it. It was a compendium of all the main works on history, geography, mathematics, ethics, and other subjects which were extant at the time. The compilation was finished in 1407, in 11,095 volumes; but it was too big to print, and only three manuscript copies were made, of which less than 400 volumes have survived.

Among the books which an early Portuguese visitor obtained in China were, 'Manie herbals, or bookes of herbes, for phisitions, shewing how they should be applied to heale infirmities.' But the work of this kind which has been called the greatest scientific achievement of the Ming period was yet to appear; Li Shih-chen's great pharmacopoeia, *Pen-ts'ao kang-mu*, which took twenty-six years to compile, was not published until 1596. It lists about 1,000 plants and other medicines, and has an appendix containing more

[11] For Taoism *see* Arthur Waley, *op. cit.* and D. C. Lau, *Tao Te Ching.*   332

162 Coal-mining in Ming China (*T'ien-kung k'ai-wu*)

than 8,000 prescriptions. Li Shih-chen described smallpox inoculation and the process of distillation, and discussed the value of many substances still in common use, such as iodine, mercury, kaolin, and ephedrine. Previous botanical work had laid the foundation for this achievement, such as the *Chiu-huang pen-ts'ao* (Herbal for Famine Relief), published in 1406, which lists and illustrates with woodcuts plants thought to be suitable as food in time of famine.

Another important book yet to be compiled was the technical treatise, the *T'ien-kung k'ai-wu* of Sung Ying-hsing (1637), which describes and illustrates every kind of manufacturing and productive process, some of which were fairly new at the time, but most of great antiquity.[12]

In the kinds of literature regarded as 'orthodox' – poetry and essays – there was little achievement during the Ming period. But in the drama and the novel, forms looked upon by the literati as frivolous and often subversive, there was great development. Under the Mongols, foreign influences were assimilated from central Asia

[12] There is now an English translation of this book: Sung Ying-phsing, *T'ien-kung k'ai wu, Chinese Technology in the Seventeenth Century*, trs. E-tu Zen Sun and Shiou-chouan Sun. *See also* Joseph Needham, *Science and Civilisation in China*.

MAP 15   China in the Ming period

and beyond to enrich the somewhat limited dramatic tradition of China. At the same time, the rejection by the Mongol rulers of the literati as administrators of their Chinese Empire, weakened the commitment of these scholars to traditional Confucian values and, perhaps from necessity as well, turned their creative activities to the writing of dramas and fiction in the vernacular. So the Yuan and Ming dynasties saw the flowering of these two forms of popular literature. They were still frowned upon by serious Confucians, but more and more people flocked to see the musical dramas. Where before people had gathered in tea-houses and temples to hear story-tellers, now those who could read could enjoy fully-fledged novels and stories which had evolved out of the repertoire and the prompt-books of the same popular story-tellers.

Although they did not win recognition as literature until the twentieth century, the best of these novels achieved extraordinary popularity. *San-kuo yen-i* (The Romance of the Three Kingdoms) by Lo Kuan-chung, was probably written in the first decades of the Ming dynasty.[13] It is an historical novel about the wars between the three kingdoms into which China was divided at the beginning of the third century A.D., and is full of colourful scenes of battle, tales of bravery, treachery, and cunning. One of the characters, the great statesman and commander Chu-ke Liang (181–234), mainly as a result of the account of him given in the novel, is immortalized in everyday speech in China to this day, his name being used as a synonym for a cunning plan or a brilliant solution to some problem. On one occasion, when his army was short of arrows, he created a fleet of twenty or more ships heavily laden with soldiers – made of straw. They deliberately went into battle in a fog, the few real soldiers and the boatmen making enough noise for all the others. Their indistinct but menacing advance provoked a hail of arrows, which Chu-ke collected from the straw dummies and then withdrew.

Shui-hu chuan (The Water Margin) by Shih Nai-an is a picaresque novel about Sung Chiang and his followers, bandits of the Robin Hood variety, who lived about A.D. 1000.[14] They are the heroes,

[13] *See The Romance of the Three Kingdoms*, trs. C. H. Brewitt-Taylor.
[14] Translated by Pearl Buck as *All Men Are Brothers*. For other Ming literature *see Stories from a Ming Collection, Anthology of Chinese Literature*, trs. Cyril Birch; *The Golden Casket: Chinese Novellas of Two Millenia*; *The Courtesan's Jewel Box: Chinese Stories of the Xth–XVIIth centuries*, (Peking 1957); *The Golden Lotus*, trs. Clement Edgerton.

courageous, loyal, and honourable; the cowardly and oppressive villains are the officials and ministers. The influence of this book was undoubtedly subversive and it is no wonder that it was frowned upon by officialdom; but perhaps this contributed to its popularity.

No art forms had greater prestige in China than painting and calligraphy. They were the main hobbies of educated men, whether officials, or gentry, or recluses, and even of some of the emperors. The Ming dynasty was no exception; a great many paintings have survived, and the names of over 1,000 painters, including that of the Hsüan Te emperor (1426–35) are known today. But Europeans remained for a long time unappreciative of their achievements, and were particularly disturbed by the lack of perspective.

Foreign Relations

Portuguese curiosity about China had been stimulated at the turn of the fifteenth and sixteenth centuries by the occasional presence of Chinese ships trading to Malacca. As far as Chinese law was concerned these ships had no right to be there; relations with foreign countries, even purely for trading purposes, were not the business of private individuals.

On his accession, the first Ming emperor had sent envoys to neighbouring countries and had established relations, it is said, with seventeen different states, including Korea, Japan, the Ryūkyū Islands, Annam, Cambodia, Siam, Champa, Sumatra, Java, Borneo, and Cola in south India. In doing so he was attempting to reassert an age-old tradition: the dominance of China in what was thought to be a Confucian universal order, and the Chinese emperor's paternal responsibility as the 'Son of Heaven' to attract 'outer barbarians' to come and be transformed by the civilizing essence of Confucian values.

This exalted concept of China's role in the world had its roots in the reality of her history. It had developed, as Chinese civilization grew increasingly sophisticated, in an oasis surrounded by a cultural desert of nomadic or tribal barbarity. Until the nineteenth and

163   (*opposite*) Landscape by Shen Chou, fifteenth to sixteenth centuries

336

164　A grain tribute
boat (*T'ien-kung
k'ai-wu*)

twentieth centuries, when Japan emerged as a modern power,
China's superiority, conceived in cultural rather than in political or
economic terms, had never been challenged in the East. No rival
civilization was conceivable.

The practical application of this concept was in the tributary
system. Barbarians who wished to benefit from Chinese superiority
and from her civilization were expected to acknowledge the emperor
as the 'Son of Heaven', the ruler of mankind, and take their place
in a political and ethical world order. The vassal ruler would be
granted a seal, he could profit from a defensive alliance, which might
be strengthened by a royal marriage; but there would be no
interference with the way he ran his country.

The system was important to China because it was part of the
traditional mystique of the emperor that his charismatic aura should
be felt in distant parts. It brought prestige which might be vital in
ruling China itself. The tribute system was also the normal channel
for diplomatic relations, and could be used for negotiation, for
bringing about alliances, for espionage, or for threatening other
countries. For the barbarians it meant association with the most
powerful state in the world.

But if all foreign relations of the Chinese Empire were contained

338

within the tributary system, this does not by any means exhaust its significance. In practice it had a very important, even fundamental commercial basis, and was the only legal form of foreign trade in many periods of Chinese history. The commercial aspect no doubt grew from the simple exchange of gifts between lord and vassal; but eventually large quantities of goods were involved, and the ritual significance was overshadowed by the practical. Tribute missions which came to China usually included either private merchants, or else agents of vassal rulers who had monopolies of foreign trade. Before the Ming dynasty trading points had already been established near the frontiers, and at Canton for instance, through which all foreigners and their goods had to pass. Here the government had the first choice of the merchandise. The rest was sold on the spot under official surveillance, or might be transported to the capital, where the merchants were allowed to trade for a few days. The prospect of such trading was sufficiently attractive to make it a common occurrence for foreign merchants to win the privilege by pretending to be tribute-bearers. In 1502 there were more than 150 self-styled rulers trading with China from central Asia under the cloak of tribute relations.

The states which the founder of the Ming dynasty tried to bring within his tributary empire were all on well-established trade routes, and it is possible that commercial relations had already existed with them in the previous two dynasties. So the need to reassert imperial control over this trade may well have been as important a consideration as internal and external prestige. At the same time, in order to strengthen the state monopoly, Chu Yuan-chang also pursued a strict policy of forbidding private trade, and contact between Chinese individuals and foreign states or tribes. The export of gold, silver, copper, iron, and weapons was forbidden, even by state emissaries sent abroad. There was also a ban on the use or sale of 'foreign spices and foreign goods' in China, and merchants were given three months to get rid of their stocks.

There were also political reasons for Chu Yuan-chang's policy. The defeat of his rivals had driven several of them to the offshore islands or other states, from which they hoped to stage a come-back. Then, nine years after the death of one of his prime ministers, the Ming emperor discovered that he had treacherously sent envoys to

339

Japan and to the Mongols who had been chased out of China. Such dangers led Chu Yuan-chang to break off relations with other states and only allow the Ryūkyūs, Siam, and Cambodia to continue sending tribute; he pressed on with the strengthening of coastal defences and forbade people to travel the seas or communicate with foreign countries.

Another important reason for this isolationist policy was the serious scourge of Japanese piracy. In Ming times the whole of China's coastline from Shantung to Canton was subject to the depredations of these maritime adventurers, samurai who combined piracy with trading, not unlike the gentlemen pirates of England a century or so later. The phenomenon was connected with the breakdown of central authority in Japan and the struggles between feudal barons. Large, highly organized bands fell upon the badly defended towns and villages along the coast of China to loot and take hostages; as the social crisis deepened in the fifteenth century, Chinese increasingly took part in these enterprises and alarmed the Ming rulers with the traditional spectre of trouble at home coinciding with danger from abroad. Sometimes they attacked major cities and their raids came to resemble full-scale invasions. Later, when Europeans began to arrive on the coast of China, they were not unnaturally mistaken for the same kind of visitors, and the memory of the Japanese 'dwarf robbers' coloured Chinese reactions to the coming of the West.

In the thirty years of Chu Yuan-chang's reign, as we have seen, the Chinese economy prospered; the financial needs of the régime, its desire for luxury goods and its urge for greater prestige and magnificence all increased. In an expansive and confident age, when China seemed at last to have the upper hand in her struggle against the nomads to the north, the isolationist policy must have seemed anachronistic. The Yung Lo emperor, although he did not dare to reverse openly the decisions of his brother, allowed increasing laxity in the application of the rules putting the seas out of bounds. So when the ruler of the Ryūkyūs in 1404 privately sent someone to China to buy porcelain, the emperor was ready to excuse him on the grounds that 'men from afar only know about seeking profit; how should they know about China's bans?' He also relaxed the rules against private Chinese merchants going abroad, and this increased

165   An audience of leave at the Chinese court, engraved
by T. Basire

foreign trade. But there were always disapproving voices to be heard,
with accusations about 'causing disturbances amongst the barbarians'
or 'enticing them into piracy'; moreover, illegal behaviour, such as
that of officials engaging in overseas trade, perhaps by pretending to
be imperial envoys, was later a pretext for renewing the bans.

   In general, however, the Yung Lo emperor made active efforts to
stimulate foreign trade. In the third year of his reign (1405) began
that remarkable series of seven maritime expeditions which rank
among the great feats of seamanship of all time. They were commanded by a Chinese Muslim, a court eunuch called Cheng Ho.
On the first voyage his fleet consisted of sixty-three ships, constructed
with watertight compartments, the largest of which are said to have
been over 400 feet long and 180 feet wide, with four decks. The total
complement was 27,560, including troops, officials, and officers, and
180 doctors. This expedition reached India. In subsequent voyages
Cheng Ho's ships visited more than thirty countries in the Indian
Ocean and archipelago, the Persian Gulf, Aden, and the east coast

341

of Africa. The rulers of Palembang (Sumatra) and Ceylon were brought back to China by force, so it is no wonder that the king of Malacca later came four times to Nanking of his own accord.

It is important to remember that as a Muslim Cheng Ho would have no prejudice against trade, indeed his ancestors could have been central Asian merchants; as a eunuch, he would not have been so deeply indoctrinated with Confucian values as a member of the scholar-bureaucracy; he would have none of their disdain for commerce and cannot have shared their ethnocentrism. He was a personal servant of the emperor, for whom trade was important and quite respectable when carried on in the guise of tribute.

Even today the reasons for this burst of maritime activity are not entirely clear. Some believe that the main motive of the Yung Lo emperor in sponsoring the expeditions was his desire to lay hands on the young emperor he had deposed in 1403, who was said to be abroad and plotting a counter-*coup*. But it is highly unlikely that the search would have continued for so long or ranged so far afield.

166   Macao, colonized by the Portuguese.
A sixteenth-century engraving

The desire for glory may have been part of their motivation, the urge to show the flag in foreign lands and increase the prestige of the empire at home and abroad. Perhaps the rulers of China felt the need for an ally, possibly in India, against the resurgence of the Mongols under Timur. In fact, however, that formidable conqueror died in 1405, before Cheng Ho set out on his first voyage, and afterwards there was no longer any danger of a Mongol attack on China; but this was not known in China at the time, so it is still possible that in the first instance the expeditions did have some connection with this threat. There seems little doubt that the most important reason was the desire to develop official trade by expanding Ming tribute relations with other countries. The former policy of isolation had reduced government revenue from foreign trade to the minimum; but in the Yung Lo reign there was not only economic growth but also a considerable increase in imperial expenditure, on the building of palaces in Peking, on military campaigns, and so on. So from the first Cheng Ho's expeditions had a commercial aim. His ships were called 'treasure ships'. They carried large quantities of gold, silver, silks, and porcelain, and returned with 'innumerable precious objects', rhinoceros horn, ivory, pearls, and spices. More small states were drawn into tribute relations with China, so that court-controlled trade increased, and the government seems even to have had a large surplus of some goods. In 1433 the salaries of officials in the two capitals were paid in pepper and sapan-wood. Whether the expeditions were economically profitable in themselves is another matter. Indeed, they were attacked by officialdom on the grounds that they were a costly extravagance and a drain on state resources.

While they lasted, the expeditions must also have stimulated domestic trade in China and the production of such goods as porcelain and silk, though we have no information as to the amounts exported. They increased China's knowledge of South East Asia and the Indian Ocean; they enhanced the techniques of maritime engineering, navigation, and the knowledge of wind and tides. Cheng Ho's ships used nautical compasses, as Chinese navigators had done since at least the early twelfth century. The Spanish friar Martin de Rada noted in the 1570s:

343

They also have a compass-needle, but not like ours, for it is only a very sensitive little tongue of steel which they touch with a loadstone. They place it in a little saucer full of sea-water and on which the winds are marked. They divide the compass into twenty-four parts, not into thirty as we do.[15]

Cheng Ho and his captains must have been able to add to the already considerable number of manuals of sailing directions available at the time. Their skill is shown by the fact that they circumnavigated Malaya through the Singapore Main Strait, a passage which was not found, or at least not used, by the Portuguese until 1615.

If the complex motives behind these spectacular and promising maritime expeditions are still the subject of speculation, so too are the reasons why they suddenly came to an end after 1433 and were never repeated. As primarily eunuch enterprises, they certainly aroused the hostility of the scholar-officials, who were unlikely to approve of any activity of their hated rivals, even if it had been profitable to the state. There were presumably other reasons of a more political nature, but we do not know them. Indeed Cheng Ho's achievements were given little attention in the official records of the time, and when another expedition was planned it was found that the bureaucracy had conveniently lost vital documents dealing with navigation and sailing directions.

The consequences for China of this failure to maintain sea-power in Asia were considerable. Sixty-four years after Cheng Ho's last voyage Vasco da Gama sailed into the Indian Ocean and inaugurated a long era in which the seas of the East were dominated by European powers.

Decline

By the dawn of the sixteenth century Ming China had already entered a period of slow decline. The emperor (Wu Tsung) who came to the throne in 1505 after forty years of ferocious struggles between rival cliques, was an inexperienced, weak, and pleasure-loving youth, who rapidly fell entirely under the influence of the eunuchs who had brought him up. His wedding cost the state a whole year's revenue of gold and silver. He then built himself palaces and gave himself up to the pursuit of pleasure; within 100 or 150 miles

[15] C. R. Boxer, *South China in the Sixteenth Century*.

344

167   An engraving of a Chinese junk, by de Bry

of the Huai Valley, it was said, no girl was safe.

During his reign the power of the imperial secret service agencies was greatly increased, and became completely dominated by court eunuchs. In 1508 a new secret police organization was established, which acted as a kind of coordinating headquarters for all such agencies, and terror and spying was extended throughout the whole country. The emperor resigned his authority to his eunuch favourite, who filled every post with his own supporters and amassed an enormous fortune.

Eunuch-controlled secret police government poisoned the political life of the nation. Officials were terrorized and corrupted by the necessity to protect themselves by bribery against vindictive dismissal. Those who enjoyed the protection of the powerful at Peking could do as they wished, and could seize land or kill without any restraint. Ultimately the burden of corrupt and oppressive government fell upon the ordinary people. 'The people are worse treated by these mandarins than by the devil in hell. Hence it comes that the people have no love for the king and for the mandarins, and every day they go on rising and becoming robbers', wrote a Portuguese who had been in a Chinese prison.

There was increasing concentration of land into fewer and fewer hands. In 1489 five royal estates in the Peking metropolitan province occupied 269,000 acres of land; another half million acres were taken up by 312 aristocrats' estates. By 1505 more than 3 million acres of land in the same region had been swallowed up by the great land-owners. Some estates grew to be ten times, and in one case fifty times, their former size in the space of a few years. Smaller landlords were not slow to take advantage of this trend. For the state it was disastrous, since the more powerful a landowner became the easier it was for him to evade paying taxes, and the more the state had to lose. By 1502 taxes could be levied on just over half of the total amount of land under cultivation – 74 out of 126 million acres. Since there was no decrease in state expenditure, the burden of taxation fell increasingly on those who could least afford to carry it. In the region of Suchow, for each acre of land which had not been absorbed into one of the great estates, the owner had to pay the tax rate for fourteen which had. In addition, after 1436, the land tax could be paid in silver, at a rate which was then 1 ounce of silver to 4 piculs of grain; but by the later fifteenth century 1 ounce of silver was equal to only 1 picul of grain, yet no provision for such depreciation had been made in fixing the taxes.

As the result of land-grabbing, official oppression, and the control of water resources by the rich and powerful, countless peasant proprietors were dispossessed and reduced to destitution. At the beginning of the dynasty there had been over 16 million households on the registers; in 1491 only 9 million could be registered as having fixed abodes. The main reason for this was that hundreds of thousands of people had become vagabonds or had put themselves and perhaps their land into the hands of the great landowners in order to avoid taxes and *corvée*. Thousands drifted into the towns, or became workmen, petty traders, beggars, soldiers, or monks. The rulers feared banditry and the undermining of social stability; they were also concerned at the loss of revenue which this increase of vaga-bondage involved. But they were incapable of acting until rebellion showed them that their own survival was in the balance. Laws could be passed ordering the destitute to return home, but economic reality was stronger than mere commands.

In the metropolitan area the tribulations of the rural population were most acute: in addition to other burdens the people were obliged to support thousands of horses of the army reserve; their

346

proximity to the capital made official oppression more direct. It was here, therefore, that the biggest popular rebellion of the mid Ming broke out in 1501. It lasted for three years and affected five provinces. Before it was finally suppressed it had involved almost half a million rebel fighters. Once rebellions had been put down, masses of destitute vagabonds could be forced to return home, where they were soon decimated by starvation and disease. Only after 1522 were desperate efforts made to reform and simplify the tax structure in order to increase revenue and spread the burden more equally.

Under corrupt and incompetent emperors there was no thought for maritime enterprise and tributary trade declined with the prestige of the empire. Between 1488 and 1493 only two tribute missions went to Peking, from Siam and Cambodia. Former vassal states had discovered that they could still carry on a profitable trade without the necessity of pretending subservience to the Ming rulers. They could contravene with impunity the laws of a weakening empire and continue trading with private Chinese merchants or smugglers.

As China grew weaker her nomad neighbours grew stronger. By the beginning of the fifteenth century there were two main Mongol groups in the northern steppe, the Ta-tan (Tatars) in the east and the Oirats to the west. Chinese policy was to divide and rule, to play one group off against the other and prevent fatal unity. But by the sixteenth century China was buying peace in the north by paying subsidies to her nomad enemies – a kind of tribute in reverse. There was little glory for China to receive Mongol tribute missions of 2,000 or 3,000 men, who looted all the way to the capital and had to be wined and dined when they got there. They had to be given gifts, and took away quantities of silk, for which in return China received horses – disproportionate both in number and in quality – and periods of peace on the frontier.

In spite of these signs of dynastic decline, many of the Portuguese and Spaniards who succeeded in penetrating China in the decades after the first official Portuguese mission in 1517 were impressed by what they saw. They were struck by the material wealth and technological skills of the 'mightie kingdome', and by its complex and sophisticated organization. Europe was at the dawn of a great age of invention and discovery which was soon to make China seem to be in a state of 'eternal standstill'; but at the time the vision of these

347

early travellers was as yet relatively unclouded by the pretensions of superiority which too many later visitors had. What better way of terminating this account of Ming China than by some of their observations?

In spite of the deterioration of government practice which seems so clear to us now, they thought that 'this mightie kingdome is one of the best ruled and gouerned of any that is at this time knowen in all the world'.[16] They noted that 'the cities be very gallant, specially near unto the gates, the which are marvelously great, and covered with iron'. In some of these cities, 'The walls . . . are very broad, in such wise that three or four men abreast can walk along them; and in some parts they are all paved on top with bricks. . . .' Within, '. . . the streets are so noble and broad, that ten or fifteen men on horseback can ride abreast along them, although there are very good covered ways along the sides, where live many merchants trading in many and diverse wares, and under the same covered ways are sold many fruits and many other things'. The towns were so crowded 'that at the entering of the gates . . . you can scarce get through'. 'I do not believe,' wrote Martin de Rada, 'that there is as populous a country in the world.' There were said to be 1,177,525 villages and 60,187,047 'tributers' (tax-payers). 'Some indication of their multitude is given by the fact that the fighting-men alone number nearly five millions.'

[16] Donald F. Lach, *op. cit.*, p. 764.

'Their ordinary apparel is long gowns with long plaits after our good ancient use; they curve over the breast and are tied down the side, and they all in general have very long sleeves to their gowns. They wear commonly black gowns of linen, or of fine or coarse serge of diverse colours.' Another visitor wrote: 'Their ordinary dress is a long loose upper-coat reaching down to the stockings, and a pair of long narrow drawers, and shoes made of straw. Some of them put underneath the coat, instead of a shirt, a silken net-work vest with a very wide mesh through which you can put your finger. . . . The important people . . . wear long silken gowns, usually of damask, reaching down to the ground, with very large and wide sleeves, and wide and large boots of dark colour, with the point of the toe turned up. . . . The bonnets of the common people are round, and those of the gentry square like clergymen's birettas, and all these are of horsehair.' Chinese women 'are very secluded and virtuous, and it was a very rare thing for us to see a woman in the cities and large towns, unless it was an old crone. Only in the villages, where

169   Ming Emperor Hsian Tsung (1487–1505)

it seemed that there was more simplicity, the women were more often to be seen, and even working in the fields.'

The men from Europe were impressed by such a 'well husbanded country' – 'Only the mountains that are high and beaten with the weather, and are not fit to plant any thing, remain unprofitable.' Finally, 'They are a plain, humble and obliging people, save only the mandarins who set themselves up as gods. They are great workers and very active in their trades, so that it is astounding to see how diligently they furnish their works, and in this they are most ingenious.'[17]

[17] C. R. Boxer, *op. cit.*

Simplified Chart of Chinese Dynasties

Ch'in	221–207 B.C.
Western Han	202–8 A.D.
Eastern Han	25–220
Three Kingdoms	221–280
Period of Disunion	280–589
Sui	589–617
T'ang	618–906
Sung	960–1279
Yuan (Mongol)	1280–1367
Ming	1368–1643
Ch'ing (Manchu)	1644–1911

The Japanese Scene in the Sixteenth Century

RICHARD STORRY

The Political Situation

SO FAR AS IS KNOWN, the first Europeans to set foot on Japanese soil were Portuguese, whose boat, bound for Macao, was driven ashore on an island off the Kyushu coast in 1542 or 1543. The fact that these sixteenth-century mariners and merchants were evidently the first people from the West to reach the country testifies to Japan's geographical separation from the European world. Indeed, in terms of Europe's 'discovery' of the world, only Australia, New Zealand, the Pacific islands, and the South Pole were more remote.

Thanks to Marco Polo's account of his travels 'Cipango' (Japan) was thought to be a land rich in gold; and it was, of course, in the hope of reaching 'Cipango' that Columbus sailed across the Atlantic. However, a more realistic picture of Japanese conditions was gained after Portuguese and Spanish vessels penetrated the seas of China and the Philippines. For Japanese traders were carrying on a lively commerce along the China coast and in South East Asia well before the Europeans arrived in those parts. So it was possible for the inquisitive traveller to pick up some broadly reliable information about Japan even if he never made the long northward voyage to that country. He would know that it comprised at least three principal islands and hundreds of smaller ones. He would know that Japan was split into a number of 'kingdoms', whose rulers owed allegiance to a shadowy emperor in the great city of Miyako (Kyoto), a city more populous than any in Europe. He would discover that the inhabitants of Japan, like those of Burma and Siam, worshipped the Buddha and enjoyed a considerable reputation for valour and ferocity in the martial arts. As for Japan's resources, examples of these could be seen both in China and the Indies, in the shape of silver and copper bars, lacquerware, and swords. A perceptive European visitor to the Far East would soon conclude that despite certain broad similarities, such as the use of much of the same ideographic script, Japan was not at all like China.

170   The arrival of the Portuguese and St Francis Xavier
in Japan

Japan in fact was another world. To begin with the apex of
society, the Son of Heaven, the supreme ruler of China, was unques-
tionably much more powerful than his counterpart in Japan. Politically, the Japanese emperor was virtually powerless. Yet the position
of his House was more exalted, more secure, than that of the Ming
sovereign in China. For the Japanese monarchy was sacrosanct.
The emperors enjoyed ineffable prestige not only as high priests of
Shinto, the indigenous faith existing side by side with the Buddhism
that had come from China, but also as linear descendants of the sun
goddess, Amaterasu O-Mikami. If the emperors of China were
mediators between Earth and Heaven, effective only so long as they
governed with virtue, firmness, and benevolence, the emperors of
Japan partook of an inherited divinity irrespective of any public or
personal virtue which they may or may not have possessed. Thus in
China one imperial dynasty could be replaced by another. Through
gross misgovernment a ruler could lose 'the mandate of Heaven'. In
certain circumstances, then, rebellion was legitimate, and the crea-

tion of an entirely new line of emperors was regarded as a proper undertaking. In Japan this was strictly inconceivable. An emperor could be forced to abdicate, but his successor must be found from within the historic dynasty. There could be no usurpation of the throne by a family unrelated to the Imperial House. The very idea was blasphemous.

How was it, then, that by the sixteenth century the venerated emperors of Japan had long lost their governmental powers? When considering this question the first thing to remember is that from the earliest recorded times up to the constitution of 1946 they were *in theory* the ultimate source of all authority and the final arbiters in all matters of government. Whoever actually ruled Japan in the real sense did so, invariably, in the emperor's name.

The real power of the emperors had withered as early as the tenth century A.D.; for by that time the Fujiwara family of the court nobility, intimately and continuously linked through marriage with the imperial house, were the effective rulers of Japan. During the twelfth century the emperors, either on the throne or in retirement, were able to recover a measure of administrative power from their Fujiwara ministers. But this success was short-lived. A military family, the Taira, gained an overriding influence at court until it was totally destroyed in civil war by another military house, the Minamoto. The latter, under Yoritomo, established the characteristically Japanese institution of the *Bakufu*, or 'Camp Office', a form of government designed by and primarily for the warrior class.

The head of the *Bakufu* was the shogun. This word is an abbreviation of the title *Sei-i tai-shogun*, which means 'barbarian-suppressing generalissimo'. The title was not a new one when Minamoto Yoritomo was given it by the reigning emperor (a boy of thirteen) in 1192. It had been granted in times past to commanders engaged in campaigns against the Ainu, the aboriginal inhabitants of the country whose resistance in the east and north had to be overcome before Japanese control of Honshu, the main island, could be fully assured. But from the end of the twelfth century the shogunate became a permanent office, traditionally reserved for members of the Minamoto house.

The first *Bakufu* was founded by Minamoto Yoritomo at Kamakura, far from the imperial capital at Kyoto. It endured for about

150 years. But it was only in the early part of that period that the Minamoto shoguns exercised more than nominal power. Yet another warrior household, the Hojo (loyal vassals of the Minamoto), held the *Bakufu* together, once it was apparent that Yoritomo's heirs tended to lack both ability and force of character.

It was the Hojo who successfully rallied Japan's warriors, in the name of emperor and shogun, against the two Mongol invasions in the late thirteenth century. But Hojo hegemony collapsed some fifty years after that crisis. Power now came into the hands of the Ashikaga (themselves of the original Minamoto house); and Takauji, the first Ashikaga shogun, established his *Bakufu* in the Muromachi district of Kyoto, ushering in what is commonly known as the 'Muromachi Age', which lasted until just after the middle years of the sixteenth century.

The Muromachi Age was one of violent domestic upheavals combined with new and important developments in both economic life and the cultivation of the arts. The civil strife of the fourteenth and fifteenth centuries presents a complicated and unedifying spectacle. For a time there were even rival imperial courts at war with each other. The period was marked by what the Japanese call *gekokujo*, or 'the overthrow of seniors by their juniors'. In other words it was an age during which many old-established warrior families were overthrown by upstarts greedy for land and power. Loyalty – perhaps the most important of the great traditional virtues – did not flourish in this era of civil wars. Treachery was the order of the day. An English scholar sums up this state of affairs as follows:

> In Ashikaga times the turncoat is a common figure. His feats are startling but they may be explained if not justified by the inconstancy of the great leaders, whose conduct was rarely guided by thoughts of rectitude. Their subordinates, the general run of warriors, were for the most part concerned with the private interests of their own families and not with matters of principle. They wanted rewards, and civil wars offered the best opportunity for gain, since the victors could take the land of the vanquished.[1]

The same scholar, however, has pointed out that Japan's economy was if anything stimulated rather than depressed by the civil wars. The economic foundation of the country was its ricefields and forests, and the damage done by warfare to these national assets was

[1] George Sansom, *A History of Japan, 1334–1615*, p. 91.

171 Minamoto
Yoritomo

evidently so small as to be negligible. Moreover, those actually
involved in all the fighting were mostly, if not exclusively, members
of the samurai class. Many of these of course were, at that time,
farmers as well as warriors, but they formed only a minority of the
total farming population. The peasants as a whole suffered, it is true,
many trials – typhoons, crop failures, and, at certain times in certain
areas, the depredations of bandits (as that famous Japanese film
The Seven Samurai illustrates most vividly) – nevertheless, it was
uncommon for ordinary peasants to be pressed into combat service.

The movement of armies across the country, so it is claimed,
created 'a need for the services of local entrepreneurs in the pro-
curement, storage, and transport of supplies and the improvement
of communications'.[2] Be that as it may, it is certainly true that during
the Ashikaga period there was a notable increase in the use of metal
currency. This was one of the consequences of the renewed trade
with China after the establishment of Ming rule in 1368. For among
the leading imports from China were large quantities of copper coins.

If there were long periods when the authority of the *Bakufu* was

[2] *Ibid.*, p. 181.

scarcely felt in areas remote from Kyoto this meant that local lords had every inducement to enhance their own power. Those possessing good harbours took care to encourage not only coastal trade but also trade with China. It should be admitted, too, that such harbours were at times the bases for the dreaded *wako*, or Japanese pirates, who raided the shores of China. It was the lure of foreign trade, as well as a marked interest in foreign weapons (firearms in particular), that inclined provincial lords in Kyushu to give a friendly reception to the Portuguese, when these strangers first appeared.

At this important moment of time, the middle of the sixteenth century, when the Portuguese arrived, the Ashikaga shogunate was scarcely more powerful than the imperial house itself. Broadly speaking there were two main concentrations of power, at least in military terms. One was towards the east of the country, in the region of Kamakura and the Kanto plain (where modern Tokyo stands). The other was in the west, in Kyushu and the area of Honshu facing the Shimonoseki Straits. Power in the east was divided between four warrior lords and in the west between three. Over these barons Kyoto exercised only the most shadowy authority. When Portuguese missionaries, reporting to Macao or Rome, spoke of Japanese barons as 'kings' they were by no means wholly distorting reality.

172   Ashikaga Takauji (1305–58), the first Ashikaga shogun, either on the battlefield or shortly after a battle (one of his arrows is broken)

356

Despite the rivalries and divisions between provincial barons that gave rise to frequent civil wars, Japan remained a unified country in the cultural sense; and this cultural unity held the promise that once Japan was politically reunited under firm central government the advantages of such government would be generally perceived. The problem in the sixteenth century was how such central government could be established, and by whom. It was a problem that would not be solved satisfactorily until the last twenty years of the century. But the first signs of the future unification of the country, by armed force, were perceptible in the 1560s, with the emergence of Oda Nobunaga as the dominant warrior in central Japan.

Nobunaga

Nobunaga (he is always called by his personal, rather than family, name) took as his motto (it was engraved on his seal) the aphorism, 'Rule the Empire by Force'; and most of his life was spent planning or fighting battles. He was one of the first Japanese of his day to understand the proper tactical handling of firearms. He was able to equip most of his foot-soldiers with muskets, since he gained control

173 Oda Nobunaga, who had brought half the Empire under his domination by the time of his death in 1582

357

of territories noted for the excellence of their gunsmiths. In one of his decisive engagements he made devastating use of these weapons, having lined up his musketeers in rows behind barricades against which the horsed warriors of the enemy charged, only to be annihilated. It was a battle that revolutionized warfare in Japan; for it marked the transition from individual to collective combat.

Only about thirty years had passed since the first Portuguese muskets – two of them – had come into Japanese possession. It was not long before native muskets, copied from foreign models, were being made in large numbers. But until Nobunaga exploited their use to the full the new weapons were not employed with notable skill.

Like many of the barons of the *Sengoku Jidai*, 'the period of the country at war', as this age is known in Japanese history, Nobunaga was implacable when faced with opposition. In victory he could be merciless indeed. Among the various centres of local power were the monasteries of certain sects of Buddhism, exerting a decidedly secular influence in the politics of the time, their monks being well armed and their abbots renowned, like eleventh-century Norman bishops, for their martial prowess. The fighting monks of Hieizan, on the hill-crests near Kyoto, incurred Nobunaga's enmity. He destroyed them and their numerous monasteries – some 3,000 buildings – putting to death without exception all who fell into his hands; and the captives included many women and children.

Possibly because of his suspicion of Buddhists who dabbled in secular affairs, and because he himself seems to have had no religion, Nobunaga was more than tolerant in his attitude to the few foreign missionaries, Jesuit fathers, who had entered the country. To one or two of them he showed considerable kindness; and letters to Europe from Jesuits in Japan show that they had the highest regard for this autocratic, rough-mannered warrior, who was (as one such letter puts it) 'contemptuous of all other kings and nobles of Japan'. Jesuit dislike of institutional Buddhism may well have inclined Nobunaga to favour the missionary priests. At all events, he extended his cordiality towards one missionary so far as to issue a licence permitting him to live in Kyoto and threatening severe punishment against anyone who dared to harm the foreigner.

This act of goodwill took place in 1569, by which date Nobunaga was the master of the capital, having in the previous year secured the

174 Portuguese merchants and priests land in Japan

installation of Yoshiaki as the fifteenth and, as it turned out, last Ashikaga shogun. In keeping with tradition, Nobunaga treated the reigning emperor with immense respect; and this took a practical form, for he contributed generously to the building of a new imperial palace. Outward deference, too, was shown by the king-maker to the shogun Ashikaga Yoshiaki. But the latter fell out with him and he deposed him in 1573. This marks the end of the Ashikaga shogunate as an institution. There was to be no revival of the office of shogun until 1603, when the appointment was given to Tokugawa Ieyasu.

Nobunaga's death occurred before he could accomplish his life's ambition – to be the *de facto* ruler of the empire. In 1582, in his forty-ninth year, he was killed in a surprise attack made on him by one of his main supporters, in revenge, it is said, for a personal insult earlier suffered in silence. Had he lived, Nobunaga might have succeeded in bringing the whole country under his control. As it was, he dominated half the provinces of Japan.

These occupied a key position geographically, stretching in a wide belt across the centre of the empire, embracing two alluvial plains of great agricultural value: namely, the Kinai Plain, which included both Kyoto and the important trading port of Sakai (near the present Osaka), and the Nobi Plain at the head of Ise Bay (the area of modern Nagoya). To symbolize his ascendancy Nobunaga, during the last decade of his life, built an impressive fortress on the shore of Lake Biwa, guarding one of the main approaches to Kyoto. This was Azuchi Castle, completed in 1579. It combined great strength with considerable aesthetic appeal. The combination is typical of Japanese castle architecture, as visitors to modern Tokyo can understand, when they see the walls and watch-towers of the imperial palace in the heart of the city. Water forms the first line of defence, contained in wide, often concentric, moats: in the case of Azuchi the waters of Lake Biwa provided a natural defence, since the castle stood on a promontory so nearly surrounded by the lake as to be almost an island. At Azuchi the main tower or keep rose seven storeys above ground-level, and the interior of each was painted with decorative

175 The tower of Osaka Castle, as restored in the mid twentieth century

designs by famous artists of the day, such as Kano Eitoku. A Jesuit father from Lisbon, Luis Frois, on good terms with Nobunaga, has given us a description of Azuchi Castle, which, he declares, 'as regards architecture, strength, wealth, and grandeur may well be compared with the greatest buildings of Europe'. Frois goes on:

> In the middle there is a sort of tower which they call *tenshu* and it indeed has a far more noble and splendid appearance than our towers. It consists of seven floors, all of which, both inside and out, have been fashioned to a wonderful architectural design. . . . Some are painted white with their windows varnished black according to Japanese usage and they look extremely beautiful, others are painted red, others blue, while the uppermost one is entirely gilded. . . . As the castle is situated on high ground and is itself very lofty, it looks as if it reaches to the clouds and it can be seen from afar for many leagues.[3]

It may be thought that this description is not free from hyberbole, and unfortunately Azuchi Castle does not survive for us to check such statements against reality – it was destroyed not long after Nobunaga's death – but Frois's observations are probably fairly accurate. It is said that among the castles that survive in Japan today the keep at Himeji (about 1600) resembles the famous *tenshu* of Azuchi Castle; and Himeji seen from ground-level certainly 'looks as if it reaches to the clouds'.

Nobunaga's fortress set the style for a new, more massive, type of Japanese castle, a structure built upon a base of gigantic stones. (One of these, at Osaka Castle, is 47 feet long and 19 feet high. Kipling, during his visit to Japan, was impressed by its size and wrote that although the stone was granite 'the men of old had used it like mud'.) Thus at a moment in time when the castle in Europe was beginning to lose its military importance the Japanese castle was entering a new stage of development, becoming, in fact, more formidable both as a stronghold and as the nucleus of a thriving commercial community. For Nobunaga evidently intended Azuchi to be the headquarters of his government when, as he hoped, he was in a position to rule the whole country in the emperor's name. So he built a town as well as a castle at Azuchi, a town that would be populated by merchants and artisans as well as by warriors.

This was a period when many *joka-machi*, or 'castle towns',

---

[3] Michael Cooper, S. J. (ed.), *They Came to Japan*, p. 134. The quotation comes from Frois's *Historia de Japam*.

176 A *daimyo*'s procession through the streets of Yedo. All the citizens kneel respectfully until it has passed

began to flourish. A land survey carried out in the last decade of the sixteenth century shows that there were 160 fiefs, and most of these had one or more castles and castle towns. Their main purpose, of course, was military defence; but, as time went by and more peaceful conditions prevailed, they achieved growing importance as economic and cultural centres of the provinces in which they were located. A very large number (perhaps as many as 200) of modern Japanese cities and towns – Nagoya, Sendai, Hiroshima, Fukuoka are examples – came into being originally as castle towns. Indeed Tokyo itself springs from Yedo, the greatest *joka-machi* of them all, after the completion of the Tokugawa fortress there early in the seventeenth century.

Subservient, inevitably, to the *daimyo* (the feudal lord) who occupied the castle, the merchants of the *joka-machi* were by no means an oppressed class. Some profited enormously. Indeed, in certain cities, such as Sakai, merchant houses had won exemption from *daimyo* interference; and the Jesuits, reporting to their superiors

362

in Macao and Rome, speak of 'free cities', of a type with which they were familiar in Europe.

Nevertheless, it was the *Sengoku Daimyo*, 'the lords of the country at war', who shaped great events. The merchants of sixteenth-century Japan, important as they may have been, were not qualified, and probably cherished no desire, to compete with the warrior lords.

Hideyoshi and His Era

It was of course among such military commanders that the successor to Nobunaga would be found, after his violent death in 1582. For a few days it looked as though his assassin might maintain himself in power in central Japan. But he was rapidly defeated by the most famous of Nobunaga's generals, one of the outstanding figures in Japanese history, Toyotomi Hideyoshi.

Hideyoshi completed the work of unification – more strictly, *reunification* – begun by Nobunaga. He is a rather more attractive figure than his predecessor. Nobunaga's vindictiveness and cruelty stamp him, when all is said in his favour, as a callous tyrant. Hideyoshi seems both more complex and more human. And he was a better strategist and commander in war. An exceedingly well-known

177 Toyotomi
Hideyoshi (1536–98)

story, part of the nation's folklore – the Japanese equivalent, we might say, of Bruce and the spider or King Alfred and the cakes – tells us something of the contrasting characters of Hideyoshi and Nobunaga. Faced with a valuable cage bird that refused to sing, Hideyoshi is supposed to have said: 'I'll force it to sing for me'; whereas Nobunaga is reported to have shouted: 'I'll kill it if it doesn't sing.'[4]

Hideyoshi's rise to power was more remarkable than Nobunaga's. The latter was the son of a minor chieftain of some substance, known to the court in Kyoto and a man of a certain standing in his own province. Hideyoshi's father was a humble foot-soldier, barely on the borderline of the gentry class. Hideyoshi rose (as a Spanish Franciscan in Japan put it) 'from the dust of the earth and originally was a poor unknown fellow'. In the sixteenth century as in the twentieth (until dietary improvements began to have their effect) the physical height of most Japanese was notably less than that of most Europeans. Hideyoshi, however, seemed so short of stature as to be almost a dwarf among his compatriots. Yet this particular disadvantage is often allied with passionate ambition; and this was certainly so with Hideyoshi. He was scarcely more than thirty when he had become indispensable to Nobunaga as a most gifted improviser of plans for any military emergency. At forty-six he was Nobunaga's principal lieutenant; and he was attacking with some success a castle in the west (Takamatsu) when Nobunaga was killed in Kyoto. A courier brought the news to Hideyoshi the day after the event took place. Hideyoshi kept the information to himself, came to an immediate accommodation with his foe in battle, and marched his force east towards Kyoto with great speed. Only nine days after Nobunaga's death he overwhelmed the army of the assassin (Akechi Mitsuhide, sometimes called 'the nine days shogun') who was killed while escaping from the field.

To recount the campaigns and battle whereby Hideyoshi secured the allegiance of every *daimyo* in the land – the task took him eight years – would be an excursion into Japanese geography and into the logistics of moving scores of armed men from east to west, and west to east. But the tale would be less filled with horrors than the story of Nobunaga's scramble to power. Hideyoshi took pains to win beaten

---

[4] The story goes on to relate that Tokugawa Ieyasu – the founder of the Tokugawa shogunate and, like Hideyoshi, rather younger than Nobunaga for whom he fought – declared (when faced with the obstinate bird): 'I shall wait until it does sing.'

178   Hideyoshi's army sets out for Korea in 1592

opponents to his side, often treating them with generosity after their
defeat. In the suppression of turbulent Buddhist monks, for example,
he did not put all enemy survivors to the sword once the fight was
over. This punishment was reserved for a few of the leaders alone.

But it is perhaps unnecessary to discuss here the martial operations
that Hideyoshi conducted in different regions of the country, culminating in 1590 with the overthrow of the lord of Odawara, at the
western edge of the Kanto plain – an event that persuaded the barons
of the north to lose no time in submitting to the new master of Japan.
Now at last, for the first time in over a century, the land was unified
and at peace.

In the accomplishment of this ideal Hideyoshi received invaluable
help from a redoubtable *daimyo* named Tokugawa Ieyasu.[5] Hideyoshi had been Nobunaga's direct vassal. Ieyasu had been a junior
ally, and his relationship with Hideyoshi was much the same. For a
time, after Nobunaga's death, the two warrior lords quarrelled, but
firm reconciliation followed hostilities; and until his death, in
1598, Hideyoshi ruled Japan in the knowledge that the powerful
Ieyasu would support him. And Ieyasu was to consolidate the

---

[5] A confusing aspect of their careers is that both Hideyoshi and Ieyasu had more than one
name. The former was known, for example, as Kinoshita Tokichiro in earlier life; while
Ieyasu's earlier surname was Matsudaira.

national unity established by Hideyoshi. So the three *Sengoku Daimyo* – Nobunaga, Hideyoshi, and Ieyasu – are linked together in history, as in their lives; for between the three of them a new Japan was forged after years of centrifugal strife. Nobunaga, it has been said, quarried the stones; Hideyoshi shaped them; Ieyasu set them into place.

In order to cement his position, in terms both of political ascendancy and personal wealth, Hideyoshi rearranged from time to time the pattern of feudal fiefs, ordering a *daimyo* together with all his retainers to move from one region to another. He regarded this drastic uprooting of households as necessary in order to isolate potentially hostile barons from likely allies. On one occasion no less than twenty-three fiefs had to change their masters in one day. Father Frois – Nobunaga's friend – tells us that when these compulsory transfers took place a *daimyo*'s retainers.

> must needs pack up and leave with what they could carry, without speaking or saying a word, and if they did not bestir themselves speedily,

179 Feudal lord, followed by Samurai, approaches Ieyasu's castle in Yedo

those who came in with the incoming daimyo would as likely as not seize their goods and let them lump it.[6]

Needless to say, the redistribution of fiefs usually involved, as part of the operation, the surrender to Hideyoshi of some valuable parcels of land; and thus his own resources were enhanced. In the end he acquired an immense personal fortune.

But Hideyoshi was more than a mere feudal overlord. He himself had come from what could be called the yeoman class, of small farmer-warriors. Once in supreme power, however, he showed his disapproval of the social mobility of which his own career was an example. He decreed the confiscation of all weapons in the hands of those who were not clearly of the samurai class. This was known as his 'Sword Hunt'. To sweeten the pill he announced that all such weapons would be melted down for use as nails in the fashioning of a giant Buddha, to be erected in a new monastery in Kyoto. The enforced surrender of swords, spears, and muskets for this end would assure the contributors of religious merit in the next world, and in this. He also insisted that farmers stay in their own localities, that they remain firmly attached to the soil they cultivated. Nobody was permitted, for example, to leave his land to become a tradesman or labourer in the nearby town. To perfect the control required by such regulations a census of population was taken and a series of land surveys carried out. In short, 'Hideyoshi was determined to separate the peasants from all other classes, and in particular to distinguish them from the military class at every social level.'[7] This stratification of society was to be carried further and eventually systematized by Ieyasu and his successors.

By the year 1590, as we have seen, Hideyoshi had satisfied a great ambition – to be the arbiter of his nation's fate – and this, it might be thought, would be enough for one man. But, according to an old story, he had vowed at the shrine in Kamakura of Yoritomo, founder of the first *Bakufu*, that he would not rest content with bringing all Japan under his sway but would go on to conquer China. No doubt there was more than a touch of megalomania in Hideyoshi's make-up, as in Nobunaga's. But a simple desire for conquest may not be

---

[6] C. R. Boxer, *The Christian Century in Japan*, p. 173. The quotation is from a letter by Frois dated 20 February 1588.
[7] Sansom, *op. cit.*, p. 332.

the whole, or even the major, explanation for Hideyoshi's huge overseas expedition, his invasion of Korea, in 1592. It can be argued that his principal aim was to give vent to the energies, and deplete the ranks, of the armies of warriors whom he had subdued, but whose continued good behaviour could not be completely guaranteed. It is significant that Hideyoshi himself never crossed the water to lead the great host he dispatched to Korea, although he planned and directed the strategy of the forces in the field. A generalissimo obsessed, like Ghengis Khan or Timur, with lust for the conquest of new lands could not have resisted the temptation to command his armies in battle.

This continental adventure was a disaster for the people of Korea, whose king had refused to allow the Japanese free passage for their projected attack on Ming China. For the invaders were unable to advance beyond the Yalu. Therefore, the fighting – involving, perhaps, half a million men, Japanese, Koreans, and Chinese – took place entirely on Korean soil. In addition to the normal hazards of warfare – the requisitions and manifold brutalities of intruding armies – the Korean peasantry were subjected, thanks to the Japanese invasion, to the miseries of famine and disease. Indeed, the entire undertaking brought little glory and no permanent gains to Hideyoshi and his warriors.[8] There were in fact two expeditions, the second in 1597. But this was withdrawn the following year, after Hideyoshi's death and in accordance with his last injunctions.

Art and Culture

Hideyoshi's era is noted for a certain distinctive style in art and culture generally. Its chief characteristic may be said to be a decided liveliness, as though reflecting a new burst of energy on a national scale. Nor is this in any way a misleading impression. Japan in the second half of the sixteenth century did witness a rapid growth in the production of all kinds of commodities. Foodstuffs, for example, appear to have been plentiful; and there was a very considerable expansion of trade, stimulated of course by contact with the Portuguese. The output of the gold- and silver-mines was much improved.

---

[8] Another view is put forward by a Belgian scholar, Father Goedertier. 'The two expeditions ended with a great loss of men and materials. However, one result was good – the Japanese had brought home thousands of Korean artisans and scholars, and the arts of printing, dyeing, weaving, and ceramics were studied in a new light.' Joseph M. Goedertier, *A Dictionary of Japanese History*, p. 23.

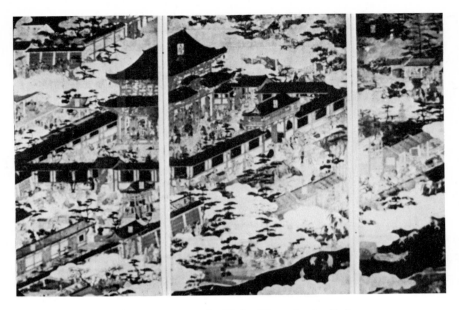

180 Great Buddha's sanctuary in Hoko Temple, built by Hideyoshi

One consequence of the movement of large armies was a general development of land communications, the upkeep of roads receiving particular attention; and this of course had favourable effects on the national economy. Furthermore, both Nobunaga and Hideyoshi were fond of conspicuous expenditure, and they set an example followed on a lesser scale by others – the rich merchant as well as the *daimyo* – who could afford it.

If Nobunaga's rough gusto found expression in Azuchi Castle, Hideyoshi's vitality was reflected in the great edifices built under his supervision, for example, the castle at Osaka, larger than Azuchi, and the splendid Jurakudai ('Mansion of Pleasure') at Kyoto, and the palace at Fushimi south of the capital. Nothing survives of the Jurakudai or of the Fushimi palace;[9] but the latter has given the name of the rising ground on which it stood – Momoyama – to

[9] This needs some qualification. Nothing survives on the two *sites* of these palaces. But a temple in Kyoto, the Nishi Hongan-ji, is fortunate enough to have in its grounds a villa, the Hiunkaku ('Flying-Cloud Pavilion'), that was once part of the Jurakudai. Also in the same temple are to be seen the very impressive audience hall from Fushimi, together with some other rooms, the Noh stage, and an imperial envoy's gate from Fushimi.

181　Sixteenth-century Japanese market scene

Hideyoshi's Age. Indeed, art historians commonly refer to the Azuchi-Momoyama period, a brief span of years – 1579–98 – from the completion of Nobunaga's castle to the year of Hideyoshi's death.

Mr Langdon Warner, the well-known authority on traditional Japanese art, describes Azuchi-Momoyama as the era in which the Great Decorators began their work.

> Our English term Great Decorators for the artists of that day is most apt. And even if it implies mere decoration and suggests a question as to what they decorated, and if we suspect a lack of deep intellectual purpose, the term is not unfair. Their subject-matter was never profound like that in the religious icons of former ages or in the philosophical landscapes by the monkish ink painters of the Ashikaga period. And yet a pair of screens by Sanraku or Eitoku, standing quite alone, decorating nothing, gives one an almost physical shock; we are not concerned with intellectual content.[10]

[10] Langdon Warner, *The Enduring Art of Japan*, pp. 64–5. Kano Eitoku (1543–90) was an outstanding painter of what became known as the Kano School. Kano Sanraku (1559–1635) was one of Eitoku's students. 'The greatest painter of this period, however, was not a member of the Kano school and for this reason was neglected until his rediscovery in recent times. He was Hasegawa Tohaku . . . who lived from 1539 to 1610.' (Hugo Munsterberg, *The Arts of Japan*, p. 131.)

For those who adorned their interiors with paintings on walls and screens the castles and palaces of the age (these two terms are almost interchangeable) provided a grand setting on a new scale. The size of such paintings was larger than had been known in earlier years, and it seems likely that Western painting, examples of which entered Japan during this period, may have had some influence here. It is certainly true that the new castles of Japan owed something to European models.

Although it was built after Hideyoshi's death, the Nijo Castle (begun in 1602) in Kyoto is perhaps the most impressive surviving example of the Azuchi-Momoyama style in terms of architecture and interior decoration. The visitor there today can see the superb audience hall, revealing that mixture of elegance and strength which is a characteristic attribute of Azuchi-Momoyama. Here great paintings on the walls – huge pine trees against a background of gold – are contrasted with the severe simplicity of the *tatami* (woven rice-straw matting) covering the floor, where more than 100 retainers knelt in attendance on Ieyasu and his heirs.

This kind of contrast, between the gorgeously decorated and the austere, is typical of the period, and also of later years under the Tokugawa *Bakufu*, when Japan cut herself off almost entirely from the Western world. A decided simplicity or plainness seems to represent the true aesthetic tradition in Japan. Of this the finest illustration is to be found in the Grand Shrines at Ise, near Nagoya, which are structures in an archaic style, wholly undecorated and most pleasing, because of their clean lines and fair proportions in a setting of great natural beauty. With their unpainted wooden walls and steep, thatched roofs, the Ise Shrines are at first as plain as cowsheds. There is no space here to dwell on the interesting question of why such uncompromising simplicity should appeal so deeply, as it always has, to Japanese taste. For one thing, there is the influence of age-old Shinto standards and practices, especially the obsession with purification and cleanliness, the removing of all accretions to what is felt to be originally pure and uncluttered.[11] There is also the influence, enormous and pervasive, of Zen Buddhism, which abhors all that is elaborate and high-flown. But bread without any jam on it can become tedious to the most ascetic. The decorative arts – meaning the

[11] Nothing gave more offence during the period of the Occupation, after Japan's surrender in 1945, than the well-meant practice of many American officers, who lived in houses commandeered from the Japanese, of *varnishing* the wooden surfaces in order to preserve them.

adornments added as *extras*, so to speak, to plain surfaces – have flourished in Japan because their function has been to provide colour, in contrast to the admired simplicities, or, as one could put it, to supply the jam; and this was spread really thick for the first time in the Azuchi-Momoyama period.

It is tempting to find in the artistic movements of Azuchi-Momoyama a parallel to the European Renaissance. Some Japanese scholars believe the parallel to be fairly close. Against this it is argued cogently that 'the comparison is far-fetched since the great energy displayed by Momoyama culture was inspired by the material concepts of feudal society and was lacking in humanistic elements'.[12]

But if we look beyond the artistic movements as such to the general culture and educated life of the time we discover a very interesting phenomenon, namely, a decided *secularization* of the human spirit. This statement needs to be explained. At one time all peoples appear to have been religious; or at least it may be said that the consciously religious outlook was the greatest force controlling man everywhere. Particularly after the introduction of Buddhism, the Japanese were profoundly impressed by the transitoriness of human existence. Buddhism brought in the concept of sin, the fear of hell, and the hope of paradise. The next world was at least as important as the present one. But by the sixteenth century the emphasis was changing quite radically. Then, the most active members of Japanese society, the great lords, warriors, and merchants, were more concerned with existing reality, with their own powers and capacities, than with the prospect of other-worldly salvation. In Japan, as in Europe, the human spirit was forsaking the transcendent realm of heaven in order to explore and conquer the present world. And this can be described as a process of secularization. It involves a turning away not from religion necessarily, but from superstition as one of the main operative forces in society.

In this sense, if in no other, a parallel exists between sixteenth-century Japan and that many-sided change in outlook that characterized the Renaissance in Europe. Was there a real link between the two worlds? Did Europe, through the Portuguese, affect Japan so deeply as to induce the process of secularization? On the whole this seems unlikely. A more profound influence, no doubt, was that of Zen.

[12] Sansom, *op. cit.*, p. 384.

In many ways it is highly misleading to speak of Zen as a form of Buddhism. One might go further than this and admit that any discussion of Zen is apt to be misleading. A famous Zen master, on being asked what Zen was, maintained an unmoving silence, as though he had not heard the question. But if Zen resists definition it is at least possible to deal with the subject by pointing out the attributes that do *not* belong to it. For example, spirituality – the sense of 'other-worldliness' – can be an obstacle barring the way to *satori*, the sudden enlightenment attainable by those who follow the way of Zen. Zen has no theology and no body of consistent ethical teachings or philosophical doctrine, although there exists a plethora of esoteric writings, which could be described as sacred texts. But these have little to say to the ordinary man unacquainted with Zen discipline. In the words of a German adept:

182   The Grand Shrines at Ise, built in an archaic style, and remarkable for their simplicity

183 Rock garden of the Ryoanji Temple (Buddhist temple of the Zen sect). The garden contains only white pebbles and rocks

They have the peculiarity of disclosing their life-giving meaning only to those who have shown themselves worthy of the crucial experiences and who can therefore extract from these texts confirmation of what they themselves already possess and are independently of them. To the inexperienced, on the other hand, they remain not only dumb – how could he ever be in a position to read between the lines? – but will infallibly lead him into the most hopeless spiritual confusion, even if he approaches them with wariness and selfless devotion.[13]

Most important of all, in the context of what we are discussing, the followers of Zen (as a sixteenth-century Italian Jesuit in Japan observed) 'generally agree in saying that there is no heaven or hell in the next world'.[14]

Since this was the belief common among the followers of a sect whose standards dominated warrior society, it is not surprising that the feudal Japan of Nobunaga and Hideyoshi should have been

[13] Eugen Herrigel, *Zen in the Art of Archery,* p. 20.
[14] Cooper (ed.), *op. cit.,* p. 320. The Jesuit was Alessandro Valignano (1539–1606), Visitor to the missions in the Orient. He spent a total of some ten years in Japan.

remarkably down-to-earth and secular. Now this prepared the way for the scientific, rational, outlook of the Tokugawa Age. It created, in other words, an attitude of mind that made the Japanese in the nineteenth century, more than many other Asian peoples of the time, ready to embark on a programme of modernization. Thus Zen, itself a form of mysticism,[15] helped to blow away the cobwebs of superstitious taboos and to promote that pragmatic, experimenting, scientific cast of thought which, in the context of Europe, was the most important fruit of the Renaissance.

Japan, then, by the close of the sixteenth century, seemed on the brink of the general material expansion and scientific advance that were to bring such great changes in western Europe in the years to come. In 1600, for example, she was much on a par with the contemporary European world. She had an energetic population, a sophisticated culture, and an efficient administrative system. Her vessels traded with South East Asia, and in that region there were thriving communities of Japanese settlers. Innovations from Europe, such as firearms and spectacles for poor sight, were soon understood in Japan and readily copied. And the Japanese could marshal and supply great armies of disciplined, intrepid warriors.

But in 1637 the country was closed to the outside world, except to the Chinese, and to the tiny group of Dutch merchants maintaining a trading station in conditions of severe isolation at Nagasaki. The closing of Japan seemed logical enough at the time. Christianity, once regarded with tolerance and even with friendly sympathy by the authorities, had come to be looked upon as potentially subversive, as dangerous to the security of the ruling Tokugawa house. The story of the Philippines depressed the Japanese. For in that archipelago conquest had proceeded hand in hand with conversion by the missionaries. In Tokugawa eyes there was always a danger that a *daimyo* in Kyushu, in the south-west, far from the shogun's capital at Yedo (the modern Tokyo) might so strengthen himself through his contacts with Europeans as to pose a threat to the central government. Thus the trickle of foreign trade at Nagasaki was put under the control of shogunal officials, who made certain that the handful of Dutch merchants had few dealings with any but a selected group of

---

[15] The late Professor R. H. Blyth and others have denied that Zen is a form of mysticism. The late Dr D. Suzuki, however, and other Japanese experts seem to agree that mysticism is a feature of Zen. This is certainly my own view.

Japanese. The Dutch, being Protestants, were not thought of as Christians. Only Catholics were placed in this category. The Dutch on their little island prison of Deshima, at Nagasaki, provided Japan with her window on the world, and it was neither large nor particularly transparent.

By the decision to close the country the Japanese inflicted severe injury on themselves. They lost nearly all touch with the progress of scientific inquiry in Europe, and they missed an excellent chance of becoming a great maritime and colonizing power. They could have anticipated Great Britain in the settlement of Australia and New Zealand. Such expansion to the south would have involved, no doubt, an early clash with the Spaniards in the Philippines; but the outcome of such a struggle can be seen as certain victory for the Japanese. Moreover, it seems at least possible that the humanism which flowered in at least some important regions of the West, following the Late Renaissance, could have penetrated and even pervaded Japanese society in such a way as to undermine the traditional supremacy of the warrior class – a consummation that did not occur until the twentieth century and then only after hideous warfare and vast destruction.

376

185 St Francis Xavier (1506–52), celebrated for his missionary journeys in India and South East Asia

·P·FRĀCISCUSXAVERIVSSOCIE·ATIS·

It is in many ways remarkable that, following the closing of the country, Japan was able to survive more or less unviolated by intruders until Perry's arrival in 1853. The Russians, it is true, had knocked hard on the closed doors of secluded Japan. The British sent vessels to Japanese ports from time to time. But no successful attempt was made until the middle of the nineteenth century. When this occurred the existing structure of government, built on foundations first laid by Nobunaga, Hideyoshi, and Ieyasu, began to totter; and its final collapse took place in 1868, the year that formally marks Japan's entry into the modern world.

Japan's first contact with the West, in the sixteenth century, proved to be a false start. The period from the 1540s to the 1630s, it is true, has been called Japan's 'Christian Century', because in that era European missionaries achieved a striking measure of success in winning converts. These included several influential lords, together with their retainers and families. That such conversions were genuine is proved by the extreme bravery shown by so many of those who suffered persecution after Christianity was firmly banned and fiercely suppressed. It is worth noting that while the foreign missionaries could make headway in most directions at first, they discovered that their toughest opponents were the monks and committed followers of Zen; and in the highest rungs of power they met men such as Nobunaga who might be personally well disposed but were hopeless as possible converts, not so much because such leaders were hostile but because they were, at bottom, profoundly secular and therefore indifferent. The fact is that the total impact of Europe upon Japan, right up to the time of Perry in the 1850s, was not enormous. Only one foreign country exerted a cultural influence – directly or indirectly – that was continuous and, at times, pervasive. This was China. Compared with Chinese ideas those of Europe were of small account in Japan, until little more than 100 years ago.

Chinese models, it is true, were so adapted to suit Japanese conditions as to change very often almost beyond recognition. Japan, as we said at the outset, was another world. But the cultural debt to China was, none the less, immense. Buddhism (including Zen, of course), Confucian ethics, Taoist metaphysics, medical lore, military arts, techniques of craftsmanship – all these, and much more, came originally from China. And during most of the long years of domestic peace under the Tokugawa shoguns, from the beginning of the seventeenth century, the orthodox ideology of the ruling class was neo-Confucianism. The Japanese felt familiar with Chinese traditions; and they understood, or thought they understood, China and the Chinese. The *Nambanjin*, 'the Southern Barbarians' – as the European visitors were called – were curiosities. They appeared, surely, much stranger to the Japanese than the men of Han, who were after all the inheritors of an advanced and impressive civilization seemingly as old as time.

'The Christian Century', then, is perhaps a misnomer. As things turned out, the Portuguese caracks trading with Japan established links that were fragile indeed. Yet the story could have been very different; and it is sad that a relationship so full of promise should have been broken with such harsh finality barely a century after it began.

MAP 16   Japan in the sixteenth century

Civilizations of Pre-Columbian America
HAROLD BLAKEMORE

ON 12 OCTOBER 1492 three small ships from the Spanish port of Palos dropped anchor off the shore of an island in the warm waters of the western Atlantic. Their commander, Christopher Columbus, claimed the land for Castile and thus began that spectacular movement in human history which, within two generations, discovered, conquered, and colonized an unexpected continent. The New World, soon to be called America, revealed to the wondering eyes of Europe not only a continent unsurpassed in its range of climate, scenery, flora, and fauna, but also the spectacle of remarkable civilizations and varieties of culture totally different from anything the Old World had experienced. No matter where the Spaniards went, native peoples had preceded them, adapting their lives to the local environment and creating patterns of living no less varied than the physical landscape itself. But in aboriginal America in 1500 two areas stood out for the civilizations they produced: Mexico and Central America, and the Andean region of Peru, Bolivia, and Ecuador. In Mexico the martial Aztec dominated a mosaic of tribes who shared a common urban culture, while far to the south the empire of the Inca knit together in one net of authority regions and peoples of extraordinary diversity. Yet a third civilization, the Maya of Central America and Yucatan, had already fallen into decay by the end of the fifteenth century and need not concern us further, though it was no less distinctive at its height than the Aztec and the Inca. These two civilizations, however, on the eve of the European conquest had recently reached the zenith of their power.

To understand and appreciate the achievements of the Aztecs and the Incas requires two preliminary considerations. The first is a knowledge of the lands which produced them, for it was only through meeting the challenge of their environment that they survived and developed. And, secondly, we must trace the growth of Indian culture from its origins to its final flowering in Aztec and Inca civilizations, since their indebtedness to the past was great.

380

Mexico and Central America

Much of Mexico is mountainous and barren. Where the North American Rocky Mountains enter the country they become the Sierra Madre, whose western ranges run north-west to south-east, while another escarpment in eastern Mexico runs roughly north to south. From this latter wall to the Caribbean stretches a hot and humid plain but between the converging ranges the land itself is high, an arid plateau over 3,000 feet above sea-level. Further south, where the mountains meet in the heart of Mexico, lie a number of natural basins and it is one of these, the Central Valley, 7,000 feet above sea-level and 3,000 square miles in extent, which is the stage of our human story. Here, until fairly recent times, shallow lakes, dammed in by the upthrusting rocks of volcanoes to the south-east, made the valley ideal for settlement, until a long process of dessication made them disappear. The surrounding hills were then covered with timber, the lake-shores abounded with water-fowl and other game, and the near-by mountains provided varieties of stone, including obsidian, volcanic glass, which played the role in Mexico that flint played in the Old World for the tools of early man. Cultivated crops flourished on the valley floor and on the margins of the lakes. The Aztecs, in fact, built up gardens on the lakes themselves – *chinampas* – consisting of alternate layers of mud and water plants, secured by the roots of overhanging trees: they may still be seen at Xochimilco, a little south of Mexico City.

Water-supply – rivers and rainfall – is always a determinant of human settlement. Between the mountain chains of Mexico rivers drain wide valleys and make cultivation possible. In the south-east, however, the rivers Papaloapan, Grijalva, and Usumacinta flow north from the mountains of southern Mexico and Guatemala through a coastal plain where rainfall is so high that the terrain is covered with thick forest. Here cultivation is only possible if the fight with the forest can be maintained. This area, like the coastal plain of eastern Mexico, was, and still is in many places, characterized by the *milpa* system of agriculture: trees are felled, forest cover burnt, and crops planted in the resultant clearing for two or three years until soil exhaustion forces cultivators to repeat the process elsewhere. Yet it was this shifting basis which supported the Olmec civilization, to which we shall return, and also that of the Maya.

381

LA MER DV SV;

MER PACIFIQVE
OV DE MAGELLAN

186   Detail of a map of the world made for Henry II of
France (1547–59) showing South America

Mexico and Central America form a region of extraordinary contrasts. Not only is the area climatically and physically diverse; it is also a land of violence. Earthquakes and volcanic eruptions occur not infrequently, and sudden storms of torrential rain sweep across the Caribbean. Faced with the capricious nature of the elements around him, and equally unpredictable forces beneath the ground he tilled to live, man in Mexico saw himself as a puny animal at the mercy of the universe. It is not surprising that, as we shall see, the nature of the land and of the elements played a crucial role in the formation of Mexican ways of thought.

The Andean Area

The region ultimately embraced by the Inca Empire at the beginning of the sixteenth century covered some 350,000 square miles. It included the present state of Peru, except the tropical eastern lowlands; the southern half of Ecuador; the high plateau of Bolivia; the north-western provinces of Argentina – Jujuy, Tucuman, and Catamarca – and the northern part of Chile as far as the River Maule. But its heartland was Peru.

Three distinctive geographical areas make up the state of Peru. First, along the Pacific coast lies a narrow plain, intersected along its length by short, west-flowing rivers. Some twenty-five of these are permanent streams, fed by the snows of the Andes; the rest flow only in the mountain wet season. Secondly, behind this plain, and rising breathtakingly from it, are the western walls of the Andean *cordillera*, part of that enormous mountain chain which is the backbone of South America and its continental divide. The Andes are wide as well as high, with parallel and abutting ranges separated only in certain places by broad river valleys. Here the rivers run north continent unsurpassed in its range of climate, scenery, flora, and fauna, escarpment and pour down to the Amazonian basin. The third region, of little further historical importance since no Peruvian civilization ever conquered it, covers the tree-clad eastern heights of the Andes, and the jungle lowlands below.

Along the coast, outside the permanent river valleys, the land is desert where little or no rain falls. So it is from northern Chile's Atacama Desert to Ecuador. In that state, however, at about latitude

7° south, the traveller is struck by two sudden changes from the coast-lands further south. One is a marked rise in temperature; the other, a sudden change of scenery from barren sand to luxuriant rain forest. This line marks the limit of effect of the cold ocean current known as the Humboldt which is responsible for both the coolness and dryness of the Peruvian and north Chilean coasts. The cold current sweeps up from the south, and is accompanied by upswelling from the ocean depths of a coastal current some 50 to 100 miles wide. South-west winds from the Pacific cross this stretch of water but take up little by evaporation and are cooled in the process. When they rise over the coast, low temperatures and low humidity make for sluggish condensation; as a result fogs form but no rain falls until its clouds reach the higher mountains inland.

Consequently, outside the river valleys, the coast is desert, and mountain spurs also cut off the valleys from one another. Hence, from man's first settlement in the region, for long periods of time cultures developed in relative isolation. Yet the coastal current with its curious climatic effect offers other compensations. It makes the waters off Peru ideal for the growth of plankton, those minute organisms on which fish feed, and these seas are among the world's richest fisheries. More than this: such quantities of fish attract birds in untold millions, and the birds' droppings, preserved by the dry climate, form guano, the rich natural fertilizer, used to increase yields on the limited cultivable land available.

As desert imposed an isolation on the coast, so inland the mountains separated communities. Here again water-supply was crucial, and life could only be maintained in the river basins between the ranges. There are about six of these basins in highland Peru which are capable of supporting large populations and they have been the home of man since the earliest times. But all round are high mountain walls preventing a wider unity.

In ancient Egypt, Mesopotamia, India, and China large political units developed from the need for some central authority to plan the use of water in the valleys of the Nile, Tigris and Euphrates, Indus, and Yellow River. Geography imposed its own unity. But here in Peru the opposite obtained, and if men were to create large units of government they had to do it in defiance of their environment. This, in effect, was the Inca achievement.

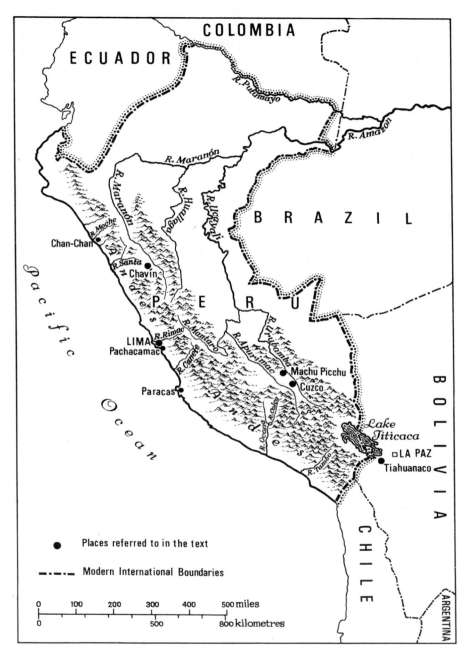

MAP 17 Peru: physical features

187 Cortés, his followers, and Indians watch ten
Spaniards attempting to climb Mount Popocatépetl –
only two succeeded

Hunters, Fishers, and Farmers

It is now generally accepted that the first inhabitants of America
came from Asia. During the last Ice Age so much of the world's
water took the form of great ice-sheets that sea-levels were much
lower than they are now. Consequently, what is now the Bering
Straits between Alaska and north-east Asia was a land connection
between the continents. Though the ice presented a barrier to
migrants in the far north of America, a milder climatic period
sometime after 10,000 B.C. opened up a route southwards, to the
east of the Rockies and, while it is quite probable that man entered
America from Asia before this date, it is clear from the archaeological
evidence that the main migrations began to take place then.

Men came from Asia overland as hunters after game, their food
and source of clothing, and they moved south, probably in small
groups but over a very long period of time, reaching Patagonia some
9,000 years ago. For millennia the quest for food dominated man's
activities. Thus, along the shores of Chile and Peru deep deposits of
shells and fishbones, with hooks and harpoons of bone and wood,
reveal his long dependence on the harvest of the seas. Inland, how-

ever, man was a hunter, and his remains, often in association with weapons, tools, and bones of now-extinct animals, are dated back beyond 10,000 B.C. in Mexico and to 8000 B.C. in Peru. Food-gathering was also important, and, in Mexico and Central America particularly, a typical early tool was the grinding-stone for crushing wild seeds and grains. Scarcely altered in form, this is still the chief utensil of Indian housewives; known as the *metate*, it grinds the corn which makes their daily bread. That corn is maize, and its discovery and domestication were crucial for American development.

The precise origin of cultivated maize is still unresolved but its significance is clear. Together with other plants, such as beans and squashes, this food staple released man from his near-absolute dependence on the chase and it greatly increased available food-supply, permitting population to grow. By 2500 B.C., if not earlier, permanent villages were emerging in favoured locations, such as the Valley of Mexico, and hunting and gathering were progressively replaced by agriculture as the key economic activity. Within another 1,000 years, pottery was well established, and art and religion were beginning to appear. Both were represented by thousands of tiny clay figures which are characteristic of this stage in central Mexico. Many of these figurines were of females, and it is not too fanciful to suggest that to these agricultural peoples there was a parallel of the miraculous process of nature, in which crops are sown as seed and ripen into grain, and that of the cycle of human life of which woman is the centre. What is less conjectural is the fact that by about 500 B.C. religious ideas were finding architectural and communal expression in the building of great artificial mounds. Again, to agriculturists dependent on sun and rain, it might have seemed logical to build structures towards the heavens for the worship of the powers which ruled the seasons. At any rate, these 'mock-mountains' certainly required huge amounts of human labour since pack-animals were unknown in Mexico before the Spaniards came, and so were metal tools and the wheel. To get the labour to build these mounds suggests a directing group and probably an emergent priesthood, while the fact that these labours required a high degree of social cohesion implies sizeable communities with common beliefs.

The agricultural revolution also took place in Peru. Although maize did not appear there before 1200 B.C., in the coastal valleys and highland basins other crops were cultivated centuries before this date, and a similar growth of communities which a more assured food-supply made possible occurred there as well. Man did not cease to be a hunter with the advent of agriculture, but the balance of his life was changed: where food could be grown, he had more leisure, and leisure is essential to the growth of civilization. Elsewhere, of course, in places such as the great plains of North America and the *pampa* of southern South America, man remained essentially a hunter until very recent times.

Mexico in the Pre-Aztec Period

From the agricultural communities great civilizations developed. The governing classes which emerged were usually priestly in character, and these theocracies elaborated the simple worship of the elements into complex religious systems, involving a large pantheon of deities. It was also largely for religious ends that the rulers devised calendrical systems and invented forms of writing, and organized the people to construct great ceremonial centres. Nothing testifies better to the dominance of the hierarchy than these centres themselves, often covering several square miles. Moreover, in the elaboration of the centres, many skilled sculptors and craftsmen worked to priests' orders, creating magnificent art in a variety of forms. It seems unlikely that the authority wielded by those who ruled was based on physical force, but was accepted by the people as necessary for their survival.

The earliest manifestations of these developments date back to beyond 1000 B.C. and were located not in the Central Valley of Mexico but in the more unlikely region of the Gulf coast, in southern Vera Cruz and Tabasco. Here, at the time of the Spanish Conquest, lived a people known as the Olmecs, and that name has been given to the civilization which preceded them by hundreds of years. The Olmec culture was distinguished by ceremonial sites (of which that at La Venta is the most significant), by elaborate sculpture, and by a distinctive art. Colossal carved heads, up to over 8 feet in height, and weighing up to 50 tons are the most monumental expressions of this art, while tiny jade figurines, fashioned no less skilfully, are the most delicate. Yet the stone for the monolithic figures was cut from quarries some 80 miles away and probably brought to La Venta by raft along the rivers. Other carvings, in light relief and in the round, show men in ornate dress, jaguar-like figures, and babies with large heads, weeping eyes, and curiously feline snarling mouths. The ubiquitous appearance of these motifs leads to the conclusion that jaguar-worship was the key feature of the religious life of the people. Since, in later cultures, representations of the rain god suggest a derivation from the jaguar-gods of La Venta, it is a fair conjecture that the latter were themselves associated with rain in this region of high rainfall.

Many Olmec characteristics turn up hundreds of miles from their original homes, coinciding with the rise of ceremonial civilizations elsewhere in Mexico, and strongly suggesting that Olmec influence was important in their early growth. Local styles, however, soon predominated, though each civilization rested on the same basis of maize cultivation and was characterized by similar social structures and religious beliefs. Thus, in southern Mexico, the Zapotecs, whose descendants still speak the distinctive Zapotec tongue, built a great

188   An illustration from Las Casas' *Cruelties attributed to the Spaniards in the New World.* The Conquistadores found Aztec society, with its bloodthirsty gods, repellent, but their own actions were often greedy and cruel

189 Line drawing of monuments
of warriors from Oaxaca

centre at Monte Alban in Oaxaca and created a culture which produced elaborate subterranean tombs with ornate burial pottery, its own pantheon of gods of maize, rain, fire, and water, and its own writing and calendrical system, which have Olmec affinities. This, like so many other sites of the period A.D. 300–900 elsewhere in Mexico and Central America, was a ceremonial centre for communal worship rather than a city in which people lived. But in the Central Valley of Mexico arose a true city, Teotihuacán.

At its height, between A.D. 300 and 600, Teotihuacán covered some 7 square miles. Its centre was a complex of religious buildings, dominated by the Pyramid of the Sun, now 200 feet high and measuring 700 feet along its sides. Near by is the stepped-temple of Quetzalcoatl, patron deity of the city, of whom legends tell that he first taught men agriculture and the arts. His symbol is the serpent crowned with feathers, and his temple was decorated with carved heads of this creature, alternating with masks of the rain god Tlaloc.

The arts flourished at Teotihuacán. Sculptors and architects designed palaces as well as temples, and mural painters executed mythological scenes in bright colours. Other artists in stone made delicate masks of jade and jasper while potters, to whom the potter's wheel was unknown, produced polychrome wares of great elegance. The city's influence spread far and wide; typical Teotihuacán pottery turns up in tombs on the Gulf coast, in highland Guatemala and in other parts of Central America, and aspects of its culture persisted into Aztec times. Quetzalcoatl and Tlaloc were worshipped by the Aztecs, 1,000 years after the fall of Teotihuacán, and even today the highly distinctive mural art of Mexico, which may be seen on public buildings such as those of University City, has more than a casual link with the ancient city.

Teotihuacán was destroyed about A.D. 600, probably by semi-barbarous nomads from the north and north-east. Internal decline had also set in, for the climate was getting drier and crops were beginning to fail. The city, indeed, helped to sow the seeds of its own collapse: its construction required huge amounts of plaster which was obtained by reducing limestone under heat but, since the only fuel was timber, the surrounding hills were thus deforested, accelerating the erosion of the countryside. Teotihuacán paid the

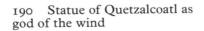
190   Statue of Quetzalcoatl as god of the wind

penalty in crop failure, followed probably by the collapse of organized government precisely when the barbarians were appearing at the gates.

There followed some 300 years of confusion in which the character of the high civilization survived only in attenuated form. Incursions of hardy nomadic tribesmen from the north, probably impelled by increasing drought, pushed southwards, becoming more civilized in the process. By about A.D. 1000, the Toltecs, one of the invading peoples, had risen to prominence, and in their city of Tula, north of Teotihuacán, they re-created high culture, absorbing much of what had gone before but also adding new elements of their own. Perhaps the most significant of these was a change in religious thought which had profound consequences.

The cult of Quetzalcoatl, inherited from Teotihuacán, was a cult of peace, associated with a bringer of light. But in the early years of Tula a religious schism seems to have taken place between the

191   The gods Tezcatlipoca and Yacatecutli

devotees of this god, and those of the Toltec deity, Tezcatlipoca, 'Lord of the Smoking Mirror', patron of the warrior classes. The triumph of the latter marked the expansion of the Toltec domain, and victory in war itself confirmed the rise to power of the military orders. Religion soon came to buttress social change and art to record it. There emerged a body of belief which held that the powers controlling the universe could only be appeased and, indeed, sustained, by human sacrifice and human blood. The religious necessity to placate the gods through human sacrifice put a social premium on military prowess, and thus emphasized the central role of war in society. The art of Tula – colossal statues of warriors, low-relief scenes of conflict, and of serpents eating humans – is art for war's sake, far removed from the peaceful art of Teotihuacán.

But Tula itself, like Teotihuacán before it, succumbed to external forces, as the tribes from the north pressed south. The city was abandoned by the Toltecs in the middle of the twelfth century. Meanwhile, in southern Mexico, the Zapotec site of Monte Alban had been abandoned for a new centre at Mitla, while another tribe, the Mixtecs, 'Cloud-People', took over much of Oaxaca in the seventh century. The Mixtecs survived as a separate culture until the coming of the Spaniards, being distinguished for their superb pottery, magnificent gold-work, and painted histories. These are folding books of deerskin on which were written in pictographic and rebus form the story of the Mixtec people and the histories of their royal houses. This civilization also had a profound influence spatially and temporally for the excellence of its artistic products, and, like the cultures of central Mexico, contributed much to Aztec greatness.

The fall of Toltec Tula late in the twelfth century ushered in a period of chaos, in which various tribes – all newcomers – established separate states, deriving much of their culture, including religion, from their predecessors and from Toltec 'islands' which survived the waves of barbarism. These tribes spoke a common tongue, Náhuatl, as their Indian descendants do today. Cities sprang up as tribal centres, and inter-tribal warfare became endemic, but in culture and belief these states had much in common. Towards the close of the thirteenth century, the last tribe of uncultured invaders reached the Valley of Mexico, bearing the image of their tutelary deity, Huitzilopochtli, a sun god who was also a god of war. He was

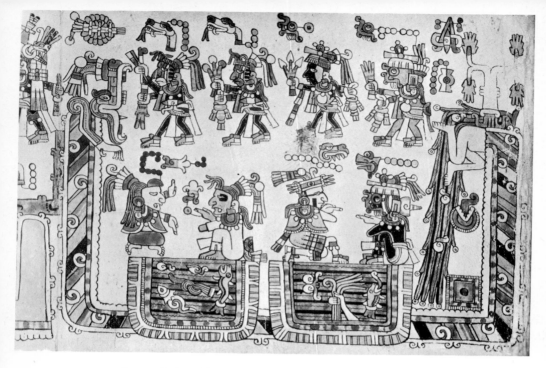

192   A pre-Columbian Mixtec pictograph manuscript,
painted on deerskin, probably depicting the creation of
the Mixtec people

to do great things for his people in a short space of time, for he was
the deity of 'those who come from Aztlán', a region no one knows,
but one which gave its name to the inheritors of Mexican culture –
the Aztecs.

The Aztecs of Mexico

The Aztec tribe entered the Valley of Mexico as a poor, nomadic,
uncultured people, seeking a place to settle. Other tribes, arriving
before them, had already established their jurisdictions in the better
areas, and built towns and cities round the lakes, sharing the common
culture they derived from the Toltecs. But a state of inter-city
warfare prevailed and, in fact, the Aztec newcomers first gained a
precarious foothold in the region as mercenary troops to one of the
established towns before they began to build their own city.

Tradition gives the year 1325 as the founding date of the future

394

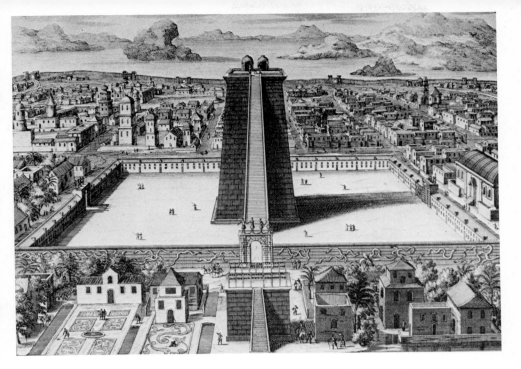

193　The great Temple of Huitzilopochtli in Mexico-Tenochtitlan, engraved by Picart

Aztec capital, Mexico-Tenochtitlan. One free translation of these Náhuatl words is 'the town in the middle of the lake of the moon where the prickly pear grows' and, while scholars still dispute the derivation, these words do enshrine historical facts. The town was established on an island in the middle of Lake Texcoco, called in myth the 'Lake of the Moon', and *tenochtli* is the cactus popularly called the prickly pear. Now Aztec legend runs as follows: when the tribe was wandering into central Mexico, the oracle of its god told the chief priest that its settlement would prosper where he saw the sign of an eagle perched on a cactus. And today Mexico's national flag includes this emblem, embodying the essentials of the myth.

For decades the Aztecs were a despised people, notorious for their barbarism even among the other tribes who all practised human sacrifice, and their gods were more bloodthirsty than most. However, during the late fourteenth and early fifteenth centuries, a succession of wily rulers began to evolve a policy of opportunist warfare, dynastic marriage, and helpful alliance, playing astutely on the system of power politics within the Valley of Mexico. This culminated in a triple alliance with the states of Texcoco and Tlacopan and from that point the Aztecs never looked back. Though the alliance continued to the Spanish Conquest, in practice Mexico-Tenochtitlan became by far the dominant partner. By that time too, an imperialist urge under resolute leadership had carried Aztec hegemony far beyond the Central Valley, east to the Caribbean coast and southwards into Oaxaca. Continuity of policy through several kingships seems to have been maintained by a remarkable and long-lived statesman, Tlacaelel, counsellor to those who reigned.

The city of Tenochtitlan reflected the rise of Aztec power. From a squalid settlement on an island no one else wanted in 1325 it had developed by the sixteenth century into one of the largest conurbations in the world. Linked to the mainland by three causeways, the island city with its lakeside dormitory towns probably contained over half a million people, though Aztec rule in Mexico embraced ten times that number. To the Spaniards, who first saw the city in 1519, it was a revelation, and no one captured their amazement better than Bernal Díaz del Castillo, comrade of Cortés in the conquest of Mexico and, in his retirement, unofficial chronicler of the expedition, who wrote:

> When we saw so many cities and villages built in the water and other great towns on dry land and that straight and level causeway going towards Mexico (Tenochtitlan), we were amazed . . . on account of the great towers and temples and buildings rising from the water, and all built of masonry. And some of our soldiers even asked if the things that we saw were not a dream?[1]

He describes the city's market at Tlatelolco:

> Every kind of merchandise was kept by itself and had its fixed place marked out. Let us begin with the dealers in gold, silver and precious stones, feathers, mantles and embroidered goods. . . . Next there were other traders who sold great pieces of cloth and cotton. . . . There were those who sold cloths of hennequen and ropes and the sandals with which they are shod. . . . In another part there were skins of tigers and lions, of otters and jackals, deer and other animals. . . . Let us also mention the fruiterers and the women who sold cooked food . . . in their own part of the market; then every sort of pottery made in a thousand different forms . . . then those who sold honey . . . and those

[1] Bernal Díaz del Castillo, *The True History of the Conquest of New Spain* (tr. A. P. Maudslay), pp. 269–70.

who sold lumber, boards, cradles, beams, blocks and benches. . . .
Paper which is called in this country *amal*, and reeds . . . full of tobacco,
and yellow ointments . . . and much cochineal is sold under the arcades
which are in that great market place. . . . There are also buildings
where three magistrates sit in judgement, and there are executive
officers . . . who inspect the merchandise. I am forgetting those who
sell salt, and those who make the stone knives. . . . There are for sale
axes of brass and copper and tin, and gourds and gaily painted jars
made of wood. . . . Some of the soldiers who had been in many parts
of the world, in Constantinople, and all over Italy, and in Rome, said
that so large a market place and so full of people, and so well regulated
and arranged, they had never beheld before.[2]

There was much to marvel at. Tenochtitlan, the island-city, was
honeycombed with canals spanned by wooden bridges, and much
of its traffic went by boat. The city was supplied with fresh water
by means of an aqueduct from the hill of Chapultepec on the mainland, and oases of colour could be seen amidst the buildings since
every house had its garden or inner court. Indeed, the Aztecs, who
loved flowers and trees, seem to have lavished more time and care
on their surroundings than on the houses in which they lived. The
latter were mostly of one storey only, though noblemen's houses

[2] Bernal Díaz, *op. cit.*, pp. 272–3.

194   Aztec sacrifice

might have two storeys, and were built of volcanic stone and sun-dried bricks, with a veneer of plaster. Furnishings were very sparse, even in the royal palaces, and consisted of mats – which served as beds – low, wooden chairs and sometimes tables, wooden screens and wickerwork baskets to keep things in. The screens could be used as room dividers, draught excluders, and fire-screens, and were often, in the best houses, richly carved or ornamented with gold. The better-class residences would also have internal walls painted with frescoes or hung with animal skins and embroidered cloths.

Dwellings, of course, denoted social status. Peasants on the fringes of the suburbs made do with one-roomed structures of mud and wattle with grass-thatched roofs, whereas Montezuma's palace in Tenochtitlan was a spacious building with many apartments. What impressed the Spaniards more than the palace itself was its gardens, its lakes teeming with water-birds of every kind and colour, and its menagerie, a microcosm of Mexican fauna. The Aztecs, apparently, knew something of landscape gardening, and they were keen on botany and zoology, but this is not surprising for a people who led more of their lives in the open air than indoors.

The centre of the city was a great paved square with important buildings all around. Though some of these were secular – Montezuma's palace was located here – the area was largely given over to religious purposes. The most imposing edifice was the Great Temple, really two temples in one, dedicated to the war god, Huitzilopochtli, and to the ancient rain god, Tlaloc. A smaller temple was sacred to Quetzalcoatl, and there were at least four others in the central plaza as well as other structures of religious significance. Here stood the Calmecac, the monastery school of the priests, and a masonry court where a game was played with balls of solid rubber. This game also had religious connotations and had been played in Mexico since Olmec times. A more forbidding feature, at least to the Spaniards who saw it in 1519, was an enormous rack on which were laid in grisly rows the skulls of those sacrificed to the gods. Another object, suggesting the crucial link between religion and war which was the chief characteristic of Aztec belief, was the great stone of Tizoc, emperor from 1481 to 1486. This was a massive circular stone, richly carved with warrior figures and used as a public platform for ceremonial combat in one of the rituals of Aztec religion. All in all,

195 Late fifteenth-century Aztec sacrificial knife with chalcedony blade and wooden haft ornamented with a figure of the 'Eagle Knight' inlaid with turquoise and shell

it was entirely fitting that the very centre of the Empire, the heart of the Aztec metropolis, should be dominated by religion, as the sacred plaza was, for religion itself dominated so many aspects of Aztec life.

To come to terms with Aztec religion requires a particular effort by the European mind. To the Spanish conquerors of the sixteenth century there was no better justification for their violent subversion of native society than the extirpation of its religion, and they saw nothing paradoxical in the fact that they waged bloody and cruel wars against the Indians to that end. But even our own age, accustomed to ideas of toleration for strange beliefs of others, finds it hard to comprehend, let alone justify, the religious practices of the Aztecs with their emphasis on human sacrifice and occasional cannibalism. It is probably because these features were characteristic and commonplace, rather than infrequent and exceptional, that we find Aztec culture so abhorrent, and, clearly, the sacrificial knife used on countless individuals is less clinical than the gas chamber or the hydrogen bomb.

Aztec religion was extremely complex. It was the result of an evolution of beliefs in a land characterized by nature's violence, and the amalgamation of elements from many parts of the country. But at its heart was the idea of life's impermanence, and the puny strength of man when pitted against universal forces. He could only appease but not control them by offering the most precious gift of all – human life – in the attempt to maintain a precarious balance for the continuation of his known world against the unknowable intentions of the gods.

The Aztecs believed that, since time began, successive worlds or 'suns' as they called them, had been destroyed by awful cataclysms – flood, the fall of the sky, fire, and wind. Their age would end in earthquake but a persistent effort was required to postpone the day of wrath, and the daily sun, whose rising guaranteed a little more time, needed to be fed with human hearts. Yet there was more to it than that: life had to be governed by prescribed rituals to keep the world in balance, and Aztec religion had its own practices of confession for sins committed, penance for wrongs done, and absolution for contrition. The moral code was very severe. Clearly, as in all societies where wide distinctions exist, religious belief and practice varied greatly in sophistication. The peasant-farmer, close to gods of earth and rain, was moved by a simpler philosophy than the sophisticated nobleman of Tenochtitlan, intellectually prepared by position and environment to speculate and imagine. Nevertheless, bound by the cement of society, both peasant and noble were part of an ordained order under heaven, and each was obliged to play his part in maintaining it.

The Aztec pantheon of gods was characterized by its enormous size, the unpronounceable names of its members, and their apparently insatiable desire for human blood. Some gods were very ancient in Mexico. Tlaloc, god of the rain, and therefore connected with things that grow, to whom in times of drought children were sacrificed so that their tears, like drops of rain, might induce the god to relent, goes back in time to Teotihuacán if not earlier. An ancient god of fire, Huehueteotl, was even older, and the fact was marked at Aztec festivals, when priests dressed up as gods, by him appearing last and moving slowly, befitting an aged figure. Quetzalcoatl, 'Feathered Serpent', the revered god of wisdom, was, on the whole, a benevolent deity but most gods were characterized by a dual nature – good and bad. Thus, Tlaloc, chief god of the peasant-farmers, was not only he who sent rain to make crops grow, and therefore benevolent, but also he who might send storms to destroy the growing vegetation or send no rain at all. In either case, his goodwill was critical for human survival and it could best be assured by a plentiful supply of sacrificial victims.

Other gods were either specifically Aztec in origin, or adopted by the Aztecs from conquered peoples. Huitzilopochtli, god of war,

196 Stone mask representing the flayed god, Xipe Totec

came nearest to being the patron deity of this warlike people, and he and Tlaloc were the supreme gods at Tenochtitlan. Xipe Totec, 'the Flayed One', was imported from the Mixtec peoples of the south. God of growing vegetation, it was in his honour that a peculiarly repugnant rite was carried out, the skin being flayed from a sacrificial human and worn by a priest to represent the decaying plant within which new life lies. He was also the patron of goldsmiths because, it was said, flayed skin has the pallor of beaten gold.

But not all deities had such a sombre character. Mayauel, patron goddess of the maguey cactus, was revered because the plant itself provided so many useful things. Its spines were used as needles, its beaten fibres provided cloth, and the fermented juice from within its haulms was *pulque*, the intoxicating beer of Mexico. With Mayauel were associated the Centzochtotochtin, the 'four hundred rabbits', minor gods of drunkeness. And Xochipilli, god of flowers, presided not only over the beautiful blooms which Mexicans love but was also a god of dance and song, love and pleasures, games and amusements, a very benevolent deity.

Thus, while it is true that Aztec religion was dominated by cults of human sacrifice, bloodletting, and war, there were happy feasts, songs and flowers, pointing to that duality which was characteristic of the gods themselves, and which reflected the human condition.

It has already been suggested that the peculiar character of Aztec religion was not simply a theological matter but that social and political factors played an important part. The dominant strata in society were the priesthood and the military orders, and it is easy to see how they would have a vested interest, for social and economic reasons, in the maintenance of a religious system which required their particular attributes. The priests, as the intermediaries between men and gods, were in a particularly powerful position but their hold on society, and their privileged status in it, depended on military support. Without the warriors to engage in war and secure captives for sacrifice, as well as tribute exacted from conquered peoples, the priesthood's hold would have been that much weaker. As it was, the alliance between these two sets of interests reinforced them both, and they jointly maintained their high position in society by co-operating in the workings of a religious system which benefited them in the material sense. But we must be careful of assuming that,

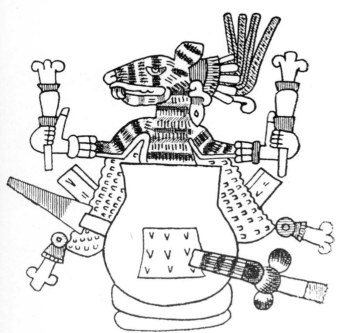

197 Octecomatli, the Pulque jar, and Tochtli, symbol of the Centzochtotochtin, the 'four hundred rabbits', minor gods of drunkenness

402

because of this alone, the system was oppressive to the people themselves, and that they were dragooned into acceptance. For it does seem clear that the beliefs associated with human sacrifice had permeated the society, and there are many stories of captured warriors preferring sacrifice to the gods of the next world to freedom in this one. Those whose hearts were cut from their bodies to sustain the strength of the gods were destined for eternal bliss, and many rituals involving sacrifice also entailed granting to the individual concerned everything he desired in the months before his death.

Another 'rational' argument about Aztec religion claims that population pressure in the Valley of Mexico was acute, and that a religious system involving permanent war and human sacrifice was a safety-valve to relieve the pressure of numbers on means of subsistence. There is probably something in this also but its assumption that the leaders of society calculated the situation to that extent seems over-large. Endemic war and a sacrificial religion may well have relieved population pressure but whether they were designed to do so is another matter.

At all events, it was the warrior-nobility and the priesthood who made up the ruling classes, and they were linked by family relationships and education, apart from ideology and function. Their holdings of land were tilled for them by the common people, and it was the nobility which administered and judged, as well as serving as regimental commanders in war. These great lords were the aristocracy, chiefs of the districts of Tenochtitlan or tributary towns, high officials of various kinds connected with the central administration, and judges of the most important suits. By 1500, what had formerly been elective procedures to high office, in which clan members chose their leaders, had become very much a matter of direct appointment by the emperor or confirmation by him of a locally chosen appointee. Since, in addition, there was, even in the more democratic system, a tendency to appoint a relative of a defunct leader to succeed him, clearly a hereditary element had become paramount and a virtual caste system was in the making. In other words, the aristocracy was now self-perpetuating, and its role was closely geared to the development of a centralized administration which the growing complexity of a large city-state required. The system was not entirely closed: common men still had war in which to prove their quality, and an outstanding warrior might by merit break into the high nobility. But the natural democracy of the wandering tribe, in which heads of families formed a council and consulted together as equals, had quite disappeared. The nobleman, appointed to office or confirmed in it by the emperor, was now part of a machine, responsible to those above but not to those below. Yet he was the 'speaker' for his district in the councils of the nation, as the emperor himself was the 'chief speaker' for all Aztecs to the outside world.

The elective principle, curiously enough, did survive at the very highest level. The emperor himself and his four chief officers of state were confirmed in office by the highest councils of the nobility and the priesthood. This was not democratic but simply the selection of the first among equals. And, while the emperor himself lived like a god and was treated as one, government was more conciliar than autocratic. Bernal Díaz gives a good picture of Montezuma II when he first met Cortés.

> . . . the Great Montezuma got down from his litter, and those great Chiefs supported him with their arms beneath a marvellously rich canopy of green coloured feathers with much gold and silver embroidery. . . . Montezuma was richly attired . . . and he was shod with sandals, the soles were of gold and the upper part adorned with precious stones . . . many other Lords . . . walked before the Great Montezuma, sweeping the ground where he would tread and spreading cloths on it, so that he should not tread on the earth. Not one of these chieftains dared even to think of looking him in the face, but kept their eyes lowered with great reverence, except those four relations, his nephews, who supported him with their arms.[3]

The 'nephews' were in fact lords of four of the towns around Tenochtitlan, but closer to the emperor in decision making were the four heads of the military districts into which the city was divided. Such men, like the emperor himself, were distinguished by their richly embroidered clothes, their plumed headdresses, their jewels, and their large following.

This noble class was the first beneficiary from booty exacted from conquered neighbours. Warring expeditions had an economic purpose as well as the religious one of securing captives for sacrifice. After defeating a foreign tribe, the Aztecs would present a list of demands – such a quantity of cotton cloth, so many quills of gold-dust

[3] Bernal Díaz, *op. sit.*, pp. 298–302.

198   The first meeting between Montezuma and Cortés
in Mexico

or bags of cochineal dye, and so on – and leave officials to collect the
tribute. Here was a weakness in Aztec statesmanship which contrasts
strongly with the Inca: they failed to establish a true imperial system
of incorporating defeated areas in the body politic, a policy which
left old hatreds to rankle among their neighbours, and for which they
paid dear. The aid of Indian auxiliaries, men of other tribes, was
critical to Cortés in the conquest of Mexico.

Like the nobility, the priesthood was virtually self-contained by
1500. Recruitment to it was largely limited to sons of the nobility
but it could not be hereditary since celibacy was the rule for the high
priests. The heads of the hierarchy were those two priests who
presided over the temple of Huitzilopochtli and the temple of Tlaloc
in Tenochtitlan, and below these archbishops, if so they may be
called, were the lords spiritual, equivalent to our bishops. The functions of the priests were specialized, according to rank. Some were
responsible for the running of the monastery schools for initiates;
others had charge over church property, which was extensive – lands,

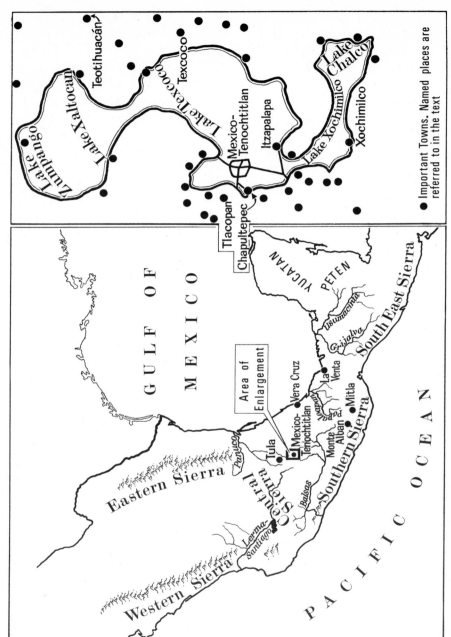

MAP 18   Mexico: physical features and Central Valley

buildings, plate, war-booty; others, again, were those specialised in sacrificial rites and in keeping records. Since the whole rhythm of Aztec life was governed by religion, and since the Aztec year was crowded with festivals, it is easy to appreciate that the Aztec priesthood was large and its power and influence great. Moreover, every god in the vast Aztec pantheon needed his ministrants, and the more important needed many. For example, each of the 'four hundred rabbits' had a serving-priest of his own. It was also the practice for the priest to take the name of the god he served. Women could enter the service of the church, and priestesses directed rites associated with some goddesses while others looked after particular temples.

The common people supported those who ruled through taxation and labour-service, and able-bodied males made up the Aztec armies. Each man belonged to a clan, of which there were about twenty in 1500, and land was held by the clan itself, its produce being apportioned to individual families. The division of land for family use was registered in a special book, and the keeper of this record was the head of the clan, elected by its members but confirmed in office by the emperor. The clan chief was advised by a council composed of the oldest and best-known heads of families and, while he had certain responsibilities for local government, law, and order, his jurisdiction was limited by the overriding powers of the local noble and the central government. The heads of the colleges to which all young free-born men went for military training and education, were appointed from above the local level, though every clan district had such a school. The priest in charge of the local temple likewise was appointed by the religious hierarchy. What, in effect, the system of clan government represented was the attenuated democracy of the original tribe, now absorbed in the powerful centralized state.

Warriors shared in the spoils of battle and could, by this means and through valour, rise in the social scale, though this was becoming increasingly rare with the emergence of a really stratified society. But all free men had their rights to the use of land, a voice in the election of clan chiefs, and the right to have their sons schooled. Warfare and agricultural skills formed the basis of the curriculum but some youths would seek a training in the arts, and go on to the guilds of gold- or silver-workers, fashioners of feather-work – a highly prized craft – and jewel-smiths. These varied craftsmen were known as the

407

tolteca, for tradition credited the ancient Toltecs with all that was brilliant and artistic. One other class in society deserves mention, since by 1500 it was emerging into a prominence which might have had interesting repercussions on Aztec society if it had not been destroyed twenty years later by Cortés. This was the *pochteca*, the guild of traders, a close-knit, hereditary class who lived in the same districts, intermarried, worshipped their own gods and supplied their own priesthood for the purpose. The Aztec economy required a wide catchment area for commodities and goods which the Central Valley did not produce itself, and war alone could not supply the lack. Animal skins and incense, as well as rubber and tobacco, came from the humid coast; feathers of the much-valued quetzal bird, with its iridescent green plumage, came from highland Guatemala; different types of pottery from all over Mexico. The *pochteca*, guided by their god, Yacatecutli, 'Lord Long Nose' who smelled out trade on their behalf, played a crucial role in the process of demand and supply, and they also, because of their contacts and

199   Aztec bas-relief showing ancient warriors, engraved
by L. Giarre

knowledge of the lands beyond Tenochtitlan, served as spies, messengers, and sometimes a fifth column. Despised by those born to rule as a class which had to work, the traders nevertheless controlled great wealth, and it is an interesting speculation as to whether there was not here a sort of middle class in the making which might have challenged in time the traditional orders of society.

Outside society were the slaves – captives deemed unfit for sacrifice, natives condemned for certain crimes or those sunk into debt, who were too indolent to bear the responsibilities of the free, family man. They had no rights save that of buying their freedom, if they could and if they wanted to. Many, however, preferred the certainty of regular food and shelter, and the likelihood of good treatment from their masters, to the uncertainties they saw outside.

As for Aztec women, though their place was in the home as mothers of future warriors, and grandmothers too, their status in society compared somewhat favourably with that of their later counterparts in Victorian England. They could, for example, own property in their own right; they could go to the courts for redress against a cruel or wastrel husband, and obtain divorce if need be. Aztec history contains many stories of women who rose high in society, and it should be remembered that the great war god himself, Huitzilopochtli, was born of a woman, Coatlicue, regarded with veneration and awe by the Aztec people. Moreover, most male gods had their consorts who were far from being the docile, obedient, creatures one might expect in the religion of a society dominated by masculine activities.

As in life, so in art religion dominated, and Aztec sculpture reflected the sombre philosophy which ruled the state. It is massive, brooding art in stone which characterized this people, an apparent obsession with war, death, and sacrifice. Most artists were simply craftsmen, working to priests' orders, and their technological limitations were considerable. For the Aztecs were a Stone-Age people, not knowing the hard metals, using stone to cut stone. Despite this, there is a magnificence of execution and a triumph over material limitations in the finest pieces – the celebrated head of the Eagle Knight, for example. And in the making of beautiful pottery and the casting of objects in gold and silver, Aztec craftsmen were superb. Other specialized arts, such as feather-working, mosaic

200　Aztec bowl with
roughened floor for
husking grain

inlay on wood, and carving in rock-crystal[1] or obsidian, showed a
great manual dexterity and knowledge of the material, such that the
European artist Dürer, observing an exhibition of objects sent back
by Cortés in 1524, was moved to declare: 'Never in my life have I
seen anything which has so made my heart leap in me as these wonderful and artistic objects from a strange land.'

Aztec society and culture were born in war and blood, and lived by
a creed which glorified militarism and exalted human sacrifice.
There is, perhaps, some historical consistency in the violent fate
which awaited them at the hands of their European destroyers.

Pre-Inca Peru

Though differing markedly in detail, the story of the rise of Peruvian
civilization shows some interesting parallels with that of Mexico. In
the river valleys of the Pacific coast and in highland basins there was a
similar growth of agricultural communities to sophisticated levels.
Moreover, while geographical factors imposed a relative isolation on
individual regions for long periods, and thus made for great diversity, there were also ages when a dominant influence arose – like
Teotihuacán and Tula in Mexico – to overlay the local cultures for a
time. Thus, from about 800 to 300 B.C. most of the northern part of the
coast and highlands was affected by a culture characterized by worship of a feline deity, by a solid and heavy type of pottery, and by a

[1] See fig. 211, page 430

unique and elaborate art style. These traits seem to have emanated from a place in the northern highlands, Chavin de Huantar, where they were found in association with impressive stone structures, and it is as the Chavin that the period is known. Probably a vital seminal influence in cultural growth, like the Olmec in Mexico, the Chavin culture declined as mysteriously as it had begun, but it preceded a phase of great technological improvement. Pottery techniques are one indication; another is the growth of irrigation and hill-terracing for agriculture, and this also suggests considerable population growth. From 300 B.C. to A.D. 500 these and other developments rise to form an era of high achievement, contemporary with Teotihuacán in Mexico, and of artistic brilliance.

Given the extraordinary diversity of pre-Inca culture in the Andean area, selection here is inevitable. Two cultures, however, stand out: that of the Moche on the north coast of Peru, and that of Paracas on the south. The Moche is the name of a river valley but the culture which has been given its name covered a number of neighbouring valleys as well. It was characterized by enormous man-made structures of dried mud brick, the most prominent being a platform 750 feet long and 450 feet wide, standing high above the plain and probably built for religious purposes. Other public works, such as aqueducts and canals, testify to a highly organized state with a stratified society, developed religion, and flourishing arts and crafts. Writing was unknown in Peru before the Spaniards arrived, but much of the character of Moche society and culture is known to posterity from a unique historical record: thousands upon thousands of modelled and painted pots, recording in detail virtually every aspect of life. From this record, it has been possible to determine such questions as what animals, birds, and fish the Moche knew, and even what diseases they suffered from. A scene of warfare on one vessel; a family at home on another; an animal hunt on yet a third: it is from the cumulative and painstaking study of these 'documents' that Moche culture is re-created. And, although we lack the history of the Moche, we have representations of historical personages, since the ceramic art reached its peak in numerous 'portrait' vases of actual people, no less accurate than Europe's painted portraits.

While Moche culture itself had declined by about A.D. 900 its artistic traditions persisted on the north coast of Peru, though the products of later ages were somewhat less refined. Nevertheless, Moche technology and art – in gold-working as well as ceramics – was one important strand in Peruvian cultural tradition of which the Inca were the ultimate heirs.

If the high achievement here was pottery, that of the Paracas peoples was textiles. Yet we know little of these ancient craftsmen, not even where they came from, since Paracas itself was but a burial ground, a virtually rainless peninsula on the south coast of Peru. What is clear, however, is that perhaps as early as 300 B.C. people began burying their distinguished dead here, wrapping the eviscerated corpses in garments which the dry sand has preserved down the ages. In techniques of working, pattern and design, application of colour, and brilliance of overall effect, Paracas textiles are outstanding, particularly in view of the limited technology which produced them. The clothes were funeral garments since many had been made to fit an already padded mummy, and designs include demoniacal figures, clearly of religious significance. Of the society and religion of this people little is known, but their skill with textiles is unquestioned, and here again is another cultural heritage handed down to later ages.

The vigorous local cultures, of which we have seen but two examples, were profoundly affected between A.D. 500 and 1000, at least in south and central Peru, by influences coming from a single centre. On the Bolivian plateau, where the Andean ranges converge and Lake Titicaca stands, lies the extraordinary site of Tiahuanaco, some 13,000 feet above sea-level. Here high stone walls enclosed courtyards and other stone structures, a natural mound was artificially reshaped and faced with stone to form a stepped pyramid. Colossal stone figures – the largest was 24 feet high – were carved and erected, and a massive gateway, 10 feet high and $12\frac{1}{2}$ feet wide, was cut from a single block of andesite, carried several miles to Tiahuanaco. The whole site is vast and mysterious, and was probably the home of a powerful cult. It was not so much a place to live as a place to worship, a ceremonial centre constructed under the direction of a priesthood. The massive gateway bears a frieze in light relief of which the centre panel is a standing figure with weeping eyes, whose embellishments include condor and puma heads, and he is flanked by

412

201 Pottery stirrup vase, ornamented in relief and paint to represent a water fowl sitting on her nest in the reeds. Mochica culture, *c.* A.D. 600

forty-eight carved panels depicting running figures with beaks and wings. Tradition holds that this represents Viracocha, the creator god of the highland peoples, whose messengers are the condor-like figures, for the condor is the eagle of the Andes, and it soars highest towards the sun.

Whatever the truth of this interpretation, it is clear that the motifs associated with the god of Tiahuanaco completely dominated the pottery and textiles of a very wide area of Peru and Bolivia from about A.D. 500 to 1000. This suggests the spread of the cult, possibly by military conquest, possibly by missionaries from the site where its characteristics are so pronounced and pure. This phase is, after Chavín, the second period of Peruvian prehistory in which wider unity is obtained. Whether the unity was more than religious is unknown, and whether it was imposed by militaristic expansion is conjectural. But it existed until local developments again took precedence from A.D. 1000.

The final phase of Peruvian prehistory before the Inca Empire

202 Nineteenth-century imaginative reconstruction of Tiahuanaco

saw the emergence of genuine cities, large units of population, notably on the coast, and of true states, covering wide areas. On the north coast of Peru, the empire of the Chimu, inheritors of Mochica culture, covered several river valleys and guarded its frontiers with strategically placed fortifications. Its capital Chan-Chan, near the modern city of Trujillo, covered some 8 square miles, and was laid out in a pattern of rectangular enclosures with high walls of mud brick. Some of these still stand over 30 feet high and are decorated with arabesques in light relief – birds, fish, human figures, and geometrical designs derived from textile patterns. The empire was highly organized, with road systems which influenced the later Inca engineers, and it had its own distinctive pottery and metalwork.

Similarly, on the central coast, the empire of the Cuismancu was based on the valleys of the Chancay, the Ancon, and the Rimac, with its most impressive city at Cajarmarquilla, near Lima. And, in the south, the Chincha state had a comparable structure, though sites of the size and impressiveness of Chan-Chan and Cajarmarquilla have not yet been found.

These states with their urban concentrations, communications systems, and elaborate fortifications, flourished between A.D. 1000 and 1450. By the latter date, however, a new power was arising in the highlands of Peru which within two generations was to overcome and integrate within its own empire these kingdoms of the coast. That power, the Inca of Cuzco, was also to build not only on the experience of these states in terms of political organization and control, but also to inherit the accumulated artistic traditions that they themselves were heir to. And it was to be the Inca genius to mould from Peruvian diversity the largest administrative unity that America had ever experienced.

The Empire of the Incas

If the Aztecs, in their splendid barbarity, remind us of the Assyrians, the Incas recall the Romans. Their story also began with a city – Cuzco – and continued into an empire; they, too, evolved a philosophy of rule, and they were likewise great engineers and road-builders. But their rise and fall, sudden and dramatic, more nearly parallels the Aztec story.

On the archaeological evidence, Cuzco was first settled about A.D. 1200. Later Inca legend on the origins of the tribe, however, may well embody facts about their provenance. According to one version, the great creator god, Viracocha, maker of all the elements, including Sun and Moon, formed a first race of men but they sinned against him and were punished by being turned into stone. He then called out from caves in the hillsides another race of men and women, putting at their head a brother and sister, Manco Capac and Mama Occlo. To Manco Capac he gave a golden staff, telling him that the tribe should wander abroad until they came to the place where the golden staff would sink into the earth, and there should they found their city.

South of Cuzco lies the high plateau of south-eastern Peru and north-western Bolivia, a hard land unfit for agriculture but suitable for pastoralism. Here stands the site of Tiahuanaco to which we have referred previously, with its huge stone figures. Is it too fanciful to suggest that the Inca first emerged as a tribe in the region of Lake Titicaca and wandered in a vaguely northerly direction past Tiahuanaco, which had already fallen into decay, and down into the arable

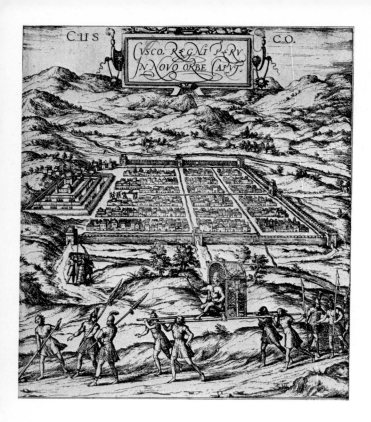

lands of the Urubamba basin where Cuzco now lies? The first race of men turned to stone might well be the figures of Tiahuanaco, and, while one would not expect a golden staff to sink into the ground on the high plateau, it might well do so in the softer, cultivable soil of a river basin. At any rate, Inca origins lie in a migration myth, and this interpretation accords well with the dating of the first human settlement at Cuzco.

For 200 years the Incas were masters of no more than 20 square miles of territory, and merely one of many warring tribes in the Peruvian highlands whose practice was to raid the neighbouring tribes and run off with their women and other booty. From about 1440, however, they began a deliberate policy of expansion, turning their backs on hit-and-run warfare, and incorporating defeated enemies into their polity. Between that date and 1530 they had made themselves masters of an enormous area in Peru, Bolivia, Ecuador, north-west Argentina, and the northern half of Chile, defeating not

416

only a multiplicity of other tribes, including some powerful kingdoms, but also overcoming the physical obstacles of high mountain ranges and desert coastal plains.

It was an astonishing transformation and it requires some explanation. But here we must be careful. For, when the Inca Empire had been established, like true totalitarians the master-race of the Andes rewrote all past history, and what emerged was a picture of complete barbarism before they embarked on their divine civilizing mission. We know from the archaeological record what a piece of unadulterated propaganda this was, and we must, therefore, take with a pinch of salt the fabulous stories handed down from generation to generation of the miraculous feats of the early Inca rulers. What does seem to be true, however, is that there emerged at Cuzco a dynasty of able rulers and that there was a slow accumulation of power, a preparation of military force, an evolution of statecraft and, finally, the flowering of policies which had long been in gestation. By the mid fourteenth century, certainly, through alliance with other tribes, the Incas had already established suzerainty over the high plateau and the eighth Sapa Inca, the emperor, extended his rule as far south as Tiahuanaco. Following him were two rulers whom it is not inappropriate to compare with Julius Caesar and Augustus: Pachacutec Inca Yupanqui (1438–71) and Topa Inca (1471–93). It was these two men of genius, outstanding soldiers and statesmen, who largely created the Inca Empire, and yet a third, Huayna Capac (1493–1527), who rounded out its boundaries shortly before the Europeans arrived.

Other key factors in Inca success were the policies of imperialism they adopted, which were often aided by the topographical situation. For example, the urbanized kingdoms of the coast depended for their survival on intricate irrigation systems in the river valleys which ran, fan-wise, from the Andes to the Pacific. Highly mobile highlanders, moving from the mountains to the headwaters and acclimatizing themselves to the lower altitudes, need only mount a *Blitzkrieg* against the irrigation works high up the valleys to disrupt completely the life of the cities of the plain. More important, in the long run, were the policies worked out in Cuzco for the establishment of the empire. They were a subtle mixture of blandishment and threat, and they usually worked. For instance, the Incas practised religious toleration, and would accept into their pantheon of gods the alien deities of others, provided that the others would worship their supreme god, Inti, god of the Sun, as chief god. No defeated tribe, therefore, need surrender its own religion but only accommodate it to the new dispensation. Similarly, chiefs of other tribes would not be done away with but confirmed in office on giving, so to speak, an oath of allegiance to the Sapa Inca, and accepting the imperial system. They might well be required to send their sons to Cuzco for schooling but this was as much to train them for office as to give the Incas hostages for good behaviour.

Other measures made for integration. It was the deliberate policy of the Incas to spread their language, Quechua, as the lingua franca of empire, as it was to impress local inhabitants by their engineering skill in building roads to bind the regions together and establishing impressive fortifications with garrisons to overawe the local population. Particularly recalcitrant areas were ruthlessly dealt with: whole populations were simply moved elsewhere and replaced by loyal subjects, but great care was taken to see that the new locations of both sets of migrants were as much alike as possible. In short, while compulsion was avoided and the Incas first tried, through a basic deference to local institutions and beliefs, to rule by the consent of the ruled, they could coerce if necessary.

The establishment of empire is one thing; the government of it another. What makes the Inca Empire so interesting a study of imperialism is the political and social underpinning of the policy of expansion. The Incas were not content to unify and rule; they also sought to create a state in which every man knew where he stood, and in which a man's obligations to society were balanced by its responsibility for him.

The Inca Empire was known to its inhabitants as Tawantinsuyu, 'Land of the Four Quarters', since, administratively, it was divided into four great regions, each with its own capital, though the capital of the empire itself was Cuzco. Each 'quarter' was divided into provinces, and each province divided into the equivalent of our counties. The smallest unit was the *ayllu*, a geographical unit based on agrarian collectivism and consisting of a number of unrelated, extended families, following certain common rules of living together. The *ayllu* probably antedated the Incas by hundreds of years as the local community and it still exists today. Each territorial unit was governed by a royal official, and the rulers of the 'quarters' formed a council of supreme government with the emperor, the Sapa Inca. These governors were usually blood relatives of the emperor, while governors of provinces were of the nobility. Under these, however, was a whole class of officials in each area which constituted the civil service, organized on a decimal breakdown of population. Thus, a senior official was responsible for 10,000 taxpayers; two others under him for 5,000 each; five under them for 1,000 each, and so on down to the last 100. Each category had its special name and down to the lowest level the office was hereditary. Clearly, the classification must have been approximate rather than precise but the point is that a chain of command existed from the emperor at Cuzco virtually down to the lowest level. There a head count was made for taxation purposes and reported to Cuzco and, in addition, there was also a classification of population into twelve age groups so that the human resources of the empire were always known, the 'statistics' being kept up to date.

Yet writing was unknown. To maintain this, and other sorts of information, the Incas had the *quipus*, knotted and coloured strings which, if one knew the meaning of the colours and the values of the

204 Inca worship of Inti, god of the Sun

205 Procession of Incas bearing offerings to the Temple
of the Sun

knots, one could compute easily. A special class of recorders and
readers, the *quipucamayoc*, was maintained specifically for this
purpose, and it could be said that the Inca emperor really had an
information bank on his kingdom in Cuzco.

Such was the administrative bureaucracy of the empire and its
instrument. What it administered was the productive potential of
the state by a system of taxation and benefits. Since money was
unknown and no payments in kind were made to the government,
taxation took the form of labour which was of two kinds. First, all
taxpayers were required to cultivate certain fields, the produce of
which supported the government and the Church; secondly, there
was the *m'ita*, special labour services such as a spell in the army or
some time on public works, roads and bridges, for example. A rather
long, but useful, quotation from the Spanish chronicler, Bernabé
Cobo, describes the way the 'land tax' worked.

420

When the Inca settled a town . . . he set up markers on its boundaries and divided the fields and arable lands into three parts. One part he assigned to Religion and the cult of his . . . gods, another he took for himself, and the third he left for the common use of the people. . . .

In the lands assigned to Religion and to the Crown, the Inca kept overseers and administrators who took great care in supervising their cultivation, harvesting the products and putting them in the storehouses. The labour of sowing and cultivating these lands and harvesting their products formed a large part of the tribute which the taxpayer paid to the king. . . . The people assembled to cultivate them in the following way. If the Inca himself, or his governor, or some high official happened to be present, he started the work with a golden *taccla* [digging-stick] . . . and, following his example, all the other nobles and officials who accompanied him did the same. However, the Inca soon stopped working, and after him the other nobles and officials stopped also, and sat down with the king to their banquets and festivals which were especially notable on such days.

The common people remained at work . . . [those] in charge of ten subjects worked all day as did the ordinary Indians who had no official position. They subdivided the work they had to do by lines . . . and . . . each man put into his section his children and wives and all the people of his house to help him. . . .

The third division of the land . . . was assigned to the people in the nature of commons, it being understood that the land was the property of the Inca, and the community only had the usufruct. . . . Sufficient lands were given to each province and town to support its population, and these lands were distributed each year . . . not in equal parts but proportionate to the number of children and relatives that each man had; and, as the family grew or decreased its share was enlarged or restricted. . . .[4]

Two types of storehouse were maintained in each .district: one held the produce of land apportioned to the Inca, by which is meant the emperor and, by extension, the whole governmental structure; the other housed the produce belonging to the Church, for the upkeep of the temples and the maintenance of the priesthood. Stores were drawn as needed for the government, the ruling nobility, the civil service, those who paid no labour tax such as the aged and infirm who were regarded as a state responsibility, and the common people in times of scarcity, such as natural disaster or drought. The system was also used for a general distribution of commodities which were not produced in particular areas, and thus rationalized

[4] Bernabé Cobo, cited by J. H. Rowe, *Handbook of South American Indians*, vol. 2 *Andean Civilizations*, pp. 265–6.

internal provision to all parts of the empire. Since the government required only labour as a tax, a thrifty and industrious family might earn a surplus from its own holding and thus increase its moveable property, diversifying it through the universal mechanism of the local markets which operated on a barter system. The use of precious metals and of other luxury objects was, however, restricted to the court and nobility. Houses and moveable property were individually owned.

The *m'ita*, additional to the 'land-tax' for able-bodied men, was a special labour service which could take many forms, and the decimal division of population enabled it to operate with a minimum of disruption. Army service was one form, mining precious metals another, while building bridges or forts might be a third. Thus, if an army of 10,000 men were required to put down a revolt on the Chilean frontier, a small proportion of the total would be drawn from a large catchment area, without unduly disturbing the work-pattern of those left behind. One hundred men from 100 areas would spread the load in a way that 1,000 men from each of 10 areas would not. Tax-exemptions for certain areas were not uncommon but they had to pay *m'ita* service in specified ways. Thus, the Rucana tribe were trained litter-bearers to the court, and the Chumpivilca furnished dancers for royal festivals.

As the 'welfare state' of the Incas mitigated the pressure of the 'land-tax' by guaranteeing the people from its storehouses in times of want, so it also tried to minimize the disabilities of *m'ita* service. A married man with family responsibilities called up on military service need not fear for his family's welfare in his absence, since the state demanded, and saw to it, that they were cared for by the local community and by the administration if necessary. An absentee's morale would be maintained and on his return he might well find, as Cobo puts it, 'that a harvest which he had neither sown nor reaped was gathered into his house'.

The keystone in the arch of the administrative superstructure was the emperor, who lived in great pomp at Cuzco. He was, in effect, an absolute ruler whose powers were checked only by custom and by personal responsibility, but it does appear that the royal house was distinguished for good and just government. The emperor, however, was not only the repository of secular authority but also the embodi-

206   The Temple of the Sun at Cuzco

ment of divine sanction, since he was regarded as a living god and
son of the Sun. Thus, his absolutism was, in one sense, logical, as
it is difficult to question the dictates of a living god. His whole life
was passed in ceremony and surrounded by splendour; specially
trained maidens cooked his food and made his clothing; all eyes were
lowered in his presence and, on his death on this earth, his mummi-
fied body was preserved in the royal palace along with those of his
ancestors, but brought out at festivals as a sacred object. Whenever
he went on progress round his realm, he was carried in a richly
decorated litter and attended by a vast retinue of soldiers, nobility,
and *quipucamayoc*. And all about him was made of precious metals,
since gold was the metal of the Sun god, Inti, and its use or possession
were denied to commoners. The sixteenth-century writer, Garcilaso
de la Vega, himself the son of a Spanish conqueror and an Inca
princess, described the royal gardens as follows:

All the royal palaces had gardens and orchards for the Inca's recreation. They were planted with all sorts of gay and beautiful trees, and fine and sweet-smelling herbs found in Peru. They also made gold and silver models of many trees and plants; they were done in natural size and style with their leaves, blossoms and fruits, some beginning to sprout, others half-grown and others in full bloom . . . they made fields of maize, copying the leaves, cob, stalk, roots and flowers from life. . . . There were also large and small animals carved or hollowed out of gold and silver – rabbits, mice, lizards, snakes, butterflies, foxes and wild cats. . . . There were birds of all kinds, some perched on trees as if they were singing, while others were flying and sucking honey from the flowers. There were, too, deer and stags . . . and all the other animals and birds that were bred in that country. . . .[5]

Small wonder that the Spanish conquerors were overwhelmed at the sight of such opulence, though we should remember that for the

[5] Garcilaso de la Vega, *Royal Commentaries of the Incas* (tr. H. V. Livermore), Part I, p. 315.

207   An engraving by Picart depicting the Incas lighting a sacred fire during the festival of the Sun

Incas the value of gold lay in its religious and ornamental significance, not in its economic worth.

Inca religion was much less complex than Aztec, though it was almost as pervasive. The society was essentially an agricultural one, and the deities were really the personification of the elements on which the people depended. Chief of the pantheon was Inti, great god of the Sun, with his consort, Mamaquilla, goddess of the Moon. Then there was Illapa, god of thunder, rain, and lightning, who carried a sling and wore a shining cloak, and was accompanied by his sister who bore a pitcher of water. When Illapa wished to send rain, he would whirl his sling-shot, flashing his cloak as he moved; the crack of thunder was the impact of the stone on the pitcher which broke to scatter its contents over the earth. There were gods of earth and sea, principally Pacamama, revered by peasants, and Mamacocha, the sea goddess who was worshipped on the coasts. Naturally, as the Inca Empire was enlarged, the policy of religious toleration and incorporation of local deities into the official pantheon led to the

208   Picart's engraving of funeral honours paid to the great lords of Peru on their death

merging of divine identities. Pacamama was originally the supreme deity of the Cuismancu kingdom on the central coast of Peru, and today the enormous archaeological site of Pachacamac, a little south of Lima, testifies to his importance in their life. As part of the deal, whereby the Cuismancu came into the Inca Empire, they were allowed to go on worshipping him but the Inca regarded him as another manifestation of their own supreme god, Inti.

A vast priesthood cared for the large number of temples throughout the empire, and participated in the numerous festivals which marked the agricultural year. The head of the hierarchy, the chief priest, presided over the Church from Cuzco and was a close relative of the emperor, though, in effect, it was really the latter, as divine king, who was head of the Church no less than of the state. An important part in the religious arrangements was played by the 'Chosen Women', the Virgins of the Sun. These were girls, chosen early on in life by royal officials for their beauty and other accomplishments, trained in 'nunneries' to the duty of working in the temples or at court, and sworn to chastity in the service of the Sun. In fact, those at court – the specially favoured ones – might become concubines of the emperor or the high nobility, and a few were set aside for sacrifice on very important occasions or in moments of crisis, such as the serious illness of the emperor. But, while animal sacrifice was a common feature of Inca religion, human sacrifice was not, and there was no comparison with the great public sacrifices which were characteristic of Aztec Mexico.

Yet, as in Mexico, there was a great gulf between the top and lower echelons of society. At the court, by the time of the Spanish Conquest, a philosophy of religion had emerged in which the central figure was not Inti but a shadowy creator god, Viracocha, who had himself created all the elements including the Sun. Viracocha as a sun god probably goes back in time to Tiahuanaco but the Inca rulers seem to have been moving towards a monotheism of which he was the core, for the name itself means 'creator-lord', like Jehovah, and is a description of his attributes rather than a proper name like Inti. Side by side with this conception, and particularly among the common people, were animistic beliefs in objects called *wacas*. The basic notion was that all kinds of things – peculiarly-shaped trees, certain hills or rivers, even stones, harboured spirits which

209 Inca aryballus with black and white designs on red

might need placating. Hence, if one made a journey up a mountain-side believed to be a *waca*, one took the precaution of placing a stone at its foot, as countless others did, to build a cairn as a testimony of belief and appeasement. The inexplicable were *wacas* – gall-stones found in the bladders of llamas, since one should not expect to find stones in such a place, and twins were *waca* since one child was normal but two at once were odd. Such beliefs posed no incongruity with the State Church: they existed before hierarchies and temples, and they survive in the Andean area today, long after the Indian hierarchies and temples have been destroyed.

The governmental structure, organization of society, and form of religion in the Inca Empire, were all cohesive factors but it is clear that the system was one which operated in the interests of a small class, at least so far as material things went. The class division of nobles and commoners was effectively a caste system as well, and while the empire had many features of a 'welfare state', in which the demands of the rulers were predictable rather than arbitrary, it is clear that, for the masses, there was no possibility of rising far from the level into which they were born. Whether they had any desire to do so is a moot point and not worth further sociological speculation. But, while the legal system might seem weighted in favour of those who ruled, it was not always so. Thus, commoners could be executed for apparently minor infractions on the ground that *any* breaking of the law was disobedience to the divine emperor while nobles might simply lose their office. But in certain cases it worked the other way. A commoner caught in adultery would be tortured and freed: a noble would be executed along with his mistress, probably less for the crime itself than for letting down his class and setting a bad example. A poor man who stole would be much less likely to be punished than the official under whose jurisdiction he fell, and whose job it was to see that he had no need to steal. In fact, however, crimes were rare, and the Incas never ceased to puzzle why the Spaniards required locks on their doors and treasure-chests. And, in the last analysis, the unqualified despotism but paternalistic régime of the Incas did seem to be based on the belief that people work better and produce more when their needs are supplied than when they suffer from want.

No consideration of the Inca Empire can ignore that final factor in their success as strategists and statesmen – their engineering skill. Their communications bound the empire together no less effectively than administrative structures and social policy, yet they lacked pack-animals and the wheel. They did have bronze and in this respect were technologically in advance of the Stone Age Aztecs.

A network of good roads knit the empire together, wide thorough-fares on the coast and in basins between the mountains, narrower trails in the highlands but traversing physical obstacles by steps and tunnels. Fixed *balsa* bridges traversed broad, slow rivers, while high suspension bridges crossed canyons and gorges. Local populations paid their *m'ita* tax by keeping these communications in repair, and special labour forces would be drafted under the same tax for big enterprises. Along the roads, at fixed intervals, stood storehouses of food, clothing, and arms, so that armies on the march or emperors on progress need not live off the countryside and thus create disaffection. At shorter spaces on the main highways, small post-houses accommodated runners trained to sprint at top speed with oral messages or *quipus* or even special foods for the imperial table, and

428

210 Pizarro meets the Inca Atahualpa and takes him
prisoner

this relay system could cover 150 miles a day. The roads, however, were literally the King's Highway, and the relay system was the Royal Mail. Special permission was needed to use the roads beyond a certain distance, and few commoners passed beyond the local area of their birthplace.

In architecture, the Inca builders constructed impressive fortifications and splendidly proportioned temples and palaces. There were several styles of building, the most prominent being in smooth-grained rectangular blocks, fitted perfectly together without mortar and held in place by friction, and the polygonal style, in which each stone was cut, and chipped, and shaped to fit precisely with its neighbour. One such stone in an extant wall at Cuzco has no fewer than twelve angles. When one stands in the ruins of Machu Picchu, a fortress town on a ridge overlooking the Urubamba in the north-eastern highlands of Peru, or gazes at the triple-tiered bastion of

429

Sacsahuaman on the heights above Cuzco, with its solid stones weighing up to 50 tons, one can see how impressive to conquered tribes was the power of the Inca revealed in this conquest of nature.

Artistically, the Inca Empire was not distinguished. It lacked writing in any form, and its pottery, while well made and not unattractive, does not have the refinement or the artistry of previous cultures. It is possible that in the working of soft metals the Incas were at their best, but little of their gold-work survived the Spanish melting-pot, whence it flowed to finance Spanish wars in Europe and, incidentally, the rise of European capitalism. Inca achievement, in the last analysis, lies in a combination of social and physical engineering, and in this respect the comparison with the Romans is apt.

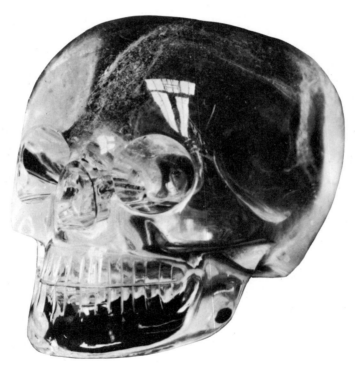

211 Fifteenth-century Aztec rock-crystal skull (see page 409)

Acknowledgements

THE AUTHORS AND PUBLISHERS wish to record their grateful thanks to copyright owners for the use of illustrations listed below:

Barnaby's Picture Library: 175
Bibliothèque Nationale, Paris: 22, 25
Osvaldo Bohm, Venice: 21
The British Museum: 1, 10, 16, 17, 20, 34, 41, 42, 45, 46, 48, 49, 51, 52, 55, 59, 60, 69, 83, 84, 140, 188, 195, 196, 203, 211
Camera Press Ltd.: 119
J. Allan Cash: 82, 93
The Percival David Foundation of Chinese Art: 157, 158, 163
Embassy of the Republic of Indonesia: 124, 125, 126, 133, 134, 135, 137
Alison Milner-Gulland: 27
Hungarian Historical Museum, Budapest: 67
Hutchinson & Co. Ltd. (Henri Lhote: *The Search for the Tassili Frescoes*): 95, 99
India Office Library and Records: 31, 114
Information Service, Government of India: 102, 107, 108, 109, 111
International Society for Educational Information, Tokyo: 171, 172, 176, 177, 179, 185
Japanese Embassy: 173, 180, 181, 182, 183
Library of the School of Oriental and African Studies, London: 29, 78, 79, 80, 86, 87, 88, 89
Mansell Collection: 23, 30, 40, 47, 50, 62, 68, 77, 104, 146, 178, 186, 202, 205, 206, 207, 208
Museo Navale, Genoa: 11
National Gallery, London: 43
National Library, Madrid: 142
National Maritime Museum: 4, 5, 6, 7, 8, 12, 14, 15, 18, 19, 73, 75, 76, 85, 92, 94, 96, 103, 123, 130, 136, 143, 167, 210

431

Palazzo Ducale, Venice: 39
Photographie Giraudon: 170, 174
Portuguese State Tourist Office: 2, 3, 9, 13, 63, 70, 74, 98, 129, 131, 166
Radio Times Hulton Picture Library: 24, 26, 33, 36, 44, 53, 54, 56, 57, 58, 61, 64, 65, 66, 71, 72, 90, 91, 128, 141, 148, 165, 184, 187, 189, 190, 191, 193, 197, 198, 199, 204
Royal Academy: 112
SATOUR: 97
Science Museum: 138
Service de Documentation Photographique de la Réunion des Musées Nationaux, Versailles, and the Musée du Louvre: 38
Sudanese Embassy: 81
University Museum of Archaeology and Ethnology, Cambridge: 201, 209
Victoria and Albert Museum: 35, 100, 101, 105, 106, 113, 115, 116, 117, 118, 119, 120, 121, 122
Victoria Education Department, Australia: 132, 139.

and for quotations:

Cambridge University Press (Hakluyt Society) for: C. R. Boxer, *South China in the Sixteenth Century* and Bernal Diaz del Castillo, *The True History of the Conquest of New Spain* (tr. A. P. Maudslay)

The Society of Authors and Mr Christopher Dawson for: Christopher Dawson, *Mongol Mission*

Smithsonian Institution Press for: J. R. Rowe, *Handbook of South American Indians*, volume 2 of the *Bulletins of the Bureau of American Ethnology*

Index

Indian, 241; Japanese, 360–1, 371; S.E. Asian, 254, 271

Ardabil, 109

Armenia, 70; captured by Turks, 73

Ashikaga period, the, 354–7, 359

Asia, attraction of for the European, 253

Asoka, Emperor, 219, 225, 226; relations with the West, 51, 53

Assassins, the, 78

astrolabe, 18

Atacama Desert, 383

Atahualpa captured, 42

Atjeh, 281, 290

Atlantic Ocean: in early exploration, 28–35; knowledge of in 15th century, 29–30; motives for exploration, 29–30

Atlantis, 10

Atlas Mountains, 175

Attalids, the, 51

Augustus, Emperor, 62, 417

Australian exploration, 48–9

Austria, attacked by Ottomans, 137–8

avatar, 210

Avestic, 206

Ay Khanum, ruins at, 51

Aztec civilization: arts and crafts, 407–10; militarism in, 410; political organization, 402–7; pre-Aztec period, 386, 388–94; religion, 393–403; social classes, 403–5

Aztlan, 394

Azuchi-Momoyama period, 370–1, 372

B

Babur, emperor, 201

Bactria, 50, 52

Baffin Island, 45

Baghdad, 55; califate, 71; capture (1258), 86

Bagratids, the, 76

Bahmini kingdom, 199

Baikal, Lake, 78

Bakufu (Camp Office), 353–4, 355, 367, 371; see also shogunate

Balboa, Vasco Nuñez de, 36, 40

Balkh (Bactra), ruins at, 51

banana, the, 159, 164, 188

Bantu, the, 184–7, 192–3

Barbarossa (Khayr al-Din), 133–6

Barbary, 174–7

Barents, Willem, 44–5

Basil I, Emperor (812–86), 70

Basil II, Emperor (976–1025), 73

Bayezid I (1389–1403) defeated at Ankara, 94, 103

Bayezid II, Sultan (1481–1512), 105, 106, 107, 113, 114, 127

Beauvais, Vincent de, 86

Bedouin, the, 169, 175–6, 177

Behaim, Martin, 46

Belem (Panama), 35

Belgrade, 136, 138

Benin, 19, 180

Bhagavad Gita (Lord's Song), 208, 219

bhakti (path of devotion), 217, 219, 239

Binh-Dinh, 292

Black Death, 14, 102

Black Sea: Genoa in, 86–7; Ottoman control of, 98

Black Sheep Turcomans, 108

Bogomils, the, 65

Borobudur, 258

Bosphorus, 99

Brahma, 210

Brahmins: caste of, 214–16; as court advisers, 216, 222–3; Kulin Brahmins, 214; orthodox, 203; and ritual pollution, 214; in Vedic India, 213

Budak Beg, 105

Buda-Pest, 138

Buddha, the, 211, 218–19, 229; influence in

434

the West, 52, 66

Buddhism, 218–19, 223, 226; in Afghanistan, 51; expands to Asia, 231; destroyed in Bihar, 234; in Ceylon, 225; in China, 306, 331, 332; in Japan, 358; monasteries destroyed by Huns, 229; adopted by Kushans, 229; see also Hindu Buddhism, Zen Buddhism

Buganda, 191

C

Cabot, John, 32–4, 43

Cabot, Sebastian, 38

Cabral, Pero Alvares, 25

Çaldiran, battle of (1514), 116, 117

Calicut: Arab merchants at, 15; Pero da Covilhan at, 22; Vasco da Gama at, 24, 25

califate, the, 65, 66, 68, 73; gold specie in, 60; employs Seljuks, 71; and Shi'a, 109

California, discovered by Cortés, 41

camel, the: importance in African development, 169–70; introduced into Sahara, 178

cannibalism: Aztec, 399; in S.E. Asia, 264–5

Canton, 28, 339

Cão, Diogo, reaches Congo, 22

Cape of Good Hope, 22

Cape Verde, 19

Carthage, 175, 176

Cartier, Jacques, 39

cartography, 9–11, 46–8, 62–3

Caspian Sea, 109

cassava, 159

'caste' system in Peru, 427; see also Hinduism

Cathay: search for, 29, 31, 32, 45; eskimo as 'native' of, 45; and North East Passage, 43, 44

Cathay Company, 45

Caucasus, the, 102

Ceylon, 200; Buddhism in, 225; Chinese voyage to, 201, 342

Chad, Lake, 170, 182

Champa, 292–3, 300, 312

Chancellor, Richard, 44

Chan-Chan, 414

Chao Ju-kua, 85

Charlemagne, 67

Charles V (Spain), 37, 38, 42

Chavín culture, 411

Cheng Ho, voyages of, 265–6, 341–4

Chimu, the, 414

China: discontent in 14th century, 306; as seen by Europeans, 304, 347–50; famine (1329), 306, 309; foreign trade, 314, 338–44; Portuguese reach, 28; rebellion (1501), 347

chinampas, 381

Chinese administration: the Censorate, 324; central admin., 317–21; Confucian examination system, 325–7; judiciary, 324–5; provincial admin., 321–4, 325–6

Chinese *Annals*, quoted, 85

Chinese culture, 297–8, 330, 333–6

Chinese foreign relations, 188, 296, 297–8, 306, 336–44, 347–8; see also Cheng Ho

Chinese influence in S.E. Asia, 250, 265–6, 280, 281, 290, 293–6

Chingis Khan (1162–1227), 77, 78, 234

'Chosen Women' (Virgins of the Sun), 426

Christianity: Byzantine relations with Islam, 66–70; in Cebu, 270; in Egypt, 168; in India, 66, 231; knowledge of Islam, 90–1; in Japan, 358, 375, 376, 377–8; effect on Roman trade, 63; in Sudan, 169; and Timur, 79–81, 83

Christian Churches: Coptic, 65, 168; Eastern 63–8; Monophysite, 53; Nestorian, 66, 81, 83, 231; Orthodox, 64–5

435

Chu Yuan Chang, first Ming emperor (1328–98), 307, 321–2; improves agriculture, 309–13; empire rebuilt, 308, 336, 339; frontier colonies of, 310; taxes regularized, 310–11, 313, 314; trade stimulated, 315–17, 340

Cilicia, 104, 105–6; Shi'a in, 110

Cipango ('Zipangu'), 31, 33, 351

circumnavigation of the world, 38

city culture in Peru, 414–15

Cochin, Cabral at, 25

cochineal, 405

Columbus, Christopher: voyages of, 28–35; uses Marco Polo's *Travels*, 92, 351

communications: in Ming period, 312, 315, 317, 318, 342; Peruvian, 428–9; S.E. Asian, 250

compass, magnetic, 16, 343

Confucius (552–479 B.C.), 328

Confucian administration: in China, 318–20; in Viet-Nam, 297, 299, 302

Confucian examination system, 325–7

Confucian philosophy, 318, 328–31; in Japan, 378; in Viet-Nam, 297–8, 300

Congo River, Portuguese at, 184; see also Kongo

conquistadores, the, 40–2

Constantine the Great, emperor (280–337), 64

Constantinople: capture, 76, 94–5, 96; defence of (717), 53

Cook, Captain (1728–79), 49

Coronado, Francisco Vasquez de, 42

corsairs, 133–6

Cortés, Hernán, 41, 405

Cosa, Juan de la, 46

Cosmas Indicopleustes, 9, 62–3

cotton: in the Deccan, 242; in Harappan culture, 205; in Indian trade, 221–2

court life in S.E. Asia, 285–7

Covilhan, Pero da, 22, 24

Crete, 87; emir of, 66

Crusades, 66, 77, 86, 94; as impetus to exploration, 14

Cuba, 31, 32

Cuismancu kingdom, 426

Cuzco: capital of Inca empire, 416–20, 422; buildings, 429; captured, 42; dynastic centre, 417; first settled, 415

Cyprus: Ottoman invasion of, 135, 136

D

daimyo, the (feudal lord), 362–3, 364, 365, 366–7

Dai-Viet: extent in 16th century, 292; extinguishes Champa, 293; political growth in 15th and 16th centuries, 298–303

Damascus: captured by Arabs, 65; Roman traders in, 54

Danube, Ottoman campaigns, 136–9

Darien Isthmus, 36, 40, 41

Dasht-i Kipçak, 99, 102

Da'ud Pasha, 105

Davis, John, 45

Dayo, the royal city, 278

Deccan, the, 199, 205, 235, 242

declination tables, 18, 23

Dee, John, 43

Delhi sultanate, 197, 199, 234, 239

Demak (Java), 248–51, 280, 282, 289

dervish *tarikas*, 110–11

Deshima, Dutch at, 375–6

dharma (law of moral duty), 210, 216–17

Dias, Bartholomeu, reaches Cape of Storms (1487), 22

Dias, Dinis, reaches Cape Verde, 19

Digenis Akrites, 68

Diu, defeat of Turkish fleet at (1508), 26, 201

dnyana (path of knowledge), 217

Drake, Sir Francis, 48, 283–4

436

Dravidians, the, 205
drugs, see under spices
Dürer, Albrecht (1471–1528), 410
Dutch, in Japan, 375
dyeing, in S.E. Asia, 257; see also cochineal
Dynasties: chart of Chinese, 350; length of, in S.E. Asia, 276, 291

E

Eannes, Gil, rounds Cape Bojador (1434), 19
economic depression, in 15th century, 90
Edward I (England), 80, 83
Egypt, 156; Arabic in, 168, 170; Christianity in, 168; Mamluk sultanate, 99–107; Muslims in, 168; political organization, 168
Eitoku, Kano, 360, 370
El Dorado, 42
Epic Age, see later Vedic Age
Ethiopia: Christianity in, 172; conflict in south, 173–4; early settlement, 170–1; kings of, 171–2; Prester John, 172
eunuchs, Chinese, 318–20; see also Cheng Ho
European influence in Japan, 371, 372, 376, 378; see also Jesuits
Europeans in Japan: English, 377; Dutch, 375–6; Portuguese, 351, 356, 368; Russian, 377
Europeans in S.E. Asia, 288–91
Euxine, see Black Sea
exploration, reasons for, 13–16

F

Ferdinand and Isabella, 31
'feudal system' of the Ottomans, 71, 120–1; see also *daimyo*
firearms: used by Janissaries, 99, 107; by Japanese, 356, 357, 375; by Mamluks, 107; by Ottomans, 99; Portuguese ascendancy in, 16, 26–7, 28
fishing, in S.E. Asia, 254, 257, 274
Fitch, Ralph, 46
'Forbidden City', the, 318, 319, 320
'fratricide, law of', 99, 113
Frederick II, emperor (1194–1250), 74
Frobisher, Martin, 45, 58
Frois, Luis, 361, 366
Fushimi Palace, 369

G

Gabras dynasty, 74
Gama, Vasco da, 23–5: at Calicut, 14, 24–5, 129; in E. Africa, 188–9; reaches Moçambique, 23; at Sofala, 184
Gandhi, Mahatma, 210
Ganesha, 210
Ganges, river, 209, 232
Gaza, battle of (1516), 119
gekokujo, 354
Genoa: in Black Sea, 98; conflict with Ottomans, 134; expansion of, 86–90
geographical knowledge in 15th century, 9–13
Ghana Empire, 180, 183
ghazi, the, 93, 96
Gilbert, Sir Humphrey, 45
Goa, 26, 129, 200
Gold: Aztec, 404; export from Africa, 160, 178–9, 183, 184; Inca, 423, 424; hoarding in India, 61; in the New World, 42; as specie, 63; in Sumatra, 278–9
Gold Coast, 19, 179
Golden Horde, the, 78, 102
Gomes, Fernão, 19
gotong royong, 275
Grand Canal, the (China), 315
Grand Shrines, the (Ise), 371
Greeks of Bactria, 226

437

Greek influence: in India, 223, 226; in the Middle East, 50–3
Greenland, 11
Gregory IX, Pope (1154–1241), 74
guano, 384
Guinea coast, 19, 25; Columbus at, 30
Gujarat, 199, 288; Jains in, 218; Parthian invasion, 226; Portuguese at, 131
Gujaratis, in Malacca, 260, 262
Guptas, the, 223, 229

H

Haiti, discovered, 31
Han Dynasty, 57; compared to age of the Antonines, 56
Harappan culture, 204–6, 207, 210
Hartogszoon, Dirk, 48
Harunu'l -Rashid, 67
Hausa, the, 180, 182
Henry III (England), 78
Henry of Portugal (1394–1460) (The Navigator), 14, 18–19
Heraclius, emperor (575–641), 53, 65
Hideyoshi era, 368–72
Hideyoshi, Toyatomi, 363–8
hill terracing in Peru, 411
Hindu-Buddhism in S.E. Asia, 266–7, 269, 277–8, 279
Hinduism: art and science, 223–5; caste, 204, 210, 212–16; in Champa, 293; concepts and ethics, 216–17; development, 204–7, 207–12; distinctive features, 202–4; epics, 207–12; festivals, 208; and Islam, 203, 235, 244–5; in S.E. Asia, 277–9; urban organization, 221; influence on West, 52; see also, Brahmins, Buddhism, Hindu-Buddhism, Jains
Hispaniola, 32, 34, 35
Ho Quy Ly, 294

Hojo, the, 354
Honshu, 353, 356
Hormuz, 26, 55, 130, 132
Horn of Africa, 172–4
Huang Ho, river, 83, 306
Huayna Capac (1493–1527), 417
Hudson, Henry, 46
Hudson Bay Company, 46
Huitzilopochtli, 393–4, 398, 400–1, 405, 409
humanism in Japan, 376
human sacrifice: Aztec, 395, 402–3, 410; Inca, 426
Humbolt Current, 384
Hungary, 137, 138, 139
Hun invasions in India, 226–9
hunting: in Africa, 158, 178; in Mexico, 388; in S.E. Asia, 256–7
Husain Shah, 198

I

Ibrahim Pasha, 121, 130–1
Iconoclast Decree (726), 67
Ilkhanids, the Persian, 78, 80, 81, 83
Ilkhans, the, 76, 78, 83; conflict with Mamluks, 103
Inca Empire: administration, 418–22; architecture, 429–30; art, 430; conquest of, 41–2; development, 417; emperors, 417, 419, 422; gods, 425; mythology, 416; pre-Inca Peru, 410–15; religion, 425–7; social structure, 426–9
Incas, the: of Cuzco, 415, 417, 419; imperial state of, 422–4; see also under individual names
incanti, the, 88
Indo-Aryans, 204, 206–12
Indus River, 198, 205, 206
Indus Valley people, 221; see also Harappan culture

438

Innocent IV, Pope (1190–1254), 79–80
Inter Caetera, papal bull, 31
irrigation: Chinese, 312, 313; Peruvian, 411; for rice, 251, 254, 258; see also *qanat*
Ise (Nagoya), 371
Islam: relations with Byzantium, 66–70; in Ottoman Empire, 110; under Spanish and Portuguese in S.E. Asia, 290; 'Five Pillars of Islam', 270; see also shi'a; sufis
Islam in Africa, 146, 164–5, 169, 188; in Barbary, 175; in Egypt, 168; in Horn of Africa, 173; in Sudan, 183
Islam in India, 231–45; Muslim rule, 196–201
Islam in S.E. Asia, 263, 268–9, 270, 282
Isma'il, Shaykh, 110, 113, 117, 201

J

Jains, the, 218–19
Jamaica, 32, 35
Janissaries, the, 99, 114, 115, 122–5
Japan: communications, 369; cultural life, 368–78; foreign relations, 375; Hideyoshi era, 363–8; Nobunaga era, 357–63; political situation, 351–6; social structure, 367
Japanese castle-towns, see *joka-machi*
Japanese emperor, 353; contrasted with Chinese, 352
Jarakisa, the, 102
Java, Dutch route to, 48; see Demak
Java Man, 253
Jem, 105, 106
Jenkinson, Anthony, 44
Jesuits: exploration in Far East, 27–8; in Japan, 358, 360
Jews, 66, 95, 231
jihad, 93, 114
Jihan Shah, 109
John II, king (Portugal) (1455–95), 19, 22

John of Damascus, Saint, 67
John of Monte Corvino, Friar, 81
John of Plano Carpini, 12, 79
joka-machi (castle-towns): Azuchi, 360–1, 369; Himeji, 361; Nijo, 371; Osaka, 361, 369; Yedo, 362
Julian, emperor, death of (363), 54
Jumna river, 207, 209, 232, 234
Junayd, Shaykh (1447–60), 109–10
jungle products of S.E. Asia, 257, 343
Jurakudai (Mansion of Pleasure), 369
'Just King' (*Ratu Adil*), 277
Juvaini, 77–8

K

Kaffa, 87, 114
Ka'it Bay, sultan (1468–96), 105, 106
Kamakura, 353, 356, 367
Kansuh al-Ghuri, 117–18, 130
Kantakouzenoi, the, 76
Karakorum, 79
Kara Koyunlu, 108
Karaman, 105, 113
karanisa, 102
karma (law of moral consequence), 210, 216, 217, 220
Katanga, 186
Kayseri, 106, 115, 118
Khadim-al-Haramayn (Selim I), 120
khalifa, 110
Khayr al-Din, see Barbarossa
khushdashiya, the, 101
Khushkadam, sultan (1461–7), 104–5
Kilij-Arslan, sultan, 74
Kilwa, 25, 161, 188; Roman traders in, 54, 59
kiriltays, 79–80, 89, 90
Kisale, lake, 186
Kistna River, 199, 200
Knights of St John, 103, 105, 134–5

439

Manoel, king (Portugal), 304, 307, 318
Mantzikert, battle of, 73
'Manu, laws of', 220
Manuel I, emperor (1143–83), 74
Mappa Mundi, 9
Marathon, 53, 225
Marcus Aurelius, emperor (161–80 B.C.), 85;
  see also 'An-tun'
margas, the, 217
Marj Dabik, 118, 119
Massawa, 131
mathematics, Indian origins of the cypher,
  225
Mathew of Edessa, 73
maulanas (mullahs), 237–8
Mauro, Fra, 22
Mauryan Empire, 226
Maya civilization, 34, 380
maya (Hindu doctrine of), 217
Mecca, 106, 120, 183; caravan centre, 54–5;
  Covilhan at, 22
medicine, Indian, 225
Medina, 106, 120
Mehemmed (the Prophet), 54–5, 65
Mehemmed II, sultan (1451–81), 76, 87;
  establishes Istanbul, 95–6; encourages
  Jews, 95–6; controls Balkans and Asia
  Minor, 96–8, 127; controls Black Sea, 98;
  defines Ottoman state, 98–9; ends Kara-
  manid resistance, 97, 108; death, 105
Menander, king, 226
Mercator, Gerard, 44, 47, 48
Mexico, conquest of, 41; see also Aztec
  civilization
Mexico-Tenochtitlan, see Tenochtitlan
Michael VIII, Palaiologous, 76
milpa system of agriculture, 381; see also
  ladang
Minamoto Yoritomo, 353–4, 367
Minangkabau, 278–9

Ming Dynasty (1368–1643), 306–50; art,
  332–6; belief and ethics, 328–32; decline,
  344–50; economy restored, 309–13; foreign
  relations, 306, 336–44; literature, 333–6;
  politics and administration, 317–27; production and commerce, 313–17; scholarship, 332–3
m'ita, 420, 422
Mitanni, the, 206
Mitla, 393
Mixtecs, the, 393
Moche culture, 411–12, 414
Moldavia, 98, 127
Moluccas, see Spice Islands
Mombasa, 24, 188
Mongols, the, 77–86; capture Baghdad, 86;
  reach Black Sea (1222), 78; threat to
  China, 78, 304–5, 307–8; threat to India,
  234–5; invade Japan, 354; *kiriltays* of,
  79–80; aid to Ottomans, 127; papal em-
  bassy to, 79–80; '*Secret History*' quoted,
  77–8, 84; indifference to West, 84–6
Monomatapa, 25, 187
Monophysites, the, 65, 66
monotheism, 64, 65, 66; Peruvian, 426
Montezuma, 41, 398, 404
Moplahs, the 232
mullahs, see *maulanas*
Muromachi Age, the, 354–5
Muscovy Company, the, 44
Mystikos, Nicholas, Patriarch, 66–7

N

Nagasaki, 375, 376
Nagoya, 371
Nambanjin, the, 378
Nanak, Guru, 245
Naples, 134

R

Q

S

444